跨文化双边对话
——第二届中美文化论坛文集

A BINATIONAL CONVERSITION BRIDGING CULTURES

The Second China-U.S. Cultural Forum
Collection of the Theses

贾磊磊 主编

Editor in Chief
Jia Leilei

文化艺术出版社
Culture and Art Publishing House

第二届中美文化论坛
The Second China-U.S. Cultural Forum

目录

开幕致辞

7　王文章　中华人民共和国文化部副部长、中国艺术研究院院长

13　[美]吉姆·利奇　美国国家人文基金会主席

第一单元　中美文化关系的历史回顾

23　主持人导语
　　[美]安德鲁·琼斯 加利福尼亚大学伯克利分校东亚语言文学系教授

27　主持人导语
　　[美]余宝琳 美国学术团体联合会主席

33　中国传统文化的现代价值
　　于丹 北京师范大学艺术与传媒学院副院长

40　中国文学传统如何影响西方
　　[美]金安平 耶鲁大学历史系高级讲师

46　我雕塑艺术中的文化观
　　吴为山 中国艺术研究院雕塑院院长、美术研究所所长

58　中美关系的历史起点与维度
　　[美]乔纳森·斯宾塞 耶鲁大学历史系斯特林荣誉教授

第二单元　文学遗产与创新性

69　主持人导语
　　[美]唐纳德·麦奎德 加利福尼亚大学英语与美国研究教授

73　21世纪人类能否在非对抗中重生
　　刘梦溪 中国艺术研究院中国文化研究所所长

81　美国大学与文学事业
　　[美] 安德鲁·德尔班科 哥伦比亚大学美国研究中心主任

90　美国文学对中国文学的影响
　　莫言 中国艺术研究院文学院院长

98　"发现之旅"与文化交流
　　[美] 克里斯多弗·梅里尔 爱荷华大学国际写作项目主任

第三单元　视觉艺术的传统与创新

111　主持人导语
　　[美] 亨利·亚当斯 美国克利夫兰市凯斯西储大学美国艺术教授

117　中国书刻：传统艺术语言的崭新表达
　　李胜洪 中国艺术研究院中国书法院副院长

127　艺术构建东西方桥梁
　　[美] 恩·荷·德尔班科 哥伦比亚大学东亚艺术系教授

140　心与象合——关于中国画文化体验
　　田黎明 中国艺术研究院副院长、研究生院院长

156　西方艺术的传统与创新
　　[美] 劳伦斯·林德 伯克利艺术博物馆和太平洋电影档案馆馆长

166　密响旁通——我眼中的中美艺术交流景观
　　徐累 中国艺术研究院创作研究中心研究员

178　在标记中表现自我
　　[美] 萨拉·辛纳克劳斯 美国南卡罗来纳大学、哥伦比亚大学绘画教授

184　建筑的艺术：内在体验与外在表现
　　[美] 钱以佳 "陶德·威廉斯与钱以佳建筑事务所"建筑师

第四单元　表演艺术比较观

197　主持人导语
　　[美] 瑞秋·格斯林斯 美国总统艺术人文委员会执行主任
201　文化时代与传统艺术的发展
　　刘祯 中国艺术研究院戏曲研究所所长
212　中美文化交流的见证与阐释
　　[美] 克莱尔·康塞逊 美国杜克大学戏剧研究教授
222　中美舞蹈交流的回首、现状与未来建议
　　欧建平 中国艺术研究院舞蹈研究所副所长
252　有意义交流的关键 —— 参与
　　[美] 达米安·沃策尔 美国维尔国际舞蹈艺术节主任
258　跨文化交流中的理解误差
　　贾磊磊 中国艺术研究院院长助理、文化发展战略研究中心主任

第五单元　中美文化关系的未来展望

281　主持人导语
　　[美] 吉姆·利奇 美国国家人文基金会主席
285　对话是人类的生活准则
　　刘梦溪 中国艺术研究院中国文化研究所所长

296 文化比政治更具影响力
[美] 埃里森·布莱克利 美国波士顿大学欧洲比较历史学教授

300 未来十年的世界与中国：从国际政治的视角
金灿荣 中国人民大学国际关系学院副院长

320 文化关系 —— 大国合作的途径
[美] 何塞·欧博 美国斯坦福大学古典学、政治科学教授

新闻综述

328 构筑新世纪的巴比伦通天塔
贾磊磊 中国艺术研究院院长助理、文化发展战略研究中心主任

360 建构中美文化交流的世纪桥梁
潘源 中国艺术研究院文化发展战略研究中心副研究员

374 重构全球化语境下的文化交流模式
肖庆 中国艺术研究院文化发展战略研究中心助理研究员

392 翻译与文化 —— 美中两国学者与艺术家齐聚圆桌论坛
[美] 梅瑞狄斯·辛德雷 美国国家人文基金会资深作家

397 **中美文化论坛历史沿革**

Contents

Address at the Opening Ceremony

10   Wang Wenzhang, Vice Minister of Ministry of Culture, People's Republic of China , President of Chinese National Academy of Arts
14   Jim Leach, Chairman of US National Endowment for the Humanities

Unit One: Historical Perspectives on China-U.S. Cultural Relations

25   Moderator's Introduction
      Andrew Jones, Professor of East Asian Languages and Cultures, University of California, Berkeley
30   Moderator's Introduction
      Pauline Yu, President, American Council of Learned Societies
36   The Value of Chinese Traditional Culture in Modern Times
      Yu Dan, Associate Dean of School of Arts and Communication, Beijing Normal University
43   How Does the Chinese Literary Tradition Reach the West
      Annping Chin, Senior Lecturer, Department of History, Yale University
52   My View of Culture in Sculptural Arts
      Wu Weishan, Director of Institute of Fine Arts, Director of Institute of Sculpture, Chinese National Academy of Arts
60   The Historical Start Point and Aspects of China-U.S. Relations
      Jonathan Spence, Sterling Professor of History Emeritus, Yale University

Unit Two: Literary Heritage and Creativity

71   Moderator's Introduction
      Donald Mcquade, Professor of English, University of California, Berkeley

77   Can Humanity be Reborn without Confrontation in the 21st Century
     Liu Mengxi, Director of Institute of Chinese Culture, Chinese National Academy of Arts
85   American University and Literature Career
     Andrew Delbanco, Director of American Studies, Columbia University
94   The Influence of American Literature on Chinese Literature
     Mo Yan, Dean of School of Literature, Chinese National Academy of Arts
101 Life of Discovery and Cultural Communication
     Christopher Merrill, Director of the International Writing Program at the University of Iowa

Unit Three: Tradition and Innovation in The Visual Arts

114 Moderator's Introduction
     Henry Adams, Professor of American Art, Case Western Reserve University
122 Chinese Calligraphy Engraving: A New Expression of Traditional Artistic Language
     Li Shenghong, Deputy Dean of School of Chinese Calligraphy, Chinese National Academy of Arts
136 Bridging Cultures with Arts
     Dawn Ho Delbanco, Professor of East Asian Art, Columbia University
148 The Integration of Mind and Image — Cultural Experience in Chinese Paintings
     Tian Liming, Vice President of Chinese National Academy of Arts, Dean of the Graduate School of Chinese National Academy of Arts
161 Tradition and Innovation in Western Art
     Lawrence Rinder, Director of the Berkeley Art Museum and Pacific Film Archive
172 Silent Voice, Permeating Echoes
     — The Sino-American Artistic Exchanges in My Observation

Xu Lei, Research Fellow of Research Center for Creation, Chinese National Academy of Arts

181 Finding Ourselves within the Mark
Sara Schneckloth, Professor of Drawing, University of South Carolina, Columbia

187 The Art of Architecture: Inner Experience and External Manifestation
Billie Tsien, Architect of *Tod Williams Billie Tsien Architects*

Unit Four: The Performing Arts: Comparative Perspectives

199 Moderator's Introduction
Rachel Goslins, Executive Director of the President's Committee on the Arts and Humanities

206 Cultural Era and the Development of Traditional Arts
Liu Zhen, Director of Institute of Traditional Operas, Chinese National Academy of Arts

217 The Witness and Interpretation of China- US Cultural Exchange
Claire Conceison, Professor of Theater Studies, Duke University

237 Dance Exchanges between China and U.S.A.: 100 Years' Retrospective, Present Situation & Suggestions For the Future
Ou Jianping, Deputy Director of Dance Research Institute, Chinese National Academy of Arts

255 The Key to Meaningful Exchange — Participation
Damian Woetzel, Director of the Vail International Dance Festival, USA

266 Misinterpretation in Cross-cultural Exchange
Jia Leilei, President Assistant of Chinese National Academy of Arts, Director of Cultural Development Strategy Research Center

Unit V: The Future of China - U.S. Cultural Relations

283 Moderator's Introduction
Jim Leach, Chairman of US National Endowment for the Humanities

291 Dialogue is a Principle for Human Life
Liu Mengxi, Director of Institute of Chinese Culture, Chinese National Academy of Arts

298 Culture is More Powerful than Politics
Allison Blakely, Professor of European and Comparative History, Boston University

310 The World and China in the Next Decade: A Perspective from International Politics
Jin Canrong, Associate Dean, School of International Studies, Renmin University of China

323 Cultural Relations — The Way of Cooperation Between The Powers
Josiah Ober Professor of Classics and Professor of Political Science, Stanford University

News Roundup

344 Building the New Century's Tower of Babel
Jia Leilei, President Assistant of Chinese National Academy of Arts, Director of Cultural Development Strategy Research Center

367 Constructing A Century Bridge of China-U.S. Cultural Exchange
Pan Yuan, Associate Research Fellow of Cultural Development Strategy Research Center, Chinese National Academy of Arts

383 Reconstructing the Pattern of Cultural Exchange Under the Context of Globalization
Xiao Qing, Assistant Research Fellow of Cultural Development Strategy Research Center, Chinese National Academy of Arts

394 Translation and Culture— American and Chinese Scholars and Artists Gather for Roundtable Discussions
Meredith Hindley, Senior Writer at the National Endowment for the Humanities

401 **Evolution of China-U.S. Cultural Forum**

Jim LEACH

Opening Address

开幕致辞

中华人民共和国文化部副部长、中国艺术研究院院长王文章开幕式致辞
Address at the Opening Ceremony by Wang Wenzhang, Vice Minister of Ministry of Culture of P.R.C,
President of Chinese National Academy of Arts

美国国家人文基金会主席吉姆、利奇开幕式致辞
Address at the Opening Ceremony by Jim Leach,
Chairman of the National Endowment for the Humanities

中华人民共和国文化部副部长王文章与美国国家人文基金会主席吉姆·利奇
庆祝签署继续举办论坛的谅解备忘录
Vice Minister of Ministry of Culture of P.R.C. Wang Wenzhang and Jim Leach,
Chairman of NEH Celebrate Signing a Memorandum of Understanding for Future Conferences

王文章

中华人民共和国文化部副部长
中国艺术研究院院长

尊敬的美国国家人文基金会主席吉姆·利奇先生，
尊敬的美国总统艺术人文委员会执行主任瑞秋·格斯林斯女士，
女士们，先生们，
大家上午好！

今天，由中华人民共和国文化部和美国国家人文基金会共同主办、以"跨文化双边对话"为主题的"第二届中美文化论坛"在美国加利福尼亚大学伯克利分校隆重举行。在此，我谨代表中华人民共和国文化部，对论坛的开幕表示衷心的祝贺！对出席论坛的中美两国专家学者、艺术家表示热烈的欢迎！

中美两国虽然远隔千山万水，但两国人民之间并没有因为空间的距离而相互阻隔。特别是1979年1月中美正式建交，联合签署了《中美文化交流协定》，开创了中美文化交流与合作的新纪元，两国之间的文化艺术交流空前活跃，且真正被对方更多的了解和接受。

今天的中国处在改革开放的新世纪，我们更以开阔的胸襟和悠远的眼光吸收世界各国的优秀文化。中国的学者和艺术家也通过越来越多地了解和借鉴美国的文化艺术，开阔视野，加深对外来文化的认识。现在，根据中美双方的有关协议，包括美国电影在内的多种美国文化产品进入了中国的文化市场，中国的表演艺术等也更多地进入美国观众的视野，这些都为双方的公众所认同，中美文化交流正在迈向一个不断升华的历史时代。这不但沟通了两国人民的心灵与情感，增进理解和信任，还对推进中美两国关系健康、稳定地发展起到了重要作用。两国人民在文化上的这种友好交往，使我们想到了美国学者托马斯·弗里德曼先生在他的《21世纪简史》中所说的，我们现在生存的世界是平的。世界经济一体化和现代化进程缩短了人们之间的距离，当今时代，文化的沟通和交流更显重要。

2008年12月，由中华人民共和国文化部与美国国家人文基金会共同主办，中国艺术研究院承办的"第一届中美文化论坛"在北京成功召开。论坛围绕"数字化时代的文化遗产保护和展现"这一主题，针对数字技术在文化遗产保护中的作用、数字技术与当代文化发展等多个论题进行了广泛、深入的对话与研讨。它是中美两国主流文化机构进行的第一次学术合作，也成为中美两国在文化领域进行高层学术交流新的历史起点。中美两国从此在文化艺术领域建起了一个具有公共性、学术性、开放性、互动性的文化艺术高端交流平台。

2009年11月，中国国家主席胡锦涛与美国总统奥巴马在北京举行会谈，发表了《中美联合声明》，其中特别强调了人文交流对促进中美关系具有重要意义，并提出建立新的双边交流机制，举办中美文化论坛，以制度化的方式全面推动中美两国在文化艺术领域的相关合作与密切交流。

2010年5月，中华人民共和国国务委员刘延东和美国国务卿希拉里·克林顿联合主持了"中美人文交流高层磋商机制成立仪式暨第一次会议"，双方再次强调办好中美文化论坛，加强人文交流的共同愿望，显示了两国领导人对中美文化论坛和两国文化领域加深交流的高度重视。

在这种背景下，我们双方在美国加利福尼亚大学伯克利分校举行的第二届"中美文化论坛"，显示出其所具有的独特时代意义。它标志着中美两国文化交流与合作正在不断走向深入，并向着制度化、高端化的境界迈进。此次论坛以"跨文化双边对话"为主题，旨在从文化艺术的各个领域全面回顾中美交流的历史，探讨两国文化交流的现实路径，展望中美文化关系发展的未来，通过多种文化交流方式，增进中美两国在人文社会科学和文化艺术领域中的交流与合作，从而推动文化的多样化协调发展，开辟中美文化交流与合作的新天地。

今天参加论坛的中国艺术家和学者，都是以自己的艺术创造和学术研究在文化艺术界享有盛誉的杰出人士。他们中的许多人曾多次到访美国，与美方学术界、艺术界有友好的交往。中国古代的哲学家曾子曾经说，"君子以文会友，以友辅仁"，讲的是人与人之间可以通过文化的交流增进友情，并通过加深友情，修养仁德，从而达成对美好生活的共同向往。

当代中国非常注重政治、经济、社会、文化的协调发展，文化建设已经摆在中国现代化发展的重要位置，文化艺术百花齐放、百家争鸣的局面正在形成。我们在努力进行当代文化创新、弘扬民族优秀文化的同时，也将不断努力学习和借鉴世界各国的优秀文化，与世界各国携手并进，走向人类美好的未来。

站在21世纪的地平线上，回顾中美文化交流的历史，我们将以积极务实的态度展望更加美好的未来。中国有句古语，"万物并育而不相害，道并行而不相悖"，不同文化的交流会使我们更加了解对方而尊重对方，会使我们在学习与借鉴对方的同时提高我们各自在文化艺术领域建设发展的创造性。文化因交流而丰富，因交融而多彩。我相信，在双方共同努力下，中美两国的文化合作必将迈上一个新的台阶。中美两国文化机构和专家学者、艺术家们不断加强交流与合作，符合两国人民的根本利益，有助于增进两国人民的了解与友谊，它必将造福于两国和两国人民，同时也有利于促进东西方文明的相互沟通与和谐发展，成为推动人类文明不断进步的重要动力。

最后，向共同主办此次盛会的美国国家人文基金会和为论坛承办付出智慧和辛劳的加利福尼亚大学伯克利分校表示诚挚的感谢！预祝第二届中美文化论坛取得圆满成功！祝中美两国人民的友谊地久天长，中美文化交流与合作不断结出丰硕成果！

谢谢大家！

Wang Wenzhang

Vice Minister of Ministry of Culture,
People's Republic of China
President of Chinese National Academy of Arts

Respected Mr. Jim Leach, Chairman of NEH,
Respected Ms. Rachel Goslins, Executive Director of PCAH,
Ladies and Gentlemen,
Good morning.

Today, the Second China-U.S. Cultural Forum, jointly held by the Ministry of Culture of the People's Republic of China and the National Endowment for the Humanities and themed by A Binational Conversation on Bridging Cultures, has commenced at the University of California, Berkeley. On behalf of the Ministry of Culture, I want to express my heartfelt congratulation and extend warmest welcome to experts, scholars and artists from both China and the United States.

Geographically, China and the United States are oceans apart, but the peoples of our two countries have never been alienated from each other due to the long space distance, especially when China and the United States established formal diplomatic relations in January, 1979, and jointly signed the China-United States Cultural Exchange Agreement, which initiated a new era for cultural exchange and cooperation between the two countries. From thereon, cultural and artistic exchanges between both countries have become unprecedentedly active, and the culture and arts of both countries have come to be truly known and accepted by each other.

Today's China is in the new age of reform and opening-up. With a great breadth of mind and a long-term view, we absorb the best of all cultures from countries around the world. Chinese scholars and artists broaden their horizons and deepen their understanding of foreign cultures through increasingly getting to know and borrowing from American culture and arts. At present, under relevant agreements entered into between China and the U.S., a wide array of American cultural products, including American films are being introduced to the Chinese cultural market, and more and more Chinese performing arts, etc. are also coming into the American spectators' sight, all of which are agreed by the peoples of both countries. China-U.S. cultural exchange continues to grow and is approaching a historical time.

Cultural exchange allows peoples of both countries to better communicate, improves rapport, fosters understanding and builds trust, as well as plays an important role in sustaining a sound and stable bilateral relationship. As we are seeing a growth in cultural exchange between our two countries, I am reminded of what Thomas Friedman said in *A Brief History of the Twenty-first Century*: The world is flat. The process of integration and modernization of world economy have shortened the distances among people. In contemporary times, the communication and exchange of culture stand out to be of greater importance.

The First China-U.S. Cultural Forum, jointly held by the Ministry of Culture of the People's Republic of China and the National Endowment for the Humanities, and organized by Chinese National Academy of Arts, took place in Beijing in December 2008. The Forum was a great success. The theme of the Forum was the "Preservation and Exhibition of Cultural Heritage in the Digital Age". Participants engaged in a wide range of in-depth dialogues and discussions, including the role digital technology plays in preserving cultural heritage, and the relevance of digital technology to modern culture. This was the first academic event jointly held by mainstream academic organizations in China and the United States. It marked a new historical starting point for our two countries to engage in high level academic exchange in the cultural realm. Since then, China and the United States have established a public, academic, open and dynamic cultural and artistic high level platform for the two sides to engage in exchanges in the realms of culture and arts.

In November, 2009, Chinese President Hu Jintao and U.S. President Obama held talks in Beijing and issued the *China-U.S. Joint Statement*, which in particular stresses the significance of exchange in humanities and arts to promoting bilateral relationship, and proposes the establishment of a new bilateral mechanism and holding the China-U.S. Cultural Forum, in an attempt to fully push forward relevant cooperation and exchange in the cultural and artistic dimension in an institutionalized way.

In May, 2010, P.R.C. State Councilor Liu Yandong and U.S. Secretary of State Hillary Clinton jointly hosted the Establishment of the *China-United* States High Level Humanities and Arts Consultative Institution and its First Conference. Both Sides reiterated their common aspiration of holding the China-U.S. Cultural Forum and enhancing exchange in humanities and arts, which showed that leaders from both sides attached great importance to the China-U.S. Cultural Forum and the deepening of cultural exchange between the two sides.

In this context, the Second China-U.S. Cultural Forum that we hold at the University of California, Berkeley bears unique significance of our time. It signifies that bilateral cultural exchange and cooperation between China and the United States will continue to be deepened, and move towards institutionalized and high-end development. The theme of this forum is A Binational Conversation on Bridging Cultures. The purpose of this forum is to, through various aspects of culture and different forms of arts, review thoroughly the history of China-U.S. exchange, seek a practical path for bilateral exchange, and discuss the prospect of China-U.S. cultural exchange. Through various means of cultural exchange, this forum hopes to strengthen bilateral communication and cooperation in the areas of humanities and social sciences, culture and arts. This will in effect promote cultural diversity and create a new chapter in China-U.S. cultural exchange and cooperation.

The Chinese artists and scholars participating in this forum are remarkable public figures in China who enjoy high reputation in the cultural and artistic circles for their artistic innovations and academic researches. Many of them have visited the United States multiple times, and have friendly contact with the American academic and artistic circles. An ancient Chinese philosopher, Zengzi, said: "A gentleman makes friends through literary pursuits, and friendship ennobles benevolence", which indicates that people can enhance their friendship through cultural exchange, thereby cultivating benevolence, and finally reach common aspiration for a better life.

Today's China attaches great importance to economic, political, social and cultural development in a coordinated manner. Cultural development has occupied a key position in China's modernization effort. We are witnessing in China the inception of an era where a wide range of arts and academic schools are emerging and thriving. As we endeavor to encourage cultural innovation and promote our national culture, we are also making continuous efforts to draw experience from other cultures in the world, in the hope of making progress together with other countries of the world and moving ahead to a bright future of humanity.

As we stand on the horizon of the 21st century and look back on the history of China-U.S. cultural exchange, we should be proactive, and practical, and hope for a promising prospect. There is an old Chinese saying: "All living creatures grow together without harming one another; ways run parallel without interfering with one another." Cultural exchange makes it possible for us to better understand and respect each other. As we learn from and draw on the experience of each other, we become more innovative in the construction and development of cultural and artistic fields. Cultural exchange and integration is what makes a culture grow and thrive. I believe that with joint efforts, cultural cooperation between China and the United States will reach a new height. For cultural organizations, experts and scholars and artists of China and the United States to engage in more frequent exchange and cooperation is in the interest of our two countries and peoples. It is conducive to strengthening bilateral understanding and friendship and will benefit both sides; furthermore, it is conducive to reinforcing communication and harmonious development between the civilization of the East and that of the West, and shall be a key driving force to promote the continued advancement of humanity.

Finally, I would like to convey my sincere gratitude to the intelligence and diligence devoted by the National Endowment for the Humanities and the University of California, Berkeley. I wish the Second China-U.S. Cultural Forum a complete success. May the friendship between our two peoples last forever and cultural exchange and cooperation between our two countries continue to yield fruitful results.

Thank you!

吉姆·利奇

美国国家人文基金会主席

王部长、高领事,以及来自华盛顿和中国的好朋友们,我们欢迎你们的到来!
此外,能在伯克利这所著名的美国大学举办此次盛会,我们深感荣幸!

19世纪时,有一位非常伟大的美国诗人,名为沃尔特·惠特曼。他曾经提到自己有一个梦想,就是希望有朝一日,全世界的诗人和诗歌有机会汇聚在一起,组成一个由个人及其作品所构成的更大群体,一起为世界带来和平。两千五百年前,孔子曾说,地球上的人们如果能够多花一点时间欣赏音乐,了解礼仪,战争将不复存在。

昨天,我有幸采访这个杰出代表团中的一个成员莫言。我问他,对于世界的更好理解是来自政治家和政治主张,还是来自小说家和关于文化的作品。他认为答案显而易见,"无疑,"他说,"是来自对文化有深刻理解的人,来自世界各地的优秀文学作品。"

然而,对很多所谓的现实主义者而言,这听上去似乎很不现实,且过于幼稚。大概四五年前,恰逢胡锦涛主席就任不久,我正巧在北京,大使馆帮我安排了与胡主席的见面会谈。会面结束时,我对胡主席说,我要去见一位在政府机构中级别比他还高的人。他有些困惑地看着我,问道:"那个人会是谁呢?"我解释说,我要去拜访文化部部长。我说文化比政府政治要大得多,政府只是文化的一部分,而非相反。他笑了,说有可能如此。正是在这种尊重文化、理解不同文化的氛围下,我们欢迎各位莅临此次盛会。

谢谢!

Jim Leach

Chairman of US National Endowment for the Humanities

Minister Wang, Council General Gao and good friends from Washington and China,

We welcome you all.

We are particularly honored to be at this great American university of Berkeley!

In the 19th century, we had a very great American poet named Walt Whitman. He once suggested that he had a great dream, and the dream was that all of the poets of the world and all of the poems of the world would come together, and that would serve as a greater group of individuals and a body of work to bring peace to the world.

Two and a half millennium earlier, Confucius wrote that if peoples of the earth would spend more time appreciating music and understanding courtesy, there would be no war.

Yesterday, I have the honor to interview MO Yan of this wonderful delegation. And I asked him if he thought greater understanding of the world would come from politicians and assertions of political doctrine or from novelists and writings about culture. And he took this as an obvious and not difficult question. "Of course," he said, "It would come from those who understand culture, from the great literary works of the world."

Well, to many so-called realists, this may sound very unrealistic and very naïve. For four or five years ago, I happened to be in Beijing shortly after President Hu took office, and the embassy set up a meeting between President Hu and me. At the end of the meeting, I said to President Hu, I was going to see a person in the government of higher rank than he was. And he looked at me somewhat quizzically and said, "By chance who would that be?" And I explained that I was going to visit the Minister of Culture. And I said culture is much bigger than government politics. Government is part of culture, not the other way around. He laughed and suspected that might be the case. It is under this atmosphere of the importance of culture and of culture understanding that we welcome all of you to this great conference.

Thank you!

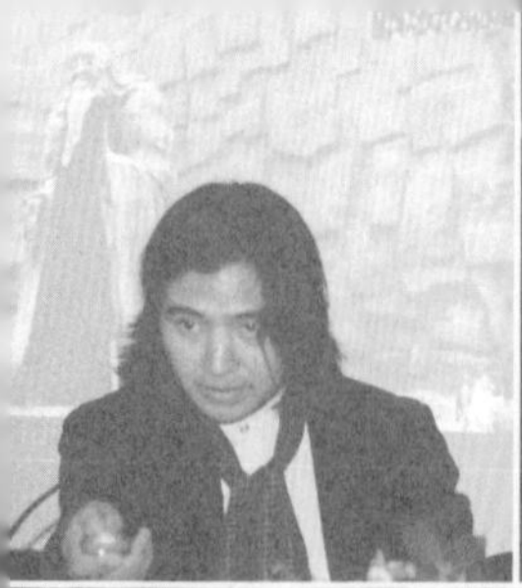
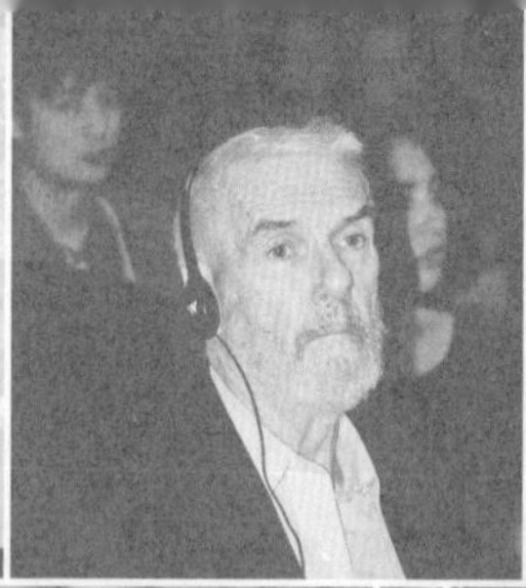
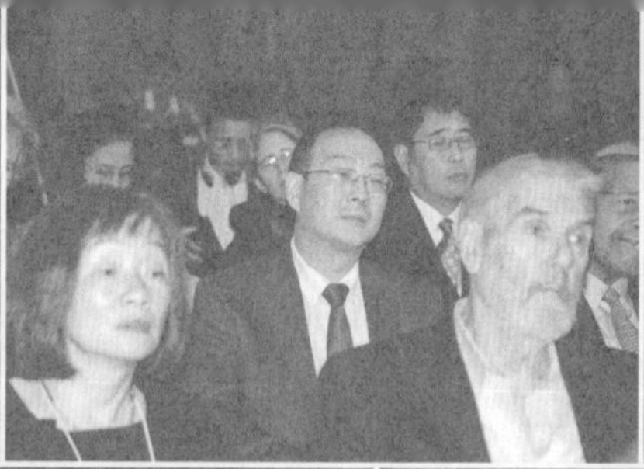
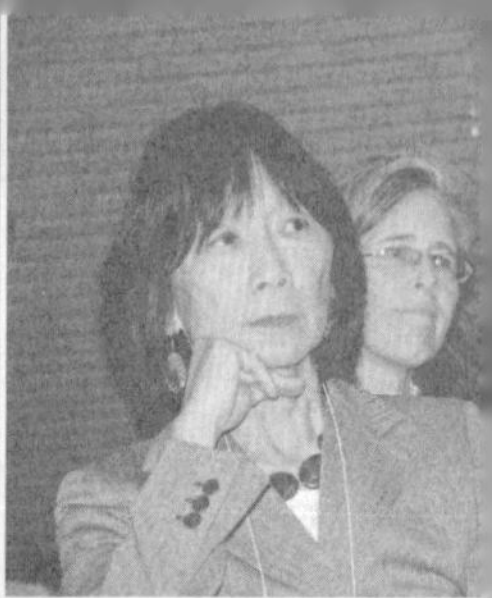
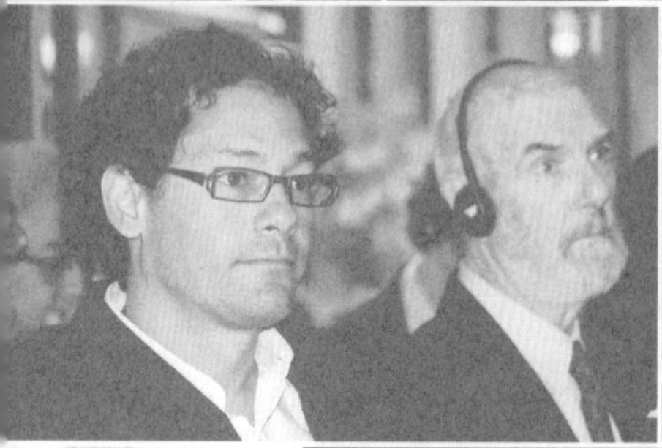
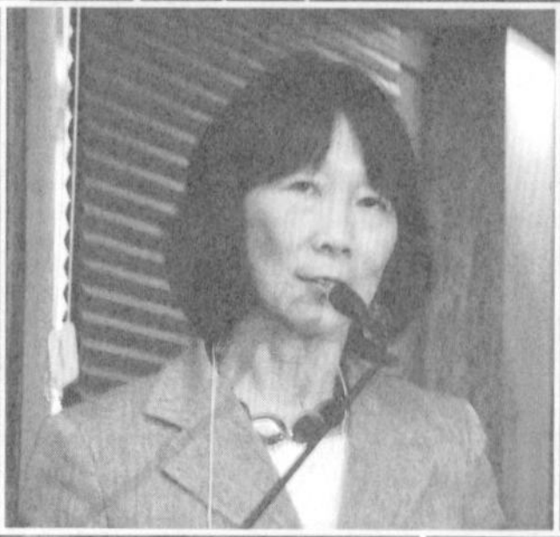
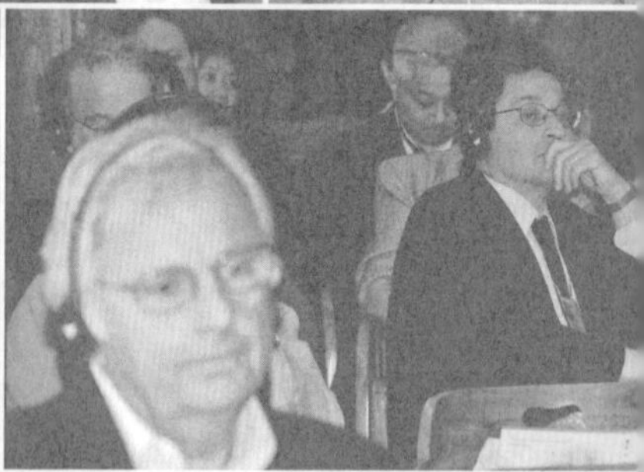
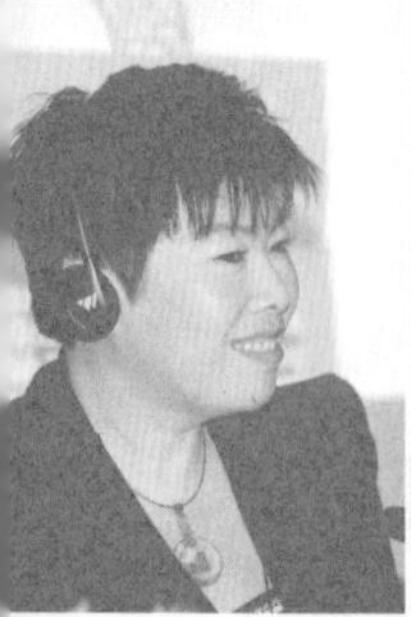
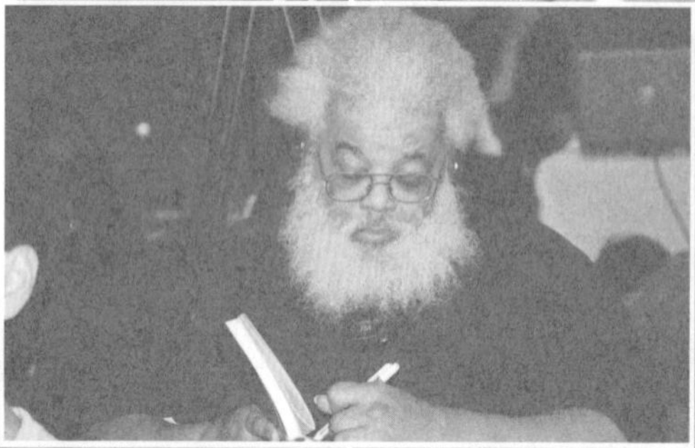
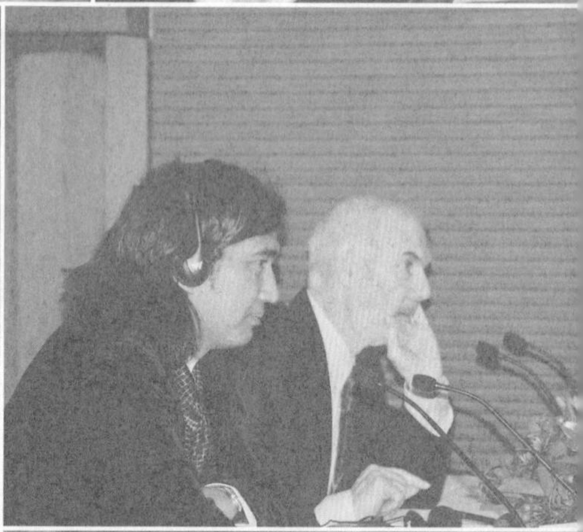
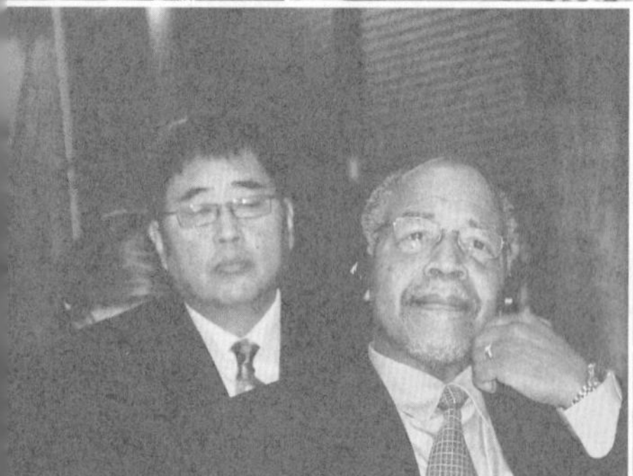
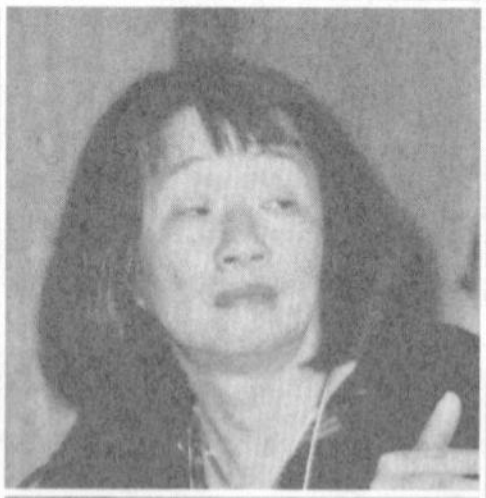
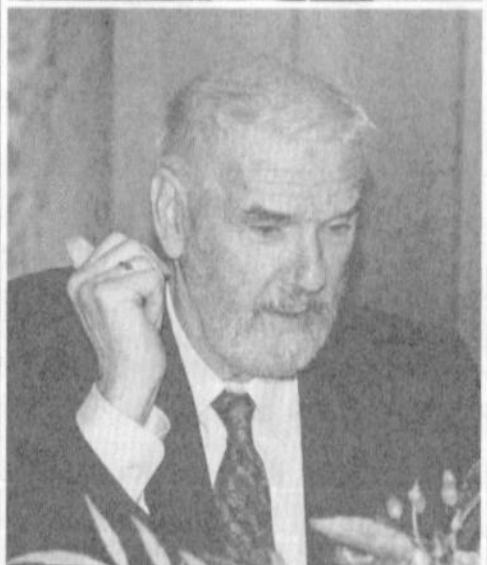
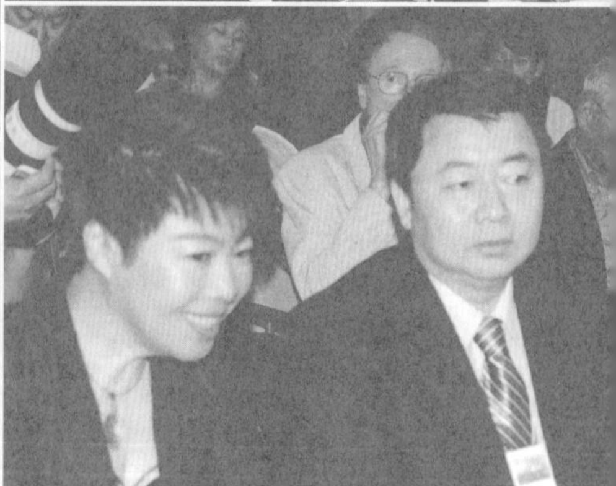
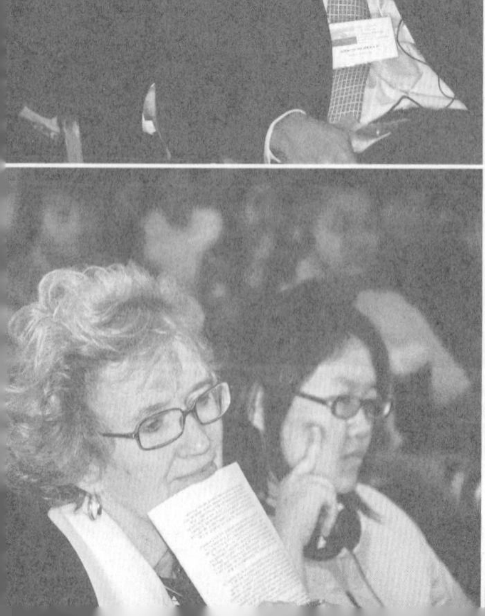
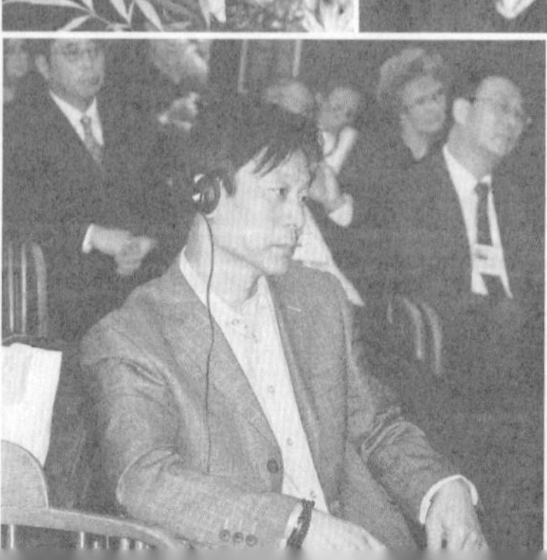
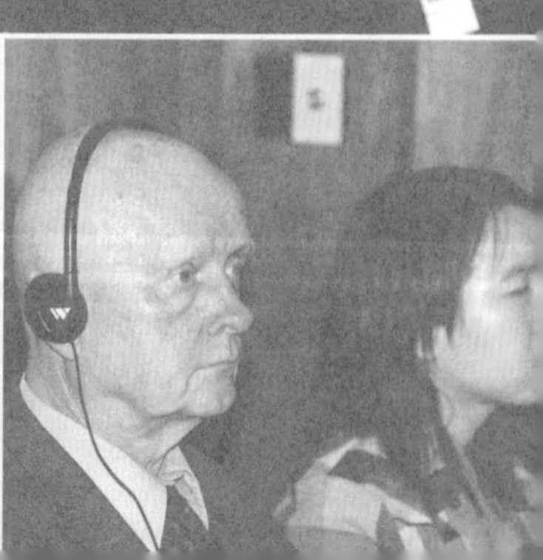

UNIT ONE: HISTORICAL PERSPECTIVES ON CHINA-U.S. CULTURAL RELATIONS

第一单元 中美文化关系的历史回顾

加利福尼亚大学伯克利分校东亚语言文学系教授安德鲁·琼斯
主持人导语
Andrew Jones, Professor of East Asian Languages and Cultures, University of California, Berkeley
"Moderator's Introduction"

美国学术团体联合会主席余宝琳
主持人导语
Pauline Yu, President, American Council of Learned Societies
"Moderator's Introduction"

北京师范大学艺术与传媒学院副院长于丹教授做主题发言
《中国传统文化的现代价值》

Yu Dan, Professor and Associate Dean of School of Arts and Communication,
Beijing Normal University
"The Value of Chinese Traditional Culture in Modern Times"

耶鲁大学历史系高级讲师金安平做主题发言
《中国文学传统如何影响西方》

Annping Chin, Senior Lecturer, Department of History, Yale University
"How Does the Chinese Literary Tradition Reach the West"

中国艺术研究院雕塑院院长、美术研究所所长吴为山研究员做主题发言
《我雕塑艺术中的文化观》
Wu Weishan, Research Fellow and Director of Institute of Fine Arts,
Director of Institute of Sculpture, Chinese National Academy of Arts
"My View of Culture in Sculptural Arts"

耶鲁大学历史系斯特林荣誉教授乔纳森·斯宾塞做主题发言
《中美关系的历史起点与维度》
Jonathan Spence, Sterling Professor of History Emeritus, Yale University
"The Historical Start Point and Aspects of China-U.S. Relations"

主持人导语

安德鲁·琼斯

加利福尼亚大学伯克利分校
东亚语言文学系教授

　　欢迎大家参加第二届中美文化论坛。我是安德鲁·琼斯，加利福尼亚大学伯克利分校中国研究中心的主席。今天非常荣幸地在此和大家一起讨论有关文化和艺术在中美两国关系中的角色问题，我相信将会是非常富有成效。我也很高兴这次活动能在加利福尼亚大学伯克利分校举行，因为该校从19世纪以来一直是中美文化交流的中心。加利福尼亚大学伯克利分校是美国最早设立中国研究教授职位的高校之一，当时是1872年，加利福尼亚州人口仅为一万九千多人，还不及如今伯克利市的人口数量。当时开始教授汉语时，伯克利还没有成为一个城市，学校毕业生仅有12名。

　　当然，中文教学并不是中美文化交流唯一的项目。我们之间的关系还有更悠久的历史。比如三年前我们建立了C.V.斯塔尔东亚图书馆，馆中图书的所有者是约翰·弗赖尔（中文名字为傅兰雅）先生。他是19世纪上海江南制造局的首席翻译之一，在将现代科学译成中文、引进中国方面，他发挥了重要作用。

　　多年以来，伯克利分校曾接待很多中国现代艺术、文学方面的专家和文化名人，并吸收他们在此执教。其中包括"五四"时期伟大的知识分子和语言学家赵元任、作家张爱玲，以及现代作家北岛和余华等。今天的伯克利仍是一个充满活力的中文研究和教学中心。

　　在大学外面，从当年的淘金热到如今的硅谷热，加州湾地区和加利福尼亚州北部的建设都有中国移民参与。加州北部的文化、文学和建筑都受到中国和亚洲文化不可磨灭的影响。实际上，今天我们所在的这个名为"教工俱乐部"的建筑，就能反映出亚洲文化对我国建筑风格的影响。

　　我衷心感谢国家人文基金会、中华人民共和国文化部以及加利福尼亚大学伯克利分校中国研究中心的各位同仁安排了今天这样一个非常有意义的盛会。

Andrew Jones

Professor of East Asian
Languages and Cultures,
University of California,
Berkeley

Moderator's Introduction

Welcome to the Second China-U.S. Cultural Forum. I'm Andrew Jones, Chair of the Center for Chinese Studies here at the University of California, Berkeley. It's a real pleasure to see all of you here at the beginning of what promises to be a fruitful program of discussion of the role of art and culture in Sino-American relations. I'm also gratified that this conference will take place here, at the university and in a region that has been from the 19th century onwards a center for Chinese-American exchange. Berkeley was one of the very first American universities to establish a chair in Chinese in the year 1872, when the population of California was 19,000, less than the population of Berkeley, the city today. The year Chinese started being taught here, Berkeley was not yet a city, in fact, and the university only graduated 12 students.

These connections of course go much deeper than just teaching Chinese, of course. For instance, the collection in the C.V. Starr East Asian library, which was just constructed 3 years ago, I believe, actually belongs to a man named John Fryer. John Fryer was known in Chinese as Fu Lanya, and he is one of the crucial figures in the introduction of modern science into China in his role of the head translator at the Jiangnan Arsenal in Shanghai. He played a crucial role in translating modern science into Chinese as one of the translators at Jiangnan Zhizao Ju in Shanghai in the 19th century.

Over the years Berkeley has also played host to, and actually become home to many luminaries in modern Chinese art literature and culture, So including figures as famous as the great May Fourth intellectual and linguist Zhao Yuanren as well as the writer Zhang Ailing, and contemporary writers such as Bei Dao and Yu Hua. And Berkeley continues as a vibrant center for research and teaching in Chinese studies.

Outside the university, this California bay area and northern California was built in part by Chinese immigrants, from the Gold Rush to the Silicon Rush of more recent times. The Culture, the writing and the architecture of northern California are indelibly affected by Chinese culture and Asian culture. Actually the very building we are in today, the Faculty Club, is an example of that influence of Asian culture on our own architecture here.

So, I want to thank everyone at the National Endowment for the Humanities, the Ministry of Culture as well as our Center for Chinese Studies for arranging such a beautiful conjunction of occasion and place.

主持人导语

余宝琳

美国学术团体联合会主席

我是美国学术团体联合会的余宝琳，非常荣幸能担任第一专题讨论小组的主持人。今天上午圆桌会议的主题是中美文化关系的历史回顾。在讨论开始时，我还有另外一个任务，就是谈一谈中美文化理解和交流的主要基础之一，即我们简称为中美学生和学者之间的学术关系以及大学关系。我要强调的有三点：就是这一关系是悠久、持续和广泛的。

当然，当我说中美关系历史悠久，我们不得不说这是相对而言。与中国五千年的历史相比，我们不能说美国的历史很长。中美大学的关系以及现代美国大学的历史始于19世纪。那时，建立紧密的双边文化关系的目标早已确立，并已开始实施。

实际上，有关这一问题，最早的重要声明之一便是1872年出任加利福尼亚大学第一任校长的丹尼尔·科伊特·吉尔曼在伯克利做出的。他认为，伯克利应成为一个真正的跨文化研究中心。他问道："是否应该在此区域成立一所高校，即便不与加利福尼亚大学相连，也可建在学校附近，一方面向美国人传授东方的语言、文学和历史知识，另一方面教授中国人和日本人欧洲和美国的现代语言和科学知识？"现在，这样的一所高校或许尚未成形，但正如安德鲁所提到的，就在那年，第一个中国研究中心在校内建成，教授东方语言和文学。吉尔曼校长将这一发展赞誉为加强加利福尼亚和东亚文化与人民密切联系的开拓之举。

中国文明的迅速扩展及其文化生产力的深刻内涵吸引美国人研究中国。让我感到骄傲的是，我所在的机构——美国学术团体联合会——在其1919年成立之后不久即已成为中美学术交流研究的推动者之一。在过去的70年中，美国学术团体联合会至少赞助了一个、有时是多个学术委员会，为以中国为主题的研究、会议和出版物等提供奖金。同样值得一提的是，自1980年起，国家人文基金会已拨款逾6200万美元支持与中国相关的研究。

第二，中美大学之间的联系尤为持久，也许是全球高等教育史上最为突出的联系之一。我敢说，从19世纪的传教式活动开始直至今天，中美两国在教育方面的联系比中国与任何其他国家、乃至日本等地理位置更近的国家的联系更为持久，且影响更为深刻。1949年以前，前往美国学习的中国学生比前往其他国家学习的中国学生人数更多。我的父母就在其中。20世纪50年代，这一合作关系受到阻碍。但其很快得到了恢复的事实恰恰印证了我的观点。即使两国的政治关系紧张，学术和文化的交流仍兴盛不衰。为之做出贡献的机构包括美国与中华人民共和国学术交流委员会。该委员会斥资3000万美元向中国输送美国学生和学者。如今，大批的中国学生来到美国北部的院校学习，最新的统计数字为十万，表明中美两国的学术互通充满了生机与活力。

第三，在今后，我认为我们可以推动更为广泛和紧密的学术合作，这要归功于正对教育和文化模式起改型作用的经济制度和技术改革。今天，中国和美国在经济方面有着千丝万缕的联系，这一联系比以往任何时候都更为紧密。从费城到波特兰的学校系统已在美国引入了中文课程，一些学校甚至从幼儿园起就开始教授中文。美国高等院校中的中文课程与其他人文课程相比更为有力和兴盛，并在不断发展。如今，每年约有一万五千名美国学生前往中国学习，奥巴马总统可能希望这一数字上升到十万，我相信这一目标将会实现。

据《纽约时报》报道，中国进行了蔚为壮观的现代教育拓展，本科生人数越来越多，拥有博士学位的人数在十年内增长了五倍。如今，中国大学入学人数已居世界首位。此情况对真正意义上的跨国学术交流的合作和开发造成了负担。我们必须将这些活动建立在对文化深刻而广泛的理解基础之上。我们必须坚持把文化和人文知识作为中美文化和经济联系的基础。美国学会是全世界有关中国文化及其古代和现代表达的最重要的知识库之一，而目前选择来我们学校学习或工作的年轻中国学者的见解和专业知识正定期更新和重塑这一知识库。我们需要这里以及中国的学者们多样化的视角和见解，以进行真正意义上的成功合作。我们终究是在各种文化之间建立桥梁，目的不是消除不同的价值观，而是欣赏、理解和解释这些价值观。历史显示，我们已经为这一最终目标开创了良好的开端，现实要求我们做更多的工作，尽更大的努力。

Moderator's Introduction

Pauline Yu
President, American Council of Learned Societies

I'm Pauline Yu of the American Council of Learned Societies, and it's my pleasure to moderate the first panel. This morning's round table has been asked to provide historical perspectives on U.S.-China cultural relations. But I was also asked to begin the discussion by focusing on one of the main foundations for China- U.S. cultural understanding and exchange that we may just simply call the academic relationship between students and scholars in the United States and China, the University relationship. And I have three central points to make: it has been long, it has been durable, and it has been extensive.

Of course when I say that the Sino-US relationship is a long one, we have to think of it as a relative statement, and we can't call the history of United States very long compared with the five-thousand-year history of China. But the history and the history of the modern university here really only goes back to that 19th century. Within that period, the goal of building a strong bilateral cultural relationship has been long stated and acted upon.

In fact, one of the most important first statements was made right here at Berkeley, when Daniel Coit Gilman, who was the first president of the University of California assumed office in 1872. He envisioned Berkeley as a true intercultural study center. He asked, "would it not be fit that in this vicinity, near to, if not in connection with, this university, a high seminary should be founded, having the double purpose of enlightening Americans in respect to the languages, literature and history of the East and of instructing the Chinese and Japanese in modern languages and sciences of Europe and America?" Now the seminary may never quite have taken shape, but as Andrew mentioned, that very year the first study center was created on campus the legacy of professorship of oriental languages and literatures, a development President Gilman praised as an early recognition of this intimate relationship that must be developed between California and the cultures and people of East Asia.

It was upon the rapid expansion of Chinese civilization and the impressive substance of its cultural productivity that fuel the American people to study China. And I'm very proud that my own organization, the American Council of Learned Societies has been one of the major promoters of research on the scholarly exchange with China, began shortly after our Council was founded in 1919. For the past 70 years, ACLS has sponsored at least one and sometimes several scholarly committees, charged with the awarding funds for research, scholarships, conferences and publications on China. It is also worth noting that since 1980, the National Endowment for the Humanities has spent more than 62 million dollars in support of China-related research as well.

Second, I think we should take heart from the fact that the China-U.S. university relationship has been especially durable, perhaps one of the very remarkable appearing in the global history of higher education. Indeed I would argue that from the 19th century missionary policies until today, the US-Chinese educational relationship has proved more long lasting and influential than China's relationship with any other nation, even those with greater cultural and geographical convenience, such as Japan. Before 1949, more Chinese students and scholars went to the United States to study than to any other country. My own parents were among them. That partnership was decisively stagnated in the 1950s, of course. But the fact that it was restored with such relative ease and enthusiasm only underlines my point. Even when political relations were strained, scholarly and cultural exchange flourished, thanks to such organizations as the Committee on Scholarly Communication with the People's Republic of China, which has spent 30 million dollars to send American students and scholars to China. The impressive numbers of Chinese students coming to us in the ordinary American institutions today, nearly 100,000, by latest count, shows that there is great evidence a vigorous academic traffic in both directions.

Third, in the years ahead, I think we can force even more extensive and intense academic partnership, thanks to economic institutional and technological changes that are transforming the language of education and culture. Today, China and the US are economically entwined as never before. School systems from Philadelphia to Portland have introduced Chinese language programs in the United States with instruction and some school beginning as early as kindergarten. Chinese programs with US colleges and universities in some contrast to other programs in the humanities have been relatively strong and flourishing, and are growing. Approximately 15,000 American students now go to China, probably Obama would like that number to rise to 100,000 a year, and we will get there.

The New York Times reports that China has already pulled up one of the most remarkable expansion of education in modern times, increasing the number of undergraduates and people who hold doctorate degrees five folds in ten years. Enrollment in Chinese colleges and universities, you know, are now the largest in the world. So with this expanded field for action, the possibilities for partnership, collaboration, and development of genuinely transnational scholarly communities have burdened. We must ground these activities, I think, in a deep and broad understanding of culture. We must insist on the importance of culture, of humanistic knowledge as a foundation for any China-U.S. cultural and economic relationship. The American Academy is in fact one of the world's great reservoirs of scholarship concerning Chinese civilization and its antiquely and its contemporary expressions. And that reservoir is now also regularly renewed and reshaped by the insights and expertise of young scholars born in China, who have chosen to pursue their education or careers in our universities. We will need these multiple facets of perspectives of scholars here and scholars in China for truly successful collaboration. We build bridges between cultures after all, not to eradicate differences in values, but to appreciate, understand and interpret them. History shows we have already made a good start at this final task, the present demands that we do much more.

中国传统文化的现代价值

于丹

北京师范大学艺术与
传媒学院副院长，教授

内容提要：儒家、道家、佛家，都不提供结论，而只提供提点；它不提供大家统一的行为准则，但它提供思考方式。一个良性的文明，从来不是强制性的。它心平气和，包罗万象，以一种宁静的呈现去完成一种生态的平衡。当前，文明的意义分为三个步骤，第一是文明的传承，其次是文明的融合，第三是文化对于问题的解决。因为所有传承的目的是在今天建立一个新的文化生态，为今天世界上面临的所有共同的困惑提供一种出路。

  中美文化论坛以文明对话的方式呈现对当今社会和历史文化的态度。这种态度的交流比结论更为重要。在各种文明中，对于当代的意义分为三个步骤，第一是文明的传承，其次是文明的融合，第三是文化对于问题的解决。因为所有传承的目的是建立一个新的文化生态，而为今天世界上面临的所有共同的困惑提供一种出路。

  按照中国人的理解，什么是文化呢？ 在《周易》上曾经给出最早关于文化的定义，叫做"观乎人文，以化成天下"。所谓观乎人文，就是观察人间世象百态，以化成天下。就是提炼出来某种理念，再来流化于心，所以观察、凝聚，再去化生，这是文而化。在过去的文化研究中，我们过多地强调文化作为一种文明成果的属性，而忽略了它流化天下的动态的过程。

  在今天这个文明交流的世界里，文化作为动词存在，作为行为存在，作为过程存在。也许要被特别的放大，是我们这种文明的对话。可以说所有文化的语言是国际的，但文化的语法是民族的，我们只不过以本民族的语法共同完成一个世界文明语言的交流，如何成为一个新的生态，那么刚才王部长提到一些话，说今天的世界是一个平面的。这样的一个世界上，再去完成化生天下，已经不是某一个民族、某一个文化态度内部的事情。

所以中国的文化思想是什么呢？儒家、道家、佛家形成了它共同的源头，简而言之，它对于世界能够提供一种借鉴意义，就是中国的儒家教我们关注人与社会之间的关系，中国的道家教我们关注人与自然和环境之间的关系，而中国的佛家教我们关注人与内心、自我之间的关系。我想无论哪一个民族的人都会面临我们在社会中自我结论的建立，人和自然环境之间的身心平衡，以及一个人在内心中的自我确认。

可以说儒家、道家、佛家，都不提供结论，而只提供提点，它不提供大家统一的行为准则，但它提供思考方式，所以一个良性的文明，从来不是强制性的。它心平气和，包罗万象，它以一种宁静的呈现去完成一种生态的平衡。中国的文化思想在跟美国文化的对话中，能够呈现出来什么样的普适价值呢？

以中国的儒家文化为例，我想起码在这三个方面，它是耐人寻味的：首先君子的标准与现代公民的标准之间有没有关联？如果说现代公民社会，大家都会很熟悉，但是中国的好公民是什么样的呢？在《论语》中有大量对于君子的阐述。它所提出的是一个人发自内心的反省，来确定它跟世界关系的调整。

那么这种反省是否过时呢？大家都知道君子日三省乎己，要每天做多次的自我反省，反省了哪些方面呢？我们可以站在今天的理性上去重新解读它的三个标准。孔子说的第一个标准，叫做为人谋而不忠乎？就是一个人在社会上做职业的时候，做到忠诚了吗？恪尽职守了吗？第二个标准叫做与朋友交而不信乎？在社会伦理中跟朋友的承诺，完成了吗？守信了吗？第三个标准叫做传不习乎？在如今这个快速传播时代中，所得到的外在信息，是否通过学习转化成了个人的生命经验呢？

这三个标准，我们用21世纪的视角来看，它评价了人的职业角色、伦理角色和生命自我角色。这同样也是世界上每一个人都面临的角色。在社会角色中做到一个字，忠诚。在伦理角色中守到一个底限，信。在个人生命角色中以学习的方式完成更新与成长。大家看，这是不是在美国、在欧洲、在全球都有它的借鉴意义呢？所以简而言之，我认为君子的方式，提供了一种个人融入社会、取得自律的可能。

第二点价值，就是对于整个社会的态度，中国儒家提出和而不同，也就是说和谐的前提是尊重不同的个性，每一个人不同的取向，这种坚守融合在一个社会中，才是一种正确的文明。文明不以完成统一的强制标准去泯灭每个人的个性，但是每一个人的个性又要在大社会的体系中达到均衡，这是一种现代法律和制度下理想的公民社会的状态。

第三点就是中国儒家提供了"仁"这样一个知行合一的伦理起点，就像我们所看到的，在美国、在欧洲，很多人从小是去教堂的，他可以有自己在与神的交流中得到个人生命经验平衡和提升的一种方式。但中国人的信仰在哪里呢？在于伦理。所以我开玩笑说，中国人跟美国人，不小心都绊了一个跟头，美国人可能本能地说"Oh, My God！"而中国人会说，"哎哟，我的妈呀！"也就是说一个美国人不会本能地说"Oh, my mum！"一个中国人也不会说"哦，我的神啊！"因为我们从小没有培养这样一种文化习惯，所以这只是文明的差异，不存在高下。每一种文明当下态度的呈现，一定带着它的基因和传承。

那么从伦理出发，中国人是从哪里去开始呢？就是"仁义"的"仁"字，这个中国字很简单，单立人，一个"二"字，在中国的民间说法中，这叫做"二人成仁"。两个人之间的人际关系协调好是世界上最大的仁爱，所以孔子才会说，一个人的仁爱，就是"己欲立而立人，己欲达而达人"。一个人用立自己的心帮别人树立价值，用发达自己的心去帮别人一起发达，这就是"仁爱"，所以它既是一个理念，又是一个行为，它是一个知行合一的起点。

中国的儒家思想实在是博大精深，我只是站在21世纪的坐标上举这三个例子，君子与现代公民的关联，社会"和而不同"的标准，与知行合一、仁爱的起点。我相信它不仅仅是中国的，它也是国际的。我们完成这种呈现，是为了最后在全球化的范围中，能够让一种新文化的体系化成天下，带我们去解决共同的迷惑，走向大同世界！

The Value of Chinese Traditional Culture in Modern Times

Yu Dan

Professor and Associate Dean of School of Arts and Communication, Beijing Normal University

Abstract: Confucianism, Taoism, and Buddhism do not provide conclusions; instead, they provide suggestions; these schools of thinking do not provide a uniform standard for conducts; instead, they provide different perspectives. A good civilization is never forceful. It should be peaceful and all-embracing. It seeks to strike balance through a serene manifestation. In the present day, the significance of civilization is three-fold: first, the preservation of civilization; second, the integration of different civilizations; and third, civilization as a solution to today's challenges. The purpose in preserving civilization is to create a new cultural sphere, in hope of providing a solution for the common challenges the world faces today.

Through civilized dialogue, the China-U.S. Cultural Forum aims to discuss our respective views on the cultural aspect of the modern world, and on the values of our traditions. We might not reach a conclusion, but I think the exchange of our viewpoints is more important than reaching a conclusion.

In the present day, the significance of civilization is three-fold: first, the preservation of civilization; second, the integration of different civilizations; and third, civilization as a solution to today's challenges. The purpose in preserving civilization is to create a new cultural sphere, in hope of providing a solution for the common challenges the world faces today.

From a Chinese perspective, what is "culture"? The earliest definition of culture can be found in the Chinese classic *I-Ching* (The Book of Changes). Culture is defined as "observing the hundred different aspects of the world, and using the result of that observation to educate people under heaven." In other words, a specific notion is extracted from observation and used to educate people. So, culture is about observation, extraction, and education. In past cultural studies, we put too much focus on culture as an attribute of the legacy of civilization, and neglected the dynamic role of culture in educating people.

In the present day world where civilizations engage in exchanges, culture exists as a dynamic notion; culture is action as well as a process. Sometimes, it may be necessary to study culture under a microscope; for example, when we engage in this kind of dialogue. It can be said that all cultures share the same language, but every culture has its own grammar. We use the grammar of our own nationality to engage in an international dialogue, for the purpose of finding a new cultural sphere. I am reminded of what Vice Minister Wang said about how today's world is flat. In the world that we live in, it is not merely the job of one nationality or one culture to guide the world with principles, but a shared responsibility.

So what is Chinese culture about? Chinese culture originated from the teachings of Confucianism, Taoism, and Buddhism. In short, the significance of Chinese culture is such that others may draw from its experience. The teaching of Confucius is about the relationship between man and society; the teaching of Taoism focuses on the relationship between man and nature and the surrounding environment; and the teaching of Buddhism is about man and enlightenment from within, about self-identity. I think these notions can be found in every nationality: we all face the dilemma of finding our place in a society, finding physical and spiritual balance between man and nature, and finding selfhood from within our hearts.

Confucianism, Taoism, and Buddhism do not provide conclusions; instead, they provide suggestions; these schools of thinking do not provide a uniform standard for conducts; instead, they provide different perspectives. So I think that a good civilization is never forceful. It should be peaceful and all-embracing. It seeks to strike balance through a serene manifestation. So in the present day, as we engage in dialogue with the United States, what universal values can be brought forward from Chinese culture?

Let's take Confucian teaching as an example. I think there are three things worth looking into: firstly, what is the relevance between the criteria of a gentleman (man of noble character) and those of a present day citizen? We are all familiar with the notion of civil society. So in the context of Chinese society, what defines a good citizen? In Confucius' Analects, there are plenty of discussions on what defines a "gentleman". The Analects holds that a gentleman is someone who self-reflects from deep within to affirm his relationship with the surrounding world.

Can we say such self-reflection is no longer relevant in the present day? We all know the saying that a gentleman should self reflect many times on a daily basis. So what exactly does a gentleman self-reflect on? There are three things, and we can interpret them from a modern, rational perspective. According to Confucius, the first thing a gentleman should self-reflect upon is "devotion to your profession". A gentleman that assumes a profession should think whether he has been devoted to his profession, and whether he has expended every effort. The second criterion against which we gauge a gentleman is whether he has "fulfilled his promise to his friends"? Has he kept his words to his friends? The third criterion is "internalize external information". We are living in the age of communication. A gentleman receives information, and should learn to internalize the information into part of his personal experience.

If we speak about these three criteria using the perspective of the 21st century, we say that they represent an individual's professional role, ethical role, and the assertion of one's self-identity. These are things relevant to everyone regardless of which part of the world they're from. As members of a society, we have certain devotion to our professions. With regard to ethics, we adhere to integrity as the bottom line. With regard to ourselves, we grow into better people through learning. As you can see, these notions can be applied in the United States, in Europe, and anywhere else in the world. So, in short, the way of a gentleman provides one possible means for an individual to find his place in society and to abide by a set of disciplines.

The second value with respect to culture is the Chinese perspective on society as a whole. Confucianism proposes the notion of "harmony despite differences". This means that the prerequisite condition for achieving harmony is respecting individual personalities and preferences. Only by firmly adhering to this principle could we have a justified civilization. Civilization is not about achieving a single set of standard and forcing it onto everyone at the expense of individualities; yet at the same time, it is necessary to strike a balance among the various individualities. This is the ideal state of a civil society under the general framework of rule by law and a modern system.

The third notion proposed by Confucianism is the notion of "benevolence". Benevolence lies at the core of one's moral principles, bringing an individual's moral belief in line with his actions. In the United States and in Europe, many people go to church as part of their lifetime routine. Through conversing with God, they find a sense of balance and transcendence. What about Chinese people? What is our belief? Our belief lies in ethics. There is a joke I used to tell. It is about a Chinese and an American, both tripping over something. When an American trips over, he/she might say "Oh My God!" When a Chinese trips over, he/she is more likely to say "Oh My Mother!" In other words, Americans don't subconsciously say "Oh My Mother", just like Chinese don't subconsciously say "Oh My God!" We say certain things because we grew up hearing them. They are present in our culture. Civilizations are different, which does not mean one is better or worse than the other. Every civilization carries its unique genes and legacies, and consequently, every civilization manifests itself differently.

So from the Chinese perspective, what is the root of our moral principles? It can be summed up in the notion of "benevolence". The Chinese character for "benevolence" is simple. It is made up of a left half and a right half. The left hand side radical means "People", and the right hand side means "two". So we say, "Benevolence is born from two people". Good relationship between any two people is the greatest benevolence. So Confucius said "help the other person establish his values the way you would help yourself; and help the other person obtain prosperity the way you would help yourself." This is what benevolence is about. Benevolence is not just a concept. It should also be put into action. Benevolence is the starting point from which one aligns one's thinking with one's action.

We can only touch upon the tip of Confucian teachings today. I've only talked about three examples from the perspective of the 21st century, namely, gentleman and civil society; "harmony despite difference" as social standard;

and benevolence as the starting point from which one aligns one's thinking with one's action. I believe that these notions not only apply to the Chinese culture; they belong to the world as well. Within the context of globalization, our purpose is to construct a new cultural structure, in hope of providing a solution for our common challenges, so that one day we will live in a world of harmony.

中国文学传统如何影响西方

金安平

耶鲁大学历史系
高级讲师

内容提要： 如何使中国的历史及其早期的文学传统和文本触及西方观众、西方读者，让西方观众意识到早期中国人讨论的问题、早期中国人感兴趣的问题从很多方面而言都与他们今天在现代世界个人生活中所面临的问题相关？孔子之前的文化传统对于孔子的思想和教学有着巨大影响。《诗经》就是一本在中国早期时代对孔子影响比较大的诗歌总集。如果能有这样的早期文本呈现给西方读者，他们也一定能够得出同样的感悟。

今天我不是谈论中美文化关系的历史回顾，当然，这是我们这个专题讨论小组的讨论主题。我想要思考一个相关的问题，即如何使中国历史及其早期的文学传统和文本触及西方观众、西方读者，让西方观众意识到，早期中国人所讨论的问题、早期中国人所感兴趣的问题，从很多方面而言都与他们今天在现代世界的个人生活中所面临的问题相关？事实上，正是因为这个问题，我和利奇主席才有了第一次的接触。我们讨论了有关早期中国以及孔子的问题。于是我们回到了孔子的话题。

当我第一次跟利奇主席提到，孔子之前的文化传统对于孔子的思想和教学有巨大的影响时，他跟我说："这怎么可能？孔子不是中国的先师吗？"

我们的谈话就是这样开始的。我们讨论了一本名为《诗经》的诗歌总集。我很高兴，利奇主席在他的介绍中提到了沃尔特·惠特曼以及他说的一段话。所以我谈到《诗经》，这是一本在中国早期时代对孔子影响比较大的诗歌总集。其中的颂诗和歌赋都是从古代中国民间各个地区搜集而来,起止年代约为公元前9世纪至孔子所在的公元前6世纪。

从民间搜集而来的这些诗歌经宫廷乐师配乐而成为歌曲,在宫廷演奏。孔子认为,这一诗歌总集中总计300首左右的诗都有重要的意义。他喜欢这些诗歌之中协调的措辞以及表现出的多种情感。例如其中一首诗《駉之什》。该诗描写在野外骑马。孔子说,《诗经》中300多首诗中的义理都可以用《駉之什》中的一句话加以概括,即"思无邪"。他所要表达的意思是,虽然是在野外驭马,但驾驭时要有力量且方向明确,才不至于偏离正道。他认为,这首诗所表达的重点在于坚持正确的方向,不要偏离。

他以同样的方式解读了另一首非常有名的诗,名为《关雎》。这首诗也是《诗经》中的第一首诗,描述一位君子对淑女的追求。孔子认为,在这首诗中,虽然有深切的情感,却没有乱了分寸的行为,虽然有求而不得的苦恼,却没有过激的行动,亦即所谓的"爱而不淫,爱而不伤"。因为诗中的求爱者,虽然因自己思慕的淑女而感到渴望和焦虑,由于还没得到而翻来覆去无法入睡,"求之不得,寤寐思服。悠哉悠哉,辗转反侧"。但他没有对自己心爱的女人作出任何不轨行为,而是借助邻里的帮助,以音乐的形式,即"琴瑟友之,钟鼓乐之",表达自己对她的爱慕。

正是这种文学传统影响了孔子,这种影响是微妙的。如果能有这样的早期文本呈现给西方读者,他们也一定能够获得同样的感悟。换句话说,他们需要更深的文学影响以及更丰富的历史接触。身处西方的早期中国学者正是做了这样的尝试。他们认为应该让这样的文本真正触及更多的西方读者。那么,就出现了翻译问题。怎样以一种有趣而吸引人的方式将这些知识结合起来呈现给西方读者呢?怎样借助传统知识将一句简短的隽语,如"思无邪"解释得完整而透彻呢?

《诗经》首次译成西方语言时是译成了拉丁语。这一工作由大约20位学者耗时30年时间才在17世纪末完成。翻译完成后,译者们发现作品很难在西方出版。拉丁语版《诗经》直到1687年才得以出版。之后不久,拉丁语版的《诗经》被翻译成了英语。这一版本是将400页的手写稿缩减成为60页的版本,译后内容很多易于造成误解。

但是近一个世纪以来,情况已有很大改观。事实上,20世纪早期,出现了很多非常学术性的《诗经》英语、德语、法语和荷兰语译本。但我还是要说,要做的工作仍然很多。近5年来,出现了5个新的不同版本的

《诗经》译本，译者均为优秀的学者。当然，我们已经有了完整的译本。熟悉《诗经》的中国读者知道，其中的所有诗歌都已在50年前译出。但正如我所说，还有很多工作要做，而我也有自己的期许。

Annping Chin
Senior Lecturer,
Department of History,
Yale University

How Does the Chinese Literary Tradition Reach the West

Abstract: How to use Chinese history and her early literary tradition and her early text to reach the western audience, to reach the western reader, and let the western audience see that topic discussed in early China? The questions that interested the early Chinese are in many ways relevant to the problems they right now are facing in their own personal lives in the modern world. The literary tradition before Confucius had an enormous influence on Confucius' thinking and teaching. Book of Poetry is a work that persuades Confucius. That's the literary tradition the western reader certainly could relate to if an early text like that was presented to him in this way.

Today instead of talking about the historical perspectives on China-U.S. cultural relations, which of course is the subject of this penal, I would like to consider a related question and that is, how to use Chinese history and her early literary tradition and her early text to reach the western audience, to reach the western reader, and let the western audience see that topic discussed in early China? The questions that interested the early Chinese are in many ways relevant to the problems they right now are facing in their own personal lives also in the modern world. In fact, this was how Chairman Leach and I first made our connection. Through discussion, we had talked about early China and about Confucius. We come back to the topic of Confucius.

When I first mentioned to him that the literary tradition before Confucius had an enormous influence on Confucius' thinking and teaching. Chairman Leach asked me, "how was that possible? What could have influence Confucius, Wasn't Confucius an original thinker, wasn't he China's first philosopher, first teacher?"

So this is how we begin our discussion. In a sense, I believe, we actually talked about the book of poetry, about Shi Jing, I'm so glad that Chairman Leach in his introduction mentioned Walt Whitman, and what Whitman said. So I believe that we talked about the Book of Poetry, which is across China's earliest, first anthology, a poem, a work that persuade Confucius. The odes and songs in that anthology were collected from all regions of early Chinese Empire, from about 9th century B.C., up to Confucius' time in the 6th century B.C.

And these poems that were collected, they were actually set to music , and they were set to music by the court musicians, and they were performed at the court during periods of official function. Confucius, Kong Zi, thought it is of great importance of the 300 or so poems in that anthology. He liked the balance in the diction and also the sentiment of these poems, and of one poem, the Jiong poem, for instance, the Jiong means noble talent. Of that particular poem, a poem that described the act of driving a horse in the wild, Confucius said about that poem, he said that actually the 300 or so poems in that anthology were like the horses, never swerve from the path. In Chinese, he said "Si Wu Xie". So what he was trying to say is that even though these horses are being driven in the wild, there is a lot of spurs on and reins in, so that the horses were able to still keep on the track. He thought that the point of the poem was to be able to catch that idea of never swerving from the path.

This was also the way that he read another poem, called Guan Ju poem, which is Osprey, such a well-known poem, the first from that book of anthology. This is a poem about the love in yearning in courtship. And of this poem, Confucius said, there is joy yet no wantonness; there is sorrow yet no self-injury. 乐而不淫，哀而不伤，because the wooer, the suitor in this poem, though he was made anxious and miserable by his yearning for the women he desired, wanting, the poem says in Chinese, 求之不得，寤寐思服。悠哉悠哉，辗转反侧。Even though this was so, the young man did not make a cruelled display of his feelings toward his beloved, instead he resorted to the help of his community, and together they made music to harden her and to gladden her, 琴瑟友之，钟鼓乐之。

That's the literary tradition that influences Confucius with this kind. It's something that is subtle; something that the western reader certainly could relate to if an early text like that was presented to him in this way. That is to say, with deeper literary written emphasis and a rich historical contact. And this is the work that scholars of early China in the West have tried, the text that they assume, or they have to assume if they really want to reach a broader western audience.

And then, of course, there is the question of translation. How to bring all these knowledge together in an interesting and compelling way for the western reader? How to convey the fullness of fragment of a comment, such as "they never swerve from the path", somehow to convey this, the fullness of such a fragment with the help of traditional scholarship, so that the integrity of the original is apparent.

The first translation of the anthology into a western language, in this case, was translated into Latin took about 20 scholars over a span of almost 30 years to get the job done. And this was done in fact in the late 17th century. And when it was finished, these scholars, these western scholars found a really hard time to get it published in the west. It was not published until 1687 in Latin. And very soon after that, this text was translated into English from the Latin version. But this major version, well, I'll say the English version was on something that was condensed into about 60 pages from a manuscript of about 400 pages. It was condensed still into about 60 pages. The text set in English was often misleading.

But things have changed a lot in the last a hundred years. In fact, in the early

20th century, there are many very learned translations of the anthology into English, German, French, and some of it into Dutch. But still I would say that there is a lot work to be done. In the last five years, there are about five different new translations of the anthology, all done by very good scholars. And then, of course, we have complete translations. This is again for the Chinese, and if you are familiar with the early text, all these have been translated to for about 50 years or so already. But still, as I said, there is a lot more to be done, and I have my own wish list.

我雕塑艺术中的文化观

吴为山

中国艺术研究院雕塑院院长、美术研究所所长，研究员

内容提要： 中国传统文化中有"文以载道"、"诗言志"，这与海德格尔的"诗人何为"有共通之处。我的雕塑艺术传达了我的人文理想与我的文化观。二十多年来，我创作了四百多件雕塑作品，分布于世界二十多个国家，内容涉及重大历史事件、重要历史人物、普通人物，以及作者的生活感受。每件作品的背后都有故事。它们是我的经历、情感、艺术研究与实践的体现，也是我文化价值观的体现。在此，我从四件代表作品的创作来阐发我的文化观。

今天使我想起1998年，我应邀在旧金山举办雕塑展，其中一件作品《女儿》被一位中年美国妇女收藏，她说要将这件作品送给她八十多岁的妈妈。时光飞逝，十多年来，我一直牵挂着我的《女儿》，也许我的《女儿》已习惯并融入了这世界，成了美国妈妈的心肝宝贝……

无独有偶，1999年，美国约翰·霍普金斯大学校长布罗迪教授访问中国，到南京大学我的工作室参观，看了我根据我家乡的小男童创作的雕塑《小小少年》，便真诚地要收藏。他的夫人称之为"领养"。我于2000年专程去美国看望了被布罗迪校长"领养"的男童，他依然在阳光下微笑，成了美国家庭的"成员"。

此刻，我心系着在西岸的"女儿"和东岸的"男童"，虽不能相见，但我想，他们一定能感应到一个艺术家父亲的思念。我也相信，领养他们的美国"爸爸"和美国"妈妈"与我心灵相通，这种父爱带着美好，带着祝愿。

当然，我还记得12年前，我第一次来美国，一位老华侨告诉我，他到美国20年，时常产生徒步金门大桥的意念。听者有心，我竟于第二天独自步行跨越了这座桥，并以过桥的体验写成散文《桥不过如此长》，阐发了我跨国家、跨文化交流的人文理想和渴望人类在信息时代以英特网为桥梁沟通内心、消除隔膜以漫步人类最美好的精神家园。这篇文章被新加坡世界科技出版社译成英文收录到我的文集《雕塑的诗性》，很快传播到美国、英国、荷兰……

中国与美国虽远隔重洋，但是两国人民在人类普世价值上的共同追求，在中美关系上曾有过值得纪念的重要事件和历史的转折。今天的论坛便是一座金桥。

了解是交流的基础，交流增加了解。这正是高层论坛目的所在。

中国传统文化中有"文以载道"、"诗言志"，这与海德格尔的"诗人何为"有共通之处。我的雕塑艺术传达了我的人文理想与文化观。二十多年来，我创作了四百多件雕塑作品，分布于世界二十多个国家，内容涉及重大历史事件、重要历史人物、普通人物，以及作者的生活感受。每件作品的背后都有故事。它们是我的经历、情感、艺术研究与实践的体现，也是我文化价值观的体现。

下面，我从四件代表作品的创作来阐发我的文化观。

一、普世的情感 ——《睡童》

中国古代《三字经》中有"人之初，性本善"之说，也有"人之初，性本恶"之说。关于善与恶本性的争辩，无据可考。然而，人个体的童年与人类的童年相似，系混沌状，未经过文化净化的自然属性，处于本我层面。其喜怒哀乐本能使然。我作《睡童》是因为我在友人的家中看到他刚出生四个月的孙儿，那天使般的面容给予我灵感。这熟睡的婴儿没有烙上文化的印痕，超越民族，超越地域，超越国家，超越政治与宗教。它是人类普遍情感的寄托。在世界美术史上以儿童为题材，以母与子为题材的作品不乏，法国雷诺阿的作品反映的是儿童的天真稚趣，通过色彩的

《睡童》，青铜，高13cm，作于1991年。

美表现了一个温情的世界。美国画家萨金特的油画《海边的儿童们》则是以优雅而纯粹的写实语言歌颂了母爱的温润与儿童的聪慧。从某种意义上讲，儿童题材的艺术作品反映了人类情感深处的善与爱。荷兰女王贝娅特丽克丝在看到我塑的儿童时说："吴先生通过塑造儿童，发现并升华了童性，体现了人类对童年的真实情感。"这些无声的语言，不分语种，是超越时间和空间的共同语言。这个题材，从古希腊到文艺复兴直至20世纪现代主义均有大师表现。中国的民间木雕、泥塑及年画中也多有绘刻。从西方的天使到中国的娃娃，普遍表现的是祥瑞与和谐。我为这件《睡童》题诗："睡吧，宝贝，梦乡里有一个甜美的梦乡……"这件作品2003年在英国皇家雕塑家协会年展展出时，获得了皇家"攀格林"奖，同时受到百姓的喜爱。英国的同行们称我是《睡童》的爸爸。这孩子睡了，有着全人类儿童一样的表情，有着所有善良人们的安详与幸福。

二、包容的哲学 ——《老子》

作为中国传统文化主干之一的道家思想创始人和表征者——老子是一座恍惚悠然的精神奇峰。他的形象悠远模糊，却于混沌中透发着光明。他的身影虚幻缥缈，在细微与广阔间，在沉寂与铿锵间，展示出无穷的文化魅力。唯神与物游，思接千古方能臻其境，对语圣哲而成形象。老子尊像何如，无从以考。虽历代画工有所描绘，然而凭各自想象，只能是面目多殊。近人作古人像，乏内在古意与神韵。关于老子的长相，史书上记载"体弱而头大，眉宽而耳阔，目如深渊，珠清澈，鼻含双梁中如辙。"《玄妙内篇》里记载，老子一生出来就"生而皓首"。这些描述近乎神话，甚至违背客观规律，但表现了人们心

《天人合一 ——老子》，青铜，高18米，作于2005年。

目中"仙化"了的老子。以雕塑的手法表现老子重在表现出老子的哲学思想、精神内核,以使人们一目了然,由形象而对应上"老子"。老子对宇宙起源的认识,表现在《道德经》四十二章第一句:"道生一,一生二,二生三,三生万物。"老子对最高境界的善行以"上善若水"而概之。水的品性,润泽万物而不争名利。老子提出的重要处世原则是"虚怀若谷"。先秦·李耳《老子》:"敦兮其若朴,旷兮其若谷。"人要有像山谷一样深广的胸怀和宽容的胸襟,居上谦下。老子说:"上德若谷",意即最高的"德"像山谷那样幽深空阔,谦虚为怀。这种内藏生机、蕴涵力量的虚怀,对中华民族美德的形成有着重要影响。

虚怀若谷,要能容。老子说:"知人者智,自知者明,胜人者有力,自胜者强。"只有容纳万物,善于包容,才能至"大"。

虚怀若谷,要能谦。老子说:"我有三宝,持而宝之:一曰慈,二曰俭,三曰不敢为天下先。"老子"道"的发扬,开阔了中华民族宽广的文化襟怀。巨川非一源,容而后大。今天我在这里,在加州伯克利大学与美国的同道们讲我们的文化祖先——老子,不是讲课,不是讲故事,而是讲我们文化心理构成的基础。任何一个人,一个民族,其文化发散的方向与发散原点的方位有着密切关联。因此,根植于中国人心理深度的处世原则是"包"、"容"。我塑老子以虚怀若谷为造型特征,雕塑满刻《道德经》,谓之满腹经纶。这"空谷"能包罗万象,吐故纳新,接天地正气,幻化自然。

三、和谐的文化 ——《孔子》

刚才于丹教授谈论孔子,讲《论语》。于教授非常形象地表述了

《孔子》,青铜,2006年,高2米。

她对儒家思想的认识。我以为人与人，人与社会的和谐强调伦理。伦理重在秩序，善、和、仁、礼……至圣先师——中华传统文化的纪念碑。

以雕塑的形体、神韵表现出孔子的思想和精神特质，表现出这种秩序与伦理，不仅是艺术的情感，也是艺术的哲学。孔子像的意义不言而喻。在时空里，他是云中之巅峰；在文化里，他是和煦之春风。当然，他更是一尊凛然的化石，那仁慈，从脸上道道皱纹中绽出，似山脉水系，流韵弥长。手的礼仪传达着"仁"，孔子之仁，二人为仁，乃人与人，人与社会之伦理关系。

孔子的造型便在人的生理结构与山体之间找到了结合点。自上而下纵观，山脚、山腰、山顶，层层递进；自左而右横看，道道天沟，一泻而下，纵横万里。或峭壁奇凸、或峰壑互生。孔子面含温润，满怀慈爱，智者仁相，巍然山巅。

四、和平的诉求 ——《侵华日军南京大屠杀遇难同胞纪念馆主题群雕》

1937年12月13日，侵华日军占领南京，灭绝人性的大屠杀开始。30万平民和放下武器的俘虏惨遭屠戮。

如何看待这历史事件？

我曾于2005年4月樱花时节应邀访问日本东京并举办雕塑绘画展。作品中内蕴的汉风唐韵感动着一衣带水的邻国观众，他们依依抒怀，谈及唐僧鉴真，也论到当年徐福率众男女东渡日本求仙草之往事。文化渊源的共通当获得彼此的理解。然，也有不解，《朝日新闻》记者问，60年过去了，中国为何还不放过"大屠杀"事件！

我的回答只能是：以史为鉴，则后事可师矣。

类似世界近代史上的三大惨案——奥斯威辛集中营的法西斯大屠杀——南京大屠杀——广岛原子弹爆炸，在未来人类会重演乎？在当今和平环境中提出这个问题似乎耸人听闻，但细想则是令人忧心忡忡。

因此，侵华日军南京大屠杀遇难同胞纪念馆工程的扩建是历史的需要，是人类的灵魂工程。扩建工程首先是建筑，它是载体，也体现精神。史实——物证陈列是基础。作为凝固历史、铸造国魂的雕塑，则是直接进入人心灵的。它为人们对客观史实的认识提供价值判断之参照。

雕塑首先是立意，立意的基础是立场。是站在南京看待这座城市的血泪,同情当年市民的苦难遭遇;或是站在国家民族的方位,看待吾土吾民所蒙受的劫难? 我认为只有立足于人类、历史的高度来正视、反思这段日本军国主义反人类的兽行,才能升华作品的境界,超越一般意义上的纪念、仇恨。回顾一下我国自上个世纪至今所有表现抗战题材的作品,几乎是再现场面。那种国仇家恨溢于作品的内容与形式,这是时代的必然。但今天的中国日益强大,今天的世界日趋文明,中国有自信来倾诉历史的灾难与蒙受的污辱。作为受辱者,中国有责任控诉战争,有责任告诉世界,和平是人类精神所栖。一个遍体鳞伤的弱国是没有能力祈求和平的! 因此凝固平民悲怆的形象,表现祖国母亲蒙难,呼唤民族精神崛起,祈望和平应当是整个作品的表现核心。

整个组雕,没有出现一个日本侵略者的形象,皆表现我遇难同胞,表现我中华儿女。2007年12月13日开馆前后,有许多日本观众和记者在雕塑中专门寻觅他们先辈的形象。据说,中国文艺作品(尤其是电影)中所刻画的"日本鬼子"大令今天的日本人伤感。而在这组组雕中,从遇难者群像的惨烈足以佐证日军之凶残与兽行。日方记者同样为之深思,悲情动于衷。其原因在于我们是以祈望和平之心塑魂的。是为纪念我同胞而塑魂的。它的潜台词则为:

记住历史,不要记住仇恨!

《侵华日军南京大屠杀遇难同胞纪念馆主题雕塑之 ——逃难》,青铜,高2米,作于2007年。

My View of Culture in Sculptural Arts

Wu Weishan

Research Fellow and Director of Institute of Fine Arts, Director of Institute of Sculpture, Chinese National Academy of Arts

---

Abstract: In the Chinese tradition, we say "literature for moral instruction" and "poems convey ambition", which state the same idea as Heidegger's "What are poets for". The sculptures I created bear my humanistic ideals and my perspective on culture. I have created over 400 sculptures in over 20 years. Behind every sculpture, there is a story. The sculptures I have created reflect my experiences, emotions, and the result of my artistic studies and practices. Furthermore, they reflect my cultural values. Here, I'd like to talk about my cultural perspective by introducing four of my sculptures.

Today it reminds me of the year 1988 when an exhibition of my works was held in San Francisco. One of the sculptures named "Daughter" was purchased by a middle-aged American woman as a gift for her eighty-year-old mother. Time flies and I've been always missing my "Daughter". Perhaps she has become part of this world and a sweetheart of her American mother.

Things come in pair. In 1999, Prof. William Brody, President of Johns Hopkins University, visited my studio in Nanjing during his trip to China. He appreciated my sculpture named "Little Boy" based on a boy living in my hometown and, according to his wife, "adopted" the boy. In 2000 I visited America for the boy who had become part of an American family and kept smiling in sunshine.

I always miss my "Daughter" at the West Coast and "Little Boy" at the East Coast far across the ocean and I know they can hear the affection from an artist father. I also know that the American father and mother have the same affection as well as fair wishes.

I also remember my first visit to the US 12 year ago when an old Chinese man told me that during his 20 years' stay in the US, he had always been itching for walking the full length of the Golden Gate Bridge. This aroused my interest and I walked across the Bridge by myself in the next day and wrote a prose about that experience titled It Takes Only So Long to Cross the Bridge. It was about my desire for cross-nation and cross-cultural communication, for communication via Internet in an era of information, and for a spiritual Eden without gaps. The prose was translated into English and published by Singapore-based World Scientific Publishing along with my album Poetics in Sculpture and soon introduced to the US, Britain, the Netherlands…

Though parted by a vast ocean, Chinese and American share the same universal values. Sino-US relationship casts remarkable events and historical changes. The forum today will be a golden opportunity to bridge the two countries.

Communication comes after understanding and builds it up. This is what the summit forum intends to deliver.

In the Chinese tradition, we say "literature for moral instruction" and "poems convey ambition", which state the same idea as Heidegger's "What are poets for". The sculptures I created bear my humanistic ideals and my perspective on culture. I have created over 400 sculptures in over 20 years. They can be found in more than 20 countries. Some of them record important historical events that took place in the world, and others are key historical figures and average people. I've embedded my sentiment into each and every one of them. Behind every sculpture, there is a story. The sculptures I have created reflect my experiences, emotions, and the result of my artistic studies and practices. Furthermore, they reflect my cultural values. Next, I'd like to talk about my cultural perspective by introducing four of my sculptures to you.

1. Universal emotion—Sleeping Child

The Chinese classic three-character scripture advocates that "man's nature at birth is good". We also have a saying goes "man's nature at birth is evil". We have no records to help trace the origin of the argument of good vs. evil. But the infantile stage of an individual is comparable to that of all men, both of which are in a natural state, ignorant of the surrounding, and untouched by culture. In other words, man is in his "id" state, and all of his emotions (pleasure, anger, grief and joy) come from instinctive impulses. The "Sleeping Child" was modeled after the grandson of one of my friends. I was inspired when I saw the angel, who was at the time only 4 months old – an infant not molded in any manner by culture, a symbol that transcends race, terrain, nation, politics and religion, and a universal embodiment of man's sentiment. Children, mother and children are eternal subjects of arts. Pierre-Auguste Renoir' works about pure and naïve children present a world full of love; John Singer Sargent's canvas "Neapolitan Children Bathing" sings motherhood and clever children in graceful and realistic language. In one sense,

Sleeping Child, a 13-cm-high bronze sculpture made in 1991.

artworks about children show goodness and love deep in our hearts. Dutch Queen, Her Majesty Beatrix at the sight of my works said that "Mr. Wu's works about children discover and exalt childness, exhibiting mankind's affection for childhood." Art talks in silent language that is universal, beyond time and space. Such subjects are depicted all along the history from ancient Greece to Renaissance and to the 20th century of modernism, and seen in Chinese folk woodcarving and clay figures as well as New Year paintings. Images of Western angel and Chinese baby convey the same idea of auspiciousness and harmony. The inscription of this sculpture reads: "Sleep, child, there is a sweet dream in your sweet dream." While on exhibition in the annual convention of Royal British Society of Sculptors in 2003, it received wide acclaim from the art circle and was awarded the Pangolin Prize. The visitors loved it as well. My British fellows called me father of the "Sleeping Child". In his slumber we see a calm and sweet face that belongs to all children.

2. Philosophy of tolerance—Laozi

The founder and advocator of Daoism, Laozi is a legendary sage shining amidst chaos. His image in the mist and dimness exhibits profound cultural charms and guides us between preciseness and immensity, between silence and sonorousness. How does he look like? We do not know because we could not wander to the spiritual vastness or antiquity. His image has been variously depicted along the history, however, based on imagination. Sculptures of ancient figures made by modern artists are more or less absent of historical and cultural charm. Historical records say Laozi "is weak in body, has a big head, broad eyebrows, large ears, profound and sharp eyes, and a straight nose"; and "he was born with hoary head." Though deific or even contrary to objective laws, people believe that is Laozi, a man of deity. So when I made this sculpture of Laozi, I focused on bringing out his philosophical thinking and the essence of his spirit, so anybody who takes one look at the sculpture could recognize that it is Laozi. His idea on origin of the universe, according to phrase 1, Chapter 42 of Tao Te Ching, "Dao gives birth to one, one to two and, two to three and three to all beings." He also

The Harmony between Men and Nature—Lao Zi, an 18-meter-high bronze sculpture made in 2005.

says "The Greatest Good Is Said to Be Like Water". Water nourishes all beings but remains its simplicity. He also concludes the principle of life—"be modest and open-minded". He is recorded "honest as if unsophisticated, open as if a deep valley." He says "the greatest virtue is like the valley, tolerant, open-minded and modest." His Golden Mean, embedded with vigor and energy, is of great significance to Chinese morality.

Laozi advocates tolerance. He says "it is wise to know others, while knowledgeable to know himself; it is powerful to conquer others, while overwhelming to conquer himself." Greatness comes after inclusiveness and tolerance.

Laozi also advocates modesty. He says "I have three treasures: love, frugality and modesty." His Dao leaves Chinese with cultural tolerance. An enormous river comes more than one stream. Today I bring Laozi to my American fellows in Berkley University, California. I am not giving a lecture or telling a story. I am talking about the foundation of our cultural psychology. A man, an ethnic group, sees his cultural radiation closely related with the core. It is inclusiveness and tolerance that are deeply rooted in Chinese mind. This sculpture reflects Laozi's modest and open-minded nature, and his erudition. The sculpture is carved with words from Laozi's Tao Te Ching, and tells the notion of "all-embracing".

3. Culture of harmony—Confucius

Prof. Yu Dan talked about Confucius just now and her view of Confucianism. I think Confucian teaching is about man existing in harmony with himself and within his society, and about observing moral principles. Moral principles stress on order, kindness, harmony, benevolence, and rites. Confucius was a sage and a great teacher of monumental importance to Chinese culture.

It is an artistic affection and artistic philosophy to present Confucius' thoughts and spirits by means of sculpture. The artwork is of great significance: Confucius represents the summit of Chinese culture at that time. He is the high-commanding mountain and flowing river, conveying from his wrinkles

Confucius, a 2-meter-high bronze sculpture made in 2006.

kindness and by his hand posture benevolence, the moral principles on man existing in harmony with himself and within his society.

The sculpture is designed combining human structure and mountain. Taking a bird's-eye view, it stands alongside the mountain; looking from left to the right, gullies run all the way down, carving out alternate prominences. And imposing Confucius stands there full of benevolence and wisdom.

4. Appeal for peace—Theme sculptures for the Memorial Hall of the Victims in Nanjing Massacre

On December 13th, 1937, Japanese invaders captured the city of Nanjing and committed the heinous act of murdering 300,000 civilians and disarmed soldiers.

How should we view the Nanjing Massacre?

I was invited to Japan in April 2005 for exhibition of my sculptures and painting. Japanese visitors were deeply moved by the traditional Chinese charm in my works, which also reminded them of historical figures such as Buddhist master Jianzhen of the Tang Dynasty, and Xu Fu who led virgin boys and girls sailing to Japan for fairy herbs. We share the same cultural root, and should reach mutual understanding. However, we still hear disharmonious voices: Asahi Shimbun asked me why China could not forget Nanjing Massacre after 60 years?

There is but one answer: learn from the history.

Will the world see massacre after the three biggest mass murders in the history of modern world-Auschwitz, Hiroshima and Nanjing? It sounds horrible but is indeed something to worry about in the current seemingly peaceful world.

In this sense, expansion of the Memorial Hall is a spiritual project needed by the history. Buildings of the Memorial Hall embody the spirit and physical evidences proving the history. And the sculpture captures historical moments, explains national spirit and touches our hearts as reference to evaluation of historical facts.

The soul of a sculpture is conception based on certain viewpoint. Shall I start from the viewpoint of Nanjing and narrate the suffering? Or shall I start from that of the country and depict the national calamity? I think we must look from a human and historical height to face and reflect animal-like Japanese militarism. Only in this way can we bring artistic works out of the bond of commemoration and hatred. Taking a look at the last century, or even at today, most works on anti-Japanese war are noting but represent and pass down hatred. They were limited by the times. Today China is becoming more and more powerful, and the world more and more civilized. China is confident to tell her historical hardship and obligated to accuse the war and tell the world that human destination rests in peace. A miserable weak country is incapable to appeal for peace. Thus, I focused on pathos of civilians and calamity of our motherland to call for Chinese ethos, and appeal for peace is the core of this work.

While I was working on this group of sculptures, I chose no scene of killing; instead, I focused on my fellow countrymen, including those killed The Memorial Hall was open on December 13, 2007 and many Japanese visitors and journalists came to see how I carved their ancestors—it is said that Japanese feel shame for the "Japs" in Chinese artistic creations, especially in movies. However, in my work, Japanese brutality and inhumanity is show through the victims in awful tribulation. Japanese journalists were also touched and burst into tears. I made it in this way to appeal for peace, and to commemorate my fellow countrymen. We could read from it:

We should remember history, but not pass down hatred.

Flee from the War—one of the Topic Sculptures in the Memorial Hall of the Victims in Nanjing Massacre by Japanese Invaders, a 2-meter-high bronze sculpture made in 2007.

中美关系的历史起点与维度

乔纳森·斯宾塞

耶鲁大学历史系
斯特林荣誉教授

内容提要：我很感兴趣的一点是，各个国家在进行中国历史教育时所选择的时间起点是什么时候。因为选择的历史时期不同，我们所得到的关于中国历史的视角就会不同，差别将非常显著。不同的国家选择了不同的方式以及从不同的日期起点看待中国。

我将就美中关系，具体而言是美中关系的一些历史视角作几分钟的发言。因为我觉得当我们看待美国时，要将之与我们对欧洲和我长大的地方、也就是英国的看法区分开来。

首先，我想强调的一点是，中国和美国的联系始于中国处于弱势地位的时期。我很感兴趣的一点是，各个国家在进行中国历史教育时，选择的时间起点都是何时，从哪个日期开始。因为选择的历史时期不同，我们所得到的关于中国历史的视角就会不同，差别将非常显著。不同的国家选择了不同的方式以及不同的日期起点看待中国。美中关系开始于中国处于弱势地位时，这就与欧洲人、比如英国人之前看到的中国有所不同。他们是最开始来到中国的西方人，他们看到的是清代早期十分强盛的中国，当时的中国在世界上非常强大。而美国与中国建立联系时，中国则处于一片混乱之中。那是在1784年，第一艘美国船来到中国。从那时起，动荡从乾隆统治时期到嘉庆年间，再到鸦片战争，战乱开始，之后又到了太平天国起义以及之后的时期。所以，如果美国人以消极观点看待中国，则不足为奇。尤其是当时的中国被各个国家入侵，所呈现出的并非其本身原貌。

我提到了1784年，因为正是那时中国开始与美国建立联系。最初这种联系主要与贸易有关。我们存有一些早期的美国人航海日志，可以帮助我们了解与他们进行交易的中国人的情况。当时，使用相同语言的英国人和美国人正开展美国独立战争。美国人最初到达广东省广州市时，因与英国人形象相似，所以结成某种联盟，以满足中国的最终需求。

因此，中美之间的文化关系有四个方面。我刚刚提到的只是其中的一个方面，即最初的合法关系，包括最初所进行的合法尝试，以及司法方式。还有管辖权的问题。美国与中国的贸易是否能拓展到广州以外的其他地方？天津的可能性如何？台湾可能发生些什么？香港可能会发生些什么？所有这些在成为管辖权问题。

第三个方面有关宗教。从最初的时候开始，美国人即非常注重传教工作，在传教方面所做的工作比英国人多得多。英国人主要是在澳门传教，而美国人则想进入中国内陆的每一个地区，开始传教布道，并在各处传播宗教音乐。这是美国强势的宗教渗透的一个方面。

第四个方面有关商业贸易。商业利益是第一只来中国谋利的商船最重要的目标。他们的确盈利了，但利润不大，因为美国人发现，想要找到中国人需要的商品十分困难。在一些方面他们做得甚至还不如英国人。他们试着找一些东西出售给中国人。他们向中国出售人参、海豹皮，总之他们找到的可以大量出售的商品少之又少。所以我想，在贸易的早期，美国人多少感到了一些失望。

美国在外交文件的翻译方面也发挥了重要作用。此方面的重要人物包括之前提到过的约翰·弗赖尔（傅兰雅）。约翰·弗赖尔实际上是英国人，后来去了中国。这一点我们可以从他写的一些书信中得知。这些书信仍保存在伯克利的图书馆中。弗赖尔在给英国父母的信中写道，你们应该过来看看我，看看我生活得怎样。他出生于英国的一个贫困家庭，到中国后却成为一名大人物。他工作的领域从我之前提到的商业、宗教、司法领域到国际法。在19世纪中期从事国际法的翻译工作，尔后转为科技翻译这一重要领域。这应归功于美国与中国的联系，弗赖尔引进了大量的教科书，翻译了西方化学、物理、地理等书籍。

因此，当时的中美关系是一种非常务实的关系。在这一关系中，美国是需求的提出者，中国则花了很长时间平衡这一关系，直至19世纪末20世纪初。

The Historical Start Point and Aspects of China-U.S. relations

Jonathan Spence
Sterling Professor
of History Emeritus,
Yale University

Abstract: I'm very interested about the question of when you started teaching Chinese history. By choosing different periods of stories, we can get very, very different perspectives on China's history, and different countries have chosen different ways and when, from which date to start looking at China.

I was thinking about a few minutes of phrases so that I can look at some historical perspectives on China-U.S. relation, and specifically, the US and China. I'll stick with that, because I think when we look at the U.S., it's expected that we saw the difference from looking at the European, also the British in which I was brought up.

First of all, the thing I want to emphasize is that the relationship between China and the United States starts in a period of Chinese weakness. I'm very interested about the question of when you started teaching Chinese history, what date, and by choosing different periods of stories, we can get very, very different perspectives on China and its history, and different countries have chosen different ways and when, from which date to start looking at China. In the question of the United States with China, China was in a period of extreme weakness, and this was very different from the situation when the Europeans such as British people, the first westerners who come to China, when they saw an extremely strong country in the early Qing period, China was acted globally very tough, we regarded it as a very tough country with us western. American relations start with China in a period of great disarray. It's in 1784, we get the first American ship coming to China. And from then on issues flurried from the Qianlong Reign and through into the Jiaqing Period, and then into the Opium war, the disasters military results from there, and then into the Taiping and later period. This is not surprising that American will give an extremely negative view of China, particularly because it seems to be trapped in a series of global conjunctions, and not to its own making.

I mentioned the date to 1784, because then when China in fact encounters with the United States, it's largely in terms of trade from the very beginning, and in definition of culture I think we should include trade. And we have some of the log books kept by the earlier Americans on their ships, as we see it help us to deal with and to understand how the Chinese they are meant to be trading with. And in fact it was the common language that the Britain and the American had been fighting a serious war for American's independence. As soon as the Americans got to Canton, to Guangzhou, they imagely associated with the British and form over by course a united front in a position to meet the China's final demands.

So the relationship, the cultural relationship between the United States and China has about four different aspects, I only mentioned just the first one of being legal, from the very beginning, there were a series of legal relationships, about how trials to be conducted, and work on the justice means, and so on. They were jurisdictional about how far could trade with Chinese reach. Could it be extended into other areas beyond Guangzhou? What were the possibilities of Tianjin? What might have happened to Taiwan? What might have happened in Hong Kong? All of these are becoming important jurisdictional questions.

The third one of religious, from the very beginning, the Americans put much more emphasis in missionary work, and promoting missionary work than the British have ever done. The British has mainly stayed in Macao, the Americans wanted to go to each of China's inner land and just started preaching as much as possible and distributing tracks, written tracks as much as widely as possible. So again, this was a very aggressive side of American through religious that we should remember.

The fourth one was commercial. The commercial interest is always paramount and the first ship was expected to make good profit. And they did, but these were comprised margins, because the Americans found it almost impossible to find products that the Chinese wanted. And so they did even worse in some ways than the British have done. They tried to find something. The Americans tried to sell ginseng to China, They tried to sell seal skins, and so they found very, very few products that they could get to the kind of scale that they were hoping for, so there was a real disappointment in these early years.

There is a strong American practical side here in translation of diplomatic documents, and so, many of the people, like John Fryer was mentioned here. John Fryer was in fact an English man. And Fryer went out to China, as we know from his letters, which I think are still stored in Berkeley's library. Fryer wrote to his parents in England, and said, you should see me now, how I lived. He was from a poor family in England, and in China, he began a big person. And he was able to expand his various operations. Americans moved from the areas I mentioned on commercial, religious, jurisdiction grounds to ideas of international law, translation of international law in China in the 1850s, and from then to the crucial aspect of scientific translation, and that owes a great deal to the American early relationship with China, the introduction of classical textbook text, not only Confucius, translated classical text of western chemistry, physics, geology, and so on.

So it was a very practical relationship. It was one in which America was the presenter of demand, and it took a long time for the Chinese to work out a kind of balance until the very, very end of the 19th century and the beginning of the 20th century.

Christopher MERRILL

LIU Měngxī

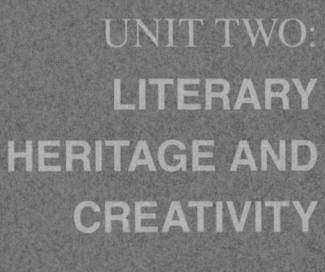

UNIT TWO:
LITERARY HERITAGE AND CREATIVITY

第二单元
文学遗产与创新性

加利福尼亚大学英语与美国研究教授唐纳德·麦奎德
主持人导语
Donald Mcquade, Professor of English, University of California, Berkeley
"Moderator's Introduction"

中国艺术研究院中国文化研究所所长刘梦溪研究员做主题发言
《21世纪人类能否在非对抗中重生》
Liu Mengxi, Research Fellow and Director of Institute of Chinese Culture,
Chinese National Academy of Arts
"Can Humanity be Reborn without Confrontation in the 21st Century"

哥伦比亚大学美国研究中心主任安德鲁·德尔班科做主题发言
《美国大学与文学事业》

Andrew Delbanco, Director of American Studies, Columbia University
"American University and Literature Career"

中国艺术研究院文学院院长莫言研究员做主题发言
《美国文学对中国文学的影响》

Mo Yan, Research Fellow and Dean of School of Literature,
Chinese National Academy of Arts
"The Influence of American Literature on Chinese Literature"

爱荷华大学国际写作项目主任克里斯多弗·梅里尔做主题发言
《"发现之旅"与文化交流》
Christopher Merrill, Director of the International Writing Program at the University of Iowa
"Life of Discovery and Cultural Communication"

主持人导语

唐纳德·麦奎德

加利福尼亚大学英语与美国研究教授

本轮圆桌会议的讨论主题是文学遗产与创新性。创新性的形成，与我们所珍视的其他事物一样，需要长时间的努力工作。而这一工作的基础就是要充分了解什么是已知的，以及如何知晓的；什么是未知的，以及在众多未知事物中，哪些才是重要的，需要我们去了解。在我们创造出任何新事物之前，我们需要知道哪些事物是已经存在的。

我想以我对当代中国的观察和建议作为本轮有关文学遗产和创新性的专题讨论的开端。多年以来我曾多次造访中国，并与中国的教育领域和政府领导人交谈。我观察到的现象是，创新和创造力已成为中国的一项国家使命。这一使命最近的一次表现是北京奥林匹克运动会的开幕式。当时所展现出来的富有创造力的表演令人惊叹而优美，使多年以来外国人对中国的陈旧观念和印象在2008年8月8日晚奥运火炬点燃的一瞬烟消云散。

中国继续以一种惊人的方式建设体现创新与创造力的基础设施与机构。例如，2020年，中国的高速公路系统规模将超过美国。公司采取大量措施引入创新机制，专家和人才在中国各大城市的厂区中不断涌现。进一步观察，我们将会发现，创新随处可见，不仅存在于设计、时尚、媒体等商业艺术中，在附近的咖啡馆、艺术工作室和画廊、以及剧院、人行道和街角等地方也有丰富的体现。

中国的创造性遗产，尤其是其文学传统，体现了数千年的成就。因此，接下来刘梦溪博士以及莫言先生的发言将会对我们了解中国目前的文学状况，尤其是小说及其与中国文学传统的关系，以及文化和教学条件提供很大的帮助。目前，创造力正在中国的学校以及创造性艺术家，尤其是作家的思想中、心中和手中不断繁荣成长。我相信，我们杰出的中国同仁将有兴趣参与有关创造力之所在、尤其是其文学遗产的讨论，以及有关当代美国大学中，尤其是本科教育的严峻环境中的诗歌和形成这一环境的美国文学教育传统的视角的讨论。

在邀请我们的专题讨论小组进行发言之前，我想提出一个诚挚的邀请。我建议我们的来宾们参观 C.V. 斯塔尔东亚图书馆。此图书馆作为田长霖东亚研究中心的一部分，曾为伯克利在我们今天上午所讨论的三个方面，即文学、传统和创造力方面做出最精彩的诠释。C.V. 斯塔尔东亚图书馆是收藏东亚语言和文化材料最为全面的美国图书馆之一。其建筑师托德·威廉姆斯和钱以佳将这一建筑比喻为"由光线分割的对称包厢"。我很高兴得知钱以佳今天就在观众之中。

C.V. 斯塔尔东亚图书馆坐落在格莱德纪念馆旁，位于伯克利校园的中心，深嵌在一个陡峭的山坡上。学校表现校园经典核心的设计方针是要有倾斜的黏土瓦屋顶，对称的外观和使用白色的花岗岩。钱以佳和托德·威廉姆斯以对一个重要的中国建筑元素 —— 屏风的重新诠释创造性地将这些元素结合起来。在这一建筑中，他们既使用了传统的碎冰，也使用了当代的网格花样。这一巨大的圆形屏风尺寸为120英尺乘35英尺，充分体现了亚洲风格。其外部结构统一，并以非对称的窗户排列创造出了对称的错觉。从外部来看，外观结实、有力而富有神秘感。从内部看，透过屏风我们可以看到周围生动的景色。

C.V. 斯塔尔图书馆及加州伯克利大学校园都坐落于东向的山坡之上，面向东方，越过旧金山湾，朝着东亚的方向，这绝不是一种巧合。斯特尔图书馆的古朴典雅正是永久联系中国和美国以及斯特尔图书馆及其周围世界的伟大遗产。这些事物让我们这些伯克利大学的成员感受到了创造力和传统是如何发展和繁荣的。

Donald Mcquade

Professor of English, University of California, Berkeley

Moderator's Introduction

The focus of our conversation in this round table session is literary heritage and creativity. Creativity is built like everything else we treasure with long, hard work. And that work begins with a foundation, a thorough understanding of what is known, and how it came to be known, what is unknown, and what among the many unknown, is important for us to know. Before we create anything new, we need to know and to understand what is already present.

So I'd like to begin this round table discussion on literary heritage and creativity with an observation about contemporary China, and a recommendation based on my many years travelling to China and speaking with educational business and government leaders there. The observation is that innovation and creativity have become a national mission for China. Perhaps most recently, a spectacular expression, the opening ceremony of Beijing Olympic Games, the purposefully and breathtakingly elegant calligraphy of creativity displayed on that occasion sent generations of stereotyped and clichéd ideas about China and images of it up in smoke when the Olympic torch was lit the night of August 8, 2008.

China continues to build an infrastructure of innovation and creativity in an astonishing way. For example, by the year 2020, China's highway system will be larger than that of the United States. Innovation driven companies led in appreciable measures, experts and talents are popping up in old warehouses, and factory districts in China's major cities. And in a closer look of views, creativity is surfacing more visibly, not only in the commercial arts in design, fashion, media and the alike, but also with abundant evidence in nearby cafes, art studios and galleries, as well as in the theatres, and sidewalks and street corners.

China's creative heritage, and especially its literary tradition, reflects thousands of years of achievement. So it would be especially informative to hear from Dr. Liu Mengxi, and Mr. Mo Yan about the current state of literature, and especially the novel, and its relationship to China's literary heritage, as well as the culture and pedagogical condition within which creativity continues to flourish in China's schools and universities as well as in the minds, hearts and hands of creative artists, and especially, its writers. I trust also that our distinguished Chinese colleagues would be interested in engaging in dialogue about the place of creativity, and especially, its literary heritage, and we believe, more particularly, poetry within the contemporary American University, and particularly within a pressured context of undergraduate education and the angle of American tradition of literary education that forms it.

Before inviting our panelists to speak, I'd also like to offer a respectful recommendation. I would like to encourage our guests to visit the C.V. Starr East Asian library. The Starr library, which is part of the Chang-Lin Tien Center for East Asia Studies, is used to be Berkeley's most splendid realization of the intersections of the operative terms of our conversation this morning, literary, heritage, and creativity. The C.V. Starr library contains one of the most comprehensive collections of materials in East Asia languages and literatures in the United States. The architect, Tod Williams and Billie Tsien, described this building as a symmetrical box broken by light. I'm delighted to know that Billie Tsien will be in the audience today.

The C.V. Starr East Asian Library is situated on Memorial Glade, the heart of the Berkeley campus, and its cut deeply into a steep hillside. The university design guidelines for representing the heritage of the classical core of the campus required a pitched, clay tile roof, a symmetrical façade and use of white granite. Billie Tsien and Tod Williams creatively blended these elements by re-interpreting the use of a screen, an important element of Asian architecture. In this instance, they use both a traditional cracked ice and contemporary grid patterns. This monumental round screen is 120 by 35 feet. It's a building of an expression of its Asian identity. It unifies the exterior and creates the illusion of symmetry from the asymmetrical arrangement of windows. From the exterior, the façade is solid, powerful, and mysterious. From the interior, the screens offer a dynamic and filtered view of the surrounding landscape.

It is no coincidence that the C.V. Starr libraries as well as the larger campus of U.C. Berkeley are perched on the fragile east based hills and looked directly out across San Francisco Bay towards East Asia. The elegant simplicity of the Starr library celebrates the magnificent heritages that forever link China and the United States, the Starr library and the larger world around it. These are reflections and remind us of inner Berkeley community of how and where creativity can flourish and heritage can thrive.

21世纪人类能否在非对抗中重生

刘梦溪

中国艺术研究院中国文化研究所所长，研究员

内容提要： 就像一个人不能离群索居一样，一个国家也不可能逸世独存于当代世界。而文明的融合，首先需要文化沟通。文化沟通不仅是文明人的礼仪，而且是文明人的智慧和生存方式。正是在这个意义上，我认为国与国、区域与区域、民族与民族之间，是互为依存的关系。东方离不开西方，西方也离不开东方。"同"和"异"是就达至目标的途径而言，最终归宿常常是相同的。

世纪的转换，是历史的恒常现象，照说不应该对人类社会有什么影响，可是复按历史却不尽然。当19世纪末、20纪初的时候，也就是上一个世纪转换的历史时刻，全世界都害起了"世纪病"。

当时东方许多国家面临西方强势文化的冲击，迎退失据，陷入了自身价值系统崩塌的严重危机。西方也发生了危机，主要是强势国家的殖民化政策，加剧了宗主国与殖民地之间以及宗主国与宗主国之间的矛盾。东方的危机迫使人们通过变革来改变现状，因此反倒看到了希望。西方的危机似乎更加深在。后来终于爆发第一次世界大战，是危机的直接结果，也是试图摆脱危机的一种方式。正因为如此，上一个世纪转换时期，也就是19世纪末、20世纪初，才有西方物质文明已经破产的观点出现。

一个世纪过去了，虽然中间又有第二次世界大战发生，多少世纪累积的人类文明成果遭受重创。但西方的物质文明并没有破产，不仅没有破产，而且在20世纪差不多走到了巅峰的位置。当然东方也没有破产，不仅没有破产，而且在磨难中逐渐苏醒过来，纷纷获得独立，不少国家用自己的方式完成了民族国家的整合过程。从大历史着眼，如果说西方赢了，那么东方并没有输。中国站立起来和重新走向世界，不就是20世纪惊世骇俗的一大景观吗？何况还有印度，还有日本，还有当时的"亚洲四小龙"。

历史过程本身，是不可以简单用输赢、胜负、成败来计量的。当然我这里所说的东方和西方，是历史地理和文化类型的概念，而不是单一的政治意识形态概念。

这次20世纪和21世纪的转换，至少到上一个世纪的90年代中期和后期，人们还是相当平静的，没有什么危机感，西方没有，东方也没有，不但没有，反而为一片乐观的情绪所笼罩。西方浸沉在因前苏联和东欧的解体而进入冷战后的喜悦之中，东方为自己的经济奇迹而沾沾自喜。特别是亚洲一些经济发展势头强劲的国家，情绪高蹈，对未来做出了乐观的估计。因此"21世纪是东方文化的世纪"、"亚洲的世纪"等话语，都出现了。

但没过多久，1997年开始，席卷亚洲的金融危机爆发，泰国、印度尼西亚、马来西亚、韩国，传染似的连锁反应，全球为之震惊。于是"东方文明破产了"、"亚洲价值崩溃了"一类话语又大行其时。但三年过后，亚洲经济又开始复苏。如果仅仅以经济的浮动指标作为现代文明的尺度，对于亚洲价值作价值判断，就会像华尔街股指那样变得不可捉摸。

现在以金融危机为潮头的经济危机，又一次汹涌而来，"金元帝国"美国始作俑，席卷西方，弥漫全球。相对这次亚洲所受冲击要轻一些。但没有置身局外的幸运者。即使三流四流的政治家，也不敢有所轻忽，更不敢幸灾乐祸。现在中国流行三个成语：未雨绸缪、亡羊补牢、同舟共济。此时此刻，需要的是信心和胆魄，而不是扭捏不清的"高兴"或"不高兴"的矫情计较。也许现在已经像专业人士设想的那样，一年见底，二年回升，三年重振。我们当然希望如此。可谁都不是预言家，无法预测这次以及下一次人类在21世纪已经或者还要面临哪些严峻的挑战。

我想21世纪和20世纪一样，仍然是充满变量的时代。当人们处在19世纪末的时候，谁想到20世纪会发生两次世界大战。历史的发展、社会的变迁、文明秩序的建构，从来都不是一帆风顺的。不断地挫折，不断地重生，是人类社会发展的恒常现象。可是人性的弱点就是最容易犯重复的错误。不肯吸取教训是人类的痼疾。现在一些国家拥有的最先进的大规模杀伤性武器，超过历史上任何一个时期。大家都在扩军备战。连产生圣雄甘地的"非暴力主义"的印度，也在沾沾自喜地以武力自炫。本来危机尚不算深的东北亚，也被那只看得见和看不见之手，搅扰得危机重重。

人类大约没有想到，刚进入21世纪之初，就晕眩地站在了十字路口。看来奥巴马去年的复活节演说流露出来的"世界重生"的闪光一念，只不过是策略性的权宜之计，也许在他个人是真实的，但权力中枢和利益集团，并未因胜心不胜而累积出新世纪的绝地猛醒。

然而，并不很聪明的人类可曾知道：我们的居住之所地球已经远不像从前那样硕大无垠了，所谓地球有无穷无尽资源的想法已变得荒唐可笑。当金融家、政客、金钱和权力万能论者，用各种神话编织全球化的奇妙网络的时候，他们忘记了地球在21世纪会做出怎样的回应。现代文明唯一被遗忘的角落是地球的超负荷运转。其实地球被迫做出回应的预兆我们已经看到了：气候变暖，那是地球在慢性发热；赤地千里，那是地球的饥渴；洪水泛滥，那是地球流的泪水；火山喷发，那是地球的叹息；地震，那是地球的愤怒。

一个国家的现代化进程，不可能在与世隔绝的情况下单独完成，需要不同文化背景、不同文化系统、不同文化理念的点燃与嫁接。20世纪最后一年的早春，恰值我在哈佛大学作访问学者，当时哈佛大学的资深学者史华慈教授亲口对我说，语言并不像人们想象的那样对思维有那样巨大的作用。他说这个话不久，就离开了人世。他是坚定的跨文化沟通的倡导者，为了鼓舞人类沟通与对话，他勇敢地提出了关于语言与思维的关系的也许是尚待证实的新理论。

就像一个人不能离群索居一样，一个国家也不可能逸世独存于当代世界。亨廷顿教授的偏颇，是过分强调了文明的冲突，而轻视了文明的融合。而文明的融合，首先需要文化沟通。文化沟通不仅是文明人的礼仪，而且是文明人的智慧和生存方式。正是在这个意义上，我认为国与国、区域与区域、民族与民族之间，是互为依存的关系。东方离不开西方，西方也离不开东方。"同"和"异"，是就达至目标的途径而言。最终归宿，常常是相同的。《易经》上说："天下同归而殊途，一致而百虑。"说的就是这个道理。

东方文明中，譬如说中国传统文化里面，是不是也含有供全人类取资的普世价值？我想那是毋庸置疑的。作为中国学术思想经典源头的"六艺之学",也就是"六经",其义理内涵与人类的普遍精神追寻可谓同一旨归。而孔子的"仁"、"恕"思想、"己所不欲勿施于人"的学说,显然应该成为人类的共德。还有源于孔孟而由宋儒集大成的"主敬",也应该是属于全人类的德律资源。不过西方传统中,同样也有近似或者相同的价值呈现,不是孰好孰不好的问题,而是对话互阐的问题。

人类既然从轴心文明中走过来,就会回到轴心文明中去。所谓"21世纪是东方的世纪"、"亚洲的世纪"——我个人不作如是观。我更倾向于这样一种看法,即世界是多元的、文化是多元的、现代文明模式的建构是多元的。社会制度是历史的阶段性型态,文化精神的理性之光是永恒的。21世纪既属于东方,也属于西方;21世纪是我们的,是你们的,也是他们的。总之21世纪是大家的,它属于全人类。

因此如果需要对21世纪的进程做出某种预测,我认为经济的全球化、现代文明的普世化是必然之趋势,但各个国家的经济模式和文明的类型却不必也不可能完全整齐划一,本土文化资源的整合必定是各民族国家追寻的既定目标。"全球化"的理想是令人神往的,因为每个国家都是地球村的一个住户,谁不希望有一个好邻居?但"全球主义"则是一个危险的口号,因为那意味着人类将接受霸权的主宰。当然我同样不能认同"新亚洲攘夷论",我认为那里面也隐含有不祥之兆。

距今一千多年的宋代思想家张载,为了启发人类的良知,写了一本书叫《正蒙》,书中第一篇是"太和",里面有四句有名的话:"有象斯有对,对必反其为;有反斯有仇,仇必和而解。"这是对宇宙世界图景的一种哲理认知。我相信他的话 —— 这个万象纷呈的世界,虽然有"对",有"反",有"仇",但最后必然是"仇必和而解",从而归于"太和"。已故的佛学大师赵朴初先生引述的两句诗,写的也很好,即"渡尽劫波兄弟在,相逢一笑泯恩仇。"他说出了全世界每一个人的心里话。

看来能够给人类未来带来真切曙光的,是中国的一个字"和"、两个字"和合"、三个字"将无同"(晋时吊诡清谈的"三语掾",即无不同的意思)。

Liu Mengxi

Research Fellow and Director of Institute of Chinese Culture, Chinese National Academy of Arts

Can Humanity be Reborn without Confrontation in the 21st Century

Abstract: A man cannot live in complete seclusion; likewise, a nation cannot exist isolated from the modern world. Cultural communication is the precondition of integration of civilization; it is not only etiquette of civilized people, but also their wisdom and way to live. Right in this sense, I believe that, regardless of whether we are talking about nations, regions, or ethnic groups, the relationship is one of mutual dependence. The East cannot exist in isolation from the West, or vice versa. I believe humanity shares a set of common goals, and different approaches are taken to realize these goals, which is how I see our similarities and differences.

Time goes as the rule of nature. It should have had no influence on human society, but history proves otherwise. At the historical turn of the 19th and 20th centuries, the world suffered from the "Century Disease".

At that time, countries in the East were challenged by forceful Western culture and gradually losing their own value systems. The West also suffered from crisis, mainly from aggravated conflicts between colonies and their metropolitan states and between various metropolitan states resulted by colonial policies of powerful countries. Crisis in the East compelled reform that brought hope; while crisis in the West seemed worse. World War I was the immediate result and also an attempt to recover from crisis. Just because of this, there came at the turn of 19th and 20th centuries an idea that the Western material civilization has come to its end.

Another century has gone, during which happened the painful World War II that ruined civilization fruits achieved over centuries. However, the Western material civilization was not over; instead, it reached the summit in the 20th century. The Eastern countries also survived from hardship. They won independence and national unification in their own ways. From historical perspective, the West wins and the East is not a loser. China has stood up on her own feet and came to the world, and astonished the world in the 20th century. We were also impressed by India, and the "four little dragons" in Asia.

History cannot be valued simply by winning or losing. Of course the West and East I mentioned are historical, geographic and cultural, rather than simply political or ideological concepts.

During the turn of the 20th and 21st centuries, people stayed calm and felt no crisis either in the West or East, at least until 1990s. It was an optimistic world. The West was happy to see the end of the Cold War marked by disintegration of the Soviet Union and the Eastern Europe, and the East enjoyed its economic miracles. Economic powers in Asian, in particular, were highly encouraged and gave optimistic outlooks. This was why we heard "the 21st century belongs to East" and "the century of Asia".

But soon the world was shocked by the financial crisis in Asia started in 1997 affecting Thailand, Indonesia, Malaysia and Korea. Therefore, notions such as "the Eastern civilization is over" and "Asian value crashes down" prevailed. However, three years later Asia saw economic revival. If modern civilization was measured exclusively by economic fluctuation, evaluation of Asia would be as uncertain as stock index in the Wall Street.

Following the financial crisis, another economic crisis broke out in US, sweeping Europe and then the globe once again. Comparatively Asia is not so affected but did not escape which even low-class politicians have to admit and cannot crow over. Current prevailing notions are three Chinese phrases which mean respectively precaution, remedy and mutual assistance. It is faith and courage that are in need, not reluctant haggle over a penny. Perhaps it is like what pundits anticipated, "down to the bottom in the first year, rebound in the second and revival in the third". Certainly it is our hope. However, we are not prophets. We cannot tell what challenges are waiting ahead of us in the 21st century.

I think the 21st century, just as the 20th century, is full of uncertainties. Did we foresee in the 19th century that the 20th century would witness two World Wars? Historical development, social evolution and building of civil order are never easy; social development is based on setbacks and rebirth. I feel that one of our weaknesses is that we tend to repeat our mistakes, and that we refuse to learn from the past. The number of mass destruction weapons held by countries today has reached a historical high. Every country is engaged in arms expansion and preparing for war. Even India, the birthplace of Mahatma Gandhi, who embraced nonviolence, is flexing its military muscles. And northeast Asia, which I thought did not have much to worry about, is now deeply stranded in crises.

Humanity probably did not see itself standing bewildered, at a crossroad, right after the onset of the 21st century. It seems that the sparkling "rebirth of world" proposed by Barack Obama in last Easter just served as a strategic stopgap; or maybe it was the voice from his heart but the central power and interest groups remained in their dream of conquering human faith in the new century.

Furthermore, is the less-than-bright humanity aware that our home – Earth, is no longer as vast and boundless a treasure trove as we used to think?. The notion that the earth's resources are endless has become a laughable one. As financial brokers, politicians and money worshippers weave the curious web of globalization through one myth after another, they have probably overlooked the ways through which our mother Earth will respond in this 21st century. There is but one nook neglected by modern civilizations, the fact that our earth is overburdened. The truth is, we are already seeing signs to that effect: global warming – that's the earth becoming warmer and warmer; thousands of miles of barren land – that's the earth becoming thirsty; devastating floods – that's the earth crying; volcano eruptions – that's the earth grieving; and earthquakes – that's the earth showing its wrath.

For any nation, the process of modernization cannot be completed in vacuum, cut off from the rest of the world. Modernization is a process that requires different cultural backgrounds, cultural systems and cultural notions to come into contact, and to learn and borrow from each other. In the spring of 1999 when I was a visiting scholar in Harvard, then senior scholar Professor Schwartz told me in person that language does not play a decisive role to the way we thought. Unfortunately he passed away shortly after the talk. Schwartz was a staunch advocate of cross-cultural communication who, to encourage communication and dialogue between human, fearlessly proposed his new theory about the relation between language and thinking which needs to be proved.

A man cannot live in complete seclusion; likewise, a nation cannot exist isolated from the modern world. Radical Professor Samuel Huntington puts too much stress on "clash", and not enough on the integration of civilizations. In my opinion, cultural communication is the precondition of integration of civilization; it is not only etiquette of civilized people, but also their wisdom and way to live. Right in this sense, I believe that, regardless of whether we are talking about nations, regions, or ethnic groups, the relationship is one of mutual dependence. The East cannot exist in isolation from the West, or vice versa. I believe humanity shares a set of common goals, and different approaches are taken to realize these goals, which is how I see our similarities and differences. This idea can be found in the ancient Chinese classic I-Ching (the Book of Changes): through different paths we walk toward the same destination; though we may disagree on ideas and means, all means point to the same end.

Are universal values found in the Eastern civilization, such as in traditional Chinese culture? I believe there is no doubt that universal values are found in traditional Chinese culture. The root of Chinese academic thinking – "the six classics", talks about concepts and ideas which share the same ends as the universal spiritual pursuit of humanity. Confucius' notion of "benevolence" and "tolerance", and "do unto others as you would have them do unto you", are obviously be universal virtues. And then there is the notion of "respect", which originated from the teachings of Confucius and Mencius, and was carried to full-bloom by Song dynasty Confucian scholars. I think this should also be part of the shared wisdom of mankind. Similar and identical values can be found in western traditions. So, this is not a question of which is good or which is bad. What we need is dialogue and mutual interpretation.

Humanity has gone through the axes civilization, and will return to the axes. Personally I do not applaud the notions "the 21st century belongs to East" and "the century of Asia". I tend towards a diverse world, diverse cultures and diverse modern civilizations. Social institutions are but the various phases of history, but the rationality of cultural ethos is long lasting. The 21st century belongs to the East, and to the West; it is a new century of ours, of yours, and of theirs. In a word, it is a century of humanity.

Therefore, if it is necessary to predict progress in the 21st century, I think globalization of economy and modern civilization are natural trends. It is not necessary, nor is it feasible for every nation to share the same mode of economic structure and to have the same type of civilization. The integration of local cultures is a set goal that all nationalities and countries must aspire after. Globalization is a charming idea. Every nation is a household in the Global Village. Who doesn't like to have a good neighbor? But "globalism" is a slogan embedded with risks – it suggests that humanity will be dominated by hegemony. But of course, I am equally against the notion "repel the barbarians", which is emerging in New Asia – a notion which I believe, forebodes trouble.

Over one thousand years ago, a Song Dynasty thinker Zhang Zai wanted to awaken man's conscience. To this end, he wrote the book Zheng Meng. In the first chapter, "Great Harmony", he wrote what later became a well-known line: "Everything in the world is made up of two contradicting forces, which inevitably leads to clashes. But in the end, the two opposing forces must find a way to resolve their differences and coexist in harmony." This is a philosophical interpretation of our universe. This is the notion I believe in – this multifaceted world we live in has forces that contradict and clash, but eventually, differences will be resolved and we will reach the state of "great harmony." The late Chinese Buddhist master Mr. Zhao Puchu had quoted two lines of poem that "Having gone through years of animosity, we find ourselves still brothers. We meet and smile and forget about all hatred and grudges." I believe this is a shared sentiment of the entire humanity.

It seems that the future of humanity is summed up by the Chinese word "harmony", or you could say it is summed up by two words "harmony" and "convergence", and the notion of "no difference" from the Jin Dynasty.

美国大学与文学事业

安德鲁·德尔班科

哥伦比亚大学
美国研究中心主任

内容提要：没有文学的大学，无论是美国大学还是中国大学，从多个意义上来说都是不完整的大学，而且我觉得没有大学参与其中的文学也是不完整的。这是一个很大的概括和推论，而我认为在各种文化中，真实的情况或许确实如此。

　　我想就一个相当长的时段、即大约四个世纪左右的时期发表一些评论。如果回到我们所了解和习惯上称之为高等教育的最早时期，也就是美国刚成立的时候，我们会发现两个术语，文学和大学。虽然这两个词汇早已存在，但其含义与现今大不相同。当时，确切地说，美国北部还没有大学。大学一词被如基督教牧师乔纳森·爱德华一类的人用在像"事物的集合"这样的短语里，所指的含义为上帝创造的整个世界。在这个世界中，上帝创造的万事万物相互之间紧密相联，不可分割。从某方面来说，这一含义可能与大学自身追求的构想有关。

　　"文学"一词当时指的是我们在当时的机构、更恰当的说应该是大学中的学院中所学的内容，主要是神学。我喜欢阅读美国高等教育史上最早的大学，即哈佛大学的创始者们写给英国同仁和朋友的信件，我们可能视这些信件为最初的愿景书或募款函。其内容主要是请求资金资助。抛开其金钱目的不说，时至今日，我还是觉得这些信件非常感人："在上帝把我们安全地送到新英格兰之后，我们已修盖了自己的房屋、制作了各种生活用品，修建了礼拜堂，并组织了自己的地方政府。下一步便是为了子孙后代的繁荣昌盛，需要促进他们的文化教育了。否则，当我们现在的传教士离开尘世之后，教会中继承他们事业的将是一批目不识丁的人。"

关于所谓的募款函，可说的内容很多，其中之一便是它标志着美国高等教育机构的混合性。这些机构既非完全公立，也非完全私立，总是二者兼而有之。今天我们所在的这所伟大的大学，从广义上而言就是一所公立大学，但同时也是受捐之地。不言而喻许多私人捐赠者和支持也享受到了其中的利益。所以，公立和私立的问题是美国高等教育历史上一个有趣的因素，一个我们希望探讨的话题。

另外值得一提的是，他们信中所称的"促进"是什么意思？我想，他们所要表达的含义与我们现在在大多数当代大学的愿景书中看到的常见语言的含义不尽相同。我们现在常常看到大学的愿景书中总是这样写道：我们站在知识的前沿，我们站在知识的尖端，我们希望推动知识的进步等等。我想，这些最初的大学创始者所指的是另外的含义。他们指的应该是传播业已通过检验的真理，也就是说，传播已为人们所接受并且从根本上不可动摇的真理。我们前面听到了有关美国文化的传教精神，及其多年以来在我们与中国的关系中发挥的作用。我想，那是"促进"一词最初的力量。

那么文学呢？文学主要是指圣经，希伯来语的圣经，即基督徒所称的《旧约》，与新书，即基督徒所称的《新约》，以及从某种程度上来说，对圣经的评注。随着时间的推移，人们向越来越多带有希腊和罗马传统的经典作家求教道德教育中诸如逻辑这样的问题，这也就是早期的美国高等教育机构的根本宗旨。

时光跳过大约200年，当我们来到19世纪第三季中期时，发现这些教育愿景最初所依据的知识的概念已开始发生根本的改变。正是在那样一个历史时期，我们可以恰当地称之为大学的机构出现了。它们主要以德国研究型大学为基础，向西方世界引进了学术自由，即无拘束的知识追求等基本概念。知识追求的结果不是由外部的权力机构而是由进行知识追求的同仁或其他人进行评判。

如果看一下这些新机构早期声明的内容，我们会发现它们与我之前提到的愿景书内容不同。余宝琳今天早上提到的加利福尼亚大学首位校长丹尼尔·科伊特·吉尔曼后来去了东部地区，成为美国第一所真正的研究型大学约翰斯·霍普金斯大学的第一位校长。他声称，学校的宗旨是告诉学生们如何拓展知识，哪怕是通过微小的积累获取庞多的知识。

在我看来，这时我们已经到达了一个具有现代意义的大学的时代。

支持吉尔曼这一观点的最具有影响力的人物是查尔斯·W. 艾略特。他是一位清教徒后代，本身是一名化学家，19世纪晚期成为了哈佛大学的校长。他认为，大学的重要职能之一是储存人类的知识。他指的人类，是今天普遍意义上的人类。因此，每一代人的接班人都应继承他们先辈所创造的优势。我且将它称为"人类历史的接力赛"。也就是说，一代人获得了某种知识的内涵，发现了一些事物，他们需要将这些知识内涵和发现的事物传递给下一代，使得下一代不必再费精力发现同样的事物。于是，对知识的寻求就可以从一个较之前更高的起点开始。这就是我对科学发展根本方式的理解。我们在这些学校表达宗旨的宣言中发现，科学范式在高等教育世界中占有越来越重要的地位，这一现象在美国表现得越来越明显，也是文化的骄傲，值得我们庆祝。科学的成就已成为一个传奇，并有希望继续发展，为我们带来巨大的福祉。

但是，我想，就我的学科目的而言，这一教育愿景以及教育机构的宗旨构成了一个深刻的挑战，即人文科学、尤其是文学研究如何适应这一新的理解范式的深刻挑战。我对此的理解是：他们在对自己以及公众宣布如何适应这种范式时存在很多问题。他们尝试在19世纪末这些大学成立之初推行语言学研究，也就是研究语言的体系以及各种语言之间的相互关系。这一研究多少可以以实证的方式完成，而他们进行了一些时至今日仍非常重要的工作，即建立善本，将过去不同版本的文本校对、整理成册。他们建立了档案，这曾是美国大学的显著特征之一。

但总体而言，我想，他们在适应这一范式的时候还是遇到了诸多困难。对此我暂不赘述。我想说的是，本国语言文学，即英国或美国语言文学以及其他现代语言的文学在美国高等教育史上出现和发展的时期较晚。其出现主要受马修·阿诺德的影响。马修·阿诺德在其著名的文化定义中提到，文化是对世界中已经思考和表达了的最优秀部分的理解。如今我们在认真对待世界的全球性含义上进展缓慢。但我们从这一言论中可以得知，大学文学教育的目标是向下一代人介绍人类积累的财富，不仅包括文学，也包括其他的知识领域。我们常常忽略他的定义的后半部分内容。他在该部分内容中提到，通过这些知识，我们对原有的观念和习惯进行全新和自由的思考。换句话说，我常常认为阿诺德是一个文化保守派，他实际上将文学视为对我们过去和现在的文化设想进行激进地质疑的工具。

在美国，我想那就是引入我们大学之中关于文学研究最根本的精神。而在我们看来，与马修·阿诺德相匹敌的人物则是拉尔夫·沃尔多·爱默生。我非常喜欢他对文学所下的定义。他说，文学是我们现在所处的现时观念圈之外的一个点，通过它可以进行新的描述。文学的作用是在我们需要对现时生活进行观察时为我们提供一个平台，一项我们可以藉以动摇它的方法。换句话说，从这一观点看，文学与我们称之为现时的文化结构是从根本上对立的，并对其持怀疑甚至是敌对的态度。而且值得我们记住的是，那些我们今天奉为经典的书籍，例如我最喜爱的《白鲸》和《哈克贝利·费恩历险记》等等都曾在某些时期被批为攻击性的、无礼的、可耻的、卑微的、使人迷惑的作品，并且不值得认真研究。我想这是值得我们记住的一点。

因此，大学中的文学功能，在我看来，就是帮助我们对现时处于主导地位的博士提出质疑，无论他们是自由市场中解决一切问题的博士，还是为解决人性问题而进行集中规划的博士，或者是罗素所称的高尚清白的创造物等等。

文学教育的意义在于帮助个体批判机制获得精神和创造力的独立。关于文化教育是如何被感知的，有很多话可说。鉴于时间有限，我暂不赘述。我想以两点评论结束我的发言。第一，如果我们坦诚对待美国现时的状态，这一教育的维度则存在严重问题。大约一星期以前，《纽约时报》的一位主管告诉我，纽约州立大学的相关公共机构宣布，法语、意大利语和俄语文学系都将关闭。而这里，加利福尼亚州大学洛杉矶分校，几个人文系也有可能合并。它们都是不可或缺的学科，并将在机构中发挥越来越多的作用。而我要补充说明的最后一点是，我们可以谈论和思考大学和文学之间的关系。我们同样需要认识到，在过去50或60年中，大学，尤其是美国和西方的大学对艺术的包容胜过以往任何时候以及任何其他国家。而今天，曾经受到繁荣的文学市场支持的文学看来存在很多问题。有人认为大学为今天的创造性写作提供了支持，而这是以往没有的。我认为，上述各项的前提是，没有文学的大学，无论是美国大学还是中国大学，从多个意义上来说是不完整的大学，而且我觉得没有大学参与其中的文学也是不完整的。这是一个很大的概括和推论，而我认为在各种文化中，真实情况或许确实如此。

Andrew Delbanco

Director of American Studies, Columbia University

American University and Literature Career

Abstract: Whether they are American universities or Chinese universities, universities without literature in the several senses are diminished institutions, and I suspect that literature without universities would be as a diminished institution. That's a big generalization and presumption on which I think might actually be true across cultures.

I'm going to try to make some remarks on a period of roughly four centuries which is a pretty long time. If we go back to the beginning of what we know and customarily called higher education and what became the United States, we discovered the two terms, which I'd like to frame my remarks, literature and university. Although the words existed, they didn't mean anything much like what they mean now. There were, properly speaking, no universities in North America at that time. The word university was used by people like Christian minister Jonathan Edward in a phrase like "the university of things", by which he meant the entire created universe, in which all of God's creations were intimately related to one another in all part of an indiscerptible whole, which is in some respects, perhaps the idea of aspiration that university still have for themselves.

The word "literature" as referred to what we study in the institutions of the time which were more properly called colleges in university, was mainly theological literature. And I like to read the words that were other than what we might regard as the first mission statement or the first fund raising statement in the history of American higher education composed by the funders of our first college, Harvard College, who wrote back to their peers and friends in England, basically to ask them for financial support with a following terms. Despite their mercenary purposes, I still find them quite moving today: "After God had carried us safe to New England and we had built our houses, provided necessaries for our livelihood, reared convenient places for God's worship, and settled the civil government: One of the next things we longed for and looked after was to advance learning and perpetuate it to posterity; dreading to leave an illiterate ministry to the churches, when our present ministers shall lie in the dust. "

There are a lot of things to be said about the so-called fund raising statement, so one thing that could be said about it is that it signals that sort of hybrid nature of American institutions of higher learning which have always been neither completely public or completely private, but have always some combination of the two. This great university which is hosting us here today, is a public university in a large sense, but it is also the beneficiary area many private benefactions and people who give support to it enjoy tacit advantages. So the public and private thing is an interesting dimension of the history of higher education in the United States, something that we might wish to talk about.

Another thing that can be said about that is that what they meant by "advance" and "perpetuate", but particularly "advance", they didn't mean anything very close to the conventional language that we now encounter in the mission statements of most present day universities. That is, the language that we are accustomed to is the language of, by which university says, we are at the frontier of knowledge; we are at the cutting edge of knowledge; we wish to advance knowledge in this sense. My sense is that the founders of these first colleges meant it in a different way. They meant it more in a sense of disseminating the reviewed truth that is disseminating truth that had already been received and were fundamentally unchanged. We've heard something about the missionary spirit of American culture and the role it plays in our relationship with China over the years that I think is the force of the word "advance" at the very beginning.

Now what about literature? Literature meant chiefly scripture, the Hebrew scriptures, which Christians called the Old Testament and the new books that Christians call the New Testament, and to some extent, commentaries on scripture. And as time went on, more and more classical writers from the Greek and Roman traditions who were turned to for guidance in such matters as logic in the service of morale education, which was the fundamental purpose of these early American institutions of higher learning.

Now skipping over about 200 years, when we arrive at the middle of the third quarter of the 19th century, I think we find that the conception of knowledge on which this educational mission had originally been based began to change in very fundamental ways. And it is at that moment of our history when we see the emergence of institutions that can probably be called universities. They were based primarily on the model of the German research university, which introduced into the western world such fundamental concepts as academic freedom, which is to say, the untrammeled pursuit of knowledge, and the results of that pursuit were being subject to judgment not by any external authorities but by peers or those who were engaged in that pursuit of knowledge.

If we look at the early statements of what these new institutions were about, we will find a very different note from the one that I have sounded so far. Daniel Coit Gilman that was mentioned by Pauline Yu this morning as the early president of the University of California moved east and became the first president of the first genuine American research university, Johns Hopkins, whose purpose, he said, was to show students how to extend even by minute acquisitions the Rome of knowledge. So there we arrived at the modern conception of the university, it seems to me.

The most influential proponent of that view was Charles W. Elliot☐ descended from purisms but himself a chemist, who became president of Harvard in the late 19th century and was described one of the important functions of universities as the store of the accumulated knowledge of the race, by which he meat the human race in the universal sense that we have been speaking of it here this morning. So that each successor of generation of view shall start with all the advantages in which their predecessors have one. I call this, I don't mean to be, and relay race of view of human history, that one generation arrives at certain insides, discoveries, and passes their own to the next generation, so that they don't have to be rediscovered, so that the quest for knowledge can begin anew from a more advanced point from where it was before. This is to my naïve understanding fundamentally the way science works. And what we hear in these articulations of the purpose of the university is the growing significance and dominance of the scientific paradigm in the world of higher education, which is more and more apparent in the United States, and which is the cause and main respects for great celebration and cultural pride, because the accomplishments of science have been a legend and promised to continue to be considerable and we all owe it, an enormous debt.

It is the case, however, for the purposes of my subject that this vision of education and the purpose of educational institutions constituted a very profound challenge for the humanities, for literary study, in particular, as to how they would fit in to this new paradigm of understanding. My own sense in this is that they had a lot of trouble articulating to themselves and to the public how they fit in to this paradigm. They tried to prevail at the end of the 19th century when these universities first came into existence through such exercises as the study of philology, that is, the study the genealogy of languages and the interrelationships among languages which could be done more or less empirically. They did it but through some very important works continue in some measures still today, that is the establishment of reliable texts, the collation of various versions of text from the past. They did it through biography, which was once an active feature of American universities less now than it used to be.

But in general, I think, they had a lot of trouble fitting in; I won't take more times to say more about that. What I would like to claim is that the entrance of vernacular literature, that is, the literature in English or American languages as well as in other modern languages was a very late development in the history of American higher education. And it basically came in under the banner of Matthew Arnold, who wrote famously in his own definition of culture that we have been discussing here this morning, that culture is the presumed perception by means of getting to know the best which has been thought and said in the world. Now we've been very slow in taking seriously the global implications of world. But you hear in that articulation that the teaching of literature in the university services the purpose of introducing the coming generation to the accumulated treasures of the human race, not just the literature, but in all fields of study. We less often, I think, pay attention to the second part of his definition, in which he goes on to say that through this knowledge, we turn a stream of fresh and free thought upon our stock notions and habits. In other words, Arnold was often characterized in my view as a cultural conservative actually saw literature as an instrument for radical questioning of our cultural assumptions about our past and present.

In America, I think that has been the fundamental spirit of literary study, even domesticated and came in our universities. Our own version of Matthew Arnold I might say was Ralph Waldo Emerson, who defined literature in a way that I always like. He says that literature is a point outside of our hodiernal circle, a circle of present mindedness, through which a new one may be described. The use of literature is to afford us a platform once we make command a view of our present life, approaches by which we may move it. In other words, literature in this view is fundamentally in opposition, skeptical, and even hostile to the constructions that we call culture of the present moment. And it's worth remembering that the books we now regard as classics, such as my favorite, Moby Dick, or the Adventures of Huckleberry Finn, were all at one time or another described as offensive, outrageous, degrading, demeaning, bewildering and certainly unworthy of serious study. I think that's worth keeping in mind.

So literature, in other words, once the function of literature in the universities it seems to me the function of literature is to help us question whatever prevailing doctors may be in force of the present time in the culture in which we find ourselves, whether they are the doctor of the free market as a solution for all problems or centralized planning as the solution for human nature, or by Russell, as a creature of nobility and innocence, and so on and so forth.

The function of literary education then is to assist in the development of an individual critical faculty independence of mind and creativity to use the charge of our present session. There are more things to say about how literary education might be perceived. But I'll skip over that in the interest of time. I want to close my speech with just two other remarks. One is that if we are honest about the situation at the present time in the United States, this dimension of education is in very serious trouble. About a week ago, a leader in the New York Times said that a counterpart public institution in the State University of New York announced that the departments of French, Italian and Russian classics will all be closed. And here in California, the University of California, Los Angeles, several humanities departments are, as I understand it, likely to become combine, which is intellectually indispensible but which probably means that they will play more and more role in the institution.

And the last thing I want to say just by way of a footnote of all of these is that you can talk and think about the relations of universities, the literature, we want also to recognize that particularly in the United States and particularly in the last 50 or 60 years or so, universities have taken up the role of being patience to the arts in a way that was not true in the past and has not been so true in other cultures, that is, we think about the history of literature as having once been supported by papers, and once upon a time supported by a thriving literary market place which seems to in a lot of trouble today. There is a sense in which universities are in a place of central support for the production of creative writing today in a way that has never been before. The premise of all of these is that I think universities, whether they are American universities or Chinese universities, universities without literature in the several senses are diminished institutions, and I suspect that literature without universities would be as a diminished institution. That's a big generalization and presumption on which I think might actually be true across cultures.

美国文学对中国文学的影响

莫言

中国艺术研究院
文学院院长，研究员

内容提要： 作为一个作家，我希望外国的读者能够从我们作品里读到我们在艺术方面的创新和发现。截止到目前，我们更多地从外国文学里受到影响。我想假以时日，中国作家的作品也会对外国的、包括对美国的年轻作家产生影响。

上半场的时候，我坐在两个负责同声传译的女士旁边。我看到于丹教授演讲的时候，两个同传者非常紧张：她们的肩膀不断颤抖。于丹教授的口才，中国第一，我们都知道她的口才非常非常之好，她讲的话一个废字都没有，整理出来就是一篇很流畅的文章。但是这样好口才的人是同传者的敌人。像我这种讲话啰啰嗦嗦，有很多病句的人，反而是同传喜欢的。为什么要讲到这个翻译？讲到文学交流，没有翻译，几乎是一句空话。我们的音乐家的乐曲，不要翻译，舞蹈家在舞台上又蹦又跳，不要翻译。但是讲文学交流，没有翻译是不可能的。因此我刚才看到我们的安道教授乐了，安道是美国非常年轻的汉学家，翻译了很多中国优秀作家的优秀作品，他为两国之间的文学交流做出了很大的贡献。

据中国著名学者钱钟书先生研究，中国人翻译美国文学最早是在1864年。翻译的是美国的一个诗人朗费罗的一首诗歌。翻译者是中国大清帝国驻美国的一个外交官。这种翻译跟老百姓没有关系，是他们这种高级外交官的游戏。后来到了1901年，中国一个一句英文都不懂的、叫林纾的人跟另外一个人翻译了《汤姆叔叔的小屋》。这本书在中国也产生了很大的影响。甚至对中国社会进程的改变产生了非常积极的作用。大概在上个世纪二三十年代，中国出现了翻译美国文学的热潮。美国那个时期很多重要作家的作品虽然没有全部译过来，但是做了大量的介绍。到了1949年以后，中国对西方文学、也包括对美国文学的翻译逐渐低落。那个时候中国主要翻译俄苏文学，包括法国的批判现实主义的文学作品。直到上个世纪80年代，中国开始了改革开放的巨大社会变革，美国大量的文学作品翻译过来。也就是在上个世纪80年代，中国掀起了一个翻译西方文学的热潮。美国文学首当其冲，美国文学翻译最多。像海明威、福克纳这些在上个世纪60年代非常有名的作家，我们在80年代才读到他们的作品。

当然关于中国翻译美国文学是一个很大的研究课题，而且完全可以做成博士论文。我这样没有文化的人只是简单介绍而已。我主要想谈一下美国文学对我们这批作家——包括对我本人——的影响。我记得大概是1984年的冬天，一个大雪飘飘的夜晚，我从朋友那边借到了美国南方作家福克纳的一本书，翻译成中文叫《喧哗与骚动》，也有的人说是《声音与骚动》，好像是莎士比亚的一句台词。这本书我看了我们中国非常优秀的翻译者李文俊先生写的一篇前言，这篇前言长达一万多字。读完这个前言，我觉得我对福克纳非常了解。他的小说我看了十来页，就放到一边去了。因为读完了前言，我觉得福克纳就像我们村的一个老头一样。用中国人的话说，这个人讲话"不着调"，或者现在叫"不靠谱"，总而言之，满口谎言。他明明没有驾驶过飞机，非要说驾驶过飞机，而且在天空中跟法西斯进行过空战，而且说他的脑子里残留了一块这么大的弹片。为什么他的语言那么晦涩，句子那么长，他的句子像一团乱麻一样缠绕不清，就是因为他的脑子里有一块弹片在压迫他的神经，所以他的语言这么混乱。我一看福克纳这个人跟我性格很相似。我也是一个从小喜欢胡言乱语、胡说八道的人，尽管我的名字叫"莫言"。但是我小时候恰好是一个非常非常喜欢说话的人。因为我喜欢说话，不知道挨了我父母亲多少痛打。后来我母亲说，你再乱说话，我找绳子把嘴给你缝起来。后来我姐姐在旁边说，你把他的嘴缝起来，他从那个缝里也会漏出很多话来。

到了上个世纪80年代，我开始写作的时候，我想起父母的教导，就起名叫"莫言"。当然现在已经变成了一句绝妙的讽刺。我在中国也到处说话，而且说出了国界，到美国来说了。福克纳的性格就和我的性格很吻合；第二，他的出身和我的出身很相似，他也是一个农民。他即便成了很有名的作家，他自认为还是一个农民。他写的那点事，也就是发生在他家乡的那么一点事，就像邮票大小的一块地方的事。他创造了一个县，这个县可能在美国地图上找不着。他就是以他的故乡为基础。他一辈子都在写这个地方的事。虽然这个地方小，但是这个地方带有很大的普遍性，可以说他从这个地方走向了世界。这让我意识到一个作家如果要在文坛上立住脚跟，就必须创造自己文学的一个共和国，一个国家。他创造了一个县，我就大胆地写了一个高密东北乡。高密是在中国地图上可以查到的一个地方。但是东北乡是查不到的。我也以我的故乡为基础，创造了属于我的一块文学领土。那么在读福克纳之前，我是受到了中国保守的文学思想的影响。一直找不到自己要写的素材。当时就看报纸、听广播、千方百计寻找可以写成小说的故事。但是找来找去找到的都不对。看了福克纳的作品以后，我才明白，实际上我个人的经验、发生在我家乡小村庄的许许多多的事情，都可以变成小说素材。我的村庄里、我的家庭里、我熟悉的亲人和我的乡亲们，他们都可以变成我小说里的人物。后来我写了很多长篇小说、也写了很多的中短篇小说，这个小说里也写了数百个人物。这里的大部分人都可以在生活中找到原型。

当然不仅仅福克纳对我产生了影响。海明威的《老人与海》也是。我想在中国，我们这一代作家没有一个人没有读过，但是相对福克纳而言，我不太喜欢海明威，因为海明威这个人句子比较简洁，讲话很干净利落，没有废话。我不喜欢不讲废话的人。但是有很多中国作家喜欢他。还有一个美国的小说家叫杰克·伦敦，他写过很多在阿拉斯加淘金的故事，还写了很多动物，其中有一个小说叫《野性的呼唤》，写了一条狗最后怎么样变成一条狼的故事。这样的小说我读了也很亲切，因为我本人在农村生活了很长很长时间。有一段时间我跟动物打交道的时间比跟人打交道的时间还长。我自己也养过狗，所以我看了杰克·伦敦写的狗，也调动起我当年跟狗生活的那些记忆。所以我在我早期小说里也写狗。最近的小说也写过狗。当然我还写了牛、马、驴很多动物。中国有评论家讲，你为什么写牛写得这么好？我说我上一辈子肯定是一头牛。你为什么写猪那么样的准确？我说我放过很长时间的猪。我对猪的思想很了解。我对人不了解，但是我能看透猪、牛的心理，这就决定了我就成为了这么一个写动物、写农村的作家。这是在讲我自己。

由于我们中国杰出的翻译家的努力，把美国很多作家的作品译成中文，让我这样一个一点外文都不懂的人也通过读他们的作品了解了外国作家，并且受到了影响。那么我想中国早期的翻译者翻译外国文学作品是不太讲究的，不太重视写外国作家作品的艺术性。这跟当时中国的社会思潮有关系。中国有一个大学者梁启超，他认为小说就是一个政治工具，小说应该变成推进社会变革的工具。所以林纾当初翻译美国的《汤姆叔叔的小屋》也是看中它的思想性。我想在上个世纪80年代初期，很多美国翻译家、也包括欧洲的很多汉学家翻译中国小说，最初选择的就是中国小说的政治性和思想性，他们希望他们国家的读者能够从中国作家的作品里边读到中国社会政治的变化或者经济的变化。当然这个也没有错，但是我认为真正好的文学翻译是应该把艺术性放在第一位的。那么像后来的美国的汉学家，比如我们在座的安道教授，他们的翻译开始注重小说的艺术性，把艺术性看做是第一位的。作为一个作家，我希望外国的读者能够从我们作品里读到我们在艺术方面的创新和发现。截止到目前，我们更多地从外国文学里受到影响。那么我想假以时日，中国作家的作品也会对外国的、包括对美国的年轻作家产生影响。现在我在这里说，我受到了福克纳的影响，受到了杰克·伦敦的影响。我想再过50年或者100年，会不会有一个美国的年轻作家说，我受到了中国一个名叫"莫言"的作家的影响呢？我期盼着这一天。

The Influence of American Literature on Chinese Literature

Mo Yan

Research Fellow and Dean of School of literature, Chinese National Academy of Arts

---

Abstract: As an author myself, I hope that readers who do not speak Chinese can enjoy the aesthetic explorations in our works. Up until now, there have been more Chinese readers that have been influenced by foreign literature than foreign readers by Chinese literature. I hope that given more time, the exchange can become more bilateral, where the works of Chinese authors will influence authors from other countries, including young authors in America.

During the first session, I sat next to our two simultaneous interpreters and I happened to notice they seemed very nervous while interpreting for Professor Yu Dan. I think the two ladies were literally trembling. Now, we all know Professor Yu's lectures are some of the most outstanding lectures given in China. Her eloquence is without parallel, in the sense that she says exactly what she means to and no one word goes to waste. A verbatim transcription of her speech is an essay that needs no polishing. Yet an eloquent speaker is often, at the same time, an interpreter's worst enemy. I, on the other hand, am not an eloquent speaker. I tend to be very repetitive and wordy, and say grammatically incorrect things all the time, which I reckon might be better received by our interpreters. The reason I brought up interpretation, and translation alike, is that literature exchange is nothing but empty talk without interpreters or translators. Language barrier is not an issue for other forms of art, such as music and dancing. But when it comes to literature, the role of the translator is crucial. I believe I just saw Professor an Dao smiling. Professor An Dao is a young American sinologist. He has contributed greatly to literary exchange between our two countries and has translated many excellent works by outstanding Chinese authors.

According to a study by the eminent Chinese scholar Mr. Qian Zhongshu, the first piece of American literature ever translated into Chinese was a poem by Longfellow. The translator was a Chinese diplomat to the United States during the imperial reign of the Manchu government.

At the time, of course, translation of foreign works was nothing more than a hobby for a few high level diplomats and was irrelevant to most people. By the year 1901, a Chinese named Lin Shu who understood not a word of English worked with a translator and together they translated Uncle Tom's Cabin. Uncle Tom's Cabin had great influence in China and played a role in driving forward China's social advancement. Roughly during the time period from 1920 to 1930, China saw a surge in the translation of American literature. Many key contemporary American writers and their works were introduced extensively to Chinese readers, though not all of which were translated. After 1949, the translation of western literature in general, including American literature, gradually dwindled as China shifted its focus to the translation of literature of the Soviet Union and those of France belonging to the genre of critical realism. It was not until the 1980s when China began undergoing dramatic opening up and reforms and saw great social changes that American literature began to be translated en masse. In the 1980s, there was a fervent interest in China in translating western literature, and American literatures were the most translated. So it wasn't until then that Chinese readers began reading works by American authors that had become very popular in the 1960s, such as Ernest Hemingway and William Faulkner.

But of course, the translation of American literature into Chinese is a very broad topic that warrants a PhD thesis. I feel very humbled by this topic and can but give a brief talk. I wish to talk a little bit about the influence of American literature on authors of my generation, including myself. If I remember correctly, it was on a winter's night in 1984, with heavy snow falling from the sky. I borrowed a book from a friend of mine by an American author from the south — William Faulkner. The book was The Sound and the Fury. I think the title is a line from one of Shakespeare's plays. The book had an introduction by Mr. Li Wenjun, who is an outstanding Chinese translator. The introduction was over 10,000 words in length. After I read the introduction, I felt that I understood Faulkner very well, despite the fact that I read only about a dozen pages of the novel itself and put it side. From what I read in the introduction, Faulkner was like a typical old man I find in my own village, somebody who "rants and raves" about things that are not even remotely true. He never flew a plane in actual combat, yet he wrote about flying a plane and engaged in combat with the Nazis. He wrote about how a piece of shrapnel is left in his head which he blamed for his obscure and lengthy writing style. Faulkner's writing style is so convoluted, and his language so intertwined, because of the piece of shrapnel left in his head irritating his nerves. And I thought, Faulkner is just like me. Ever since I was a kid, I loved rambling on and on about stories I made up, even though my name is "Mo Yan", which literally means "don't talk." But I was a kid who loved nothing more than talking and telling stories. I lost count of how many times my parents tried to take a beating at me because I couldn't keep my mouth shut. I remember my mother once said to me that if I didn't learn to stop talking nonsense, she would sew up my mouth. To which my sister said, even if you sew up his mouth, he will try to talk through the seams.

During the 1980s, when I began writing, I heeded my parents' advice and decided to name myself "Mo Yan", a name that has proven to be an irony. I've spoken to Chinese audiences everywhere across China, and now I'm speaking to an American audience. So, I feel that in this sense, Faulkner and I are alike. Secondly, we share a similar background. Faulkner was a country man. Regardless of the fame he later enjoyed, Faulkner insisted that he was a farmer. Most of what he wrote about took place in his home town – "his own little postage stamp of native soil." He invented a county that could not be found on the map. Faulkner based his stories on his hometown. Throughout his entire career, Faulkner set most of his short stories and novels in this imaginary county, a small place that carried universality. The county was where Faulkner began, and from there he became known to the world. This made me realize that a writer who wishes to get ahead needs to create his/her own universe. Faulkner created Yoknapatawpha County. I invented a place called Gaomi Dongbei Xiang in my stories. Gaomi is an actual place you can find on the map, but not Dongbei Xiang. This is my creative universe, and the stories that happen there are based on stories that took place in my hometown. Before I read any of Faulkner's works, I had been influenced by China's conservative literature ideology. For a long time, I didn't know what I wanted to write about. I tried to look for ideas in newspapers, on radio broadcasts, and through any other conceivable means, but nothing felt right to me. It wasn't until I read Faulkner's works that I realized I could write about the things that happened to me and to people in my little village. My village, the people in my family, and my fellow villagers – I could write about all of them. Since then, I have been able to finish many full-length novels, middle-length novels and short stories. I have written hundreds of characters, most of which are based on people I know in real life.

There have been other American authors besides William Faulkner who have influenced me, for example, Ernest Hemingway and his The Old Man and the Sea. I don't think any author of my generation in China has not read The Old Man and the Sea. But if I have to choose between Faulkner and Hemingway, I'd prefer Faulkner. Hemingway's writing style is spare and lean – no word goes wasted. Personally, I don't like authors who are too efficient with words. But many Chinese authors love Hemingway. And then there is the American novelist Jack London. He wrote about the Klondike Gold Rush and he wrote extensively about animals, such as the Call of the Wild – a story about a domesticated dog who eventually answers his primordial instincts. I love reading stories about animals. I spent many years living in the countryside, and for a while I spent more time with animals than I did around men. I used to have a dog. When I read the Call of the Wild, I was reminded of the time I shared with my dog. I wrote about dogs in some of my earlier novels and in my latest work. Of course I write about other animals as well, such as cattle, horses, and donkeys. Critics in China have asked me why I am so good at writing cattle. I answered: in my previous life, I must be one myself. They asked me why I am so good at describing pigs. I told them I spent a long time herding pigs. I know everything there is to know about pigs. I know very little about men, but I am good at describing the behaviors of pigs and cattle. These are the elements that have determined the kind of author that I am — someone who writes about farm animals and about countryside. So, that was a little bit about me.

Thanks to the efforts of many outstanding Chinese translators, the works of many American authors are now available in Chinese, making it possible for someone like me who does not speak any English to read their works, and for them to play a role in my writing. In my opinion, early translations of foreign literature were not very particular about their aesthetic aspect. This had to do with the ethos of the Chinese society at that time. Liang Qichao, an eminent Chinese scholar, held that a novel is nothing more than a political tool, which should be used to promote social changes. And in light of which, Lin Shu chose to translate Uncle Tom's Cabin for its ideology. I believe that during the early 1980s, many American translators as well as European sinologists translated what they thought were Chinese novels that above anything else carried certain political messages and ideologies, in an attempt for readers in their own countries to read about changes taking place in China's society, politics and economy. There is of course nothing wrong with this approach. But I think literature translation should place aestheticism above everything else. Now, more and more attention has been given to the aesthetic value of literature by American sinologists today, including professor An Dao. As an author myself, I hope that readers who do not speak Chinese can enjoy the aesthetic explorations in our works. Up until now, there have been more Chinese readers that have been influenced by foreign literature than foreign readers by Chinese literature. I hope that given more time, the exchange can become more bilateral, where the works of Chinese authors will influence authors from other countries, including young authors in America. Today, I am here talking about the role of the works of William Faulkner and Jack London played my career. I wonder whether 50 years from now or 100 years from today, a young American author might claim that his writing is influenced by a Chinese author named Mo Yan? That's something I'm looking forward to.

"发现之旅"与文化交流

克里斯多弗·梅里尔

爱荷华大学
国际写作项目主任

内容提要： 吉姆·摩尔在他生命的最后时刻，还在模仿约翰·艾什的诗作进行写作。摩尔是一位伟大的形式主义者，而艾什是我们最伟大的实验者之一。让我为之震惊的是，一位诗人，在他生命即将结束的时候还在尝试接受其他风格的思想，其他感知的方式。这样只能使他的视野更加开阔，而我想这也正是我们在这个我们称为"发现之旅"的项目中所努力做到的一点。我希望我们可以做更多这样的尝试。

我非常肯定，50年后，将有很多美国作家表达他们对莫言先生的感谢。在这个相互交流的经历中，他提到了阅读《喧哗与骚动》，并在阅读完10页之后再也读不下去了。当福克纳获得诺贝尔奖时，他一位并不知道他是作家的朋友，对他说，他去了图书馆并拿回了一本好像是叫《喧哗与骚动》的书，这本书的第一页他读了整整五遍。他说只想问福克纳一个问题，福克纳说，好的。于是他问道："你在写那本书的时候是不是喝醉了？"而福克纳回答说，不总是。

正如莫言先生受到一位美国作家的影响，我也受到了一位中国作家的影响。三十多年以前，我曾在这里，在加州伯克利大学，作为一名学生上了一个学期的课。我当时在这里追求过一位女生，她后来嫁给了别人。与此同时，我在这里学习了一门有关艾兹拉·庞德的课程。在这门课程中，他对唐朝诗人的介绍对于我以及20世纪许多年轻美国作家而言十分重要，使我们了解成为一名诗人意味着什么。那正是庞德从唐朝的诗人那里所得到的，无论他是否正确，它的确对几乎所有的当代美国诗歌产生了影响，刚刚莫言先生所表达的感谢我想美国诗人也想要表达。

有趣的是，当时的我与一位学习工程学的中国籍学生同住。他的厨艺和我一样差。而我们在那个学期中为对方烹饪，我们俩没有死真是一个奇迹。我一边阅读庞德的书，一边吃着他烹饪的食物，而他在吃着我烹饪的食物。从某种意义上而言，我正在为成为诗人而学习。所有年轻作家都需要通过广泛地阅读，深刻地阅读，将自己沉浸在另一个世界中而获得成长。而我的另一个世界就是庞德为美国作品引入的内容。

多年以后的现在，我一直在组织一个项目，邀请中国的作家来爱荷华大学交流三个月。我们所邀请的名家包括莫言、李锐、北岛、丁玲、王蒙、余华、苏童等等。我们与这些作家在一起共同讨论作家如何工作。我们相互影响，翻译各自的作品，并在一起加深我们对于成为一名作家的意义的理解。

几年前，利奇主席向我提议，我们可以组织一项更为正式的年轻美国作家和年轻中国作家之间的交流活动。因此我们组织了一个名为"发现之旅"的项目。我给大家简单介绍一下这个项目中一次活动的情况，让大家感觉一下两种文学文化之间是如何交流的。这次活动历时两年，我们将12名年龄在25岁至40岁之间的美国作家送到中国，中国方面也将相同人数的中国作家送到美国。重要性不在于相互派遣代表，而是将作家们集中到一起进行交谈，建立合作，看看我们能做些什么。我们邀请了很多不同类型的作家，并在一定程度上注重吸引来自美国少数群体的作家以及中国西部地区少数群体的作家。

最近在云南省组织的一次交流活动接近尾声时，我们进行了一项练习。这项练习就是每天阅读相同的作品，就中国作家讨厌而美国作家喜欢的角色进行讨论。当美国作家发现中国作家争论激烈时，他们会说："等会儿，等会儿，我们需要几秒钟时间理解。"所以我们的讨论十分热烈。除了这一类型的讨论之外，我们还会相互为对方布置写作练习。在活动的最后一个晚上，经过几个星期的共同旅行、观光、阅读相同的书籍、辩论和探讨成为作家的意义，大家对彼此都有了深刻的了解，于是提议进行最后一项练习。让我们思考我们作为作家应该做些什么，并了解来自大洋彼岸的同仁们在做些什么。看看我们能不能邀请对方写一些他们看起来忽视的事情，以及他们看起来没有兴趣的事情。

对于我们美国人来说，我们注意到中国同仁非常注重和谐。今天上午的发言很多都有关佛教、儒教和道教。然后我们想，我们的传统与之不同，这里要再提一下沃尔特·惠特曼 —— 我们认为那是美国文学的重要部分之一，他曾这样说："我是否自相矛盾？很好，我就是要自相矛盾。我辽阔广大，我包罗万象。"于是我们邀请中国朋友以一些含有矛盾的事物为主题进行写作，并尝试解决矛盾。中国的作家们看了我们一眼，然后说，你们这些美国作家，你们没有哲学。我想他们想说的是，你们这些人不思考。不过他们同时也谈及了有关哲学、甚至是宗教的问题，正如我们今天讨论的道教或儒教。然后他们就向我们的一位作家提议："我们想让你们写一首诗。这首诗要以我们一直在讨论的上海作家王安忆的作品《长恨歌》、同时也是一首非常著名的唐朝的诗歌的名字为题。"然后他们就邀请美国作家就此赋诗一首。当我们写完并围坐在云南昆明一家宾馆的桌子旁大声把它们朗读出来时，我们发现，我们当中每一位作家阅读的作品都是他们有史以来读到的最有趣的作品。

现在我要说明的是，吉姆·摩尔并非我的亲戚，我跟他并无关系，既不能继承他的才华，也无法继承他的财产，但我应该敬爱他。据我所知，在生命的最后时刻，他还在模仿约翰·艾什的诗作进行写作。摩尔是一位伟大的形式主义者，而艾什是我们最伟大的实验者之一。让我为之震惊的是，一位诗人，在他生命即将结束的时候还在尝试接受其他风格的思想，其他感知的方式。这样只能使他的视野更加开阔，而我想这也正是我们在这个称为"发现之旅"的项目中所努力做到的一点。我希望我们可以做更多这样的尝试。

Christopher Merrill

Director of the International Writing Program at the University of Iowa

Life of Discovery and Cultural Communication

Abstract: At the end of James Moore's life, he was writing imitations of poems by John Ash. Moore was a great formalist; Ash is one of our greatest experimenters. And what struck me was that a poet at the end of his life was trying to take on some other style of thoughts, some other way of perceiving. That could only broaden his perspectives, and that's the kind of thing that we managed to do in this program we called Life of Discovery. I hope we could do more of that.

I'm quite certain that in 50 years, there would be a lot of American writers who will say that they owe their debt to MO Yan. And I thought I might just say in this experience of interchange, he talked about reading The Sound and The Fury, and putting it down after 10 pages, when Faulkner won the Nobel Prize, one of his friends, who did not know he was a writer, said that he had gone down to the library and taking out a novel which called something like The Sound and The Fury. And his friend says that you know, I read the first page of that novel five times, and I have only one question for you. And Faulkner said yes. Then he said, was you drunk when you wrote that book? And Faulkner replied, not all the time.

Just as MO Yan was influenced by an American writer, so I was influenced by Chinese writers. I was here more than 30 years ago for a semester as a student at the University of California, Berkeley. I had chased a woman here. She went on to marry somebody else. But along the way I took a class about a graduate class on Ezra Pound. And in that class, his introduction to the poets of the Tang Dynasty was for me as for so many young American writers throughout the 20th century, absolutely crucial to my own sense of what have might be to become a poet. The image was everything. That's what Pound took from the Tang Dynasty poets, whether he was right or not, it informed almost all contemporary American poetry for this last century, and so that debt MO Yan talks about is a debt that American poets also feel.

What's funny is that I was thinking about this last night when I got to town, and my roommate was a Chinese engineering student, who had almost no English at all. It turns out that he was as bad cook as I was. And we would cook for each other during that course of semester. It's a remarkable that we didn't die. But I was reading Pound and eating his food and he was eating my food, and in some fashion, I was becoming a poet, I was serving that apprenticeship that all young writers serve by reading widely, reading deeply, immersing oneself in another idiom. And that idiom for me was the idiom that Ezra Pound was bringing into American writing.

All these years later now, I run a program that has been brining Chinese writers to the University of Iowa for a three month long residency, and among the luminaries, we had a good honor to host MO Yan and LI Rui and BEI Dao and DING Ling and WANG Mang and YU Hua, SU Tong, and so on. What happens over the course of our residency is that we engage in a conversation about how writers do their work. We influenced one another, we translated one another, and we deepen our perspectives on what it means to be a writer.

Some years ago, Chairman Leach suggested to me that we might try to create a more formal exchange between young American writers and young Chinese writers, so we put together a program called Life of Discovery, now I want to, I know time is short, so I'm just going to give you a brief case study of this, to give you a sense of how an exchange between two literary cultures can take place. This is something that happens within the context of our large program, but over the course of two years, we brought about a dozen young American writers between the ages of 25 and 40 to China and Chinese sent a like number of writers to America. And the notion was not just in exchange of delegations, but to actually put the writers into conversation together, to try to forge collaboration, and see what we might be able to do. So we had a lot of different kinds of writers, we concentrated to a certain extent on attracting writers from minority groups in the United States, as well as minority groups from western China.

And at the end of our last exchange, this summer in Yunnan province, we came up with an exercise. The idea was to have exercises each day, to read works in common, the role which the Chinese hated while the Americans loved. But the Americans, when they realized how fierce the Chinese were about it, they said "wait a minute, wait a minute, we need some seconds to perceive it." So we had very lively conversations. So we had these kinds of conversations, and then we were setting writing exercises for each other. And on the last night, having gotten to know one another very closely over the course of weeks, travelling together, seeing sights, reading books in common, arguing, trying to figure out what it means to be a writer, we thought let's try just for a final exercise. Let's think about what it is that we do as writers, and what we see at our colleagues from across the ocean, what they seem to do. Let's see if we can invite each side to write about those sorts of things that they seem to neglect, that they seem not to have any interest in.

So for the Americans, what we noticed in our Chinese colleagues was that there was a great emphasis on harmony. And some of the very issues that we have been hearing about this morning come out of Buddhism and Confucianism, and out of Taoism. And we thought, well, we know that there is another kind of history going on here, and to involve Walt Whitman again, we thought one of the crucial parts of American literature, which Whitman said, "Do I contradict myself? Very well, then, I contradict myself. I am large, I contain multitudes". So we invited our Chinese friends to try to write about something in that would contain a conflict that in some fashion, try to address a conflict. The Chinese writers took a look at us and said, you American writers, you have no philosophy. I think what they really wanted to say is that you guys don't think at all. But they were also talking about I think more philosophical, even more religious down to the writing, such as we might have been discussing here in terms of Buddhism or Confucianism. So they suggested to one of our writers, "We'd like you to write a poem that has to take this as its title, the title of the book that we had been discussing by a Shanghai based writer, Wang Anyi, called The Song of Everlasting Sorrow, a very famous poem from the Tang Dynasty". And they invited the American writers to write a poem about that. We invited the Chinese writers to write about some kind of conflict. What happened when we finished writing these pieces, and read them aloud around these tables in a hotel in Yunnan Province in Kunming, was that every single one of the writers read the most interesting piece they had ever read.

Now I took from that, I would have in mind that the late James Moore is not my relative, I would say that I was never close enough to have relative to heritage either his talent or money. But I should have loved him, and I understand that at the end of his life, he was writing imitations of poems by John Ash. Moore was a great formalist; Ash is one of our greatest experimenters. And what struck me was that a poet at the end of his life was trying to take on some other style of thoughts, some other way of perceiving. That could only broaden his perspectives, and that's the kind of thing that we managed to do in this program we called Life of Discovery. I hope we could do more of that.

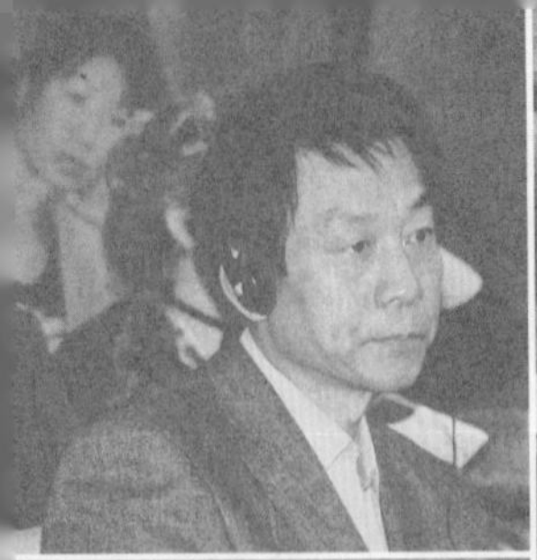
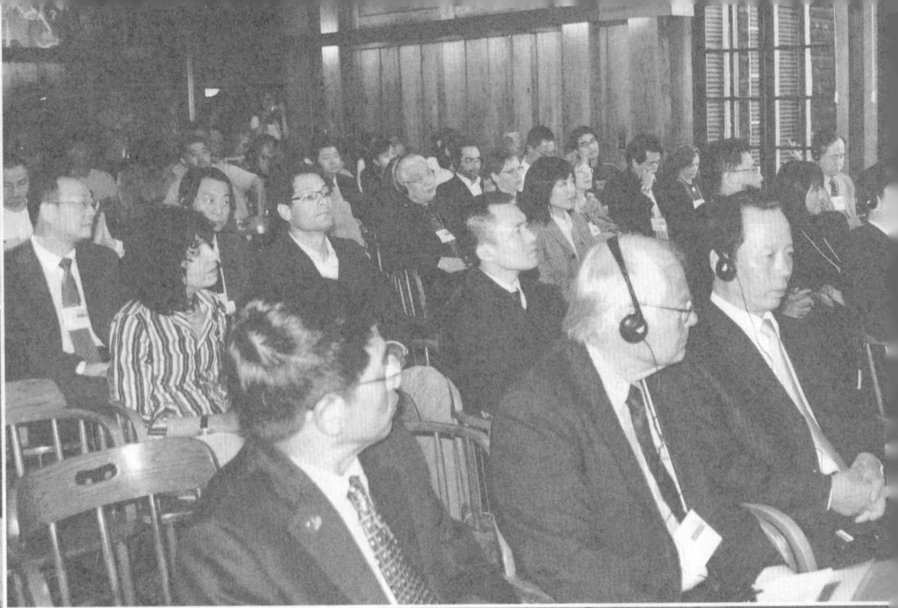
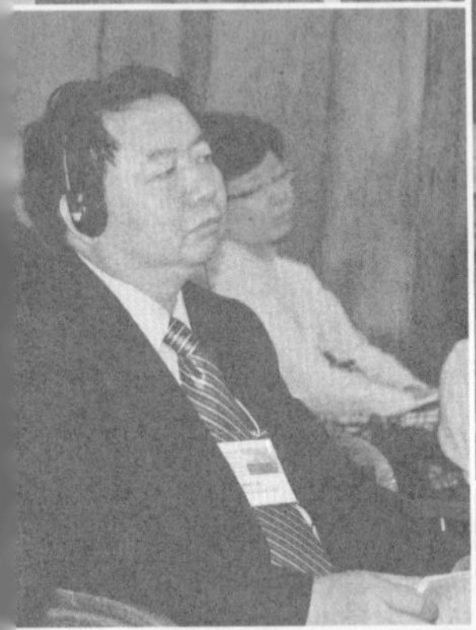
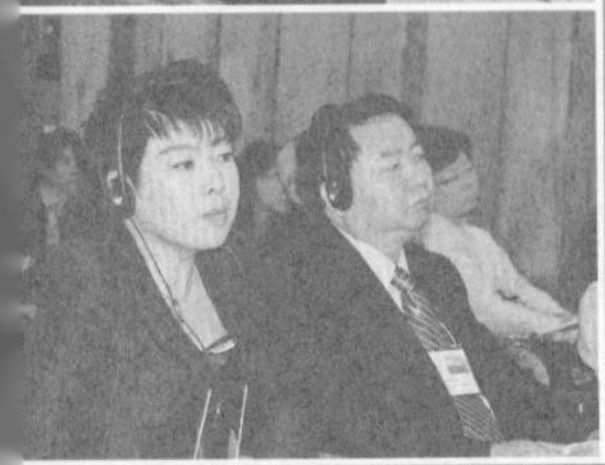
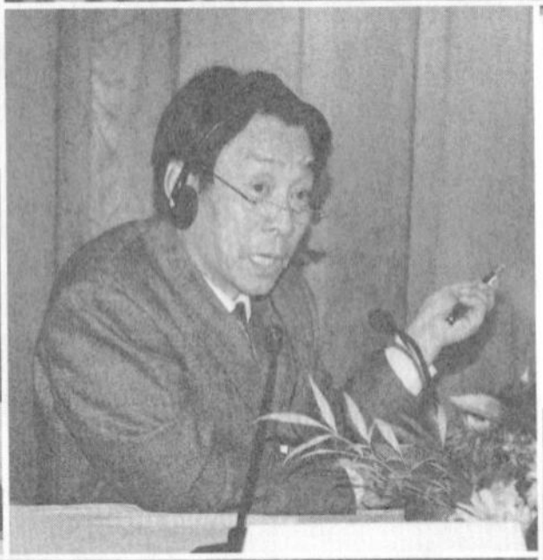
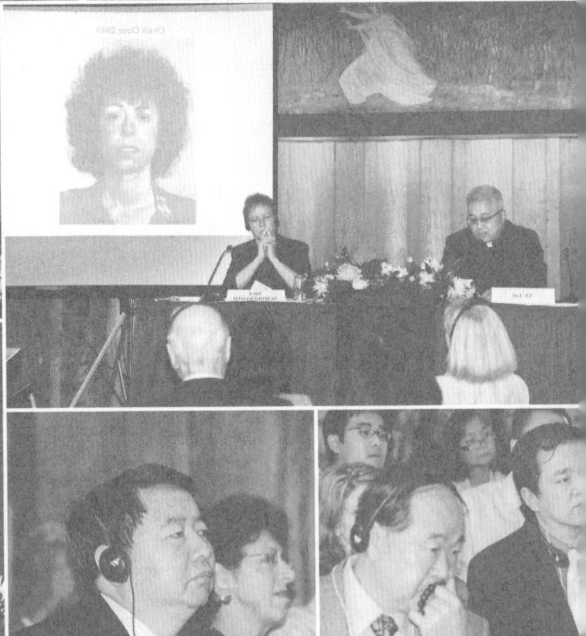
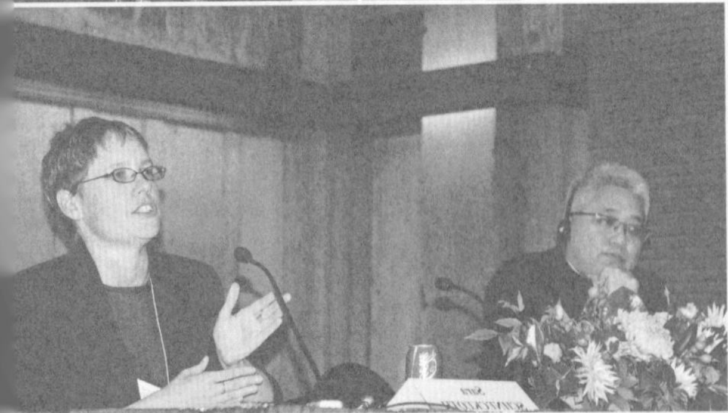
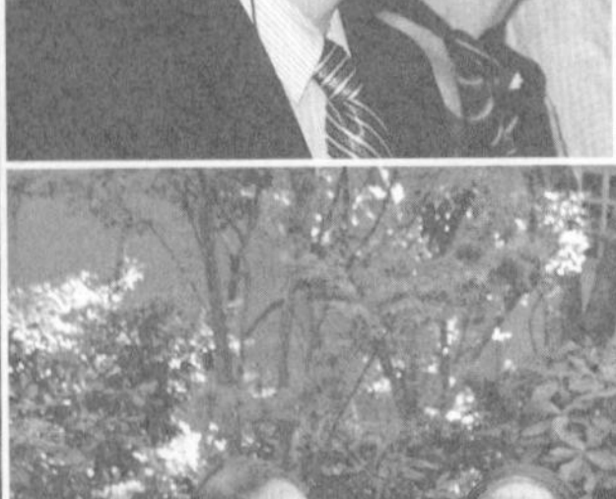
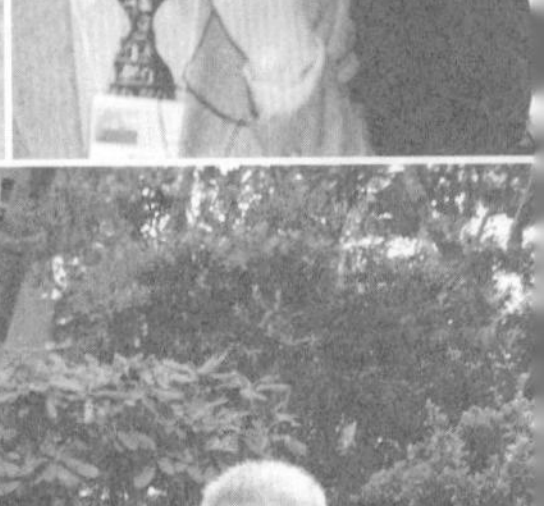
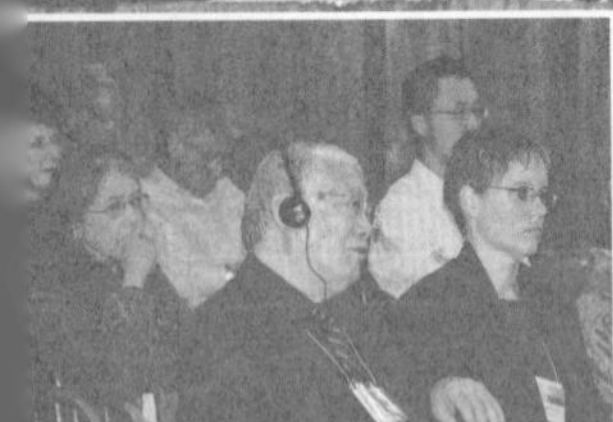
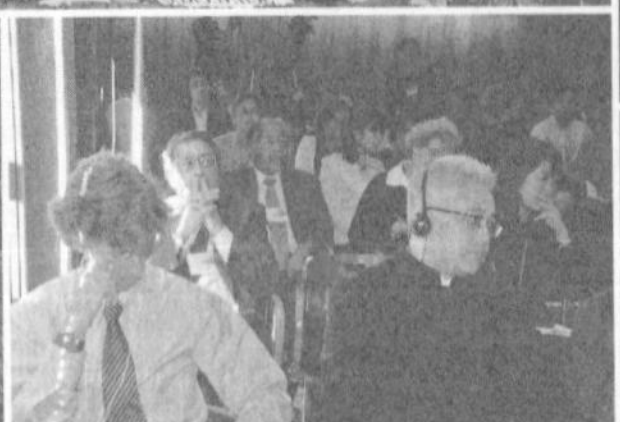
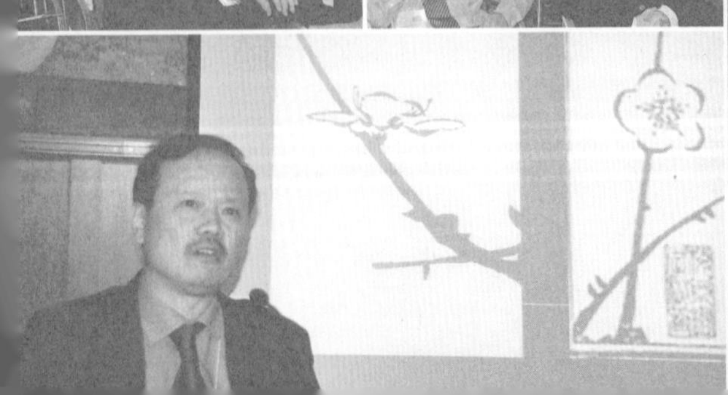
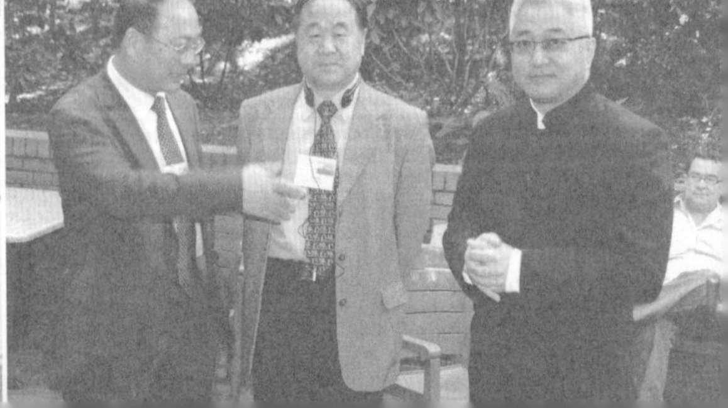

UNIT THREE: TRADITION AND INNOVATION IN THE VISUAL ARTS

第三单元 视觉艺术的传统与创新

美国克利夫兰市凯斯西储大学美国艺术教授亨利·亚当斯
主持人导语
Henry Adams, Professor of American Art, Case Western Reserve University
"Moderator's Introduction"

中国艺术研究院中国书法院副院长李胜洪研究员做主题发言
《中国书刻：传统艺术语言的崭新表达》
Li Shenghong, Research Fellow and Deputy Dean of School of Chinese Calligraphy,
Chinese National Academy of Arts
" Chinese Calligraphy Engraving: A New Expression of Traditional Artistic Language"

哥伦比亚大学东亚艺术系教授恩·荷·德尔班科做主题发言
《艺术构建东西方桥梁》
Dawn Ho Delbanco, Professor of East Asian Art, Columbia University
"Bridging Cultures with Arts"

中国艺术研究院副院长、研究生院院长田黎明研究员做主题发言
《心与象合——关于中国画文化体验》
Tian Liming, Research Fellow and Vice President of Chinese National Academy of Arts,
Dean of the Graduate School, CNAA
"The Integration of Mind and Image–Cultural Experience in Chinese Paintings"

伯克利艺术博物馆和太平洋电影档案馆馆长劳伦斯·林德做主题发言
《西方艺术的传统与创新》

Lawrence Rinder, Director of the Berkeley Art Museum and Pacific Film Archive
" Tradition and Innovation in Western Art"

中国艺术研究院创作研究中心徐累研究员做主题发言
《密响旁通——我眼中的中美艺术交流景观》

Xu Lei, Research Fellow of Research Center for Creation,
Chinese National Academy of Arts
"Silent Voice, Permeating Echoes
—The Sino-American Artistic Exchanges in My Observation"

美国南卡罗来纳大学哥伦比亚大学绘画教授萨拉·辛纳克劳斯做主题发言
《在标记中表现自我》
Sara Schneckloth, Professor of Drawing, University of South Carolina, Columbia
"Finding Ourselves within the Mark"

"陶德·威廉斯与钱以佳建筑事务所"建筑师钱以佳做主题发言
《建筑的艺术：内在体验与外在表现》
Billie Tsien, Architect of *Tod Williams Billie Tsien Architects*
"The Art of Architecture: Inner Experience and External Manifestation"

主持人导语

亨利·亚当斯

美国克利夫兰市
凯斯西储大学
美国艺术教授

　　中国拥有世界上最古老、最伟大且延续至今的文明。在中国，个体绘画的发展在形式和社会内容上都与西方极为不同。很多不同之处与这样一个事实有关，即在西方，人物绘画主要是熟练画家为了取悦地主而画，或是关注技艺的工匠为了准确表现出个体世界。另一方面，在中国，绘画由学者官员大规模创造出来。这些画更加个人化，具有知性特征，这与书法和诗歌紧密相联。

　　公元前3世纪，一个大型的中国王朝形成，其疆域与当今中国相近。这个王朝的建立很大程度上削弱了曾主宰中国文化的那个阶级。尽管文官与其他团体有矛盾，比如朝廷、地区部落或家仆等，但他们最终获得了实权，因为没有他们，王国便无法运转。在这时，书法成为中国艺术最基本的形式，形成了长达两千年的惯例。几千年以来，好的书法是居官和发财的主要途径。书法好意味着受过良好教育且品德端正。就像孔子所言，一个人的品行可从他写的每个笔划中表现出来。书法的风格成为谈论的话题。传统上，书法、绘画与诗歌搭配在一起，它们使用的工具相同，即非常灵活的中国毛笔。

　　许多伟大的画家，如王维，代表了风景画的发展，而且他还是重要的诗人。在著名画家沈周的作品里，画中有诗，诗是风景的重要组成部分。由于与书法和诗歌紧密相连，并与学者联系紧密，中国绘画的发展方式与西方极为不同。在西方，人物画是主要的表现形式，而中国在唐朝之后，人物画并不为主流艺术家所青睐，风景画成为主要的表现方式。其中的原因很难说清。通过联系风景，中国学者能够重新建立与世界大和谐之间的联系。中国艺术家最精彩的方面之一，便是他们愿意放弃表现现实世界而去达到这个目的。

美国与中国的关系可以追溯至很早的时期，几乎是在美利坚合众国建立初期。新英格兰风景不佳，缺乏自然资源。从一开始，新英格兰人便尝试寻找与大多数世界贸易的可能性以及与美利坚合众国的商业发展。商人和水手乘坐小得惊人的帆船，从波士顿出发，前往中国，带回茶叶和瓷器。事实上，引进的瓷器仍可以在许多美国人或新英格兰人的家中找到，这些艺术品颇受欢迎，直到现在还在生产。在19世纪，进口商品开始对美国画家以及法国画家产生巨大影响，首先是通过日本画家，然后是日本和中国复杂的混合影响。

人们可以认为，艺术的全部旨趣在于引向创造现代艺术和新的表现形式的主要步骤。这个转变可以从不同的方面解读，并引进了关于新的色彩、模式、竞争和表达的新观念。具有讽刺意味的是，在许多方面，所有那些具有说服力的影响来自美国。据美国人所知，中国的艺术很复杂，这是因为美国人首先是通过日本人的视角来了解中国。而众所周知，中国与日本的关系是一个非常复杂的主题。日本在很短的一段时间内把中国当作榜样，所有那个时期的日本人只是尝试模仿中国的艺术，但是日本人并没有完全理解中国艺术和中国文化，而两国之间紧张的政治局势成为20世纪早期非常显著的问题。

美国人对此的看法主要受厄内斯特·费诺罗萨的影响。他毕业于哈佛大学，然后去了日本，成为东京大学的哲学教授。当时，日本正在改革，费诺罗萨获得大量日本艺术品，现在陈列在波斯顿的美术馆里。他还撰写了第一部关于中国和日本东方艺术法则的通史，起点是日本艺术。他的理论研究最终使他发现，日本艺术成就的创造力源自中国。费诺罗萨之后主要致力于研究中国艺术，并得到日本学者的指导。他基本回顾了中国早期的作品，如汉朝、唐朝以及宋朝的作品，认为之后的中国艺术较为颓废。他的观点中的一个缺陷是没有重视董其昌在中国书画中的传统，而西方也非常欣赏这一传统。

在19世纪，美国人和欧洲人认为自己更强，因为他们开发了在信息表达上更有执行力的透视法。20世纪，中国和日本的抽象艺术作品被看做是一种目标与西方不同的艺术，在很多方面更为高级，在品质上较西方观念更加复杂。中国唐朝时期或者更早些时候的先锋艺术家可与我们这个时代的西方现代画家相比肩。比如杰克逊·波洛克的作品，在他画作右侧，其署名方式与中国书法家非常类似，这就表明他在模仿中国作品。

在做总结之前，我再提一点，英语与中文是两种非常不同的语言，事实上来源于不同的语系。世界上大多数现代语言都可追溯到六千到七千年前的农业社会。英语来源于印欧语系，起源于土耳其，然后发展到欧洲，而中文就是起源于中国。因此，我们的语言不仅是词汇不同，而且在组织现实和联系事物的方式上也有所不同。我们要铭记，我们的语言代表两种不同的现实图景。为了相互了解，我们需要超越互不熟悉的思考方式和语言的界限。

希望我们在讨论中能够考虑到这些事实。我认为这次会议有两个目的，首先是考虑中国的艺术家和学者应向何处寻求灵感，是西方艺术或西方学术界，还是中国的古老传统和书法、绘画与诗歌，或能否成功利用这两个资源。如果中国人从自己的文化中获得资源，他们应如何调整中国的传统，以反映那个不再是传统的、等级森严的社会。如果他们借鉴西方，他们应怎样扩大他们的资源，以满足人们的基本文化需求，确保这些文化不是西方的，而是中国自己的。

其次是要考虑西方人应向中国艺术学习什么，中国的主流艺术如何才能从现在这个全球化、而非狭窄的艺术视角帮助我们重新激活西方艺术，激活西方历史。中国在快速向领导地位发展的这一历史时期，是否能够以互利的方式帮助我们西方更深地了解中国人民以及他们的作品。中国发展迅速，已经成为现代艺术的主要推动人，创建了上千新的博物馆。我们应该怎样进一步推进这一文化和变革过程？此次会议不应该是孤立的事件，而应该是更长期对话的开始。

Moderator's Introduction

Henry Adams
Professor of
American Art, Case
Western Reserve
University

China has the oldest, grandest, most continuous civilized culture in the world, and in China, painting individual art developed a fashion very different from the West, but in form and in social content. Many of these differences are associated with fact that in the west, painting was largely province of skilled artisans who were working to please rich peasants and were craftsmen who were focused on techniques of accurately represented the individual world. In China, on the other hand, the painting was largely created by scholar officials. It was more personal and intellectually character which closely associated with calligraphy and poetry.

In the 3rd century B.C., an enormous Chinese empire which formed a border which was very close to those of China today, the founding of the empire largely eliminated the class that had dominated the Chinese culture. While scholar officials were in conflict with other groups, such as court units, regional clans or the family's servants,but in the end, they remained powerful because the empire could not function without them. At this point, calligraphy became the preliminary form of Chinese art established which was a routine for 2000 years. For several thousand of years, good handwriting was the main way of getting official and financial success. Good handwriting indicated both education and moral character. As Confucius declared, a man's character is apparent in every brushstroke. Styles of handwriting became the matter of disputes. Classically calligraphy painting was painted with poetry, which was also created with the same instrument, the wonderfully flexible Chinese brush.

Many of the greatest painters, such as Wang Wei, he figured the development of landscape paintings were also important poets. And in this famous work by Shen Zhou, the painting is written and the poem is the main principal part of the landscape. Because of the close connection with calligraphy and poetry, and because of its close connection with the scholar class, Chinese painting developed in a way very different from the west. While in the west, figure painting became the dominant form of expression, figure painting ceased to be the charmer practice by major Chinese artists after the Tang Dynasty. And landscape became the central form of the expression. In contrast to the west, they never play an important role in Chinese art. The reasons for this are hard to pinpoint. By connecting with the landscape, the Chinese scholars could re-establish the connection with the larger harmony of the universe. One of the most fascinating aspects of Chinese artists that they would rather early abandoned the representation of reality as its central goal.

The American relationship with Chinese goes back very far, almost to the beginning of the American Republic. New England has a harsh landscape and a few natural resources. From the beginning, New Englander tried to seek for the likelihood that form trade in the major world in the commercial development of the American Republic. Going surprisingly small sailing-ships, merchants and sailors from Boston sail to China and brought back tea and porcelains. Indeed, the transmit in China pots can still be found in many American homes and New England, and they became so popular that they're still in manufacturing today. In the mid nineteen century, all imports began had major influence on the American painters as well as painters in France, first through the Japanese painters later through more sophisticated forms of Japanese and Chinese source.

One could argue that the interests all in art were the major steps that led to the creation of the modern arts and to a new form of fashion. All in the large form shift the world can be seen in many different ways, and introduced new ideas of aspect of color, pattern, competition and expression. Ironically, all in those influences persuasive in many of forms of art that are often considered to be American. In American knowledge that Chinese arts complicated by the fact that the American first came to know Chinese are from Japanese perspective and as we knew China's relationship with Japan is complicated subject. The Japanese turn to China is a model in a narrow period and all Japanese are from that time were some degree of model than that of China, but the Japanese did not always fully understand Chinese art and Chinese culture and the political tensions between the two countries had often been a problem noticeably in the early 20th century.

The most influential figure in shaping the American views was Ernest Fenollosa who ever graduated from Howard and went to Japan to become the professor philosophy at the University of Tokyo. At that time, the Japanese were turning a way from the their traditions, Fenollosa was able to acquire a major collection of Japanese arts which is now in the museum of Fine Arts in Boston, and he also went on to write the first comprehensive history of oriental law in parts of Chinese and Japanese arts. Well, his starting point was the Japanese arts and in the courses of his theoretical research finalized his discovered the creative sources for Japanese achievements lying in China and much of his later career developed to studying Chinese arts which is largely with the guidance of Japanese scholars. Basically he reviewed the work of earlier periods, the Han, Tang and Song dynasty, but regarded the later Chinese arts as decadent. A weakness of this views is it did not pay much attention to lateritic tradition to pay such Dong Qichang at the literary tradition in the later Chinese painting is last well appreciated in the west.

In the 19th century, Americans and Europeans consider themselves superior because they have developed perspective in more executive message representations. but in the 20th century, with the works of abstract art, Chinese and Japanese arts have became recognized as an art form with different goals in many ways superior and more sophisticated in its qualities than the western opinions. Pioneers of China in the Tang Dynasty and even earlier struggled with many of issues of radically modern western painters of our time. Here for example, you can see the Jackson Pollock, on the right of the writing his name in a fashion that is very similar to which Chinese calligraphers' fashion earlier indicates that he was truly imitating the Chinese.

Let me present just one more thought before summing up, that English and Chinese are very different languages and in fact belong to different families of languages. Most of the modern languages in the world would go back to the times when the agriculture was sort of 6000 or 7000 years ago. English grew from the Indo- European language which is started in Turkey and then spread to Europe. Chinese grew from languages just started in China. Consequently, our languages are different not only in the words but in the way of organizing reality and making connections between things. Let's remember that our languages present two different pictures of reality. To understand each other, we need to reach beyond the way of thinking and speaking which were not most familiar.

I hope that we can consider some of these matters in discussions that follow in the way that I think the conference has two purposes, first is to consider where Chinese artists and scholars should turn for inspiration, whether to western art or western scholarship to ancient Chinese traditions and calligraphy, painting and poetry. Can I successfully draw on both sources, if the Chinese drawings form their own culture, how should they modify Chinese traditions to reflect society to this no longer classic and rigid hierarchy? If they borrowed from the west, how they should magnify their resources to fit the needs of the people his fundamental culture is not western but Chinese.

Second is to consider what westerners should learn from Chinese arts, how can Chinese principal arts to help us to revitalize western arts and also revitalize our history, so to this global rather than narrow art of look. And can Chinese would help us to more deeply understand the Chinese people and works with them for a mutual benefit at the time when China is rapidly moving toward leadership. China's growing very fast, it's became a major signer of modern art and it created thousand of new museums. How should we carry further with this process of culture and change and what should we do so? This conference is now not isolated event but the beginning of a longer dialogue.

中国书刻：传统艺术语言的崭新表达

李胜洪

中国艺术研究院中国书法院副院长，研究员

内容提要：中国现代的书刻艺术是一门有着自身独立的审美语言、能传达独特审美意境的崭新的艺术形式。它具有十分丰富的技法运用，而各种单项技法的审美指向以及相互组合的无穷性，使其审美意境有着无限拓展的广阔空间。它是传统技艺与现代艺术理念的结合；古典审美与现代思维与审美取向的结合；是东方古老艺术与西方艺术形式的有机结合。

中国汉字在演变、发展的历史长河中，一方面起着思想交流、文化继承等重要的社会作用，另一方面它本身又形成了一种独特的造型艺术——书法。它不仅是中华民族传统文化艺术的瑰宝，如今也已成为全人类非物质文化遗产中的代表作。

历史悠久、灿烂辉煌的中国书法几千年来，与中国的政治、经济、军事、科技、文化乃至人民群众的日常生活息息相关。上至帝王将相、下至庶民百姓都非常喜好书法。在中国，书法圣人王羲之及其代表作《兰亭序》几乎是人尽皆知。历经几千年的发展历程，书法已成为中国传统文化的一个代表性符号。

近代考古成就以大量的事实说明："契刻在文字之前"。即中国的文字是由"契刻"而产生的。商朝（约公元前17世纪—前11世纪）的甲骨文，是刻在龟甲、牛肩胛骨上的早期古文字，距今已有3600

多年的历史；秦朝（约公元前8世纪）的石鼓文，是中国最早的石刻文字之一；魏晋南北朝（公元2世纪—6世纪）时期的《始平公造像记》是魏碑书法的代表作；北齐（公元6世纪）时期刻在泰山经石峪的大字《泰山金刚经》亦是洋洋大观……书法艺术的发展与刻字艺术的发展密不可分。夏朝（公元前2224年—前1766年）以来的4000多年间，甲骨、碑刻、摩崖、石经、造像铭、墓志上的传统刻字以及木、竹、漆器，骨、角、陶瓷、砖、瓦当、印文上的书法艺术，皆保存了大量的史料、成为宝藏书迹的丰富宝库。

中国文化具有伟大的开放性、包容性、创造性，这正是中华民族历经挫折而生生不息的根本原因。就中国书刻艺术而言，虽然历史悠久、曾经灿烂辉煌，但作为传统艺术在当代并没有故步自封，而是不断吸取各种艺术养分，以极其旺盛的生命力、不断进行着崭新的艺术语言表达——在传统刻字基础之上、于上个世纪80年代发展起来的中国书刻艺术，一开始受到了汉字文化圈那些国家的艺术创新的启发和影响，之后在中国一发而不可收拾：20多年来得到了日新

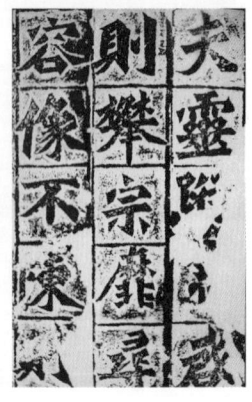

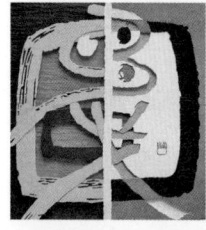

月异、突飞猛进的发展。具有时代审美和中国风格的现代书刻艺术作品,开始在国际艺坛上异彩纷呈、独树一帜。中国现代刻字艺术的成功实践,又反过来促进了中国周边汉字文化圈国家和地区书刻艺术的发展。一些欧美国家也逐渐对这个东方新兴艺术门类予以热情关注。我的刻字艺术拙作《舞》,2002年在法国展出时受到普遍理解和欢迎,给了中国刻字艺术家很大的启发与鼓舞;前不久,中国在联合国教科文总部大楼举办书法展,其中现代刻字作品引起外国友人的浓厚兴趣也是一个例证。可以说中国的现代书刻艺术,必将成为国际上了解当代中国艺术的一个新的视角。

中国现代的书刻艺术是一门有着自身独立的审美语言、能传达独特审美意境的崭新的艺术形式。它具有十分丰富的技法运用,而各种单项技法的审美指向以及相互组合的无穷性,从而使其审美意境有着无限拓展的广阔空间。它是传统技艺与现代艺术理念的结合;古典审美与现代思维与审美取向的结合;是东方古老艺术与西方艺术形式的有机结合。

中国现代书刻具有独特的审美。其审美价值的多元性,主要表现在构成、立度、色彩、肌理四个方面:

一、构成之美:合理、巧妙表现思想主题的空间安排。

"具有多层面和特殊格式的刻字艺术,基于以文字(书法)为基础的刻字艺术,维系着中国几千年来传统书画的某些(如书体、结体、章法、笔法与墨法、线条的表现力等)形式因素,既接受了少字派创造文字意境的优点,又融入了绘画的笔墨效应,既糅合了东方诗、书、画艺术的固有特色,也寓合了西方抽象主义艺术的时代精神与意念。"(耕夫:《现

代刻字的平面构成》）

二、立度之美：具有三维空间的雕塑感与凝固的流动感。

现代刻字艺术在技法上，对阴刻线条凹凿和对阳刻底部肌理等处理，展示了刀与刀之间语言的沟通，以刀代笔，把一刀一刀的痕迹与木质结构纹理的质感，一目了然地体现在具有现代感的艺术作品之中。同时，刻字在成形材料上的立体造型——线条的立体形象，有粗细、厚薄、方圆、曲直、疏密的变化，线条的力量感也随着变化，在线条内显示出力的流动，在表面可以感觉到物质材料的张力与空间压力的抗争。

三、色彩之美：充满情趣、恰到好处的色彩烘托与渲染。

色彩总是具有在特定民族文化和历史背景下的相对性的象征，是特定的语境和仪式的流露与展现。因此，色彩对现代刻字艺术意境的延伸和审美内涵的拓展，具有十分重要的意义。因为它具有无穷的表现力，并产生不同的视觉效果。作品中的色调充分体现了设计者的审美、意境、趣味等心理要求和感情倾向。

四、肌理之美：追求天趣盎然、引人入胜的特殊审美效果。

首先是材料的肌理表现。物质材料的质地结构，经过艺术家的加工，显露于表面的质地、纹理和颜色、光泽等，结合刻字艺术的点画造型，并以物质

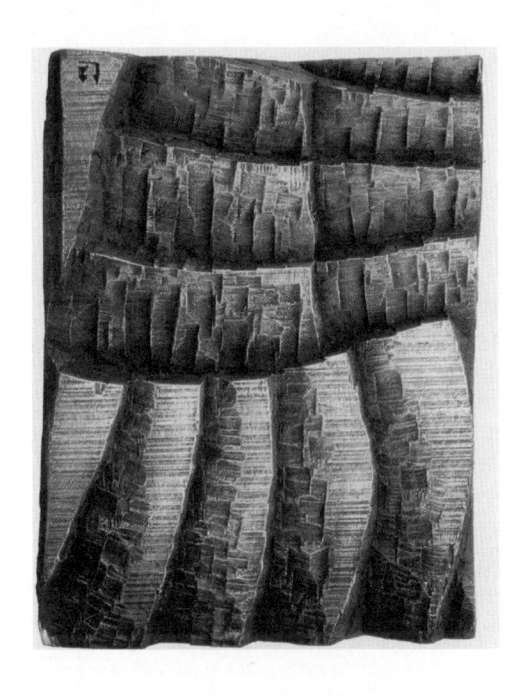

材料的肌理来烘托、表达作品的思想内容。此外还有创作过程中的凿刻肌理，如刀痕、残缺等等，即运用工艺加工手段而在材质之上创造形式美。肌理美的表现使现代书刻艺术产生了特殊的审美效果。

随着时代发展，中国书法的艺术语言会越来越丰富，表现形式也将越来越多样化。"汉字艺术"在当下与未来的发展中，已经呈现出多种可能性而我们决不能视而不见。

中国现代书刻艺术是传统艺术语言的一种崭新表达，也是东西方文化交流和有机融合而具有深远意义的一个典型案例。从外部世界来说，不了解今天中国的现代书刻艺术，就无法进而认识、深入理解书法艺术的博大精深和无限生命力，以及那种因富于创造而传承千年的中国文化精神。而对我们自身来讲，则意味着已经成为"全人类非物质文化遗产代表作"的中国书法艺术能否得到真正的传承与保护。

源自古老而悠远的民族传统艺术之光，今天仍然照耀着中国书法艺术前进的道路。中国现代书刻必将以其独特的艺术魅力展现出更加灿烂辉煌的未来。

Chinese Calligraphy Engraving: A New Expression of Traditional Artistic Language

Li Shenghong

Research Fellow and Deputy Dean of School of Chinese Calligraphy, Chinese National Academy of Arts

Abstract: Modern Chinese Calligraphy Engraving is an independent art form which can present special aesthetic experience. It is of rich techniques. Combined with limitless possibilities, this single technique can constantly expand the aesthetic experience. It is a combination of traditional technique and modern artistic idea, a combination of classical aesthetics and modern thinking and aesthetic orientation and a combination of ancient oriental and western arts.

In its long history of evolution and development, Chinese characters not only played a role in facilitating the exchange of ideas and the inheritance of cultural heritage but also developed a unique form of visual arts, namely calligraphy. It is a treasure of Chinese traditional culture and art, and moreover has become a representative work in intangible cultural heritage of all mankind.

Brilliant Chinese calligraphy has a long history of thousands years, during which it interacted with politics, economy, military, science and technology, culture and even people's daily lives. Ranging from emperors, ministers and generals to common people, most Chinese are keen on calligraphy. In China, calligraphy and the sage of calligraphy, Wang Xizhi and his masterpiece Lanting Xu (literally Preface to the Poems Composed at the Orchid Pavilion) are almost known to everybody. After thousands of years of development, calligraphy has become a representative symbol of Chinese traditional culture.

Modern archaeological achievements have revealed the fact with lots of evidence that "carving was born before writing". Chinese writing was created based on carving.

The oracles of Shang Dynasty (17th century BC - 11th century BC) are ancient text engraved on tortoise shells and cattle scapula. They were dated back to more than 3,600 years ago. Inscriptions on drum-shaped stone blocks of the Qin Dynasty (8th century BC) are one of the earliest stone inscriptions; Written Narration of Lord Shiping's Deeds of Wei and Jin dynasties and the Southern and Northern Dynasties (AD 2-6) is a representative masterpiece of calligraphy of Weibei (the style of calligraphy typified by inscriptions carved on the stone tablets of the Northern Wei Dynasty); the big characters of Vajracchedika-sutra engraved on Jingshi Valley of Mount Tai in Northern Qi Dynasty (6th century AD) is magnificent and very impressive. ...The development of calligraphy is inseparable from the development of the art of engraving. It can be said that since the Xia Dynasty (BC 2224 – BC 1766), engravings on bones for augury, stone, cliff, rock, statue, epitaph, wood, bamboo, lacquer, bone, horn, pottery and porcelain, brick, tile, and seal have preserved a lot of historical data and became a treasure for calligraphy.

Chinese culture is of great openness, tolerance and creativity, and this is the essential reason that the Chinese nation has survived various ups and downs. Though it is traditional art with long histories, Chinese Calligraphy Engraving continues to draw nutrients and constantly creates new ways of expression for traditional artistic language with great vitality in modern times.

On the basis of traditional art of engraving, the modern engraving which initiated in the 1980s began to be influenced by countries using Chinese characters and had made tremendous progress in China over the past two decades. Works of engraving corresponding to the aesthetics of the time and with Chinese characteristics are colorful and unique in the international arts circle. The successful practice of modern Chinese Calligraphy Engraving in turn promoted the development of engraving in countries using Chinese characters. The U.S. and some European countries also began to show interest in this emerging oriental art. A good example is that my works of engraving Dancing was understood and welcomed widely when on exhibition in France, 2002, which has greatly inspired the artists of Chinese Calligraphy Engraving. Not long ago, China hosted an exhibition of Chinese calligraphy in the headquarters of UNESCO, and the modern works of engraving were warmly received by foreign friends. So, it is safe to say that modern Chinese Calligraphy Engraving will become a new perspective for the international society to understand contemporary Chinese arts.

Modern Chinese Calligraphy Engraving is an independent art form which can present special aesthetic experience. It is of rich techniques. Combined with limitless possibilities, this single technique can constantly expand the aesthetic experience. It is a combination of traditional technique and modern artistic idea, a combination of classical aesthetics and modern thinking and aesthetic orientation and a combination of ancient oriental and western arts.

Modern Chinese Calligraphy Engraving is of unique aesthetics. Its aesthetic plurality is represented by constitution, stereoscopic impression, color, and texture.

1. The beauty of constitution: reasonable and clever spatial arrangement for the representation of thoughts

Based on calligraphy, the art of engraving is of multi-dimension and special pattern. It sustains the formal ingredients of traditional calligraphy and painting (style, structure, art of composition, chirography, ink technique and the strength of lines) over the past thousands of years, and maintains the merits of artistic conception produced by the works of School of Less Characters and absorbs the artistic effects of painting. It mixes together the characteristics of Oriental poetry, calligraphy and painting while absorbing the time spirit and ideas of Western abstract arts.

2. The beauty of stereoscopic impression: the three-dimensional sculptural effect and the effect of flowing solid

Modern art of engraving is the presentation of the communication between cuts in dealing with the incised lines by chiseling and the bottom texture of rilievi. Replacing pen with graver, this art marks so-produced works with the obvious texture quality of wood and cuts. Meanwhile, the three-dimensional forms of engraving – those carved lines crackles with the dynamic of changes in weight, thickness, roundness or squareness, straightness and curve, and density. These lines also show the flowing of strength. One can feel the surface tension and the resistance against the pressure from the atmosphere.

3. The beauty of color: vigorous and proper colors serve as contrast and support

Colors are symbol of relativity in the context of certain national culture and history; it is also a representation of certain context or rituals. So, colors are of vital significance for the extension of artistic conception of modern engraving and its aesthetic implication. Colors can produce different visual effect as it has unbounded power of representation. The tonality of works demonstrates fully the designer's psychological need and emotional tendency in aesthetics, artistic conception and taste.

4. The beauty of texture: modern engraving pursues a special aesthetic effect with emphasis on natural charm and attractiveness

First and foremost, there is the texture of raw material. With artist's craftsmanship, the texture quality of the raw material begins to show a surface with certain type of texture, grain, color, and luster, which together with the dots and lines carved can contrast and convey the idea of works. Moreover, the signs of chiseling on the texture, like cuts and breaks, show a certain formal beauty. The beauty of texture enhances the aesthetic effects that can be presented by an engraving product.

With the development of the world, Chinese calligraphy and its representations will be increasingly diversified. "The art of Chinese characters" has shown and will continue to show multiple possibilities.

Modern Chinese Calligraphy Engraving is a new way of expression for traditional artistic language, and is a typical example with profound meaning to prove the Eastern and Western cultural communication and organic integration. For the foreign world, without knowing about modern Chinese Calligraphy Engraving, it is impossible to understand the profound and energetic Chinese calligraphy and Chinese culture well-known for its creativity and long history. For us, it matters whether Chinese calligraphy art as the masterpiece of intangible cultural heritage of humanity can be truly inherited and protected.

As an ancient traditional art form, this national art will continue to illuminate the prospect of Chinese arts. With its unique charm, modern Chinese Calligraphy Engraving will have a more brilliant future.

艺术构建东西方桥梁

恩·荷·德尔班科

哥伦比亚大学
东亚艺术系教授

内容提要： 从事物的表面上看，传统中西方文化中好像有着不可逾越的鸿沟。实际上，在两个艺术传统中，我们发现了很多惊人的相似性和重叠。如果说中国艺术家曾经在20世纪尝试着效仿西方绘画风格，而事实上，西方现代主义艺术家们在20世纪所做的正是中国艺术家已经践行了几个世纪的艺术理念。

我本想通过举出我在自己艺术史课程中提到的例子将东西方文化结合起来，从而很好地解决为中美文化构建桥梁这一课题，具体说来，是可视文化构建桥梁这一课题。尽管本次论坛为中美文化论坛，但我不得不承认，我将仅仅举出美国艺术的例子。有些作者认为我所有的评论都指向了20世纪前的中国艺术。那么我要向所有出席今天会议的艺术家道歉。事实上，我现在仍然在努力地学习20世纪前的中国艺术和文化。我还未能让自己与时俱进，赶上当下的时代步伐。因此，我是个真正的恐龙。

我以大屏幕上的20世纪前的绘画作为今天演讲的开始。大屏幕上的图片可能会让你产生错觉，以为不是你参加错了会议，就是我参加错了会议。然而，我将这幅画放到屏幕上，是因为它可能是你们最熟悉的西方艺术中的画作——列奥纳多·达·芬奇的《蒙娜丽莎》。现在，如果你问我中国绘画中的《蒙娜丽莎》是哪一幅作品，它将是人们最熟悉的一幅中国绘画作品，肯定不是人物画像，最有可能是10世纪范宽的山水画《溪山行旅图》。现在，如果我们从不同的文化传统将这两个形象加以比较，会很清楚地发现他们截然不同。在屏幕右方，我们看到中西方很明显的区别在于，西方艺术和

文化以人物画像为主。恰恰相反，在屏幕左方，我们看到中国的艺术和文化以自然为中心。

　　从事物的表面上看，传统中西方文化好像有着不可逾越的鸿沟。诚如凯普林·怀特所宣称，东方就是东方，西方就是西方，二者不可混为一谈。当然了，我们自然知道结论是否定的。而且事实上，在两个艺术传统中，我们发现了很多惊人的相似性和重叠。因此，在初学者看来，为了指出其中的一些相似性，我将发表的言论非常具有争议性。但是我想指出的是，在左方以范宽为代表的不朽的北宋山水画作品属于宗教绘画（在传统中国的人文文化中，人性为本）。我的演讲并不包括中国的佛教艺术，这是不同会议上的不同议题。

　　因此，仅仅将左方范宽的绘画作品与法国13世纪的绘画作品《哥特式大教堂》进行对比。人们可以看到，在两幅图画上的右边有相同的层次，它是神圣的三位一体，一种神圣的三位一体的象征符号；然而在左边，你看到的是高高的以中心点为基准的绘画方式。山路上的旅人赶着驮队攀向山顶。在这两幅画中，我们都可以看到相似的表达，即向上攀登的可能。换句话说，在《哥特式大教堂》的空间中，人类可以获得神圣感；而在右边这幅北宋绘画作品中，这些小如蚂蚁的行人好像是人类处于与上帝的一种关系之中。但是从这个角度来说，在这座大教堂中，人类无法获得神圣；然而在这幅画中，行人有可能。换句话说，他们能动。行人能够离开人类那个崇山峻岭的世界，就在下方这个山巅的中心。

　　进而，考虑到从范宽（左）所处的10世纪到郭熙11世纪的《早春》（右）的变化，人们可以看到在东西方传统中有着相似的进化过程。如果要在中国绘画作品中选出第二幅《蒙娜丽莎》，那么你们可以把《早春》称作《蒙娜丽莎Ⅱ》。因此这幅画中的形象是中国绘画作品中最著名的形象。

　　在我看来，这一个世纪里所发生的变化与希腊雕塑从大约公元前600年到公元前450年所发生的变化具有惊人的相似性——即从所谓的男性青年人物到维多利亚人物以及经典的希腊艺术的发展历程。简单地说，这是我所看到的一些相似性。

　　那么从10世纪到11世纪到底发生了什么？这是一种具有里程

碑意义的形式，它在范宽的绘画和希腊公元前300年的雕像中都有所体现。尽管它是具有里程碑意义的绘画形式，但最终还是土崩瓦解。在这个雕塑中的每一个元素，手臂、腿、头发的弧线或者在这幅山水画中，前景、中景和后景，都是相互分离、独立存在，并未形成统一的整体，而且这个人并未处于一种完全平衡的姿态中，几分钟之内就能摔倒。我们可以进一步说，如果前景、中景和后景没有明显的连接的话，这位行人就很难从前景走到中景，而后再到后景。

但是在随后的画作中，如左方这幅11世纪郭熙的作品，还有公元前450年的画作作参考，山水画的不同元素，人身体的各个部分都已连接起来，形成了天衣无缝的整体，非常平衡且具有动感。通过这两个例子，我们发现，中国画家和希腊雕刻家都在其作品中发现了相似的补充原则，通过这种原则将山水画的各个部分和人体的各个部分连接起来。

事实上，这种原则在西方称为"平衡力"原则，帮助作品实现一种整体性，这种整体性不仅做到天衣无缝，而且富有动感。换句话说，这个行人现在不仅仅能够离开他那大山的世界，而且还能够攀到山的顶峰。但与此同时，这是一种在发展中形成的新的动感和能量。因此，人们有可能看到自然的富有动力的运动。这才是《早春》的景象，这幅画体现了一种剧烈的成长，一种奇迹般的成长，这种成长发生于冬季过后的早春时节。在这种富有曲线的运动中，人们可以看到这种成长，例如这里的这个人，"平衡力"是最具有平衡性的姿态，他能运用这种姿势永远这样地站立下去。但关键在于，尽管他站得很稳，但如果他要动起来，只需抬起后面的脚向前迈即可。因此，富有动感且具有平衡性是在中国和希腊艺术传统中发现的相似原则。所以，5世纪的伟大哲学家赫拉克利特曾这样描述这种"平衡力"：整体性即为对立面的一种内在和谐，一种张力的和谐。这就是经典希腊文化中对"整体性"的注解。这是否让人想到了中国的"阴"和"阳"的概念？

那么，让我们回来看看中国的山水画和西方的人物画可能有何不同？我们看一下左侧的画作，这是14世纪中国画家倪瓒的《竹树野石图》，右侧的是17世纪荷兰著名画家伦勃朗的《凝视荷马胸像

的亚里斯多德》。难道两幅画之间没有任何联系吗？难道绘画仅仅意味着描绘人物或者描绘一棵树和旁边一块不太大的石头吗？两个问题的答案是"错"。为什么我要这么说呢？我们看一下其他有关树的绘画作品。这一幅是16世纪明代画家王崇明的作品，而这一幅为11世纪郭熙画作《早春》中树的形象。通过这两个例子，我们看到中国的风景画具有非常强烈的表现力。在王崇明的画中，树展现了一种龙的形象。而郭熙的棕榈树就像是晴天里的霹雳。我们肯定能够从这两种树的形象中了解到这两位画家的个性。而相比之下，倪瓒的这些树都非常端庄肃穆，紧凑，富有刚性而受到压抑，这正是他的写照。

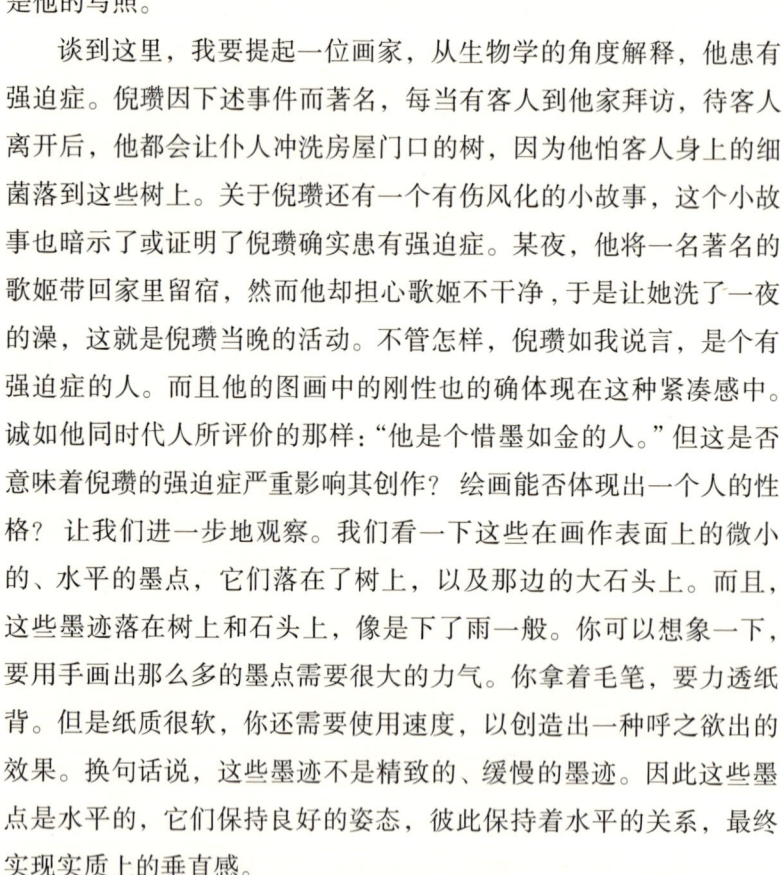

谈到这里，我要提起一位画家，从生物学的角度解释，他患有强迫症。倪瓒因下述事件而著名，每当有客人到他家拜访，待客人离开后，他都会让仆人冲洗房屋门口的树，因为他怕客人身上的细菌落到这些树上。关于倪瓒还有一个有伤风化的小故事，这个小故事也暗示了或证明了倪瓒确实患有强迫症。某夜，他将一名著名的歌姬带回家里留宿，然而他却担心歌姬不干净，于是让她洗了一夜的澡，这就是倪瓒当晚的活动。不管怎样，倪瓒如我说言，是个有强迫症的人。而且他的图画中的刚性也的确体现在这种紧凑感中。诚如他同时代人所评价的那样："他是个惜墨如金的人。"但这是否意味着倪瓒的强迫症严重影响其创作？绘画能否体现出一个人的性格？让我们进一步地观察。我们看一下这些在画作表面上的微小的、水平的墨点，它们落在了树上，以及那边的大石头上。而且，这些墨迹落在树上和石头上，像是下了雨一般。你可以想象一下，要用手画出那么多的墨点需要很大的力气。你拿着毛笔，要力透纸背。但是纸质很软，你还需要使用速度，以创造出一种呼之欲出的效果。换句话说，这些墨迹不是精致的、缓慢的墨迹。因此这些墨点是水平的，它们保持良好的姿态，彼此保持着水平的关系，最终实现实质上的垂直感。

这种绘画风格体现了当时画家所处的蒙古统治时代下的道德操守。通过这种速度、力量以及较深、而非苍白的墨色，画家赋予画作一种微妙的电能。换句话说，它们并非用来描绘叶子，它们甚至是用来描绘大石头上的植被，它们不是树枝。正是艺术家富有能量

的手，或者说艺术家的内力和力量将无形化作有形。

然而，事实上，在伦勃朗的画中，相似的事情发生了。第一眼看到这两幅画，会觉得它们非常相似，然而并非如此。亚里士多德一动不动地站在那里，沉静地注视着荷马的胸像。这幅画有一种沉静的质量。然而，在这幅画中，亚里士多德从荷马那里继承的创作灵感从两个方面展现了出来。从某种程度上说，通过这种非自然主义的手法将人的内心之光展现出来。这种创作灵感将这两位伟大的哲学家和作家联系了起来，并通过笔墨的加工，就像是亚里士多德衣袖上的印花而展现出来。就此而言，人们很难看到，亚里士多德脖子上所环绕的这根链条。这些非比寻常的有力墨迹并非用来描绘衣袖，它们与自然主义的塑造毫无联系，但是它们连接和展现了亚里士多德和荷马等人的创作能力和力量。荷马和伦勃朗很相似。换句话说，人们可以顺着这个线条，从他的手臂通过这根链条到荷马的头部或者将他的手放到荷马的头部。灵感就是这样的，它在链条和衣袖中散发出了能量。因此，它并非为即兴之作，因为它是可见的现实，我们可以看到人的灵魂。

换句话说，诚如我总是问学生的这个问题："艺术家如何展现其自身，无形的东西，精神的东西以及创作的东西？""你如何通过可视的媒介展现自我？"人们只能通过一种外化的方式来展现自我，审视自我。因此，从这个角度来说，倪瓒的山水画其实是一种自画像，与右侧伦勃朗的自画像有着异曲同工之妙。我们可能会说，这是有关自然的绘画，这是有关人物的绘画，但是归根结底，它们的落脚点都是艺术家自画像。通过这些例子，我希望你们能够明白，为何书法和绘画在中国传统的艺术中皆被视为艺术作品。

接下来，由于时间有限，我将跳过最后的一些例子。但是我希望这个例子对诸位有所启发，它体现了中国绘画的表现力，而后的西方艺术家也逐渐意识到了这一点。因此，我们看一下左侧的画和右侧17世纪画家石涛的画，这两幅画都并不关乎树和山，它们关乎艺术家的心灵，换句话说，它们通过这种富有动感的绘画表达了作者的心理。所以，毫不夸张的说，右侧的山就像是充电一般，通过画笔散发出了灵感，因此画家画出了位于画作正中高山之心的那个小东西。它并非为一幅有关大山的真实画作，相反，它反应了画家

的内心世界和艺术灵感,正如凡高的波涛汹涌的绘画作品一般 —— 反映了人类狂野的灵魂。

因此,我们可以从20世纪的抽象表现主义艺术家以及一些相似的画作中很快发现,它们与中国画家有着密切的联系。我们可以仔细看一下这幅画(下),再看一下17世纪中国画家石涛的作品(上),中国绘画与现代西方艺术有着根本的联系,这显而易见。但是,我想补充一点,石涛不仅仅与抽象表现主义有着密切的联系。他的作品与西方的现代主义也有所关联。

我们看一下石涛于公元1685年所做的题词,石涛称之为"万点恶墨"。在他的题词中,他提到了宋代两名最著名的画家 —— 米芾和董源。"万点恶墨,恼杀米颠(米芾);几丝柔痕,笑倒北苑(董源)。远而不合,不知山水之漾洄;近而多繁,只见村舍之鄙俚。"左侧为这些房子。因此,在他看来,怎么说呢,他主张反古而行之,他对先人画家提出咄咄逼人的挑战,几乎是粗暴地摒弃了传统。从这个角度来说,你可能会说,他的画是达达主义作品,某种程度上与这幅1919年马塞尔·杜尚的《带胡须的蒙娜·丽莎》并无区别(右)。这是这位画家对于以往画风的一种讽刺的评注。

因此,在我今天演讲即将结束之时,我想说,事实上,20世纪的中国艺术家进退维谷。因为如果说他们曾经在20世纪尝试效仿过西方绘画风格,而事实上,西方现代主义艺术家们在20世纪所做的正是中国艺术家已经践行了几个世纪的艺术理念。如17世纪,自唐朝之后的作品都印证了这一点。所有这些对于20世纪的西方艺术家而言都是全新的理念,而对于中国艺术家而言却是老生常谈了。用一句话来概括:"在这个年代践行着几个世纪前的理念。"

那么中国艺术家应该怎么办呢? 但是并非只有中国艺术家感到进退维谷。在这个DNA时代,艺术家该怎么办呢? 由于我在演讲的开端引用了这幅著名的《蒙娜丽莎》,那么我想引用另一幅著名的画作来结束我的演讲,这幅画好像是对《蒙娜丽莎》的一种公然挑战。这是一幅中国绘画作品,事实上,它的灵感来自于右边这幅画。但是达达是上个世纪60年代的一种流行艺术运动,当然,这是张衡图于1989年创作的作品。的确,它是一幅非常著名的作品,我举出的这两个例子说明文化具有与日俱增的全球性。而且事实上,当下,

绘画的普遍性的确能够使得绘画与所有人群进行交流，从而使人们理解绘画。换句话说，我们不应该采用在一开始谈论北宋绘画和《蒙娜丽莎》时所采用的两分法来看待问题。而且今天早上，我们欣赏了吴为山先生的动人雕塑作品，我想，这种雕塑就是最好的证明，无论它出自何人之手，只要它能够与观众交流，便是好作品。

Bridging Cultures with Arts

Dawn Ho Delbanco

Professor of East Asian Art, Columbia University

Abstract: On the face of things, it might seem that there are unbridgeable differences between traditional Chinese and western arts. And in fact there are surprising parallels and overlapping between the two artistic traditions. If Chinese artists were trying to become more modern in the 20th century by becoming more western, Well, in fact, what modernist artists in the west did in the 20th century was what Chinese artist had been doing for centuries.

I thought I could best address the theme of bridging cultures, and in this case, visual cultures, by giving you some examples of ways of which I bring eastern and western cultures together in my own art history classes. Now though this is a China-U.S. forum, I have to admit that I am only going to show you one example of American art. The other comparisons to Chinese art that I show are European. But I think they both serve to make the point. And what the authors say that some apologetically that all my comments are directed to pre-20 century Chinese art. I apologize to all these practicing artists who are here today. But the fact the matter is I am still trying to learn about pre-20th century Chinese art and culture. I haven't yet managed to bring myself up to present times. So I am a real dinosaur..

We start with a pre-20th century painting here on the screen. You must think that either you are at the wrong conference or I'm at the wrong conference, because what is this image doing up here on the screen. Well, I put it up because probably the most familiar painting in western art it this one—the Mona Lisa by Leonardo Da Vinci. Now if you are to ask me what the Mona Lisa of Chinese painting is, that is, which is the most familiar Chinese paintings is certainly would not be a figure painting, most likely it would be this 10th century landscape painting by Fan Kuan, Travelers amid Mountains and Streams. Now if we compare these two iconic images from two different culture traditions, it's obvious that they are radically different. A fundamental contrast that reflects the dominance of the human figure is central meta-form in western art and culture on the right. Versus the dominance of nature as a central meta-form in Chinese art and culture on the left.

So on the face of things, it might seem there are unbridgeable differences between traditional Chinese and western arts. Capling Write, when he declares that oh, East is east, west is west, they never between should meet. Well, of course we know the answer is no. And in fact there are surprising parallels and overlapping between the two artistic traditions. So, for starters, in order to point out some of these parallels, I'm going to make a rather controversial statement. But I think I would like to suggest that monumental landscape painting of the northern Song Dynasty as represented by Fan Kuan over here on the left comes is Kuan's to being religious painting as one finds at the predominately humanness culture of traditional China. And I don't include Buddhism art in China. These are separate matter for separate conference.

So just compare the Fan Kuan painting on the left to this diagram on the right of the 13th century Gothic Cathedral in northern France. And one sees in both images the same hierarchies are form on the right hand side. It is a holy trinity, a kind of symbol holy trinity versus on the left you have the tall central point on either side by attending peaks. And in this two images there is a similar expression of cultivate coder and possibility for transcendence. In other words, in the space of Gothic Cathedral, the human can intercept with the divine; in the northern Song painting, these tiny little travelers down here on the bottom, who are in their relationship to the nature, it would seem if they are in consequential as man is in his relationship to the questioned God in this image on the right. But the point is the human can't intercept with the divine in this Cathedral. And in this painting, there is the possibility for the traveler (take note, these figures I identified as travelers). In other words, they can move. The traveler can leave the mountain world of man, down here at the center of the heights of towering peak.

Furthermore, one can see similar direct evolution interesting enough that occurred in eastern and western traditions. Consider the shift from the 10th century painting by Fan Kuan on the left to the 11th century painting by Guo Xi on the right entitled Earlier Spring. And if I have to choose the second Mona Lisa for Chinese painting, you can call Earlier Spring on the right Mona Lisa II. So these two images are somewhat really the most famous images of Chinese painting. So what happened when one goes from the 10th to the 11th century? To my mind, what happened in this one century there are certain striking similarities to what happened from around 600 B.C.E. to 450 B.C.E in Greek Sculpture, that is from the development of the so-called young male figure on the left to the development of the figure are Victorian figure on the right and classical Greek art.

To put things simplistically, here are the similarities that I see. While it is a monumentality form in both the earlier Chinese landscape painting, that is Fan Kuan painting, and in the Greek sculpture 300 B.C.E. There is a monumentality form yet there is as yet a disconnection of parts. The individual elements, that is to say, in this sculpture, arms, legs, curves of the hair or the landscape painting, the fore ground, middle ground and back ground which exist as separate parallel plains had not yet merged in either case into a unified whole, nor is this figure in a totally balanced stance. This traveler had a lot of trouble moving from parallel plain from fore ground, to middle ground to back ground if there is no clear connection between the plains.

But in later versions, in this 11th century painting by Guo Xi in the left and in the dereference of around 450 B.C.E., the different elements of landscape, the different parts of the body had been joined into a seamless whole, perfectly balanced yet dynamic. For in both cases, the Chinese painter and the Greek sculpture had discovered a similar principle of compensation, noticed that in both cases there is what one might describe as a kind of escort that links the parts of the landscape together, links the part of human body together.

And in fact, this is a principle in the western context known as counter-balance which achieves a unity that is not only seamless, but is dynamic. In other words, not only is the traveler now able to leave his mountain world of man and follow the escort up to the top of the mountain peak. But at the same time, there is the new dynamism and new energy in this development. And therefore, it is possible also to see the dynamic movement of nature. This is after all Early Spring. This is the painting about be volcanic growth, the miraculous growth that occurs in the spring season after the depth of winter. At this kind of curving movement, one can read that growth, here to in the dereference figure, counter-balance is the most balanced pose of all. He could stand in that pose for ever with his weight on one hip. But the point there is that balanced as he is, if he needs to spring into action, all he needs to do is to move that back foot forward and he can answer the next battle. So balance yet dynamism is a similar principle discovered by both artistic traditions. So this principle of counter-balance was described in the following way, by the 5th century great philosopher Heraclitus: Unity is an inner concord of opposites, a harmony of tensions. This is what unity means in the classical Greek context. Dose this not remind one after all of Chinese concept of Yin Yang?

Now let's go back to the disparities between Chinese landscape painting and western figure painting? In this case, on the left a painting of rock and bamboo by the great 14th century painter Ni Zan, and on the right a painting entitled Aristotle Contemplating the Bust of Homer by the great 17th century Dutch painter Rembrandt. Is there no link between these two paintings? Is it means painting no more than a figure and a tree standing next to a not very substantial looking rock? The answer to both questions is no. And why do I say this? Looking at other images of trees by the 16th century painter Ming Dynasty painter Wang Chongming and a detail from the Guo Xi painting Early Spring, which is from the 11th century. We can see in these two cases how of overtly expressive Chinese landscape painting can be. What at the dragon-like coils of Wang Chongming's trees. And Guo Xi's two palm trees resemble the bolts of thunder. Surely, when comes to understand something of the nature of the two artists from their images. Now Ni Song's trees by contrast are very demure, tight, rigid, repressed, this is precisely the way the man was.

This was a man we know quite a bit about a biography who had what we would now are referring to as obsessive-compulsive disorder. Ni Song, for instance, was famously known for the following, whenever he had guest visiting him in his home, after the guest left, he would had his servant wash down all the trees that were surrounding the entrance to his house, for fear that the guest somehow gotten their germs onto the trees. There is also a risqué story about Ni Song, which also indicates or in their illustration of this obsessive compulsiveness. He was offered, in afraid of offered him the company a famous courtesan for the evening, and he had her spending the entire night taking a bath, so that was his evening activity. Whatever the case, he was, as I say, a man of obsessiveness and compulsiveness. And that rigidity is shown in this tightness and spareness in these forms. And indeed, as he contemporary said, he was the man who used the ink as if they were gold. But does this mean that Ni Zan was paralyzed by his own womentations? Is a painting without a force, a personality? Let's look at it a little bit more closely. What at this small horizontal brush stokes that doubt the surfaces of the painting, they are on the tree, and they are on the rock over here. And in fact, they hit the tree and rock like a spit of rain. It took a lot of force to make this brush strokes if you can just imagine what you have to do with your hands to make such brush strokes. You hold the brush; you have to press it down hard on the paper. The paper are soft, let it out with the speed in order to create a sense of, a certain of pointed, and almost flying away quality of the brush stroke. In other words, it is not a delicate, slow brush stroke. So these brush strokes are horizontal, they are orderly, they retain their horizontal relationship to the essential verticality and straight uprightness of this forms. This forgeable relationship perhaps of the Chinese scholar moral integrity in times of Mongo rule which is when the painting was painted. But render with the speed and force and darker ink than the pale ink of the larger forms, they impart a subtle electric energy to the painting. In other words, they are not used to describe leaves, they are even used to describe vegetation on rocks, and they are not branches. What they are dynamic hand of the artists or the inner force and strength of the man turned into visible form.

Well, in fact, something similar happened in Rembrandt. Here is where the two paintings which seem so similar at the first glance really are not the similar. Aristotle is not moving, he is standing and silent contemplation of Homer whose bust was over here. There is a silence about the painting a kind of hushed quality. Yet the creative inspiration that Aristotle has inherited from Homer is conveyed in two ways in this painting. In part, through this non-naturalistic like is an inner light that serves the inner light of the soul that is brought to the surface. But the creative inspiration that links these two great philosophers, writers is also quite literally shown through the tort of brush work that it looks like fireworks on the sleeves of Aristotle. And for that matter and it's hard to see the chain that goes around that Aristotle is wearing around his neck. These extraordinarily powerful stokes not used to describe the falls on these sleeves, there is nothing to do with naturalistic description but rather to link and convey the creative energy and powers of Aristotle, Homer and Rembrandt alike. In other words, one can follow the fire work of this brush stoke from his arm through this chain onto the head of Homer or actually goes the other way around by putting his hand on the head of Homer. The inspiration is such that it glows in dynamic brush work in the chain and in the sleeve. So this is not a brush work that is now because it is now too visible reality it is what reviewed the inner man.

In other words, as I always asked my students, how is an artist to convey extraction, the invisible, the spiritual, the creative? How do you convey extraction through a medium that is by definition visible? You can only do it through extraction when uses extraction, extract brush work to review extraction. So in that sense, Ni Zan's landscape painting is as much a self-portrait as Rembrandt's self-portrait over here on the right. We may say that this is about nature, this is about man, but in the end it's really focuses are self-portraits of the artists. And from this example, I hope you can see why calligraphy and painting eventually became synonymous arts in traditional China.

I'm now going to skip over the last few images because I'm running out of time but it is suggestive to you, I hope. Uh, the expressive potential of brush work, this is something that later western artists came to recognize Henry Shan Joe some examples of this. And so that when you want these two paintings then go separately on the left, and album leaves by the 17th century painter Shi Tao on the right. The images are not so much about trees and mountains, as they are the images of the artist's mind, all of this express, in other words, through dynamic brush work. So that this mountain on the right charged with electric current, literally, emanates through the brush hand and inspiration of the artist portray the tiny figure seated in the center of the painting in the mountain's heart. It is not a realistic image of the mountain, but rather a representation of the artistic mind and inspiration as much as the turbulent brush work of Van Gogh's painting Mirrors—the wildness of the inner man.

So when we look at the abstract expressionist of the mid-20th century and Henry Shan Joe a very similar example, we can immediately see their affinity with their Chinese painters. So you have a detail of the painting on the bottom. And a painting by the same Chinese artist of the 17th century, Shi Tao on the top. So here clearly, is a fundamental link between Chinese painting and modern western art. But let me add one more point here, Shi Tao's affinity that is the artist of the top image is not only with abstract expressionist. He had another link to modernist western artist as well.

Consider the title and inscription on this painting of 1685 on the top, Shi Tao called it 10,000 ugly ink dots. And here is his inscription. He makes reference in this inscription to the two of the most famous painters of the Song Dynasty Mi Fu and Dong Yuan. So this is what he says, 10,000 dots of ugly ink to make old Mi drop dead, what a strained strokes to make

Dong Yuan fall down with laughter. The distance does not work; there is no sense of landscape of winding and returning. All you see are a few rude shaped of houses. Here is the house over here on the left. So this kind of, in your face, almost rude he is reacting against the past, he is offering a challenge to earlier artists and throwing their tradition in their face. In that sense, you may say that his painting is a Dadaist, painting on some level no different from Marcel Duchamp's L.H.O.O.Q. from 1919 over here on the right. And like that painting, it is an artist stoical commentary as much as anything else, its relationship to the past ironic.

So let me just say at this point as I am nearing the end here, this is in fact was a dilemma for Chinese artists of 20th century. Because if they were trying to become more modern in the 20th century by becoming more western. Well, in fact, what modernist artists in the west did in the 20th century was what Chinese artist had been doing for centuries. There is certainly enough paintings like the 17th century one with reference irony, there has been since the Tang Dynasty, self-preferentiality commentary expressionism. All of these were new for the western artists of 20th century, but were old for the Chinese artists. To use a colloquial phrase:"being there, done that, century earlier."

So what was a Chinese artist to do? But Chinese artists are not alone in that. What is any artist to do in this DNA age? And I also end with a reverent image since I started with Mona Lisa, I am sort of coming by ending with a kind of defying of Mona Lisa. So I end with a Chinese work of art, that in fact is based on inspired by such a work as that on the right. But Dada is the work the pop art movement of 1960th, a piece of art by Zhang Hengtu, who did this in 1989. It is a reverent work, but what was this pairing on the other hand reflects is the increasing globalism of culture? And the fact that there is now a certain universality of images that speak to all people that all people can understand. In other words, it isn't that incredible dichotomy that one thought at the beginning of the talk between the northern Song painting and Mona Lisa. And when we saw Mr. Wu Weishan's moving sculpture this morning, I mean what better evidence do we have than that the art made by no matter who can speaks to all audience today.

心与象合

——关于中国画文化体验

田黎明

中国艺术研究院副院长，研究生院院长，研究员

内容提要： 中国艺术源远流长，其中意象文化美学形成了中国画独特的审美理念，它以澄怀观照、寓物取象、心与象合的人文体验，注重人格立足、以德观物、立象尽意的表达方式，传颂了中国画的特色和中国文化的本源。本文以立格、品物、返照、形神、心象五个层面，通过文例简述中国画所蕴涵的人文品质和精深的中国文化内涵。

"心与象合"指心性与气象合为境界，关于中国画文化体验也是关于人类所持有真、善、美心性的有关课题。中国艺术源远流长，其中意象文化美学形成了中国画独特的审美理念，它以澄怀观照、寓物取象、心与象合的人文体验，注重人格立足、以德观物、立象尽意的表达方式，传颂了中国画的特色和中国文化的本源。从中国画的语言背后来看文化的方式与生活方式，这是中国绘画的核心所在。每一代人都是以中国传统文化的精髓与自己的生活经历紧密相连，使中国画这一古老的绘画形式每一笔都有着背后的文化力量，在每一时代都绽放光芒，尤其在今天它的意义更能显现出来。本文以立格、品物、返照、形神、心象五个层面通过几个传统文例简述中国画所蕴涵的人文品质和精深的中国文化内涵。

本文主要从中国绘画的意象方式来看中国画品质与特征。

中国文化遵循"人法地，地法天，天法道，道法自然"的人文思想，以"道生一，一生二，二生三，三生万物"的自然规律来运行，这里"一"可以用一句禅语来概之"一月映一切水，一切水印一月"，道存于一切理念、物象、法理之中。中国画的意象特征作为中国文化重要载体，它以中国文化倡导的温柔敦厚为学养，体验"立天之道曰阴与阳,立地之道曰刚与柔,立人之道曰仁与义"的人文理念,逐步建构出独一无二的属于中国画的审美体系。以下从五方面用几个文例浅析中国画的意象内涵,这是中国美学重要特征之一。

一、立格

与品德、操守有关,中国画意象特征首先表现为立格,它以追寻人生境界,强调人格纯真为主体。"宋代学者周敦颐提出'文以载道'说,认为'文辞,艺也;道德,实也。'文辞是技能,道德才是实质。"(《宋代文艺理论集成》蒋述卓著)所以中国画的内容与形式的统一是以追寻品格的自由精神为基础的。

周敦颐《爱莲说》以莲为格,为操守、德行,道出君子风骨,其中:"予独爱莲之出淤泥而不染,濯清涟而不妖,中通外直,不蔓不枝,香远益清,亭亭净植,可远观而不可亵玩焉。"

此为以象立意,以莲为象,意义在于若"出淤泥而不染"有入世而超然之志,其志直指:理想、怀抱(闻一多语志、怀抱),所以有不染之格。又通过莲的"中通外直"形象,若"中和之意","和"是中国文化之道,汉《淮南子》有"万物之大,莫大于和",所以中通外直,以中和、外坚的统一,追寻内柔外刚的人文品格。而"香远益清,亭亭净植"的物象特征喻义以清风洁净之意又回到天地万物一体的自然规律之中,达到对"天人合一"的感知。(参《古文笔法百篇》之意)"中通外直,亭亭净植"借助了自然意象与语言形式之美的融合,通过"莲"普通生活的自然品物形态却能看到一种内识和人格风骨。这里引出人格的体验也需要在自然中借助物象来生发,并通过文字上升为语言的艺术力量。作者心在立格,寓物求象,而意高深邃,形象又极为平常,这是"立象以尽意"的思维感知,也是"立象以尽意"的人格风骨,古人画松、画梅、画石都以立格来自照,向着高尚的心性来品味自

然。每一处生活都内含着文化体验，印映出中国文化澄怀观道的人文力量。当心性品格在自然物中被感应，当象与意合一之时，正如唐代司空图所说"意象欲出，造化已奇"。意象更是一种以体物介入内心的文化体验。中国人立格的品质始终将个人与群体相连，将人文体验与民族文化相融，并能将个人遭遇化为境界，在自然规律中以德观物，如以松、石喻气节，以菊以莲喻心性，借助物象转换现实，物我相照，创造出中国人的美好心灵与追寻崇高美德的志向。

二、品物

借生活物象品味心性。明代画家沈周，著有一篇杂文《听蕉记》：

"夫蕉者，叶大而虚，承雨有声。雨之疾徐、疏密，响应不忒。然蕉何尝有声也，声假雨也。雨不集，而蕉亦默默静植；蕉不虚，雨亦不能使之为声。蕉雨故相能也。蕉静也，雨动也，动静戛摩成声，声与耳又相能而入也。迨若匼匼插插，剥剥滂滂，索索渐渐，床床浪浪，如僧讽堂，如渔鸣榔，如珠倾，如马骧。得而象之，又属听者之妙矣。长洲胡日之种蕉于庭，以伺雨，号'听蕉'，于是乎有所得于动静之机者欤？"

文中，沈周借助于芭蕉和雨声的描写来表达自己的感受，并感觉出一种形象的产生，这就是象。这里象是生活结晶，沉淀的形象，这个象又是由外象引出内象，也就是我们所说的得而象之。这种形象既不是芭蕉，也不是雨，而是内部深沉的一种经验，如"如僧讽堂"、"如珠倾"、"如马骧"，都是作者的亲身体会，"如僧讽堂"讲的是儒生在庙堂里念经的声音，"如珠倾"像玉珠一样的溢倾而泄的声音，

"如马骧"像马昂首的样子。这是作者的生活记忆，他又是作者的艺术形象储存及关于艺术语言的储存，由两个物象产生第三、第四个形象——这与老子"道生一，一生二，二生三，三生万物"有关。从具体描写来看，又与具体对象有所不同，它既不是对象又是对象，是从对象里转换而来，没有芭蕉、雨就难以遇见此时心象，这种互为转换互为升华的关系，只可意会不可言传。有时我们创造一种形象，心象合一时，一定是多年的感觉忽然被找到，就像一个诗人突然想到一个好句子，与他的心性相融，而不是在描述一个现象，这时它所达到的感知是"即心即境，心与象同"，象传出境界，境界贮存于自然万物事理之中。沈周的感觉是在芭蕉和雨中合体而生的，由自然之音引出主题心性之音，这些普通的生活经验，包含着淡泊清澈的品质，此时我们看到沈周已将平常景提升为一种境界。这种象我们称之为意象，中国画就是要体会和发现意象。

从《听蕉记》由听引发出的感觉，又由听觉引出心里的图像，最后又由心象回归到听，使之由原有的时空引发出多元时空的自我经验，这个经验的时空被转回为意象，沈周找到了种形式，并将形式转换为心体，他在倾听之时，其感觉正是寻找自己曾经历过的自然，这些平常的自然之景在体味中被突然化为心象之境，这样形成的艺术是真正有感而发，借物生象，物象相融，形成心象合一而达到意象，这也是中国画的人文体验方式。

中国画讲"外师造化，中得心源"，前者为自然生活，后者为文化体验，我的理解，从生活找到文化感知的内核，让心体贯穿着"一月映一切水，一切水印一月"的理念，月是一种最纯净的文化品格，水便是一种体验和承载的方式，月是理，水是事（神意：事理合一）月是心源，也是事物规律，水是生活的方式，当生活方式能映印月的品质，其规律也融入在事物之中，心性的发现与心性所达到的境界是通过整体来实现的。因此我觉得通过这样的一个禅理来理解"喻物取象"、"心与象合"的道理，对于我们理解中国画的文化基础和意象方式与水墨画创作，是有意义的。

三、返照

关于自省，中国文化讲知行合一，它是向内即自省的方式来完善自我，魏晋高僧僧肇所言"触物而一"，"立处即真"，是以自省、完善为义理，于触事中来把握自然规律与心性之真的统一。

我曾读过一位高僧日记,记录了他自省的一段文字。

高僧背上生了冻疮,每日请小僧敷药,有一次小僧用力过大,使之疼痛难忍,高僧以大声训斥,小僧低语道:"大师,您平常在大堂给我们认真传授经法,怎么到了您这,就不是那样了呢。"高僧听后非常后悔,他想,是啊,我平常在讲经的时候为什么希望别人能做到,而自己没有做到呢? 我怎么内外不一呀。

这里引出了自觉修为的心性以达到知行合一,内外合一,僧肇"触物而一""一"与老子的道相通的道理,"一"的道理在最普通事物之中,提出来就是最高道理,是自然之性。一切景、一切物、一切思都与"一"有关,如:"事理合一"、"佛身不二"、"万物与我齐一"、"一切万物不出我心",禅学里"凡与圣不二"、"天人合一"等。达到"守一不移"都是讲平常中见心性,平常中提升境界。"真"以一贯之,知行合一的品质,只有达到内外合一,才能有"立处即真"的境界。

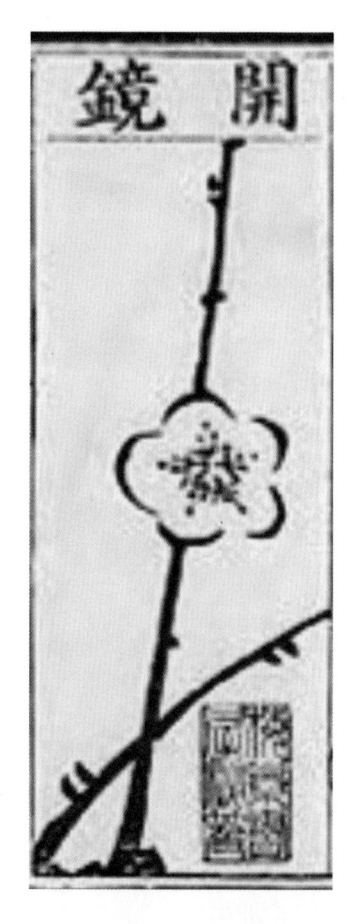

以学问讲：学向外，问向内，只有向内问，问己，学才能体悟意象。自省是做到向内求真，才能有行的真知。若内不真，其言语、其行为、其作品也难以达到感染他人。一个人画出的画一定与他进取方位有关，这里形式与内容，画法与情感如何统一是一个学问的课题。所以自省，已成为意象方式达到真知的重要进程，中国文化倡导真、善、美也是对人关于自我修为完善，向往人文精神境界的统一过程。中国画的笔墨文化正是以此来观照的。

四、形神

将平常的形象生发成有境界的形象。中国画写意性以缘物状情，借意生象，立象尽意的文化传承来体验自然与事物。宋代《宋刻梅花喜神谱》以写意、立象道出了意与形，看去最玄妙，也是最平常道理。每一幅图式都有一种境界，这是何等的奥妙。虽为梅花，却有深邃的人格精神所贮。

如《开镜》花形借镜，古人有以镜为鉴，以镜自照、自省，此图梅花盛开，借正形若镜，以自照心灵为意，从而达到立形生意，回味不尽。

如《遥山抹云》一枝梅干如山体之形斜横画面，花形似云，浮在山腰，一为花形，一为枝干之形，以形立象，借象赋意，气象自出。

中国艺术研究院当代红学大家周汝昌先生著有《永字八法》，周汝昌先生在《永字八法》中深入浅出论述了八法的意象方式。如"勒"如"侧"（点如侧，如鸟之翻然侧下），或古人用高峰坠石来引发用笔之力，通过自然借意成就下笔之形，如"策"（仰横，如鞭策、策马疾行），"啄"（由静而动，强调腾凌而速进，如鸟之啄物）如翠鸟水上捕鱼，这既是一种意象形态，也是借意象之力所成形，也内涵着造型的方法。书法的点划横撇等笔法，全因借意生力、生形，由此"意"成为书法审美的关键。

东汉蔡希综在《笔论》中谈到：

"……凡欲结构字体，未可虚发，皆须象其一物，若鸟之形（中国传统绘画有画竹之法：二笔飞燕，五笔惊鸿），若虫食禾（书法中有屋漏痕之法，人物画中有蚯蚓描都属此意），若山若树（书法有其型若山，如魏碑体，有若树型如颜真卿笔体），若云若雾，（书法有隋唐人小楷，有张旭狂草'若观夏云而得势'）。纵横有托，运用合度，可谓之书。"

由此，意象以格为本，由意生象，又以象写意，意从心生，心与象合。这虽是书法之意象，也同样形成了中国画的意象理念与笔墨的形式内涵。所以中国画的用笔、用形都与意与象有关。

五、心象

与心性中的一切景有关。中国禅学记事有这样一段情景，高僧与小僧二人行走河边，不远望去小河水面有一群鸟在戏水，小生欲前往驱赶，老者劝道，这是圣景，自然的生机，你我能看到此番景象是一种缘分。老者能将平常景看做一种境界，这是"立处即真"的修为所在，化平常为心源，这里贮存着真、善、美的心性。中国文化渗透着在普通事物中能见光明，如陶渊明句"平畴交远风，良苗亦怀新"，又如王维"行到山穷处，坐看云起时"，如赵孟頫山水画，极平常山，能出新意。在遭遇面前能见境界，陶渊明有"山气日久佳，飞鸟相与还"。清代画家弘仁，有一句题画诗"余雪冻鸟守梅花，尔汝依栖似一家。"这是一种品质的高扬，冻鸟与梅花与寒雪为友，构成一种精神，一种感慨，一种气节，这是一种向内的境界：春夏秋冬、山石苍润、树木无行、房屋错落、人无机事，人与人不猜测，不计较，人与自然不求表象，但求知己，中国传统文人往往在人格立足上是以体物进而达到静观，如中国传统的花卉梅兰竹菊、山水三远（高远、平远、深远）是关于立格的写照，而每代人和一个有感知的文人都会以独有的生活经历和人生感知来体味博大精深的文化精神，并创造出属于时代的人文境界，其过程也是作品的本体，也是自我心体的观照。心象就是一种文化精神与人格精神的统一。是一种知行合一的人生境界。比如弘仁的山水画就是他心象的写照。中国画所要表现的正是化平常为神奇，化遭遇为境界，以平常心体味自然、人生、社会，以构造澄怀观道之胸襟，追寻中国文化理想人格大境界。

中国画的文化性，以中国传统文化的自律性贯穿在每个时代人们生活和生命的审美意识和人格情趣之中，中国画当代性，继承和发展着传统意象文化的精神，使得中国画在今天展现了独有的人文高尚品质，这是中国人的精神财富，也是属于人类的共同精神财富。

The Integration of Mind and Image
—— Cultural Experience in Chinese Paintings

Tian Liming

Research Fellow
and Vice President
of Chinese National
Academy of Arts,
Dean of the Graduate
School, CNAA

Abstract: Chinese art has a long history and the image aesthetics created Chinese paintings' unique aesthetic concept, which, together with humanistic experiences of observing with a peaceful mind, creating images according to objects and achieving harmony between mind and images, and with ways of expression emphasizing being personality-oriented, integrating moral with paintings and conveying thoughts with images, demonstrate the characteristics of Chinese paintings and the origin of Chinese culture. This paper briefly describes with examples the humanities qualities and profound culture contained in Chinese paintings from the five perspectives of establishing the pattern, observing the objects, imitating the objects, forms and spirit, and mind and images.

The integration of the mind and image implies that one's personality merges with images and together they give birth to a poetic realm or in other words, state of mind. In order to appreciate the culture behind Chinese paintings, one must learn about the pursuit of truth, goodness, and beauty as human natures reflected in these paintings. Chinese arts have a long tradition. The aesthetics of culture through imagery helps to formulate the unique aesthetic concepts embodied in Chinese painting. In light of the humanistic experience of observation with peaceful mind, images through objects, and merging mind and images, this aesthetics stresses personality as foundation of morality, projecting morality onto the observed, and conveying meaning in images as the basic way of expressing. It inherits and extols the features of Chinese painting and the origin of Chinese culture. It is the core of Chinese painting that the language of painting depicts culture and lifestyle. Chinese artists in each generation never sever their close relationship between the essence of traditional

Chinese culture and their own lives. It is their pursuit that every stroke of Chinese painting embodies its cultural power which blazes through all histories, especially brightly today. In this article, the author tries to illustrate briefly with several cases the humanistic aspect and profound culture embodied in Chinese paintings from the five perspectives: establishment of personality, evaluation of objects, introspection, image and spirit, and the integration of mind and image.

This article focuses on evaluating the quality and characteristics of Chinese painting from the perspective of imagery.

What Chinese culture follows is the Chinese humanistic idea, namely, "Man models himself after the Earth; The Earth models itself after Heaven; The Heaven models itself after Tao; Tao models itself after nature". What Chinese culture operates on is the natural law that "Out of Tao, One is born; Out of One, Two; Out of Two, Three; Out of Three, the created universe." As a Buddhist allegorical chant goes, "the moon casts shadow on all the waters, and all the waters reflect the moon", the Way exists in all ideas, objects, and natural laws. The symbolism in Chinese painting is a major vessel for the essence of Chinese culture. With the gentleness and kindness advocated by Chinese culture as the fundamental academic and moral attitude, Chinese painting gradually formulated its unique aesthetic system by practicing the humanistic idea that

"Yin and Yang are the two basic elements that breed the heaven and the earth; the way to establish the earth consists of hardness and softness, while the way to establish human consists of humanity and justice." With several literary cases the author tries to illustrate briefly the symbolism, which is a major characteristic of Chinese aesthetics, distinct in Chinese paintings from five aspects.

I. To Establish One's Personality

First and foremost, as related to morality and self-discipline, the most important characteristic of the images in Chinese paintings is establishing the personality, which mainly refers to pursuing the true meaning of life and emphasizing the pureness of personality. "Zhou Duyi, a famous scholar of Song Dynasty, puts forward an argument of 'literature as the carrier of Tao'. He believes that 'diction belongs to the realm of art while morality the essential.' It means literary accomplishment is a manifestation of one's skill, while morality is what counts in life. " (Collections of literary theories of Song Dynasty, by Jiang Shuzhuo) So, the union between content and image has the free spirit of pursuing exalted personality as its foundation.

In his Ode to Lotus Flower, Zhou Dunyi has lotus flower as the model of noble personality, rigid self-discipline and morality, for its symbolist strength of

character matches that of a nobleman.

"As for me, I love lotus flower for it can keep its purity in spite of its root in the mud. Growing in clear water, it is like a shy maiden instead of an enchanting siren. Its hollow stalk grows straightly without any branches. With fragrance floating in the air, it grows like a slender maiden who can only be admired from a long distance rather than be dallied in one's hands.

Zhou Dunyi uses lotus as a symbol for ideal personality which maintains "its purity in spite of the mud-like surroundings". As this personality features ambitions beyond secular pursuit--ideals and aspirations, so it is like that of lotus. The image of lotus, being "hollow inside and straight outside", relates it to the idea of Zhong He (harmony). Harmony is the way of Chinese culture as Huai Nan Zi says that "the most important in the universe is nothing but harmony". So, being hollow inside and straight outside, the image of lotus symbolizes the unity between harmony and uncompromising principle and the humanistic character which stresses being mild inside and tough outside. Moreover, with the characteristic of being "fragrant and slender-maiden-like", lotus serves as a metaphor of what is pure and the unity between everything under the heaven. It conveys cognition of the "harmony between nature and man". (refer to the argument in A Hundred Articles for the Style of Ancient Writing) The depiction of lotus as "being hollow inside and straight outside and growing like a slender maiden" shows an introspection and strength of character via the image of a natural object, a common image in our daily life. The feeling and cognition of a powerful noble personality is expressed via the image and images in nature and uplifted by the power of artistic language. The author intends to pass on to readers a noble personality and he does so via symbolism. His intention is profound while the image he uses is very common, which is true of the practices conducted by ancients who depict pine, plum, and rock with personality as the object of introspection. This is the so-called approach and character of "representing images for expressing of meaning. With this method, the ancient artists appreciate nature with a noble heart. Cultural experience has its mark everywhere in our lives. The humanistic power of Chinese culture in purifying one's inner world and resonate with Tao is here and there. As personality, mind, and heart find their natural counterparts and as the image unites with the meaning, "Wonderful workmanship of poetry is culminated because image of poetry is not fully unfolded. Image is a cultural experience by projecting the inner world onto the outside objects. It is the traditional way of Chinese culture of cultivating one's personality by relating individual to the community, by integrating personal cultural experience with national culture and by converting personal experience into an elevated state of mind. Chinese people tend to project morality onto objects, for example pine and rock serve as metaphor for integrity, and chrysanthemum and lotus for temperament. Here, objects and images are converted into moral reality. Here, object and ego mutually project itself on the other. In this way, Chinese people pursue noble virtue and beautiful mind.

II. Experiencing the Object

This subtitle means introspecting into one's temperament via objects. Painter Sheng Zhou of Ming Dynasty said in his essay listening to the Sound from Banana Tree

"Banana tree's leaves are big and hollow, which make sound as rain fall on them. As the rain turns heavy, the sound becomes loud, the rain small, the sound low. It is not the banana leaves that make sound, but the rain does so. Without rain, the banana tree stands in silence; if the banana tree is not hollow inside, rain cannot make it sound. Rain and banana tree interact with each other and the sound is made. As the banana tree stands in still, the rain is in motion. The stillness and the motion meet each other, result in the sound which interacts with the ear. Varied sounds from rain in drops or in pour, can be confused with neigh, with pears falling on the ground, with chant by monk, and etc. It is the most wonderful experience of listeners to rain if they can relate these various kinds of sound to other objects. When did Changzhou plant these banana trees in his courtyard for the purpose of listening to the rain and learn from the interaction between stillness and motion?"

In this article, Sheng Zhou expresses his feeling via the description of banana tree and the sound of rain. Image, as the crystallization of life, and the sediment of life experience arises in the description. The image, as an inner one, is induced from the outer one. This image is not banana tree or rain alone, but a profound inner experience. The artist distills images from his experience of "monks are chanting in the hall", "pearls pouring on the ground", and "horses neighing". These descriptions are not only the author's memory of everyday life, but also the conservation of artistic images and artistic language. One image gives birth to two, and two to three, and three to four, just like the idea of Laozi: "Out of Tao, One is born; out of One, two; out of Two, Three; out of Three, the created universe." Viewed from the detailed description, image differs somehow from concrete object. Image is distilled from object, it is but not in the absolute sense object. Without banana tree, rain cannot meet the image in the mind. This relationship of mutually converting and elevating cannot be expressed in words. When creating an image, we sometimes feel the form and mind unite as one—the long lost feeling is suddenly found as a good sentence occur to a poet. It is not a depiction of a phenomenon but a projection of his state of mind. The cognition in this projection is that "the mind is the object, and the mind integrates with the image." Image, or object conveys the state of mind, and the state of mind is present in the universe. What Sheng Zhou feels is born into the integration of banana tree and rain. From the natural sound comes the sound of heart as the theme. In common life experience, there lies the personality that is indifferent to wealth and fame. So, we can put it that Sheng Zhou has elevated a common phenomenon into a state of mind. It is called image, and the purpose of appreciating Chinese painting is to find the images embodied in it.

In this article, the feeling excited by listening to the rain induces images in the mind which finally return to the activity of listening. In this process, the experience in the original space-time leads to plural personal experiences. In this process, the image is converted into the heart. As listening, he listens to his experience and thus converts the common objects into artistic images of his heart. Art in this way is generated by feelings. It is the traditional Chinese way of painting which integrates objects and images.

It is the traditional Chinese way of painting that outer factors create the universe, while the inner factors create the heart. The former originates from daily life, while the latter derives from cultural experience. According to my understanding, the core of deriving cultural experience from life is to follow through on the idea that "the moon casts shadow on all the waters, and all the waters reflect the moon". If the moon is the purest cultural representation, water is the way of experiencing and conveying this presentation. If the moon is the logic, then the water is the state of affair. (Meaning: The state of affair and the logic in it is one) If the moon is the origin of mind and the law of the nature, then the water is the way of life. If the quality of the moon can be reflected in the lifestyle, so does the law of nature in the state of affairs. It is through the wholeness that the temperament is found and the state of mind is attained. Consequently, I feel it makes sense for us to understand the cultural foundation of Chinese painting, the symbolism in Chinese painting, and the way of ink and washing painting by using this Buddhist metaphor to illustrate the implication of images through objects, and merging mind and images.

III. Introspection

As for introspection, Chinese culture extols the unity between cognition and action. It means Chinese tend to improve oneself via self-introspection. The great monk Seng Zhao of Wei and Jin dynasties said that "the essence of all things is of no difference"; "one can find the true nature of things by introspecting in any circumstances". With an emphasis on introspection and self-perfection, he argues that one can grasp the unity between the law of nature and the genuineness in contact with objects and state of affairs.

Once I read about an eminent monk's diary of his own introspection, which goes this way:

An eminent monk had frostbite on his back, and he asked a Buddhist novice to treat it with liniment. One day the novice used excessive force and caused great pain, the eminent monks yelled him and the novice felt hurt and murmured: "Master, you are usually very careful and patient when teaching us in the hall the scriptures, why things change here?" The eminent monk regretted his inconsistency after hearing this complaint. He said, ay, why I do not follow my teachings to the others? Why I am so inconsistent?

Here are the issues of the unity of cognition and action and the integration of the inner and the outer via refining one's temperament consciously. Monk Seng Zhao's argument that "the essence of all things is of no difference" corresponds with Lao Zi's Tao: the One is embodied in the common phenomenon as the highest principle of the universe and the nature of everything. All phenomenon, all things, and all ideas converge to the One, for examples, there are sayings like "affairs and reason united into One", "the being of Buddha is one", "everything and I are one", "all things are in my mind", and sayings in the teachings of Zen that "common people and saints are of no difference", "the heaven and human are one". "Adherence to the One" means to find the reflection of temperament and elevate the state of mind in daily life. "The truth" should be observed and the unity of cognition and action should be followed. Only by uniting the inner and the outer into the One, the state of mind of maintaining the true nature of everything in all circumstances can be reached.

Take studying and asking (learning) for example, studying is an outward activity while asking is an introspecting activity. Only by asking oneself can one experience and realize the images. As an action of truth finding in one's inner world, introspection lays the foundation for the true knowledge that can be attained in action. If one is not sincere inside, his words, actions, and works cannot move or influence anyone else. What one paints must relate to one's academic or artistic orientation. How the image and the content, the style and the feeling unite with each other deserves academic study. So introspection is an important way to attain genuine knowledge via images. Truth, goodness, and beauty promoted by Chinese culture are also about self-perfection and these pursuits are united in the process towards the humanistic ideal. These are the basis of introspection in Chinese painting culture.

IV. Image and Spirit

Converted from concrete images in daily life, the images of Chinese paintings are images of state of mind. Chinese paintings aim at the expression of feelings which are projected onto the object. The form conveys the image which is the projection of subjective feelings. This is a Chinese cultural heritage for the cognition and experience of nature and affairs. The Collection of Woodcut Works of Plum Blossom of Various Shapes in Song Dynasty reflects the relationship between of the expression of feelings and depiction of images. This relationship is actually very simple though it might seem to be very mysterious.

Each picture is about a state of mind. Plum blossom embodies profound personality in a metaphysical way.

Take The Mirror for example, the blossom in this picture resembles a mirror. Since the ancient people in China had mirror as a metaphor for introspection, so this picture extols the importance of self-examination. The meaning is induced by the image, which is thought-provoking.

In "Remote Mountain and Cloud", a mountain-like branch of plum tree slants across the picture with blossoms that resemble cloud floating in the midst of the mountain. The image and the association of ideas find their organic relationship in this picture. Mr. Zhou Ruchang, contemporary eminent expert on the study of Dream of Red Mansion, academician of Chinese national Academy of Arts, wrote a book entitled as Eight Strokes of Chinese Character 永 In layman's language, he discusses the images represented by the eight strokes.

"Ce (侧)" and "Le(勒)" are in the shape of the route of a bird flying slanting ways, or of the stone falling from peak. "Ce (策) " is like riding a horse, "Zhuo" reminds one of a bird pecking, for example, a kingfisher catching fish on the water. All these strokes are not only images but also a metaphorical way for expressing meaning.

As these strokes combine meanings and images, it is vital for appreciating calligraphy to understand the meaning of these strokes.

In Essays on Calligraphy, Cai Xizong of Eastern Han Dynasty said,

"... The structure and strokes of Chinese characters should model a natural existence, which could be a flying bird (the traditional way of painting bamboo emphasizes two strokes like a swallow, and five strokes like a swan), stem gnawed by worms(in calligraphy there is the way of painting leaking roof and in figure paintings there is the way of painting earthworms), mountains and trees[in calligraphy, the characters of Weibei (the style of calligraphy typified by inscriptions carved on the stone tablets of the Northern Wei Dynasty) are like mountains, and the characters written by Yan Zhengqing are like trees] , and cloud and fog (regular script in small characters of Sui and Tang dynasties, the wild cursive hand of Zhang Xu, which resembles the building cloud in summer days). To make characters be called calligraphy, these strokes must follow certain rules. "

So, the personality-oriented images are born into meanings. Images serve as the conveyer of meaning, meaning follows the heart, and heart merges with the image. It is not only how calligraphy works, but also true of the images and implication of Chinese paintings. The strokes and shapes of Chinese painting are closely related to meaning and image.

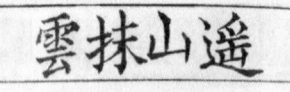

V. The integration of mind and image.

This integration is about the phenomenon in mind. An anecdote about Chinese Zen goes like this: an eminent monk walked along the river with a Buddhist novice, and not far from them, a flock of water birds were paddling in the water. The little monk wanted to drive the birds away, but the old monk stopped him and told him that this scene was holy; it was the reflection of the vigor of natural life. It is lucky for them to see such a scene. It is because of the practice of the principle that "one can find the true nature of things by introspecting in any circumstances" that the old monk can elevate a common scene to a state of mind. In this, there is the mind of pursuing truth, goodness and beauty. In Chinese culture, there is such enlightenment in common phenomenon. For example, the poetic lines by Tao Yuanming "Blowing above the Level farmland is mild wind, fine grain is teasing"; or Wang Wei's "I walked to the end of mountains and watched the building of clouds"; or the landscape paintings by Zhao Mengfu, in which you can find something new in the depiction of common mountains. In contact with nature, artists keep his noble or detached state of mind. For example, Tao Yuanming writes down these lyrics: "The unsetting in the mountain is beautiful; birds return nests one following another." Hong Ren, a painter of Qing Dynasty said in a poem that "Patches of snow and chilled birds by the plum tree, I and you are a family."

It is an ode for a noble character: chilled birds, plum tree, and cold snow befriend each other, and together they image a spirit, a sentiment, and a moral courage. This image communicates an inward state of mind. Four seasons, rocky mountain, scattered trees and houses, idle and innocent people image the basis of detached observation. People trust each other, and do not fuss. In their relationship with nature, people seek their companions without probing into the nature's representations. Traditional flowers, plum, orchid, bamboo and chrysanthemum and the three Yuan (being remote or deep or high) of landscape paintings are all depiction of personality. Cultivated Chinese People tend to pursue the profound cultural spirit with their own experiences and cognition and create their own state of mind. This process is not only the creation of artist work itself, but also the introspection of one's mind and heart. So, the unity between mind and image reflects the unity between cultural spirit and the power of personality, achieved inside, an inside realm of the unity of cognition and practice. The landscape paintings by Hong Ren are the reflection of his heart. What Chinese paintings try to represent is the process of converting the common into the uncommon, the experiences into the true meaning of life. With an idle heart to experience the nature, life, and society, and to cultivate one's spirit and broaden one's mind, is the ideal personality pursued by Chinese culture.

The essence of culture is embodied in Chinese paintings. This self-discipline of traditional culture is followed through when Chinese people live and conduct aesthetic activities. The modernity of Chinese paintings inherits and develops the spirit of symbolism in traditional Chinese culture, on the basis of which modern Chinese paintings develop its own noble humanistic quality that is the spiritual wealth of Chinese people and all humanity as well.

西方艺术的传统与创新

劳伦斯·林德

伯克利艺术博物馆和
太平洋电影档案馆馆长

内容提要： 从某种意义上来理解，典型的后现代艺术是对传统、对具象艺术、对历史艺术的一种回归。与之相较，其他时期的现代艺术唤起艺术创新中的经典传统。人们认为这种传统是对过去风格的一种选择性回归和对现代主义的抛弃，可能是对重头再来的需求。因此，后现代主义是对传统、对过去的回归，以及放弃"重头再来"。

今天我们座谈的题目为"视觉艺术的传统与创新"。由于我并非中国艺术的专家，因此，我决定将评价重点放在西方艺术的传统和创新上。或许这种对比能够减少我们两种文化和历史之间的距离，而且或许能涌现出一些相似性。

从某种意义上来理解，典型的后现代艺术是对传统、对具象艺术的一种回归，对历史艺术的回归。其他时期的现代艺术，这个新的、但可能不甚体面的内衣可能唤起艺术创新中的经典传统。人们认为这种传统是对过去风格的一种选择性回归和对现代主义的摒弃，据说是重头再来的需求。因此，后现代主义是对传统、对过去的回归，以及放弃"重头再来"。

事实上，如你们在这里所见，后现代主义并不是对过去以及对历史的惊天大逆转。也就是说，后现代主义并不仅仅是对早期艺术形式的一种模仿，而是人们通常认为，它可以通过技艺驾驭一种临界尺度。这种现代主义是对整体画面的掌握，就像这座女性半身像一样，可以凭借自己的能力在新的起点顺利自然地取代现代主义梦想。因此，拥有自身能力对于现代主义而言也是至关重要。

那么所谓的现代主义需要怎样的新起点？在19世纪和20世纪，

出现了一种有关现代主义的新理念，人们发现它是对传统表达手法的延续和创新。我们看到的是爱德华·马奈1863年的《草地上的午餐》，这幅作品在其首次展出数十年后，无论是从形式上还是内容上，都具有丑闻的意味。形式上，这个特别的人物组合缺乏透视感；在内容上，一个裸体女人与两个穿着衣服的男人共同进餐有伤风化。事实上，这幅画至少在构图上受一位1510至1520年的文艺复兴时期的画家马康托尼奥·雷蒙迪的作品的启发，那是一幅更大作品的局部。这幅作品本身参考了文艺复兴时期的画家拉斐尔的早期作品《帕里斯的审判》。再往后看，即所谓的现代主义历史时期，我们发现了20世纪60年代的毕加索，它恰恰代表了20世纪60年代的主题。因此，现代主义这一理念多少要求艺术家在每一时刻都拥有一个新的开始，都像在初始时刻诉诸一张空白画布。而实际上，在19世纪和20世纪，艺术画，即所谓的创新画并非如此。

所谓的现代主义和所谓的后现代主义之间的大战最终似乎是某种障眼的东西，将我们的注意力从艺术深远的变革中转移开来。法国哲学家雅克·朗西埃（Jacques Rancière）在他的著作《美学的政治》中，精彩地描绘并分析了这一最终的诠释，他的这本书为理解自伟大的希腊文明之后的西方文化铺垫了一条新路（除此之外，朗

西埃还发表了诸多颇具影响力的文章）。朗西埃的贡献在于，他将传统与创新的问题，或者换句话说，将前现代主义、后现代主义与现代主义的问题转换成了"感性的分配"这一问题。

对于朗西埃而言，关键问题并不是形式和内容的新或旧，而是存在问题的作品从民主地赋予制造者的权利掌控中逃离出来的程度，以及为使其制造者和观众获得解放体验所做出的贡献。朗西埃关注的是，谁有话语权以及创造形象权，以及谁有权利见证或感受这些作品。同时他也很关注效果艺术及其形成的方式，它有助于向压迫性的政权提出挑战，并朝着自由解放的生活努力。

于是，朗西埃将西方艺术史划分为三个时代，他称其为三个"政权"。第一个时代为"顶点政权"，所谓的顶点政权与希腊历史相对应，在这个时期艺术没有特殊的社会地位，人们认为艺术位于哲学之下，而且最终对于实现理想社会并无任何实质性的价值。第二个时代为"代表政权"。这一时期延续了亚里士多德的理论，即艺术可以发展其自身内部的规则和标准，同时也反应了其所处社会的等级、媒介、形式和内容，以及政治和社会等级。因此，对于朗西埃来说，所谓的"代表政权"从希腊艺术后期一直延续到19世纪，贯穿了整个文艺复兴时期，成为艺术实践的典范。最后到了19世纪中期，朗西埃注意到了一种新的政权的崛起，他把这种政权称为"动荡政权"，它摒弃了等级划分，例如，在他所谓的"代表政权"里，历史画等级最高，其次是人物画，最后是山水画，然而到了19世纪中期，这种等级划分遭到了摒弃，视觉艺术与文学之间的界限变得非常模糊，这是在西方发生的巨大变化。让我觉得有趣的是，中国的情况却截然不同，我发现在中国文化中，文学与艺术创作之间有着千丝万缕的联系。然而当这种形式于19世纪出现后，并没有带来巨大的变革。因此，朗西埃将这一时期（19世纪初期至今）称为现代主义时期。为了证明文学与视觉艺术之间的界限越来越模糊，朗西埃引用了一些人物加以证明。他还引用了一首杰出的诗作，在这首诗中，作者运用了空白区和书页以证明写作和视觉艺术都不能依靠感觉。但是朗西埃的标准将惯用的对传统和创新的提法颠倒了过来。在这个范围内，正是期待获得艺术物品独一无二的地位的参与者和观众联合了起来。朗西埃认为这个"政权"统领了当前这个时代,而他所设定的标准将会提供很多艺术性的解决方案,如环境艺术,互动形式的艺术以及看似很微型的绘画作品等,使得我们的生活更加动人,与其他人联系得更加紧密。

所以朗西埃真正吸引我的地方在于,他在前人对过去以及我们的历史进行了全面而传统的概括的基础之上,对"时代"——"艺术政权"等术语加以重新界定。有趣的是,根据他的标准,我们现在所处的时代有助于多种多样的艺术创作。这是英国著名艺术家杰明·戴拉的作品。杰明·戴拉大约40岁,为特纳奖得主,享有国际声誉。这幅作品描写了1944年的小型罢工事件,该起事件由警察挑起。戴拉在2001年组织了一场800人的罢工,参加者包括演员和当地的居民,用游行示威的方式控诉警察的行为。它是一种共同的、描述性的、展示型艺术作品。在这幅画作中,我认为很有趣也非常关键的一点在于,作者并未费尽心机地去渲染矿工的观念,而是为全社会成员创造出一种相互慰藉的机会,无论人们与矿工站在一边,还是与警察站在一边,他们都能够分享慰藉。

一方面,有些画作是这种风格;而另一方面,有些画作呈现出另一种风格,正如艺术家苏珊·弗兰克顿的这幅作品。这幅画将在未来几天内在纽约的画廊里展出。这是2010年的新作。你们可以看到这幅画同样也是绝对的抽象。你们可称之为微型画作。在很多方面,它都非常地不同寻常,然而有些方面在这幅画中并非显而易见。例如,她的作品只能在自然光线下展出,因此她的画作上无任何人工灯光,因此人们对于这幅作品的感受也不尽相同,也不是一成不变的。人们对这幅作品的感受随着云层的变化而变化,随着时间的变化而变化,还随着所处位置的变化而变化。因此,当人们欣赏这幅画时,会一直感受到每个人的独立性,事物的偶然性以及人性。

另外,由于这幅画本身捕捉阳光的方式不同,更加深了人们的感受,即通过阳光这一媒介,人们共同沐浴在阳光里。

这是苏珊·弗兰克顿的另一幅作品。她同时进行了这两幅画的创作,一幅是大型油画,而另一幅为小型水墨画。所以,正式的说,这几乎算不上一幅艺术作品。我认为将苏珊·弗兰克顿与杰明·戴拉联系起来的原因在于,她们的作品都超越了艺术的界限,触及到非艺术性的、纯物质、纯社会或者纯政治的东西。但同时又秉持了

某些仍然被视为艺术特质的东西。因此，归纳起来，朗西埃通过重新界定，将重点放在了艺术功能的研究、而非艺术表象的研究上。

Lawrence Rinder

Director of the
Berkeley Art Museum
and Pacific Film
Archive

Tradition and Innovation in Western Art

Abstract: Compared to the canonical post modern image which is understood to be, in some respect, a return to tradition, to figuration, to historical art, modern art from other period recall classical traditions of the new in art. So this is understood to be a shift from innovation to tradition. That tradition is understood as a selective return to the style of the past and renunciation of modernism, purported demand for a clean slate. So that post-modernism is a scene as return to tradition, to the past, and a renunciation of *the clean slate*.

So the title of our panelist is Tradition and Innovation of Visual Art, and not being a scholar of Chinese art, I decided to focus my comments on tradition and innovation in western art. And perhaps by contrast, this will limit some of the differences between our two cultures and histories, although perhaps some similarities will emerge as well.

Compared to the canonical post modern image which is understood to be, in some respect, a return to tradition, to figuration, to historical art, modern art from other period recall classical traditions of the new in art. So this is understood to be a shift from innovation to tradition. That tradition is understood as a selective return to the style of the past and renunciation of modernism, purported demand for a clean slate. So that post-modernism is a scene as return to tradition, to the past, and a renunciation of *the clean slate*.

In fact, what is called the post-modernism did not involve a wholesale reversion to the past, nor to tradition in their original state, as you can see here. That is it did not generally involve the expression that merely simulated the earlier artistic forms, rather post modernism through the appointment of technique which is just position as you see here, was usually understood to carry a critical dimension, critical modernism to be sure of the unitary image of the, the something like the bust of woman, but also at its own capacity to finally and coherently displace the modernism dream at the fresh beginning. So it is critical modernism also itself at its own capacities.

But how fresh a beginning did so-called modernism demand? Throughout 19th and 20th centuries, an instant idea of modernism is evoked, one finds indication of continuity as well as structure uphold as well as a factures of tradition as well as innovation. So the painting here is Edouard Manet's "Luncheon on the Grass" from 1863, a painting that was in today in fact for decades after its first being shown as scandal both in terms of its form and its content. Formally, the eras of unresolved brush work, the peculiar composition of figures that are non-perspective and in terms of the content, the supposed immoral implication of a nude woman dinning with two closed men. In fact, Manet's painting was based at least compositionally on this in grieving by Marcantonio Raimondi, a renaissance artist from 1510 to 1520 in that actually a detail of larger work. This piece itself was a reference to an earlier work by a renaissance artist Raphael, depicting the judgment of Paris.And moving forward, in the history of so-called modernism, we find Picasso in 1960, representing the very same subject in the age of 1960. So, this idea of modernism, somehow requires the artist to have a clean slate in every instance to address the blank campus as original moment. And in fact, it is not really the true story of the artist painting, so-called innovative painting in the 19th and 20th century.

So the titanic battle between the so-called modernism and so-called post-modernism appears finally to be something of a red herrings, so for the translators essentially affords to distinction, has to distract us from the more profound transition in the arts. This ultimate understanding has been marvelously described and analyzed by the contemporary French philosopher Jacques Rancière, whose book The Politics of Aesthetics which among many any other influential texts by him, laid out a potentially new way of understanding the artistic eras at least in western culture from the time of the Greeks. Rancière's contribution is to shift the question from one of tradition versus innovation, or in other words, pre and post modern versus modern to what he called the distribution of the sensible.

The key question for Rancière is not a newness or conventionality of form and content. But rather, the degree to which the work in question stands from a democratically empower producer and contribute to a liberating experience for its makers and audience. Rancière is concerned with who has the power to speak and to make images, and who have the power to witness or experience them? He is also concerned with the effective art, the ways in which it is formed, served to challenge repressive state and live towards liberating life.

So Rancière proposes three eras when he calls regimes in the history of western art. The first, the apical regime, so-called apical regime, corresponding to the period of Greek history in which art has no special status in the period of courses, epitomized by republic in which the arts were described as being beneath the consideration of philosophy and ultimately, of no essential value to the ideal community. Second, the representative regime, in which following the theory of Aristotle, art can develop itself own internal rules and criteria, while mirroring the hierarchy and medium, form and content, the political and social hierarchy of this society. So for Rancière, the so-called representative regime carried one from one period of late Greek art up through the 19th century, and it is a sort of consequential model of art practice throughout the renaissance. And then finally in the mid-19th century, he sees the emergence of something called astatic regime, which abolished the hierarchies, so for example, what he called representative regime, the highest round might be reserved for history painting then perhaps portrait, the landscape and still like in the bottom, in the 19th century, the hierarchies were abolished, there was a blurring boundary between most notably between visual art and literature, with a radical shift in the west and it is interesting to see the contrast to some of the speakers, we prefer to discuss many thousands of relationship between writing and image making in Chinese culture. When this form began to emerge in the west in the 19th century, it wasn't earthshaking transformation. And also they are becoming radically democratized in the origin and reception, so Rancière temporarily in terms of time period with a period described modernism, that is from the beginning of 19th century to the present. And many of the figures he cites, such as Nobel is consequential example of what Rancière is talking about when he speaks of the blurring boundary between text and image in the extraordinary poem in which the author utilizes the empty space, the page, the quality of hypotrophy to illustrate sensation had not been available to writing, nor to visual art. Yet Rancière's standard turned conventional notion of tradition and innovation art upside down when we consider a movement, such as the constructivism. Conventionally, consider a paragon of the modernist idiom, which by Runsier's standard, would likely fall 8 temporarily of the apical regime for the early Greek period. In so far, it is the participants and audiences aspired to an exceptional status for artistic object, united with the product of craft by their share origin in labor and binocular idioms of industrial forms. Rancière's criteria for this regime which he believes dominates the present time allows for a wide variety of artistic solutions, from situational interactional performs art, to seemingly minimal paintings, that turned the life more engagingly, more connective to the follow citizens.

So what is the thing that intrigues me about Rancière, having the extensive, very conventional notion of the past, our history, he, you know, reframes the defining terms of the era, the regime of art. And the regime that he believes that we are now, interestingly by his criteria, allows for a really remarkably diverse range, artistic practices. One project would be like this, this is a piece by Jermyn Della, who is a quite renown British artist, probably around 40 years old, the winner of Turner Prize, so very highly considered artist in Britain internationally. This particular piece consisted of restaging of a minor strike in 1944, which is broken up by the British police. And Della in 2001 organized 800 people, including actors, but also people from that town, who actually live through the original strike, to reenact the demonstration and the charges of the police against the demonstrators. And this was the art work, so was the rein active itself. It was a sort of communal, descriptive, performative art work. And one in which, I think interestingly and crucially intent without to dramatize the ideology of the miners, but rather to create a kind of an opportunity for the consolatory for all the members of the community, whether they are on the side of the police, on the side of the miners to restage this very dramatic moment in their community in order to come to some state of share of consolidations.

So on the one hand, something like this, and on the other hand, something like this, a painting by the artist Susan Frankton. This is actually for a show in New York in next a few days, you can see this painting is Gallery. You can see this painting of 2010 is also absolutely abstract. We can call it minimal. It's critically different, however in a number of important ways, unfortunately, some of which are immediately apparent in this image. For one thing, she only allows painting to be exhibited in natural light, so there is no artificial light on the painting, so one's experience of the work is contingent. It is not absolute. It is various according to the cloud cover to the timing of the day, to one position and relationship to the work. So one is reminded continuously of one's individuality, one's contingency, one's humanness, if you will. And also because of the different treatment in the circus of the painting, some area is mad, some area is shinny. The painting itself is catching the light in very different ways, and helps to heighten the sense that the light is the medium in which we are all swimming collectively.

This is another work by Susan Frankton. She works simultaneously on these two medium large scale oil painting and small water color a few inches by a few inches. So in formal it is almost not an art at all. And I think one of the thing that connects Susan Frankton with Jermyn Della is the way which is they are pushing that art out of boundary to the point, where touches on the non-artistic on the around pure material, or the purely social or the purely political, but still stay within something that could be considered art. So finally to summarize, by shifting the framing language, Rancière has allowed the focus on what art does rather than on what it appears to be.

密响旁通
——我眼中的中美艺术交流景观

徐累
中国艺术研究院
创作研究中心研究员

内容提要： 在中国当代艺术的进程中，不可否认的是，几个关键节点与美国艺术的渗入大有关系。在所有的国家中，美国是拥有中国传统艺术资源最丰富的国家，对中国传统文化的研究和推广也是相当有成就的。对中国文化来说，文化的活力代表着综合的天赋。如今我们开放的视野，对其他文明的接受的程度非常之广，这方面和美国有相似之处。文化气场的互移，文化气质的互补，是一个特别有魅力的事情，关键的问题是，我们应该在多大程度上按世界主义的方式行事，在多大程度上遵循本土与个别的原则，这是决定现代人类文明多样化的保障。

今年年初我在波士顿访问了一个美国收藏家，他特意邀请我参观了一个库房，里面居然安放了不少小型的中国塔，整齐地摆放着。他告诉我这是1915年中国参加旧金山世界博览会的展品，当时在上海有个教会组织了一些中国孤儿，用上好的木材，逼真的工艺，按1∶50的比例仿制了85座中国各地的古塔，漂洋过海送到美国展出，后来这批东西就留在了美国，辗转到了这个收藏家的手上。今年，又一届世博会在上海举办，这些95年前的"古塔"让人自然联想到中美文化交流的历史往来，无论"送经上门"或者"上门取经"，都是值得追忆的象征。

中美文化交流可以追溯的历史不仅久远，而且层次相当丰富，应该有各方面的专家作更深入的探讨。作为一个从20世纪80年代初开始成长的艺术家，我亲眼所见中美在恢复正常关系的年代里，自己观察到和参与到的中美艺术交流，如何开始，如何发展，如何聚沙成塔，而成为历历在目的证词。

在我的记忆中，第一次目睹美国艺术的大型展览是"波士顿博物馆美国名画原作展",那是在1981年的上海博物馆,当时我刚上艺术学院不久,清楚记得那幅"敲钟的人"的招贴,似乎在内心也有很大的震响。这个展览非常重要,对中国人在封闭30年后重新了解美国文化和人文精神起到先声的作用。也许考虑到中国当时的社会环境,70件作品中没有选择现代主义风格,这也恰好歪打正着,使我们很纯粹地看到了资本主义前期美国自然和民生的原生态。从触景生情的角度说,那是我对西方的第一次亲密接触。

那时的中国,百废待兴,文化上恶补不仅表现在对中国传统文化的恢复性认识,还有西方文化的传统和现代,后有古人,前有来者,对我们来说,那是八面来风、目不暇接的日子。譬如,我们不仅每天早晨起来背唐诗宋词,而且同时还能读到由美国诗人改写又重新翻译成中文的诗歌,比如爱米·罗厄尔(Amy Lowell)对中国诗歌技巧的模仿,埃兹拉·庞德(Ezra Pound)诗歌中改写的中国意象,即便是误读,也有他山之石的新鲜感。原典和新注,让我们看到了既远又近的不同的意趣。

在我看来,美国艺术的表达有一种率性,这和欧洲艺术背后与生俱来的典故、历史、隐喻略有不同。美国艺术中的直接表达,有一种人性最本初的生命活力,直通大众的朴素情感,和视觉的平等经验,所以很容易在中国的艺术家中得到回应。

简单回顾一下，20世纪80年代初期的代表作品，如罗中立的《父亲》一改原先盛行的苏俄画风，在手法上吸取了美国的照相写实主义画风，对细节的精微刻画在当时引起极大的轰动。几乎在同时，安德鲁·怀斯（Andrew Wyeth）的伤感主义风格，也与当时所谓的"伤痕"艺术融合，在何多苓的作品中表现得特别有感染力。中国这些重新提倡人道主义思想的作品，与美国艺术中大地与人的关系，生活与情感的联系，有逻辑上的对应点。这种共鸣在人本的悲悯层面上，叙述了个体的道德归属。

随着现代化进程的日益急切，艺术也同样渴望进入现代性，革新的意识在个性发挥的文化层面上有了进一步要求，尤其在年轻艺术家身上更加明显。

罗中立《父亲》（1981）

1985年，罗伯特·劳生伯（Robert Rauschenbery）在中国美术馆举办展览。当年轻的中国艺术家正在具象的范围内徘徊不定的时候，突然亲眼看到这些现成物的作品，几乎称得上是一场地震，原来艺术也可以这样妄为。接着有各种途径了解到"军械库"（Armory Show）、惠特尼（Whitney Biennial）、杜尚（Duchamp），等等，当然还有欧洲的前卫艺术。艺术上的激进派在85美术运动之后一路狂奔，直到1989年的中国现代艺术大展之后才稍有停顿。西化的热情开始消退，本土性的文化自觉成为一个新的课题。

上个世纪90年代后，一个新的潮流凸显了，那就是"政治波普"。它的兄弟是安迪·沃霍尔式的美国波普艺术，不过一个是资本主义的消费文化面孔，一个是无产阶级的政治符号，天涯若比邻。大概在这个时候，麦当劳开始进入中国，美国大片开始以每年十多部的分账模式在中国公映，中国开始领略全球化的症候。

在中国当代艺术的进程中，不可否认的是，几个关键节点与美国艺术的渗入大有关系。我也亲历了这变化的过程，一边观察，一边实践，同时也思考其中的对应关系，以及矛盾之所在。

一个事实是，以我的观察，在所有的国家中，美国是拥有中国传统艺术资源最丰富的国家，对中国传统文化的研究和推广也是相当有成就的。我在大都会博物馆看到有关中国艺术的藏品，也去波士顿博物馆的库房拜观心仪已久的唐宋以降的作品，还有一些大学博物馆里来自中国的艺术收藏，可以称得上是叹为观止。当我在美国看到这些作品，大有一种"梦里不知身是客，错把他乡当故乡"的感觉，我相信美国观众也会对这种山高水远的境界怀有一种赞赏。

美国的多元文化特点使世界各地区的文化传统得到相应的尊重，在中国艺术方面，纽约古根海姆博物馆在1998年举办了声势浩大的"中华文明艺术5000年"大展，这个展览戏剧性地分为两部分，即古代和近现代，看起来像是"一国两制"，因为社会观和美学的根本不尽相同。但新中国以后的社会主义艺术，也为美国观众理解"政治波普"的来龙去脉补了一课，集体主义的时代烙印与个人记忆是怎样的变体关系。这种联系固然有其合理性，中国当代艺术的历史追溯并不能在这里结束。

在它的上游，一个源远流长的文化传统有着更宽阔的伦理景观，一个包含深厚美学体系的文明遗嘱如何在今天有所延伸，不可能是视而不见的问题。如何沿着这样的脉络继续呈现创造性，从意识形态转移到美学，是一个更高层次更有挑战性的课题。

对传统的再生这一课题的讨论体现在中美艺术界的共同理解上，而且也以行动付之实现。例如将要在波士顿博物馆举办的"与古为徒——十个中国艺术家的回应"就体现了有意思的策划，艺术家每人选出一件波士顿美术馆举世闻名的馆藏精品来呼应创作，以当代艺术的多样性和创造性，对应古代作品并列而置，诠释今天的艺术同几千年中国文明丝丝缕缕的联系。刚刚在北京大学举办的中美专家对当代水墨的学术讨论，也是在类似的维度上开展讨论。

全球化以千篇一律的复制方式提倡经济的共通模式，这对地区文化的保存和创造性有很大的冲击。在中国当代艺术中，市场的强大魔力和推销模式,使一部分符合国际通识的艺术得到价值的认同,而那些坚持以中国传统美学体系开拓的艺术被冷落,这使得更多的年轻人出现选择的偏好。举例来说,在中国的艺术院校,过去只有最好修养的年轻人才能考入中国画科,而现在中国画科乏人问津,因为在文化修养和技术训练上,是需要相对漫长的准备时期,但现在进入了一个即时性、短暂性、娱乐性的时代,从某种角度说,这也是美国艺术的性格,它给艺术家一种幻象,似乎这是艺术的新灯塔,由此便能迈入国际化的通道,代表着成功和利益。再也没人相信技艺,也无力深入思考文化的乡愁。

2008年,我受美国国会图书馆亚洲部的邀请,在那里作了"传统的复活"的专题演讲,其中谈到中国传统美学特点在今天全球化的格局中遭遇到的尴尬和困难。简单地说,中国传统文化内敛的力量、隐喻的作风、时空的架构和宇宙的精神与美国文化的价值观是有很大的差别,而当今全球化的文化特征更多是参考了美国的价值体系,托克维尔在《论美国的民主》中说到,"民主时代的文学,它的作者只求快速,而不愿意细腻描写……作家追求的目的,与其说是使读者快慰,不如说是使读者惊奇。作家们的努力方向,与其说是使人感到美的享受,不如说是使人兴奋激动"。艺术的情形也如此。

中国文化的"植物性"和西方文化的"动物性",在气质上是不同类型。而在艺术创造的经验上,美国文化代表着一往无前的精神,目标在前方,是进化式的。而中国人的传统看法略有不同,在前进的道路上,同时需要关注前行之车的后视镜,历史的视野是他前进的动力。

对中国文化来说,文化的活力代表着综合的天赋,这样的例证有很多。如今我们在开放视

野、对其他文明的接受的程度非常之广这方面和美国有相似之处。文化气场的互移，文化气质的互补，是一个特别有魅力的事情。关键的问题是，我们应该在多大程度上按世界主义的方式行事，在多大程度上遵循本土与个别的原则，这是决定现代人类文明多样化的保障。

今年年初我在纽约举办了个人展览，希望通过自己的现代视野重新观照中国传统美学的价值，表现另一种中国当代艺术的态度。正如这个展览的主题一样，"密响旁通"——这是公元465年刘勰在《文心雕龙》中的说法，我想，个人的多样性和世界文化的多样性一样，它的力量也可以是"润物细无声"的。跨文化的相互注视、互相交流、相互修正、相互肯定，能使彼此的社会和文明提高到一个新的境界，同时也会鼓励更多的创造力来丰富人类新的文明生态。

Silent Voice, Permeating Echoes
—— The Sino-American Artistic Exchanges in My Observation

Xu Lei

Research Fellow of
Research Center for
Creation,
Chinese National
Academy of Arts

Abstract: It is undeniable that during the process of modernization of Chinese contemporary art, several key points are related to the penetration of American culture. U.S. owns the richest resources of traditional Chinese arts and has made considerable contribution for the research and promotion of traditional Chinese arts among all countries. For Chinese culture, the dynamics of culture represents the natural gift to synthesize. Nowadays, our open mindset accommodates to a very great extent alien civilizations, which resembles the American way in many aspects. It is very charming to have cultural interactions and mutual-supplementation of cultural spirit. The most important question is to what extent we should behave in the way of universalism and to what degree we should follow the principle of localism and individualism. This decision shall guarantee the diversity of human civilization.

At the beginning of this year, I visited an American artistic collector in Boston. He invited me to visit a storehouse where many Chinese Buddhist pagoda models were arranged neatly. He told me that these were exhibits for the Expo 1915 San Francisco. At that time, a church in Shanghai organized some Chinese orphans to elaborately replicate with good timber 85 Buddhist pagodas in China by the ratio of 1:50. These pagoda models were sent to the U.S. for exhibition, and then were left there. Being changed in several hands, finally, they came to this collector.

This year, the World Expo was held in Shanghai. These ancient pagoda models made 95 years ago remind people naturally the history of cultural exchanges between the U.S. and China. No matter active learning or passive receipt, it is a memorable history of symbolic significance.

The cultural exchanges between China and the U.S. can be dated back to a long time ago in several fields which should be further studied by the relevant experts. As an artist who has gradually matured since the 1980s, I witness how the Sino-American cultural exchanges started, developed, matured and stand as a testimony to history during the years of restoring Sino-American diplomatic relationship. I saw and participated in this process.

In my memory, in Shanghai Museum, 1981, no sooner had I got enrolled in the college of art than I for the first time saw an exhibition of large scale—Exhibition on the American Original Paintings of Museum of Boston. I remember very well how I was shocked by the poster of Man Who Strikes the Bell. As a forerunner, this exhibition was important for Chinese to understand American culture and society after 30 years of closed-door history. It might be out of a consideration for Chinese social milieu at that time that the exhibits were pre-modern in style. Fortunately we actually saw the original status of American natural and civic life. Personally speaking, it is my first close contact with the West.

At that time, a thousand things wait to be done in China. There are too many lessons for us to take as remedy for what we lost. We have to restore the understanding of our traditional culture and the heritage and modernity of Western culture as well. Ahead us, there are forerunners, and behind us, there are followers. So in those days, we have new things from all directions, and we found little time to cope with all of them. For instance, we recited poetry of Tang and Song dynasties while reading the English rewriting version of Chinese poetry, such as Amy Lowell's imitation of the techniques exercised in Chinese poetry and Ezra Pound's recreation of Chinese images in his poems. Even though his poems might be a misreading of Chinese culture, it brought us fresh air. Classics and new footnotes provide us both the old tastes and new enlightenments.

In my point of view, American artistic expression features unbounded freedom which differs from the existence of prevalent allusions, histories, metaphors in European arts. In American arts, there is a direct form of expression, the most original vitality, and humble feelings shared by common people, and the visual experience of no difference, American arts soon found resonance from Chinese artists.

To look back, the representative works in the early 1980s, for example, Father by Luo Zhongli discarded the popular artistic style of the Soviet Union and absorbed the technique of American photorealism with a vivid depiction of details. This picture caused a great sensation at that time. Almost at the same time, the sentimental style of Andrew Wyeth integrated with the so-called Scar Art. It was fully presented in the paintings by He Duoling especially. These Chinese paintings have logic counterparts in American art which promotes again the humanist ideas and the relationship between the earth and the humanity and the association between life and feelings. At the level of humanist compassion, this resonance narrates the moral belonging of individuals.

As the progress of modernization is accelerated, modernity is also been intensively called in the field of art. The awareness for innovation has been further inquired at the cultural level for liberating

Luo Zhongli *Father* (1981)

individual character, and it is especially obvious among young artists. In 1985, Robert Rauschenbery held an exhibition in China National Art Gallery. As young artists who were still lingering in the realm of concrete objects saw these works made of ready products, they were shocked that how could these artists be so reckless. After that, they got access to Armory Show, Whitney Biennial, Duchamp and the avant-garde arts in Europe. The artistic radicals ran like mad since the Art Movement initiated in 1985 without stop until 1989 when the Chinese Modern Art Exhibition was held. After that, the fervor of westernization began to recede and the awareness of native culture became a new issue.

Since 1990s, a new trend became prominent, called "Political Pop" which is in brotherhood with American Pop art by Andy Warhol. The only difference is that one is of capitalist consumerist culture and the other is marked with proletariat political signs – just as the saying goes: a bosom friend afar brings distance near. Probably at this time, MacDonald's began to make a landing in China, over ten Hollywood block-busters began to be shown in China a year in the income-sharing model, and China began to have the symptom of globalization.

It is undeniable that during the process of modernization of Chinese contemporary art, several key points are related to the penetration of American culture. I experienced the changes and thought about the possible relationship between them and where the discrepancy lies through my observation and practice.

According to my observation, one fact is that the U.S. owns the richest resources of traditional Chinese arts and has made considerable contribution for the research and promotion of traditional Chinese arts among all countries. Once I saw the collection of Chinese artistic works in Metropolitan Museum of Art, the works since the Tang and Song dynasties which I long admired in the storehouse of Boston Museum, and works in some college museums. I was really amazed. As I appreciated these works, I had a feeling that I had mistaken the foreign land as my hometown, or I was in my dream. I believe American audience will appreciate the feeling of enjoying being faraway from home.

All the regional cultural heritages were respected accordingly in the multicultural America. As for Chinese art, the Guggenheim Museum hosted a massive exhibition called 5,000 Years History of Chinese Civilization and Arts in New York, 1998. The exhibition was dramatically divided into two parts: the ancient and the modern. It looks like one country and two systems because of the fundamental differences in social values and aesthetics. The socialist culture since the birth of the People's Republic of China began to help American audience understand the history of Political Pop, and how the collectivism's mark turned to be individual memory. Though this association is partly rational, he history of contemporary Chinese art cannot be stopped right here.

In the upper reaches of the river of history, there is broader ethic scenery of cultural heritage. It is unavoidable to think about how to inherit the will of a civilization with a profound aesthetic system. It is a great challenge of a higher level for us to follow this route, to continue our creativity, and to shift from ideology to aesthetics.

The discussion on how the cultural heritage can be regenerated has led to a consensus and will be put into practice. For example, there will be an exhibition called "Fresh Ink: Ten Takes on Chinese Tradition" held in Boston Museum. In the interesting plan, every artist will choose one piece of elaborate works from the world-famous collections in Boston Museum to match their creation. The diversity and creativity will be posited in correspondence to ancient works to illustrate the indivisible relationship between contemporary art and Chinese civilization of thousands years of history. The academic seminar on contemporary Chinese paintings held in Peking University with attendance of both Chinese and American experts had discussions on similar dimensions.

The shared-model of economy which is promoted through the way of universal duplication has had great impact on the conservation and creativity of regional cultures. For contemporary Chinese culture, the magic power of market and promotion mode has made the arts be identified as valuable based on international standard, while those arts adhering to pioneering traditional Chinese aesthetic systems are left out. As a result, young people began to show their preference in the genre of arts. For example, in the past only those young men with finest self-cultivation can get enrolled in the department of Chinese painting while now few people are interested in it. This is because in this time of transience, instantaneity, entertainment, it is unrealistic for young men to choose a discipline which calls for long-time preparation of cultural education and technical training. From certain perspective, this phenomenon is the natural result of the character of American art which produces a vision for artists that as if this is the new beacon of art and guided by it young artists can get on the watercourse of internationalization which represents success and benefits. So, no one trusts techniques, and no one is capable of thinking deeply into the nostalgia of culture.

In 2008, I received an invitation from Asian Division of the Library of Congress and delivered a keynote speech entitled The Resurrection of Tradition on the embarrassment and challenges met by traditional Chinese aesthetics in today's globalized structure. To put it simply, the introspective and metaphorical characteristics of Chinese traditional culture, its structure of space and time, and its spirit of cosmos differ greatly from the values of American culture which are modeled by the culture of globalization. In "American Democracy", Tocqueville said that "the literature of democratic time pursues speed instead of detailed and subtle description...". What writers pursue is how to excite and surprise readers instead of how to make them feel happy. Their orientation is not aesthetic enjoyment but excitement. So is true of arts.

The vegetality of Chinese culture and the animality of Western culture belong to different genres in temperament. In the experience of artistic creation, American culture represents the reckless spirit whose goal lies ahead and whose process is revolutionary. In contrast, traditional perspective of Chinese is different. On the way of progress, the Chinese travelers have to look behind in the rearview mirror. The historical horizon is the motive power for his progress.

For Chinese culture, the dynamics of culture represents the natural gift to synthesize, and there are many illustrations for this point. Nowadays, our open mindset accommodates to a very great extent alien civilizations, which resembles the American way in many aspects. It is very charming to have cultural interactions and mutual-supplementation of cultural spirit. The most important question is to what extent we should behave in the way of universalism and to what degree we should follow the principle of localism and individualism. This decision shall guarantee the diversity of human civilization.

At the beginning of this year, I had a personal exhibition in New York. I hope I can view introspectively the values of traditional Chinese aesthetics with a modern perspective and to show another attitude of Chinese contemporary arts. As the theme of this exhibition entitled as Silent Voice, permeating echoes (a quotation from The Literary Mind and the Carving of Dragons – The Book of Literary Design written by Liu Xie in 465 A.D.) suggests, I think, the diversity of individuals as well as the diversity of cultures around the world have an unobtrusive and imperceptible power to cultivate and nurture. Trans-cultural mutual observation, communication, modification, and assurance will elevate respective society and civilization to a new state of mind and at the same time encourage more creativity to enrich the new ecology of civilizations of human beings.

在标记中表现自我

萨拉·辛纳克劳斯

美国南卡罗来纳大学
哥伦比亚大学绘画教授

内容提要： 我们能够在标记中找到自己。说到通过创造活动找寻个体的感觉，我发现我所教的学生。非常沉溺于绘画。他们受到牵引去绘画。他们被绘画所吸引，因为他们渴望绘画。绘画能够给予他们一条道路，让他们发现自我，表现自我。

我想谈的是关于积极转化的一种最终形式。我将绘画作为我主要动机的表达形式，所以我在南卡罗来纳大学教授绘画课程。我在积极转化中看待绘画，这是一种将我们周围世界以及我们内心世界转化成形象的方法，好让其他人能够进入到我们在这个世界上的经历，以及我们的思维中，它是内部与外部、他者与自我之间的交流。我认为，对于提供思想，图画本身处于一个独一无二的位置。在过去30年中，我们认为当代绘画是连接两种观点或者多种观点的枢纽。但是考虑到历史，着眼于传统，这既是新的、也是传统绘画的一面。捕捉你对面前物体新的、现实的感受，然后将其转化为标记，你实际捕捉到的这个物体，这个风景，以及与之相关联的更多的传统感觉，就是我所说的绘画。

许多人谈到绘画时，认为绘画过程是可见的。那是一个连接，二维或者三维的连接点，不只是纸上的墨水，纸上的印记，还有雕塑，你要移动材料，打碎后再堆积起来，你将关注与这些材料相关的行为。最后，当然，它是文化间的枢纽，关于这一点今天已经谈论了很多。标记本身起到了连接东方和西方的作用。这意味着将艺术家的精神在纸上表现出来。我认为绘画与这一观点息息相关。

从事绘画、在用标记语言表达的人们都以这种非常基本的"词汇"为基础，即位置、速度、持续时间、密度和压力，所有这些都与人体相关。这是一种赋予形象以生命力的方式。在梅雷图和波洛克的作品中，都使用了最基本的手迹，用墨水画的手迹，怎样让墨水在纸张上移动，怎样让我的身体成为艺术，为了创造出某种特殊的品质，触发一种反应，观看者对我而言非常重要，我的满意来自观看者，这种满意可以持续很长时间。当我开始在滑轮上运动，发现在纸上滑动的运动，这种经历让我通过身体看待我面前的一个物体，然后转化为标记，找到这些标记联系的对话。经过一段时间之后，图像本身便成为一种特别的生命形式，它开始呼吸，开始移动，你不知道会发生什么，这种开放的、试验的、充满希望以及直觉的标记，它们开始发挥作用。经过一段时间，这些标记可以激发一种创造形式，这种形式促成了对话，不再需要其他的形式。

其中，我认为我们能够在这标记中找到自己。说到通过积极的创造找寻个体的感觉，我发现我所教的学生非常沉溺于绘画，他们受到牵引去绘画，他们被绘画所吸引，因为他们渴望绘画。首先，绘画让他们认识自己，他们想要找到自身，绘画能够给予他们一条道路去发现自我，表现自我。他们想要了解世界，了解生活的方式，以及其中的内在联系，绘画成为更大规模对话的载体，更大规模的对话和绘画帮助他们了解彼此。艺术家甚至不去想纸上有什么，只是专注于物体本身，这是一种以温柔方式用眼睛去观察表面，然后你将这种经历记录在纸上。

绘画帮助我们更好地理解我们为什么要做这些事情，为什么这些事情帮助我们做出这些标记。我们寻找体系，寻找线条，寻找碎片之间的联系运动，然后尝试扩大这些运动，尝试把他们投入到更大的系统、更大的结构之中。人们可以再次看到其中的东西，关于启发本质的探讨已经有很多了，通过浓缩世界寻找我们所在世界的意义，这有一种自然的表现，所以这不是一对一的记录，而是启发，向这个世界倾诉。

我开始做剪纸，于是做了大量的三维工作。我注意到自己如何把这些纸片拼接，这件作品大约15英尺高，30英尺长，开始只是小片，一种微观有机体。但是当人们看这个作品时，发现了神奇之处，

产生好奇心，想要去触摸，想要融入其中，想要交流，因此人们很专注，很投入，而且迷失在这个小的微观世界里，这个小世界反映出我们所生活的大世界的一种联系。

我下个阶段的实践从这些共享的经历开始，从这些艺术诗歌和触觉开始，因此提出一个问题，我们怎样理解事物，不仅仅是个体，通过投入，通过行动，通过身体参与到标记的制作之中。

最后，作为结语，我想说，人们可以随时作画。我想我们今天讨论的重点是，书法标记仅是千百年来在纸上的一种工作。我认为现在是在我们的文化中作画的重要时刻，我们今天所探讨的桥梁和联系可以通过制度、也可通过个体来实现，我认为现在正是这种对话的大好时机。

Sara
Schneckloth

Professor of
Drawing, University
of South Carolina,
Columbia

Finding Ourselves within the Mark

Abstract: We can find ourselves within the mark.Talking about the sense of finding the individual through the activity of making, I find the students that I work with are drawn to drawing□ they are pulled to draw□They are attractive to draw because they have the hunger. Drawing gives them an avenue for self-discovery, self expression.

 I want to speak about a final form that in itself is an active translation. So I draw as my primary motive expression and I teach drawing around drawing program at the University of South Carolina. When I see the drawing in the active translation, it's a idea of taking the world around us and the world within us and translating it into a image that allow the access for others to entering to the world and our experience□to our minds. It's a flow between the two ways of being, the internal and the external, and the others and the self. Drawing itself ,I think, is a uniquely position to provide this kind of movement of thought. Contemporary drawing as we find in past 30 years or so is a hinge in such a way that it's connecting two sides, connecting multiple sides. But in thinking in terms of history and looking at the tradition , we cast to but on the side of traditional drawing, the active capturing the realistic of new sense of the object that in front of you and turning it into marks that you accurately to pick that thing, landscape, and the things associated with the more traditional sense of what I means to draw.

 A lot of people speak of drawing, they thought of the process visible. It's a hinge between the dependents, between the two-dimensional and three dimensional, if you thinking in terms solely of ink on the page, mark on the paper, contrasting to a sculpture practice for you are moving the materials, chuckled and piled up and you're going to be bubbled engaged with the concerns of the material. And finally, and certainly, it's a hinge between the cultures and this will be discussed extensively today. It's a mark itself that functions as a hinge between the east and west. It means to bring the spirit of the artist down to the page. I think drawing is deeply concerned with that idea.

People who are feeling with drawing, who are using this language of mark-based expressions are building on these very basic vocabularies of direction, speed, duration, intensity, pressure, all these concerned to the body. Both Mehretu and Pollock are using these very basic elemental scriptures, scripting of ink. And how the ink move across onto the page? Was my body as a art, making body need to do and in order to create a particular quality and in order to revoke a kind of reaction, and the viewer importantly to my self where I locate my satisfaction when I am making this kind of work. As I started in truckle and it was in finding that the central moment of slighting across the page and having this experience looking at something in front of me translating through my body into a mark and finding the conversation the belt between those marks overtime and image itself taking particular a kind of life and it starts to breathe, and starts to move, and through that it becomes more, and you don't know what is going to happen and this sense of openness, experimentation and hope and intuitive marking and they comes to play, and just singing overtime has the marks can inspire to create a form and the forms take on the dialogue without other forms.

And in it, I feel we can find ourselves within the mark. Speaking to the sense of finding the individual through the active of making, I find the students that I work with are drawn to drawing, they are pulled to draw, they are attractive to draw because they has the hunger, first to identify who they are, they want to find themselves and drawing give them an avenue for self-discovery, self expression. They want to understand the world, the way of living how they are inner connected and drawing being part of the larger drawing of dialogue, and a larger dialogue and drawing helps them understanding each other. The artist doesn't even think about what on the page here she is just focus on the subject and it's a gentle means wondering of eye over the surface what you observe and then you are recording this experience thing under the page.

Drawing is a way to understand a little bit better why I am making these things, why I am making help to make these mark. And I look for system, I look for lines and I look for moments of connection within a piece and then try to expend them and try to hold them out into larger system, larger structure and again people can possibly see something in, there's been a lot of discussion today about the inspirational quality of nature and finding meaning in our world through contemplation the world that has a natural referent, so it's not a one to one recording but it's inspired by and it revoked by and it speaks to being in the world.

And I had moving to cut paper and so doing a lot more three dimensional work and can see to myself how can I bring pieces figures more to lives for this piece approximately 15 feet tall 30 feet long and started with just small denomination of typhoons and kinds of micro organism to find within the ocean tycoon structures and just been amazed, but it's for people do when they look for this tycoon and finding the sense of wonder and curiosity and desire to touch and to be involved and talks to commingle, so you often go to notion found people and that would be focused, invested and lost in the small micro world that in fact mirror the larger world that we live in of a connection.

The next phase of my practice has been to go from this experience of the communal and of the artistic poetry and the tactile, so raising the question how do we understand things not just through individual and through tattoo input into, through action and through actually being physically involved in the making of mark.

So in final, in conclusion that I would like to say they can temporarily draw. I think the emphasis today in this discussion the calligraphic mark is just thousand of years of work on paper. I think it's very vital time for drawing in both our cultures. And the bridges and connections we are talking about making today are happening the institutionally but they are also happening through the individuals and I think it's a wonderful time to be having this conversation.

建筑的艺术：
内在体验与外在表现

钱以佳
"陶德·威廉斯与钱以佳建筑事务所"建筑师

内容提要： 在西方和东方，人们都是从外在评判建筑，它是一个商品，一个强烈的图像，一种广告的方式。但是一个伟大的建筑师会带给我们一个平和的缓慢的旅程，在这个建筑的内部，在我们的内心深处，这样的一个地方不是一种感觉，而是对那个地方的经历，是一个私人的领域。

我是美籍华人，或者换种说法，是第一代在美国出生的华人。几年前，我看到一本小说，书名是《典型的美国人》，作者是任璧莲。这是一个关于来自美国郊区的美籍华人青少年的故事。当我读这本书的时候，我觉得"天哪，这就是我，这就是我的生活"。当我做了一些让我父母非常非常生气的事情，我爸爸会对我说，"你就像是一个典型的美国人"。但是我并不是一个真正典型的美国人，我总是说，文化上我是百分之百的美国人，但是心理上我是个百分之百的中国人。这意味着我不会轻易表达我的情绪。当我非常生气的时候，我就保持沉默，我越是生气，就越沉默。

陶德·威廉斯是我的丈夫，合作伙伴，也是个建筑师。他说我筑造了一个沉默的长城，就像中国的长城，可以持续千年，能从月球上看到。因此对于我来说，内在即使不比外在表现更加重要，也是同等重要。作为一个建筑师，我认为建筑的主要力量在于内在。正是内在的力量使人们感动，令人们感到舒适，并给他们留下记忆。内在拥有外在难以匹敌的情感力量。想想这么一个地下室，特别当你是个孩子的时候，晚上在房中熄灯之前，想想你第一次做这些事，望向天空。这是强大的建筑经历之一，但是这个建筑的外表是静默的。事实是，正如我们所言，一个好的建筑，要平衡和满足从商品到生活的三个标准。这个实际的观点着重于人们体验的基础，而非它的外表。如今，在西方和东方，人们都是从外在评判建筑，它是一个商品，一个强烈的图像，一种广告的方式。但是一个伟大的建筑师会带着我们安静而缓慢地进入建筑的内部，进入我们的内心深处，到达可以想象的地方，那不是一种观念，而是对那个地方的体验，一个私人的领域。

这是曼哈顿的一个很小的博物馆，被称作美国图片博物馆。实际上，它是个现代艺术博物馆。但它非常小，展出非专业艺术家的作品。它非常坚固，具有造型感。没有必要马上看内部有什么。我们尝试使用非常粗粝的材料，水泥、玻璃，因为建筑师来自最不起眼的地方。可能使用一些艺术，顶部有一个很大的敞口，让阳光照射到中心。

第二个项目是艺术的边界。这是密西根的游泳池。也是一个非常安静的建筑。从外表看，它的窗户上有非常高的木质挡风棚，这个挡风棚开口很高。当你在里面时，屋顶上有两个很大的开口，直接向天空敞开，所以当你游泳时，会有一种非常强烈和集中的感受。这是你从外面无法意识到的，只有当你花些时间进入内部才能感受得到。

第三个项目是"斯塔东亚图书馆"。这是图书馆穹顶的背面。它是伯克利大学校园里的一个主要的图书馆，一座新古典主义建筑。我们想要建造一座与校园所有这些建筑浑然一体的、同时又具有东亚文学气息的建筑。所以我们决定使用屏风。再一次地，这个屏风在说，"我在这儿，我在场，但你不必认识我"。当行走在其中的时候，我想每个人都会感到惊奇，因为尽管从外部看它十分坚固，但内部非常开阔，你能感觉到与户外相连的光线，当你看着它时，没有必要特别清晰。从林间空地去看，这是一个神秘的地方，有阳光射进。那是自然天光，因为我们想要让上层楼面沐浴在自然生活之中。光线自然泻下，到达底层，就像我们所说的，将它描绘为一个坚固的盒子，打开时充满阳光。

当我年轻时，我想有所归属。但当我渐渐成熟，我意识到，我喜欢自己是两种文化的综合体。在很多方面，同处两个不同的位置是一个具有创造性的地位。你不会被具有很强文化身份的传统所束缚，你是个局外人，你可以移动，你是自由的。我问我的儿子，他是真正的东西方文化对话的产物，我问他认为自己是中国人，还是美国人，他回答说"我不是其中任何一方，我就是我"。所以从很多方式来看，这是一个周而复始的循环。最后，文化就是文化，伟大的作品就是伟大的作品。

Billie Tsien

Architect of *Tod Williams Billie Tsien Architects*

The Art of Architecture: Inner Experience and External Manifestation

Abstract: Both in the west and in the east, architecture is judged from the outside. It is a commodity, a powerful image and a way of branding. But a great architecture will take us on a quiet and slower journey inside the building, inside ourselves to that imaginable place; that is not the perception but the experience of that place, and it is the private place.

I am an American-born Chinese, other way known as ABC, first generation. A few years ago, I picked up a novel by a writer named "Gish Jen", called Typical American. This is a story of Chinese American teenager coming up from the edge of the American suburb. As I read the book, I thought "Oh, my god, that's me, that's my life". When I had done something that really made my parents very, very, very angry with me, my dad would say to me "You act just like a typical American". But I wasn't a really typical American and I often say that culturally I am 100% American, and psychologically I am 100% Chinese. This means that I keep much of my feelings inside. When I get angry, I am quiet, the angrier I am, the quieter I am.

Tod William is my husband, and partner and the architect, says that I put up the Great wall of silence and like the Great Wall of China; he says it can last 1000 years and you can probably see it from the moon. So for me, what is held inside is equally, if not more important than what expressed on the outside. As an Architect, I believe that huge part of the power of architecture lies on the inside. This was what touches people, what comforts some and what makes memories. The interior has the emotional power that seldom can be matched by the exterior, thinking of this base that was special to you as a child just before the lights were turned off in your room at night, think of the first time if you have done this, watch in the Penelope and look up the sky. This is one of the most powerful architecture experiences in the world, but the outside of the building is mute The truth is as we said the good building, balances and satisfies three criteria from this commodity into life. This actual view focus on how one's experience it is based not on how it appears. Too often today both in the west and now in the east, architecture is judged from the outside, it is a commodity, a powerful image and a way of branding. But a great architecture will take us on a quiet and slower journey inside the building, inside ourselves to that imaginable place that is not the perception but the experience of that place, and it is the private place.

So this is a small tiny museum in Manhattan, it called the American Photograph Museum. It's actually in the museum of modern arts. But it is a very, very small museum and it shows arts that made by untrained artist and it's sort of actually are all the very solid and much sculpted, it does not necessarily reviewed what's immediately inside. We try to use very humble material, concrete, glass, because the architect comes from the most humble routes. Some of these arts are maybe used, like these of whether being and it's a big opening at the top to bring the light down to the center.

The second called Art Boundary. This is a swimming pool in Michigan. To very, once again a quietly building on the outside it's very, very tall wooden shelters in the windows, this shelters opened high and when you are inside, two large opening in the roof have splendid back opening directly to the sky, so when you are swimming, it's a very powerful and central experiences, it's not one you realized from the outside but something you find when you take the time to go inside.

The third project is C.V. Starr East Asian Library. This is opposite the dome of the memorial library which is a primary library of Berkley campus, it's neo-classical building. We want to make a building that how to respond to the solidity of all these buildings on the campus but at the same time that this is the building of East Asian literature. And so we decide to use this idea of screen and once again it's the screen that says, "I am here, and I am present, but you don't necessarily know me". When you walk inside I think everyone who does is surprise because although it's solid from the inside it's rather from the outside, it is very open from the inside and you feel a sense of light connection to the outdoors and it is not necessary apparent when you see it. And from the glade and it's a kind of mysterious place with the light comes in. It's the skylight because we want to wash the upper floor with a natural life. And that light naturally move all the way down to lower level so that as we said we describe it as a solid boxes, as it is a kind of open with lights.

When I was young I want to belong. But as I grew older, I realized that I like to be a mix of two cultures. In many ways having your feet in two places is a creative place to stand. You are not bond by the tradition of strong cultural identity, you are an outsider, you can be a ship shifter and you are free. I asked our son, who is truly the product of east-west dialogue, whether he considers himself Chinese or American, and he answered "I am not one or the other, I am just who I am". So in many ways, this is cycle back to where we began, where we started. In the end, culture just is, great work just is.

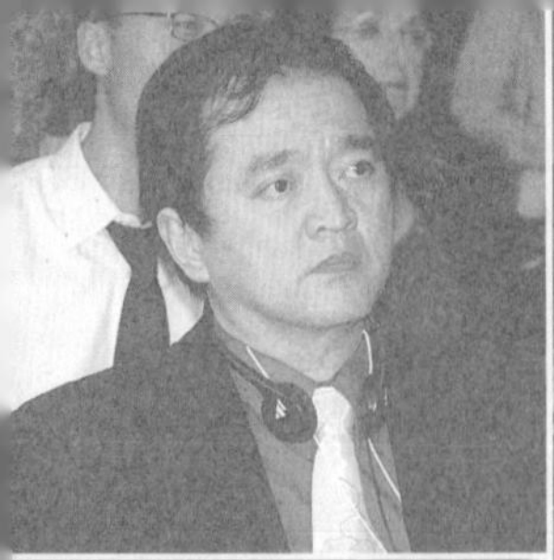
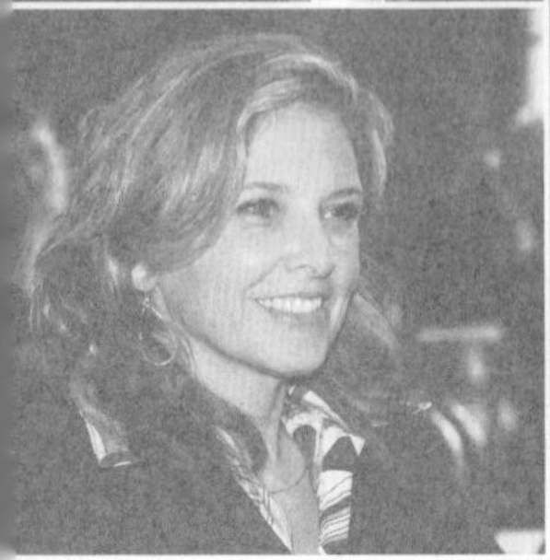
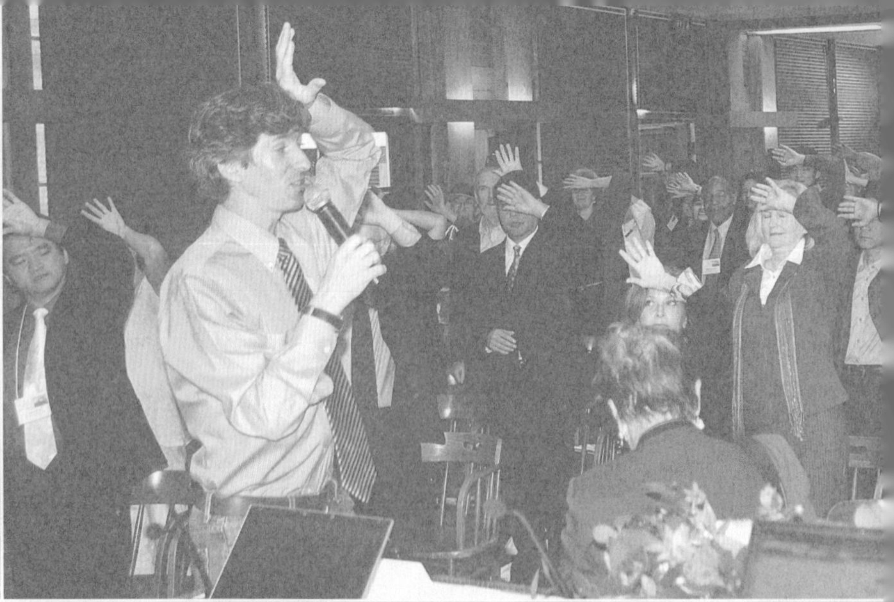
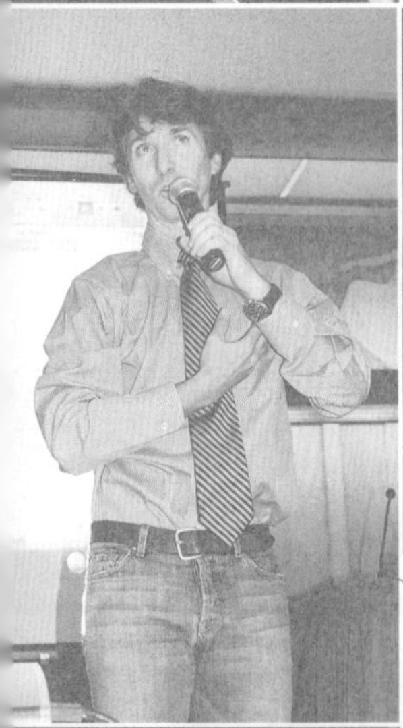
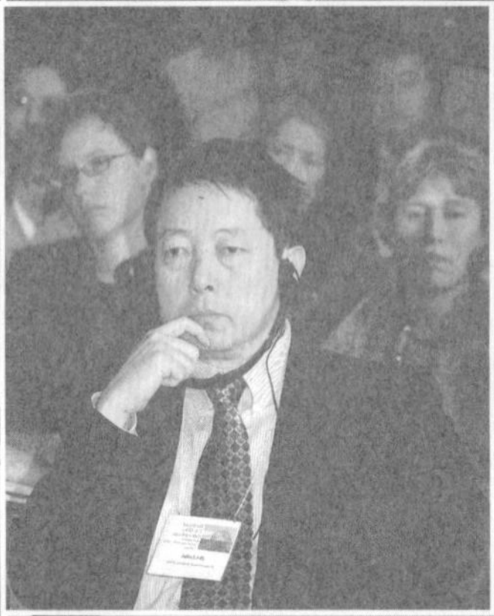
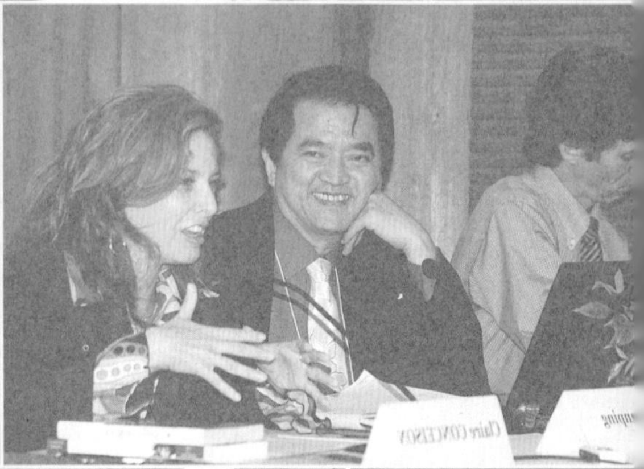
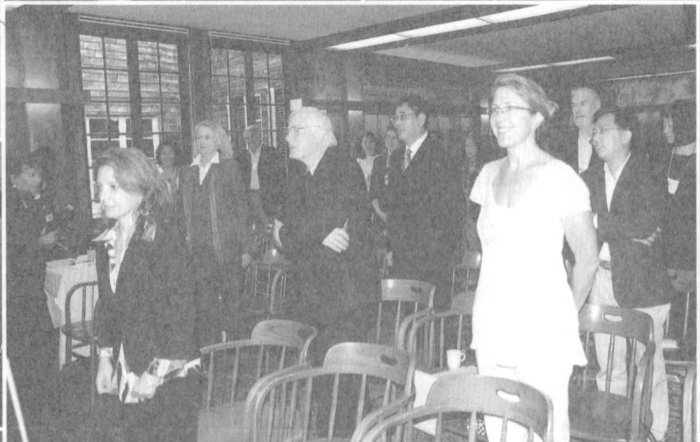
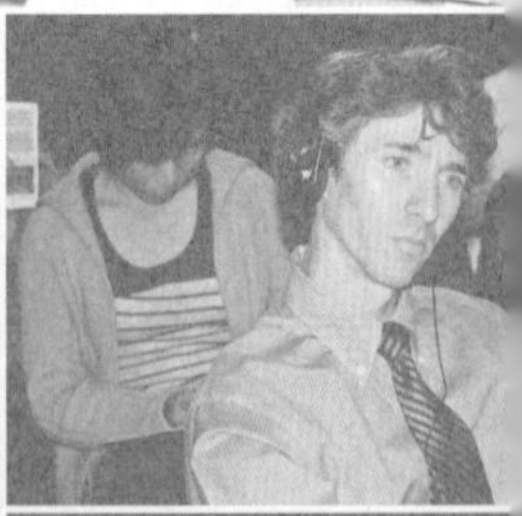
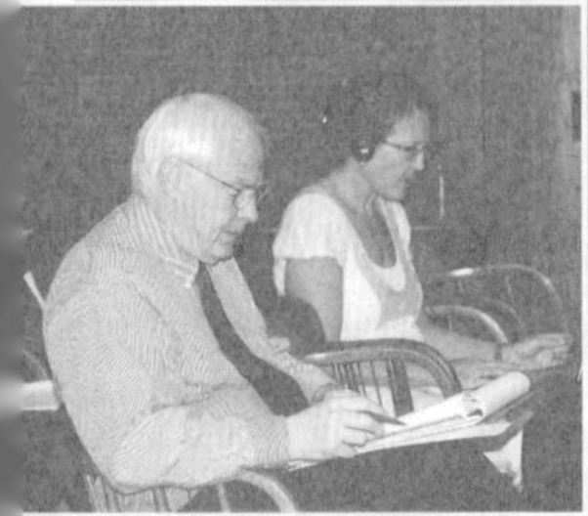
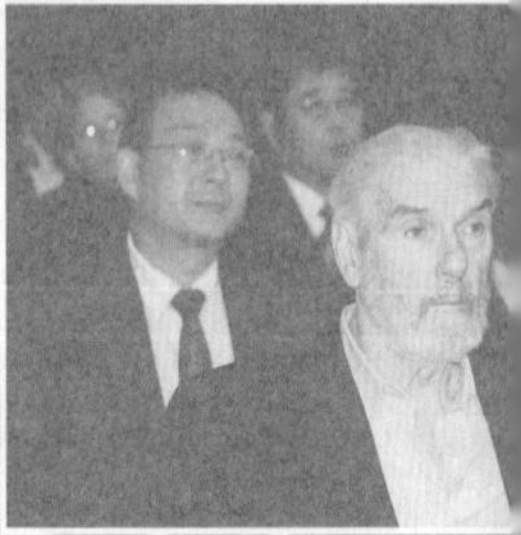
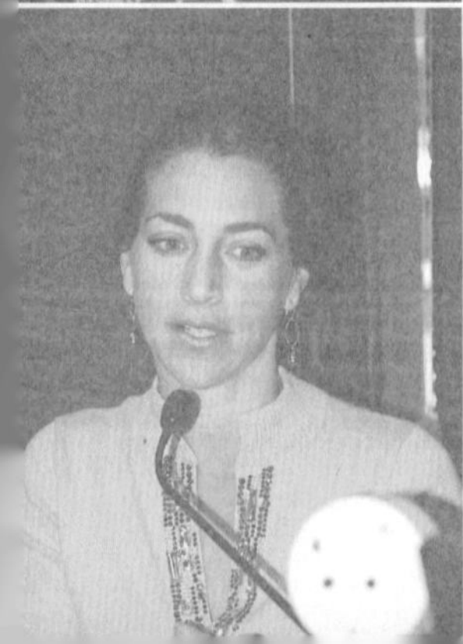
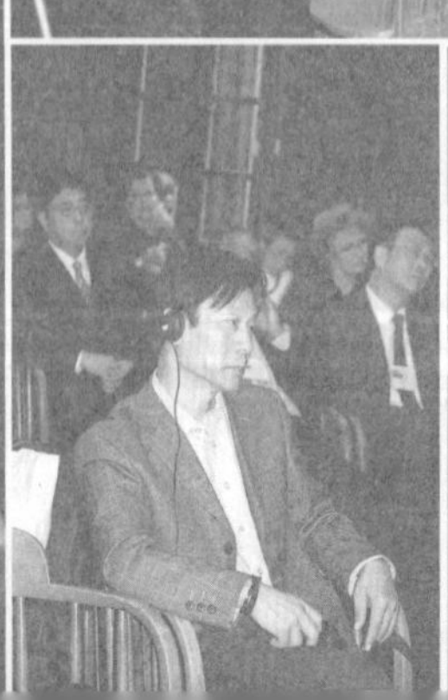
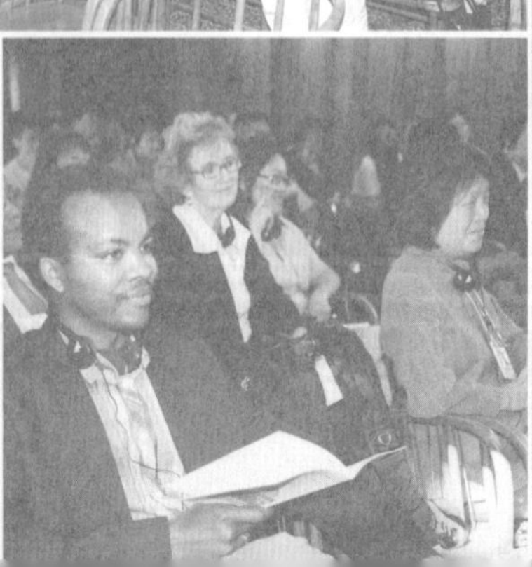
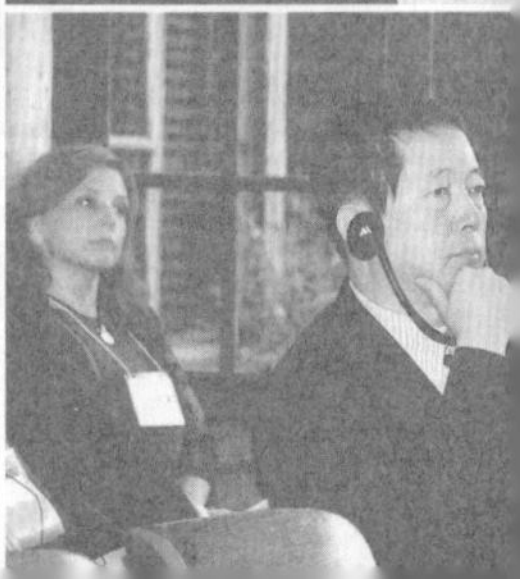

UNIT FOUR:
THE PERFORMING ARTS: COMPARATIVE PERSPECTIVES

第四单元
表演艺术比较观

美国总统艺术人文委员会执行主任瑞秋·格斯林斯
主持人导语
Rachel Goslins, Executive Director of the President's Committee on the Arts and Humanities
"Moderator's Introduction"

中国艺术研究院戏曲研究所所长刘祯研究员做主题发言
《文化时代与传统艺术的发展》
Liu Zhen, Research Fellow and Director of Institute of Traditional Operas,
Chinese National Academy of Arts
"Cultural Era and the Development of Traditional Arts"

美国杜克大学戏剧研究教授克莱尔·康塞逊 做主题发言
《中美文化交流的见证与阐释》

Claire Conceison, Professor of Theater Studies, Duke University
"The Witness and Interpretation of China - US Cultural Exchange"

中国艺术研究院舞蹈研究所副所长欧建平研究员做主题发言
《中美舞蹈交流的百年回首、现状一瞥与未来建议》

Ou Jianping, Research Fellow and Deputy Director of Dance Research Institute,
Chinese National Academy of Arts
"Dance Exchanges Between China and U.S.A.:
100 Years' Retrospective, Present Situation & Suggestions For the Future"

美国维尔国际舞蹈艺术节主任达米安·沃策尔做主题发言
《有意义交流的关键——参与》
Damian Woetzel, Director of the Vail International Dance Festival, USA
"The Key to Meaningful Exchange—Participation"

中国艺术研究院院长助理、文化发展战略研究中心主任贾磊磊研究员做主题发言
《跨文化交流中的理解误差》
Jia Leilei, Research Fellow and President Assistant of Chinese National Academy of Arts
Director of Cultural Development Strategy Research Center, CNAA
"Misinterpretation in Cross-cultural Exchange"

主持人导语

瑞秋·格斯林斯
美国总统艺术人文
委员会执行主任

我是瑞秋·格斯琳斯,美国总统艺术人文委员会的执行主任。非常荣幸能与舞蹈、戏剧、歌剧和电影领域的众多专家齐聚于此,这些都是我最喜欢的领域。与之前出场的很多主持人一样,我不仅对听我们杰出的专题讨论小组成员的发言感到兴奋,也对能有机会在这一单元结束前进行一些有趣的讨论感到激动不已。

昨天我们度过了精彩的一天,进行了引人深思的讨论。在我准备这个会议时,我曾考虑我们主题的特色是什么。我想到了两点。首先,昨天我们探讨了文学和视觉艺术,它们拥有丰富的内容可供挖掘。但今天上午,我们要谈论表演艺术。表演艺术是一个特别的领域,因为就其定义而言,它是需要观众的艺术。它不仅邀请、也强求一个共享的体验,一个叙事,需要黑暗的剧院中所有人同时相信,前提是演员、歌手或舞者恪尽其职。而这里存在非常动人的东西。

昨天,当我聆听各位杰出的发言人阐释他们的主题时,我听到了两种有趣的意见 —— 两种融合艺术的文化方法。一是个人表达的渴望,渴望冲突与解决;另一个是目的的和谐与一致。当处于最佳状态时,表演艺术能够实现这两个理想。表演艺术表达重要的、有时是激发情感的内容。通过舞者的线性表达,或演员朴实无华的独白,他们创造了一个让所有观众共同游历的神圣空间。

在这个空间里,可以交流很多事,也可以完美解决很多事。另外,关于观众而言,最重要的是使艺术家夜复一夜地保持诚实。我知道在本次论坛中提到了从孔子到沃尔特·惠特曼的很多杰出艺术家和学者。但我想要降低一些标准,提一下在中美文化关系会议上您不会想到的人，芭芭拉·史翠珊。芭芭拉说过，"观众是最好的评判者。不能对他们撒谎。真相把他们拉得更近。如果稍有迟滞，他们就会在下面咳嗽。"感谢你们还没有咳嗽，因为我即将完成任务。

关于今天早上的座谈会，我想到的第二个有趣的方面是电影类型，这也是我非常喜欢的。在这两天我们所讨论过的所有艺术学科，诸如绘画、雕塑、诗歌、戏剧等，中国都领先于美国至少四个世纪。在这些艺术闪过我们美国的艺术创始人的眼睛时，中国人已经在完善这方面的技艺了。但是电影是唯一一个同时在中美两国诞生的学科。1896年，美国第一部电影问世。1905年，中国制作了第一部记录京剧的电影。因此，我认为对这方面的必要分析是非常有趣的，可以了解到两国如何使用相同的工具以相同或不同的方式塑造其文化。

Rachel Goslins

Executive Director
of the President's
Committee on the
Arts and Humanities

Moderator's Introduction

My name is Rachel Goslins and I'm the Executive Director of the President's Committee on the Arts and Humanities. We're fortunate to have with us many experts in the field of dance, theater, opera, and film. This put together, are some of my favorite things in the world. Like many of the moderators who went before me, I'm particularly excited not only about hearing the presentations of our distinguished panelists, but also the opportunity to have some interesting discussion at the end of this session.

We had a wonderful day, a thought-provoking discussion yesterday, and as I was preparing for this session I was thinking about what was particular to our topic here. Two things came to my mind. First, yesterday we covered the literary and visual arts, which are very rich things to explore. But this morning, we're talking about the performing arts. And the performing arts are unique because they are by definition the arts that require an audience. They not only invite, but compel a shared experience, a narrative, that everyone in the darkened theater believes in at the same time. That is, if the actor or the singer or the dancer is doing their job. And there's something very powerful in this.

And as I listen to the distinguished speakers from yesterday expanding on their subjects, it was very interesting to hear two strands of thought. And two strands of cultural approaches to the arts merge. On the one hand, there's a desire for individualist expression, for conflict and resolution, and on the other, for harmony and unity of purpose. The performing arts, at their best, achieve both of these ideals. They express important and sometimes provocative content. Through the linear expression of the dancer or the quiet monologue of the actor and yet they create a sacred space where the whole audience is on the same journey together. And in that space many things can be communicated and many things resolved in perfect harmony. In addition, the great thing about an audience is that it keeps the artist honest, night after night. I know many distinguished artists and scholars have been quoted at this conference, from Confucius to Walt Whitman. But I'm going to lower the bar a bit, by quoting from, of all the people who you wouldn't expect to quote at a conference on Sino-

American cultural relations, Barbara Streisand. Barbara said, "The audience is the best judge of anything. They cannot be lied to. The truth brings them closer. And if the moment lags, they're going to cough." So thank you all for not coughing yet, I'm almost done.

The second thing that was interesting as I thought about the panel this morning is specific to the genre of film, which is a particular passion of mine. In almost all of the artistic disciplines we've discussed over these two days, painting, sculpture, poetry, theater - well, the Chinese have a head start on the Americans by at least four centuries. You were perfecting the craft in many of these disciplines before we were even a gleam in our founding fathers eyes. But film, film is the only discipline that was born in both of our countries at the same time. The first moving pictures were shown to an American audience in 1896. And by 1905, the first Chinese film was made, which was a recording of the Beijing Opera. So this is an area where, I think, it's imperative analysis will be especially interesting, to learn about the different ways our two countries have taken the same tool and used it to shape their culture in different or similar ways. And I look forward to Jia Leilei to lead this discussion on this topic.

文化时代与传统艺术的发展

刘祯

中国艺术研究院戏曲研究所所长，研究员

内容提要： 文化时代是中华民族伟大复兴的标志。传统艺术的保护和发展是建设21世纪文化时代的重要组成。文化时代，是一种文化和谐、具有文化创新机制的时代，是文化多元多样的时代，传统艺术丰厚的底蕴将极大地丰富人民群众的文化、精神需求，增强时代文化的历史感、厚重感，成为文化前行不竭的源泉和动力，使中华文化发扬光大，青春永在。

一、文化时代是人类社会发展的更高阶段

人类漫长的进化与发展经历了不同的历史时期，渔猎、农业、工业、科技和信息化、网络化时代等等，使人类从远古洪荒时代步入现代化的21世纪。这种进化由初级到高级、由简单到复杂，不断走向文明。所谓"文化"是指文治教化。汉代刘向在《说苑·指武》中说："凡武之兴，为不服也，文化不改，然后加诛。"显然，文化是一种高于、文明于兴武的行为和形态。在现代，文化是指人们在社会历史实践过程中所创造的物质财富和精神财富的总和。特指精神财富，如教育、科学、文艺等。文化时代是人类社会发展的更高阶段，恩格斯曾指出，人们首先必须吃喝住穿，然后才能从事宗教文化艺术等等社会活动。物质的满足是最基本的，却不是终极的，终极的是"宗教文化艺术等等社会活动"。亦如当代人类学家费孝通所向往的："我志在富民，这是不错的，但仅仅是富，还够不够？其实人是不会满足于吃饱穿暖的。人要安居乐业，这里的安乐就是高一个层次的追求，而这个追求要有一个物质基础，如果没有吃饱

穿暖就达不到这一点,就接触不到这最高一层。这最高一层的文化就是你们艺术家所要探索的东西。我的老师是不讲这些的,只讲到吃饱穿暖,大家满足人生的需要。需要什么呢？除了物质需要,还需要 art,也就是艺术。""现在我们人类的文化发展到哪里去,要发挥精神上的享受,发挥情绪上的感动朝着这条路线走,最终还是要走到一个艺术的世界里去,这就是人类最终的追求。"(《更高层次的文化走向》,《民族艺术》1999年第4期)费先生认为人类的最终追求是一个"艺术的世界",也即艺术的时代,亦即"文化时代",这是非常富有远见的。就20世纪后期发展来看,西方一些发达国家进入文化时代,日本首相大平正芳在1979就职典礼上讲到日本已经进入文化时代,他主张在日本的经济经历了70年代的高速发展以后,应该把经济成果投入到对文化的重视以及对地球社会的贡献,强调文化因素在当代的重要意义。1980年澳洲进入一个新的多文化时代。

二、中国的文化时代呼之将至

中国的文化时代呼之将至。关于这个问题,可以从三个方面来阐释。一、中国经济快速发展和中国综合国力的提升。经过改革开放30多年的发展,到2010年中国经济总量超越日本排世界第二,中国无论是在经济总量或者是在科技、整个综合国力方面的提升,可以看到我们经济建设为中心所取得的辉煌成就。这也是中国文化时代呼之将至的一个前提。二、在政治上,胡锦涛总书记在十七大报告里所提出来的推动社会主义文化大发展、大繁荣是前所未有的。使我们作为文化工作者深受鼓舞,它是在国家经济、科技和综合国力不断提升的历史背景下,一个国家民族文化自信心增强的反映和表现,21世纪一个文化的中国、中国的文化时代呼之将出。它吹响了一个文化时代到来的号角。三、在文化发展方面,这些年随着经济的发展,在政府的作为和对文化的重视方面,包括非物质文化遗产保护方面,应该说我们取得的成就也是有目共睹的。包括政府的一种投入,尤其是近些年来在非物质文化遗产保护方面取得的成绩特别瞩目,包括国家和省市县都在评选出各级的非物质文化遗产名录,从国家的层面、省市县不同的层面,加以保护和传承。而且在文化发展方面,这种成绩不仅体现在政府的作为和对文化重视方面,更体现在人的文化素质的提高和文化自觉方面。那我想中国改革开放这么多年以来，文化教育的发展应该说对人的文化素质的提高和文化自觉起到了积极的推动作用。

当然，中国文化时代是呼之将至，而不是已经来临，是进行时和未来时，不是已然完成。之所以这样讲，是想说在这样一种形势和趋势面前，我们所面临的任务也还是非常艰巨的。比如包括文化体制改革的问题，这些年在文化体制改革方面政府也加大了工作的力度，但问题与困难很多，探索一条符合文化艺术发展规律的运行体制是一项系统工程，牵一发而动全身，需要细致、周到考虑。无疑，改革能够取得多大成功会直接关系未来文化事业的发展和建设程度。

三、优秀传统文化是文化时代建设最基础和基本的资源

中华文化有数千年的历史，不仅创造了灿烂的中华文明，也是世界文明的源头活水。在人类漫长的历史演化中，不同种族和文化总是几经起伏，潮涨潮落，许多昔日的辉煌和神话曾几何时都已成为久远的回忆，随着历史的钟声渐远渐离。但中华文化不断经历新陈代谢，吐故纳新，以其顽强的生命力从远古走来，创造了一个个盛世佳期。它以民为本，以文化人，倡导仁爱、和谐，又有宽广的包容，所以数经浮沉和磨难而不灭。近代以来，中华民族多灾多难，备受屈辱，传统思想、文化也受到前所未有的责难和质疑，中国共产党的诞生，探索马克思主义与中国革命实践相结合的道路，开辟了中华文化新的纪元。新中国成立以来，民族民间文化、传统艺术得到保护和扶持，受到真正的重视。

党的十七大上胡锦涛总书记在报告里所提出的"推动社会主义文化大发展大繁荣"，是在这样一种历史背景和新时期改革开放以来近30年的发展、进步基础上总结出来的，它是贯彻落实科学发展观的重要内容。科学发展观的提出和社会主义文化建设新高潮的兴起，是在新时期30年来改革开放发展实践基础上认识和总结的，是中国共产党率领全国各族人民实现自己民族伟大复兴，是深刻揭示社会发展规律、被实践证明了的科学理论。在经历了经济的快速发展，科技日新月异的变化和综合国力的不断提升后，对文化、文化时代的认识和追求越来越成为人们的共识，文化的时代可以说是呼之欲出。诚如十七大报告指出的："当今时代，

文化越来越成为民族凝聚力和创造力的重要源泉，越来越成为综合国力竞争的重要因素，丰富精神文化生活越来越成为我国人民的热切愿望。"文化是一个人的思想，是一个国家的精神力量，注入了一个民族的灵魂。文化时代是中华民族伟大复兴的标志。

在一个世界经济走向一体化、人类越来越成为地球村的时代，学习、借鉴和吸收外来文化是必不可少的，但作为一个有几千年文明的中国，民族思想文化、传统艺术应该是我们建设这个文化时代最基础和基本的资源。这正如十七大报告所阐述的"中华文化是中华民族生生不息、团结奋进的不竭动力。要全面认识祖国传统文化，取其精华，去其糟粕，使之与当代社会相适应、与现代文明相协调，保持民族性，体现时代性。加强中华优秀文化传统教育，运用现代科技手段开发利用民族文化丰厚资源。加强对各民族文化的挖掘和保护，重视文物和非物质文化遗产保护，做好文化典籍整理工作。"在经历了对民族文化遗产肆意的践踏和曲解、经历了一切都是外国的好之后，新时期的中国人日益理性与成熟；在经历了一个经济快速发展和人们追求物质需求的温饱满足后，人们对文化意义的认识更为深刻。

四、当代对传统艺术的保护和发展

1949年新中国成立后，民族文化和传统艺术走过了一条不寻常的发展之路。新的社会制度的建立，思想观念的改变，使人们对历来不被重视和排斥的民间文化和传统艺术的认识，提高到一个前所未有的地位。民间文化、传统艺术历来处于文化艺术发展的边缘，不被官方和正统力量所接受，被鄙夷之为下里巴人的玩意儿。新中国成立以后，这些民间文化、传统艺术，包括戏曲、曲艺、舞蹈、民歌、年画、剪纸等等都因为其创作所蕴涵的人民性而备受推崇，过去低贱的艺人成为"人民艺术家"，是天与地的变化。20世纪五六十年代，民间文化斑斓绚丽，异常活跃，民间艺人艺术创造力空前高涨，大量民间文化、传统艺术得以重现天日，得到保护和发展。这是中国历史上从未有过的文化革命、思想革命，它的身份第一次使它那么荣耀。"文革"十年，是又一次惊心动魄的"革命"，民间文化、传统艺术作为表现才子佳人、帝王将相的主要形式，被扫除、禁止。

新时期以来所经历的比较复杂，大致有三个阶段。一是新时期伊始，民间文化、传统艺术的重现生机，在20世纪80年代初中期，如雨后春笋，扑面而来，使广大人民群众欢心鼓舞，思想解放，精神的桎梏被卸掉，带来了一个"文艺的春天"，包括许多民间文化、传统艺术在内的文化艺术长足的发展。而随着经济建设的发展，一段时间里文化地位被削减，许多人许多地方成为服务于经济建设的手段和工具。最典型的是"文化搭台，经济唱戏"，不仅物质需求上追崇西方，精神文化领域亦充斥西方文化物欲、快捷、感性的特性，传统再次跌入深谷，轰鸣的马达不仅建起了一座座摩天大楼，也铲去和切割了我们许多传统的根脉，造成新的破坏。而当经济发展到相当程度时，人们对文化地位和价值的审视更趋客观和冷静，随着民族文化自信心的提升，人们对民族文化、传统艺术愈益热爱和喜欢，经济发展与社会和谐发展就成为必然，提高国家文化软实力就显得尤其重要，贯彻落实科学发展观重大战略思想的意义愈益显示。

民族文化、传统艺术的保护、研究和非物质文化遗产的保护这些年来的发展和景象就是在新世纪这样的背景下取得的。传统艺术的保护和发展是建设21世纪文化时代的重要组成，尽管我们已经失去了许多，许多已经不能再生和复制，但尚属及时，随着昆曲艺术2001年被列入联合国教科文组织"人类口头和非物质文化遗产代表作"以来，人们——尤其是年轻人渴望了解自己的民族文化和传统艺术，越来越多的年轻人、大学生喜欢昆曲，喜欢京剧，喜欢地方戏和传统艺术。保护是手段，发展是目的，这些年传统艺术出现了"热"点，演出、出版、教育、研讨等活跃纷呈，传统艺术有个性弱化之失，但整体艺术有比较全面的提高，传统艺术不仅是当代艺术的源泉，本身依然焕发出迷人的芬芳。而文化时代的呼之将来，伴随的是文化艺术的大发展大繁荣，借此东风，传统艺术的保护和发展也成为全民共同关注的内容。传统艺术有其不适应当代审美和习惯的一面，但从内容到形式一直是百姓大众所喜闻乐见的，滋养了一代代观众群众，是人们审美和接受知识传播、教育普及的主要方式，是构成中华民族共有精神家园的内容。文化时代，是一种文化和谐、具有文化重新机制的时代，是文化多元的时代，传统艺术丰厚的底蕴将极大地丰富人民群众的文化、精神需求，增强时代文化的历史感、厚重感，成为文化前行不竭的源泉和动力，使中华文化发扬光大，青春永在。

Cultural Era and the Development of Traditional Arts

Liu Zhen

Research Fellow and Director of Institute of Traditional Operas, Chinese National Academy of Arts

Abstract: The cultural era marks the great renaissance of the Chinese nation. The protection and development of traditional arts is an important part of building the cultural era of the 21st century. The cultural era is an era of cultural harmony and diversity, with cultural innovation mechanisms. In this era, traditional arts will greatly enrich the cultural and spiritual needs of people, enhance the sense of history of the era, and become the inexhaustible source and driving force of cultural development, thereby carrying the Chinese culture forward till eternity.

I. The Cultural Era is the highest form of human society

In its long history of evolution and development from prehistoric times to modern times, humanity has been through different historical eras i.e. the fishing and hunting era, the agricultural era, the industrial era, the era of technology and information, the era of network. In Chinese, culture means 'to rule by etiquette and to educate and enlighten'. Liu Xiang, a Chinese scholar in the Han Dynasty (202 BCE-220 AD), says in his book Shuo Yuan ('Discourse'), 'Force is used in case of disobedience; when education and enlightenment do not work, punishment follows.' Evidently, in Chinese culture, 'to educate and enlighten', or wenhua, is a means superior to and more civilized than force. In modern times, culture, or wenhua in Chinese, is the sum of all material and spiritual wealth created by humanity in their social and historical practice. More specifically, it means spiritual wealth, such as education, science, literature & art. The Cultural Era is the highest form of human society. As pointed out by Friedrich Engels, people have to satisfy their fundament needs for food, housing and clothing before they engage themselves in social activities including religion, art, etc. The fulfillment of material needs is fundamental, but it is by no means man's ultimate goal. The ultimate goal is to satisfy the spiritual needs represented in 'social activities such as religion, art etc.' Fei Xiaotong, contemporary anthropologist, once expressed his yearning, saying, 'I aspire to make the people rich. There is nothing wrong about that. However is it enough to get rich? In fact, man will never be content with just feeding and clothing themselves. People often say they want to live and work in peace and contentment. Here peace and contentment represent pursuits of a higher plane. Such pursuits should first of all have a material basis – without sufficient food and clothing, they are not likely to be considered; moreover, they are not things explored exclusively by artists. But my teacher never touched upon that. He only covered sufficient food and clothing and discussed people's effort to fulfill their needs in life. What do they need? Besides material needs, they also need art.' 'Now, in what direction should human culture develop? We should seek to attain pleasures of the spirit, to get ourselves emotional touched. If we advance along this route, we will eventually enter the sphere of art. That is precisely the ultimate pursuit of humanity'. (Cultural Trend of a Higher Plane, published in the April, 1999 issue of Ethnic Arts). Mr. Fei believes that humanity's ultimate pursuit is a 'world of art', i.e. the era of art, or the Cultural Era. That is indeed very insightful. In the late 20th century, some advanced Western countries entered the Cultural Era. For example, at his inauguration ceremony in 1979, then Japanese Prime Minister Masayoshi Ohira observed that Japan was already in the Cultural Era and argued that, after the rapid economic growth in the 1970s, the economic achievements should be translated into the stress on culture and contribution to the global community. He also emphasized the significance of cultural factors in the present age. Australia announced its entry into a 'new cultural era' in 1980.

II. The era of Chinese culture is around the corner

The era of Chinese culture is around the corner. This assertion may be proved from three aspects. Firstly, both China's economy and its comprehensive national power have grown greatly. After three decades' development since Reform and Opening up policy, in 2010, China's GDP surpassed Japan's and China became the second largest economy in the world. The remarkable advances it has achieved in economy, technology, and comprehensive national strength has been universally recognized. These constitute a prerequisite for the advent of China's cultural era. Secondly, politically, as General Party Secretary Hu Jintao said in his address to the Seventeenth Congress of CPC that the government will strive to promote the unprecedented development and prosperity of socialist culture. At this we cultural workers feel particularly thrilled. That is a sign of China's boosted confidence of its national culture against the historical background of constantly growing economy, technology, and comprehensive strength. The emerging China is ushering in its cultural era in the 21st century. This goal put forth by General Secretary Hu in his report at the 17th CPC Congress heralds an era of cultural prosperity around the corner. Thirdly, in terms of cultural development, with the development of economy, these years have witnessed the Chinese government invest more on culture and make cultural development a great priority. The achievements made intangible cultural heritage protection, for example, is evident to all. China has made remarkable achievements in this regard. Lists of intangible cultural heritages have been made at state, provincial and county levels so that these valuable properties can be protected and carried forth. The work in the cultural field has been done with flying colors. Cultural development manifests itself not only in government efforts and in its more stress on culture, but, more importantly, in the improvement of Chinese people's educational level and cultural awareness. Since the introduction of the reform and opening up policy, the advancement of cultural education has played a positive role in bringing about the improvement.

The era of Chinese culture is around the corner. Of course, this does not mean that it has arrived, because, given the current situation and trends, we are confronted with arduous tasks. A case in point is the reform of cultural administrative system. Over the recent years, the government has increased its bid in this respect. However, problems and difficulties still abound. To build a new system consistent with the laws for the development of culture and art calls for systematic efforts, which may be ruined because of one tiny slip. Therefore, meticulousness and considerateness are required. No doubt, the success of this reform directly determines the future development and construction of the cultural undertaking.

III. Fine traditional culture is the primary source of momentum for the construction of the Cultural Era

Chinese culture has a history of thousands of years. Not only did it give birth to the splendid Chinese civilization, but it has also been one of the inexhaustible fountainheads of world civilization. In the long history of mankind, ethnic groups and cultures have risen and declined. Many glories have faded into legends and memories. However, Chinese culture has kept evolving constantly, retained its robust growth, and flourished many a time. Human-centered, it focuses on education, advocates benevolence and harmony, and is especially tolerant. That explains why it has sustained itself through so many vicissitudes and tribulations. In modern times, the Chinese nation suffered disasters and calamities and endured numerous humiliations. As a result, traditional philosophy and culture were subjected to unprecedented censure and skepticism. At this juncture, the Communist Party of China was founded and launched its attempt to combine Marxism and the practice of Chinese revolution, thereby ushering in a new age of Chinese culture. Since 1949, folk culture and traditional arts have been protected and supported. They began to receive serious attention.

General Party Secretary Hu Jintao said in his address to the Seventeenth Congress of CPC that the government will strive to promote the unprecedented development and prosperity of socialist culture. That goal has been set in the above-mentioned historical background on the basis of the development and progress in the nearly 3 decades of Reform and Opening up. It is an important measure of implementing the scientific outlook on development. The proposal of the scientific outlook on development and the new wave of socialist cultural construction have been based on a thorough understanding of the practice in the past 3 decades. They represent the Party's new bid to lead the people of all nationalities towards the great rejuvenation of the Chinese nation. The scientific outlook on development is a practice-proven scientific theory that sheds light on the laws of social development. After three decades' rapid economic growth, technological advancement and strengthening of the comprehensive national power, it has become people's consensus to understand and pursue culture and the Cultural Era, which can be said to be around the corner. As stated in Hu's address to the 17th Congress of CPC, 'In the present era, culture has become a more and more important source of national cohesion and creativity and a factor of growing significance in the competition in overall national strength, and the Chinese people have an increasingly ardent desire for a richer cultural life.' Culture manifests itself in a person's mind and a country's spiritual strength that can be injected into a nation's geist. The advent of the cultural era is a sign of the Chinese nation's rejuvenation.

In a time when world economy becomes increasingly globalized and the entire international community is transforming into a global village, it is necessary to learn from other cultures and assimilate their nutrients. In China, an ancient country with a history of thousands of years, national culture and traditional art should be the primary source of momentum for our construction of the Cultural Era. As stated in the address to the 17th People's Congress of CPC, 'Chinese culture has been an unfailing driving force for the Chinese nation to keep its unity and make progress from generation to generation. We must have a comprehensive understanding of traditional Chinese culture, keep its essence and discard its dross to enable it to fit in with present-day society, stay in harmony with modern civilization, keep its national character and reflect changes of the times. We will further publicize the fine traditions of Chinese culture and use modern means of science and technology to exploit the rich resources of our national culture. We will explore and better protect the cultures of all ethnic groups, attach great importance to the protection of cultural relics and intangible cultural heritage and do a good job collating ancient books and records.' After the wanton destruction and deliberate distortion of national cultural heritage in a period when 'everything foreign is superior', the Chinese in the new era are sensible and sophisticated; after people's pursuits of food and clothing are fulfilled as a result of rapid economic growth, people's understanding of culture has deepened.

IV. Protection and development of traditional art in contemporary times

National culture and traditional art have had an extraordinary history following the founding of P.R.C in 1949. Thanks to the establishment of the new social system and the radical changes in ideology, the status of folk culture and traditional art which had been disregarded was improved unprecedentedly. They had been marginalized in the development of culture and art, ignored by official and orthodox forces, and rebuffed as vulgar. After the founding of PRC, the folk culture and traditional art, including opera, Quyi (Chinese folk art forms), dancing, folk songs, New Year paintings, paper-cutting, etc. were highly regarded because of their popularity. Folk artists who had been looked down upon became 'People's artists'. Thus in the 1950s-60s, folk culture was especially vibrant and splendid; folk artists' creativity soared; and large quantities of folk culture and traditional art prospered and were put under protection. That was an unprecedented revolution in culture and ideology. The ten-year Cultural Revolution was a revolution of another kind. Folk culture and traditional art, being regarded as main means of representing 'feudal subjects', were 'swept' and banned.

The new era have seen many things happen. It can be roughly divided into three stages. The beginning years of the new era saw the reinvigoration of folk culture and traditional art. They mushroomed in the early and mid 1980s. The broad masses were in high spirits after the shackles on their mind were removed. A 'spring of literature and art' arrived. Forms of culture and art, including those of folk culture and traditional art, made considerable progress. As economy grew, for a time, less importance was given to cultural development. Many people and many places became means and tools in service of economic construction. As the saying goes, 'use culture to set up the stage and the economy to put on a show'. No only did the Chinese pursued material needs obsessively like the West, but their spiritual and cultural world was filled with the materialism and nearsightedness plaguing Western culture. Tradition was again at the nadir. The booming machines, while helping us build skyscrapers, uprooted them from the soil of tradition and scarred our land of culture. When considerable economic growth has been achieved, people are bound to make a level-headed reevaluation of culture. As the confidence in national culture is boosted, their love for national culture and traditional art are bound to grow ardent. It thus becomes inevitable for them to pursue the harmonious development of economy and society; especially important to improve the nation's cultural 'soft strength'; and increasing meaningful to implement the strategic scientific outlook on development.

The progress in the protection of national culture and traditional art, in the conservation of intangible cultural heritage has been achieved in such a context in the new century. The protection and development of traditional art is an important part of the cultural era in the 21st century. Though we have lost a lot – many of which cannot be revived – our makeup efforts have been timely. Since Kunqu opera was inscribed in UNESCO's list of the oral and intangible cultural heritage, people, particularly young people, are now increasingly eager to learn more about national culture and traditional art. More and more young people and college students have developed a liking for Kunqu opera, Peking opera, local operas, and other forms of traditional arts. To protect them is but a measure taken for the purpose of developing them. The recent years has seen revived interest in traditional arts. Activities such as performances, publication, educations, and discussions have been springing up. Though traditional art seems to have been crippled by its lack of individuality, it has improved comprehensively on the whole. Traditional art is not merely a fountainhead of the vitality of contemporary art, but it is radiating its own unique charm. The cultural era is around the corner. What will come with it will be the great development and prosperity of culture and art. In this general context, the protection and development of traditional art will become one of the entire nation's focuses. Some elements of traditional art may not be in line with contemporary aesthetics and customs. However, it has been well received by the public in terms of content and form. Having nourished generations after generations of Chinese people, it is one of the major means by which Chinese people develop their aesthetics, acquire knowledge and receive education. And it is also included in the Chinese nation's effort to construct their common spiritual resort. The cultural era is an era when culture is harmonious, self-updating, and variegated. The time-honored traditional art will address people's cultural and spiritual needs and give historicity and depth to the zeitgeist. It will provide inexhaustible strength and momentum to cultural development. Chinese culture will be carried forth and preserve its eternal youth.

中美文化交流的见证与阐释

克莱尔·康塞逊

美国杜克大学
戏剧研究教授

内容提要： 戏剧是在20世纪之交作为新文化运动的一部分特意从西方引入中国，被认为是帮助中国赶上西方，解决社会问题，并改革中国文化艺术形式。因而从一开始，这种中国的西式戏剧的作用就是要促进西方和中国的融合，并由中国的知识分子带进中国，而不是通过殖民主义，也不是通过西方影响，那是非常重要的。自从戏剧引入中国以来，话剧就像中国艺术一样被吸收，并由中国的艺术家以一种非常有趣的方式呈现给大家。我没有看出西方和中国文化之间有什么显著的二分性。一旦引进了艺术，艺术家就开始对话，这种界限也变得非常模糊。

作为一名学者，我将我的职业生涯放在作为中美文化交流的见证人和阐释者上。作为戏剧方面的翻译，以及在中国居住时碰巧进行的中西戏剧合作的临时翻译，我也是文化交流的促进者。作为中国当代戏剧的导演以及美国观众的英文翻译，我是文化交流的创建者。因此，这些视角给我提供了独特的有利机会，使我常常成为一个桥梁，这是一个令人兴奋但同时也非常复杂的位置。在听了昨天以及今天座谈会上朋友们的发言后，我认为我可以从两个方面为这些活动提供最有价值的见解。首先，我可以向不了解中国当代戏剧的人解释一些最重要的作品。其次，我可以为中美文化如何更加成功地进行交流、尤其是艺术交流提供一些精神食粮，特别是在戏剧方面。为此，我引用本周我很多同事提供的丰富见解。于丹表达了理解文化差异的重要性。金安平谈到了翻译文本及其流通的重要性。莫言说，与如音乐和舞蹈等艺术形式相比，在某些艺术形式、尤其是文学中，语言和翻译发挥了至关重要的作用。我希望把戏剧放在

语言、文本和语言交流极其重要的这一类中。乔纳森·斯宾塞指出我们所形成的跨文化关系受到初遇者历史起点的影响。安德鲁·德尔班科提到了美国文化的传教使命；最后，劳伦斯·林德揭示了传统和创新之间的错误两分法。从我的中美跨文化戏剧交流经验来看，所有这些方面都发挥着非常重要的作用。

就我个人而言，我初识中国和中国戏剧的时候正是20世纪80年代中国和中国戏剧实力不断增强的时期，当时中国正在改革开放，戏剧艺术家在国内试演，并开始到国外巡演。我亲自见证了中国观众的活力、力量和创新能力。然而，我认为斯宾塞教授的观点是正确的，即中美关系开始于中国历史上相对较弱的时期，尤其是与西方相较。我确信这是具有远见的邂逅，中国今天的艺术、经济和军事的巨大实力仍然构成了大多数不甚了解中国的美国艺术家通过国际交流项目到中国了解中国的基础。这是过去二十多年中，我在中国一次又一次目睹的情况。

我想起了劳伦斯·林德昨天发表的深刻见解，即大多数外国人将中国文化等同于传统文化，将西方文化等同于现代文化。实际上，在我们昨天听到发言中，我发现与西方的现代派运动相比，这种两分法稍微侧重于孔子和老子以及中国的国画。但是在我的中国戏剧工作中，我所接触的中国是非常现代和具有创新性的。当然，这受到我所专攻的话剧的影响。因此，戏剧形式是在20世纪之交作为新文化运动的一部分特意从西方引入的，被认为是有助于中国赶上西方，解决社会问题并改革中国文化的艺术形式。因而从一开始，我所研究的戏剧形式——话剧，我认为应该称作中国的西式戏剧，与刘祯所讨论的话剧是相对的。它的作用是要促进西方和中国的融合，并由中国的知识分子带到中国，而不是通过殖民主义，也不是通过西方影响，那是非常重要的。自从引入中国以来，话剧就像中国艺术一样被吸收，并由中国的艺术家以一种非常有趣的方式呈现给了大家。在这一点上，我想与大家分享一件小事，星期四我在斯坦福大学讲课，我的学生在上中国戏剧和社会课。实际上，在大部分学术课程上都可以展开讨论，我给他们留了一个技术性的戏剧项目，以便我不在的时候他们可以继续完成功课。他们从已经读过的四个戏剧中设计一个情景，在这次精选的讨论会上，我认为这四部戏剧是中国文化大革命前，对戏剧形式具有塑造意义的四部戏剧。因而，他们要研究这四部戏剧，他们的任务是分组，从其中一部戏中选择一个主题，然后对其进行改编，使其适应另一种文化背景，这在很大程度上也是一个文化弥合项目。但是，在中国舞台如此具有影响力的四部戏剧《汤姆叔叔的小屋》、《玩偶之家》、《雷雨》和《茶馆》中，只有两部是由中国剧作家编写的。其中一部莫言昨天提到过，将《汤姆叔叔的小屋》改编为戏剧，这是中国演员在日本留学期间改编并表演的第一部戏剧。《玩偶之家》是挪威的一部作品，该作品被翻译成中文，并在中国舞台上表演。这里就是融合，曹禺和老舍等人借鉴这些西方艺术形式，同时也加入了非常中国化的元素。我没有看出西方和中国文化之间有什么显著的二分性。一旦引进了艺术，艺术家就开始对话，这种界限也变得非常模糊。

今天我没有时间向大家介绍和我在中国一起工作过的很多剧作家、导演和其他文化工作者，以及我看到的他们所做的令人不可思议的工作。但是，今天我希望介绍其中四位我认为可以效仿的、起到文化桥梁作用的典范。在和我一起工作过的中国戏剧工作者中，有四位是我曾经非常有幸合作过、也期待将来能和他们一起工作的人。我和他们的合作非常密切，其中一位是过去20年定居法国的高行健。20世纪90年代他在法国时，他的戏剧已经非常国际化。在过去的5年中，我在法语戏剧、以及他到法国之后所写的戏剧和这些戏剧如何被全球的观众所认可等项目上与他合作过。几年前我翻译过其中的一部戏剧。第二位是孟京辉，他是过去20年中国北京的一位有改革能力的舞台导演，他实际上改变了北京戏剧的基础，将大量中国观众带到这个舞台上，开始创作有关先锋艺术、商业化和很多中国其他事物以及自己虚构的戏剧作品。从1993年开始，我与他有过密切的合作。第三位是喻荣军，一位上海剧作家，他是中国当今健在的、最多产的剧作家，他已经捕捉到了中国现、当代早期艺术的脉搏，并撰写了很多不同类型的戏剧，从独角戏、无声的试验性样本到现实主义、主旋律、独白剧和纪实剧。在中国地震后，他导演了一部名为《震颤》的戏剧，描述了这一灾难性事件。最后一位是英若诚，他已经于2003年底离开了我们，但我有幸在他生命最后的3年期间在他的自传上与他合作。我将从英若诚开始，因为在座的很多人都认识他。

我认为英先生比其他人更能代表我们所希望的中美之间的文化桥梁。在我看来，至今没有一个人像英若诚一样，我也真心希望这一代中能够出现更多他那样的人。他有着特别的教育背景。他出生于一个多语言背景的满族家庭，经一个满族皇室抚养成人。他是演员、导演，但是就我们的目的而言，我认为他更重要的是一位戏剧翻译（从中文译成英语以及从英语译为中文）。1986年至1990年期间，他担任文化部副部长。英若诚是中国的文化大使。这是对他在中国和英国、中国和美国以及为更广泛的欧洲之间所做的努力所给予的一个非正式的头衔，他将中国文化带到西方，并将西方文化引入中国。1983年，他因与阿瑟·米勒合作制作《推销员之死》而出名，他翻译了该剧，安排了全部演出工作，并担任米勒的助理和非正式翻译。米勒有一位官方翻译，但他认为英若诚能够不喘一口气地进行同传，这是一项非常难的技巧，是一种不可思议的困难事情。我想稍微提一下语言的问题。英若诚的传记有英文版本和中文版本，如果你想了解更多可以看一下该书，我认为他是我们的伟大典范。但他是一个很敏感、很有个性的人，也是一个诚实、优雅、坦率且不会冒犯别人的人。他能够解决问题，并承担像20世纪80年代末在决定改革中国和美国之间的文化交流时所承担的巨大个人风险和政治风险。他总是愿意承担这样的风险，因为他最热爱的便是将不同的语言汇在一起以促进文化之间的相互理解。相反，他看起来可能非常糊涂和理想主义，但能够坦诚地把问题放到台面上并加以解决，那也是我们应该尝试做的事情。

孟京辉，他是一位著名的特立独行的年轻人，现在在北京。我认为对于我们来说，重要的是他改编的西方作品，包括《阳台》、《臭虫》，并将两部再难不过的电影——《爱比死冷》和比利·威尔德的《桃色公寓》改编为舞台剧，他是我们所称的有趣的人。他也改革了中国的电影。他的《空中花园谋杀案》是中国一种新的音乐剧。《三个橘子的爱情》包括三段乌托邦式爱情故事，但除了标题外没有借鉴乌托邦爱情中的太多东西。他有一支摇滚乐团，在他们扮演角色的时候，他弹奏乐器。他尝试改革西方和中国的戏剧形式。《思凡》结合了薄迦丘《十日谈》的有关章节和明朝的昆曲。他拿两种文化做试验，这不仅仅是将西方戏剧形式引入中国，而是使其成为中国的文化。

最后一位是喻荣军，他是上海的一位剧作家。他扮演了有趣的双重角色，因为他是一个非常多产的剧作家，多产得让人难以想象。他撰写戏剧的速度很快，制作的速度也很快。实际上，今年春天我邀请他到杜克大学工作了6个星期。在这里，他可以在研讨会中放慢速度写他的英语戏剧。中国没有演出艺术，因此我的想法是让编剧、演员和导演合作，这样他们可以从别处借鉴一些样式。他是上海一个大制片公司——"上海话剧艺术中心"的市场总监和节目编排人。因而他是兼任行政职务的艺术家。他付出情感的其中一项工作就是促进国际文化交流以及亚洲范围内的文化交流。他创办了每年秋季举办的亚洲文化节，启动了在上海举行的校园戏剧节。几年前在北京创办的戏剧节中，孟京辉发挥了重要的作用。而喻荣军经常到国外参加文化节，并将作品带回上海，同时设法将作品从上海带到美国。因此，我们的交流自始至终都必须是双向的。我们擅长将外国人带到中国来导演戏剧，成为外国专家，向中国人展示如何做事，那才是问题所在。这是一件有趣的事，但我们需要将更多的中国作品带到美国，我们需要中国导演，而不要求他们讲英语才能在这儿工作，因为在中国，人们不需要外国人讲汉语才能在此工作。

我们真的需要注意翻译和语言的作用。对于西方来说，中国话剧第一次到美国演出是在2005年，即《茶馆》在美国的巡演。这是外国人来到中国并在中国工作数十年之后的事了。2002年和2003年，我试图将孟京辉的戏剧带到圣巴巴拉市。当一切就绪时，"非典"来了。由于"非典"，美方取消了此次活动，并且不许中国人到美国，这真的很遗憾。但对于我们来说，将中国话剧带到美国是一件新奇的事。我认为其中的一个原因是，我们认为观众不愿意观赏另一种语言的话剧。或者说更大的问题是，我们一直都在看中国的传统艺术，京剧以及其他我们认为是中国作品的其他戏剧形式。而现代剧也非常中国化。中国有一部非常精彩的都市题材作品和其他类型的戏剧，我们应该对他们改编西方经典作品及如何写关于自己经历的故事感兴趣，我们也应该看看这些故事。所以我希望能看到更多这样的事，以及人们为了获得共同尊重而努力奋斗，要知道，在建立合作关系和文化交流时，共同点和深入了解对方的文化是非常重要的。

我用一句话作为结束，钱以佳昨天说伟大的艺术作品就是伟大的艺术作品，我认为这有点不切实际。我认为伟大的艺术作品像是妙手偶得，但并非凭空出现。它们通过敏感性、深厚的知识、共同合作的精神、实际考虑到不同观众的需求以及艺术家与观众之间的有效交流而产生。我希望我们在将来的工作中都朝着这个方面努力。

Claire Conceison

Professor of Theater Studies, Duke University

The Witness and Interpretation of China- US Cultural Exchange

Abstract: Theater forms were imported deliberately from the West at the turn of the 20th century as part of the new culture movement, and that was thought to help China catch up to the West and also to address social issues and to transform Chinese culture. So from the very inception, the impetus of this kind of theater, I guess you'd call Western-style Theater in China that spoken drama, was to forge an encounter between the West and China and was brought to China by Chinese intellectuals. Not through colonialism and not through Western influence, and that's very significant, too. But it's been absorbed and it's been used in incredibly interesting way by Chinese artists since it was brought in. I just don't see a distinctive binary between what is Western and what is Chinese. Once arts are imported and artists begin dialogue, those lines become very blurred.

As a scholar, I've spent my careers afar as a witness to, and interpreter of, cultural exchange between the US and China. As a translator of plays and as an occasional interpreter for Sino-Western theater collaborations during periods when I happen to be living in China, I'm a facilitator of cultural exchange. And as a director of contemporary Chinese plays, and English translation for American audiences, I'm a creator of cultural exchange. So I think these perspective offer unique opportunity of this vantage point and often make me a bridge, which is a very exciting but extremely complex position to be in. After hearing the talks from yesterday and from my fellow panelists, I think the most valuable insights that I can offer to these proceedings are two folds. I can illuminate, first of all, for those unfamiliar with contemporary theater in China, some of the most significant works happenings there. And second, I can offer some food for thought about how Sino-American cultural exchanges, and particularly artistic exchanges, and specifically in the theater, can become more successful. In doing so, I invoke the rich comments from many of my colleagues here this weekend. Yu Dan addressed the importance of understanding cultural difference. Annping Chin addressed the importance of translated text and their circulation. Mo Yan indicated that in some artistic forms, specifically literature, language and translation play a vital role compared to other artistic forms such as music or dance. And I would include theater in this category where language, the text, and linguistic communication is extremely important. Jonathan Spence pointed out that the cross-cultural relationships we form are influenced by the historical point of the primary encounter. And Andrew Delbanco made reference to the missionary spirit of American culture. And finally, Lawrence Rinder exposed the false dichotomy between tradition and innovation. From my experience in Sino-American cross-cultural theater exchange, all of these things come in to play in very significant ways.

Personally, I encountered China and Chinese theater at a point when it was gaining strength, in the mid 1980s, when China was opening, reforming, and theater artists were experimenting domestically and begin to travel abroad. Personally, I see China's audience as having great vitality, urgency, and innovative power. However, I believe that Professor Spence is correct, that the China-U.S. relationship, began with China in a point of weakness, historically. Particularly, vis a vis, the West. And I do believe, that this is original point of encounter in spite of China's great artistic, economic, and military strength today, still form the base of that how most American artists, who know very little about China, encounter China today when they travel there for international exchange projects. This is something that I've witnessed over the past 20 years, time and time again in China.

Lawrence Rinder's insightful comments yesterday also brought to mind, for me, the fact that most foreigners equate Chinese culture with quote traditional, and the West with modern. And in fact, we saw this binary, play out, somewhat, in presentations that we heard yesterday, with a heavy emphasis on Confucius and Lao Zi, and traditional Chinese paintings, compared to a kind of modernist movement in the West. But the China that I encounter in my theater work is extremely modern and innovative. And that is, of course, influenced by the fact that I specialize in "hua ju" or Chinese Spoken Drama. So theater forms that were imported deliberately from the West at the turn of the 20th century as part of the new culture movement, and that thought to help China catch up to the West and also to address social issues and to transform Chinese culture. So from the very inception, the kind of theater that I studied, I guess you'd call western-style theater in China, that spoken drama, vis-à-vis the opera form that Liu Zhen was addressing. Their impetus was to forge an encounter between the West and China and was brought to China by Chinese intellectuals. Not through colonialism and not through Western influence, and that's very significant, too. But it's been absorbed and it's been China-fried and it's been used in incredibly interesting ways by Chinese artists since it was brought in. I think I'll share a tiny anecdote at this point, because Thursday, I was at Stanford University giving a lecture. And while I was there, my students had a class and it is a Chinese theater and society class where mostly an academic class we can actually discuss on. I gave them one kind of on your feet, a theater project that they could work on while I was away that they could work on. So they were creating a scene from the four plays you've read so far, which I consider to be four of the formative plays, pre-Cultural Revolution plays, in China in this selection forum. So, there are four plays that they're working on, and their assignment is to form groups, to choose a theme from one of the plays and then transform it and adapt it into another cultural context, so very much a cultural bridging project. But the four plays which were so influential on the Chinese stage are Uncle Tom's Cabin, A Doll's House, Thunderstorm, and Teahouse. And only two of those four were written by Chinese playwrights. One of them, as Mo Yan mentioned yesterday, just drafted Uncle Tom's Cabin into a play, and that was the first book and drama performed by Chinese actors as they were overseas students in Japan and then, A Doll's House is a work from Norway which was translated and then produced on stage in China. So there's this mixture. People like Cao Yu and Lao She were borrowing from these Western forms but also adding different Chinese elements. I just don't see a distinctive binary between what is Western and what is Chinese. Once arts are imported and artists begin dialogue, those lines become very blurred.

So I don't have time today to give you an overview of the many playwrights, directors, and other cultural workers that I work alongside in China and the incredible work that I observe them doing, but I like to introduce to you three of them today who I think are wonderful examples of cultural bridges that we can emulate. There are four Chinese theater people among, again, the many I work with, that I feel particularly fortunate to work with, to have worked with, or to be working with. And I work with them very closely. One of them is Gao Xingjian who's lived in France for the past 20 years. But whose play was hugely international in a sense for the period of 1980's. For the past five years, I've been working with him on projects such as French language plays and the plays that he has written since he went to France and how they are received globally. And I've translated one of those a few years ago. Secondly, Meng Jinghui who is a kind of the transformative stage director in China in Beijing for the past 20 years who's really changed the base of theater there. Have brought huge Chinese audiences to this stage and began the dialogue of theater about the avant-garde about the commercialization and about many other things of China and his mythology of works and I've also been working closely with him since 1993. And then Yu Rongjun, who is a Shanghai-based playwright. He's the most-produced living playwright in China today and has really had his finger on the modern-day pulse of art in China and writes in many different genres, ranging from monologues to unspoken experimental pieces to realism to 主旋律(Main Melody) to monologue play to documentary theater. He did an incredible play after the earthquake called Heartquake that had a witnessed account of the event. And finally, Ying Ruocheng who is no longer with us when he passed away at the end of 2003 but I was very fortunate to work alongside him during the last three years of his life on his autobiography.

And I'll start with Ying Ruocheng because some of you knew him. And I believe that Ying, more than anyone else, represents what we would want in a cultural bridge between China and the US to be. There is nobody, in my opinion, like Ying Ruocheng around today and I'm really hoping that this generation will produce some more people like him. He had a very unique educational background. He had been raised in a family of distinguished multicultural intellectual who was from an illiterate Manchu family. He was an actor, a director, but I think for our purposes, more importantly a translator of plays, both from Chinese to English and English to Chinese. And he became Vice Minister of Culture from 1986 to 1990. And Ying Ruocheng was known as 文化大使 or the cultural ambassador of China. It was kind of the informal title that he was given because of the great efforts that he had made between China and the United Kingdom and between China and the United States and also Europe more broadly, in bringing Chinese culture to the West and bringing Western culture to China. He's very famous for his collaboration with Arthur Miller in 1983 on the production of Death of a Salesman; he translated that play, arranged the whole gig and also played as the assistant and formal interpreter to Miller. Miller had an official interpreter but he felt that Ying Ruocheng was able to simultaneously interpret without taking a breath. And this is an incredibly difficult skill. It's something that is incredibly difficult. And I want to get to that issue of language in just a moment. So Ying Ruocheng's autobiography is available both in English and Chinese so if you want to learn more about him, I think he's a great model for us. But he was a very sensitive man, a very charismatic man, he also was a very honest man and very candid in an elegant way that didn't offend people. But he was really able to get at issues and also take risks at a time in the late 80's when it was, he took great personal risk in some of the decisions he made in innovating cultural exchanges between China and the United States and political risks. But he was always willing to take those because what he loved more than anything was languages coming together and add culture's mutual Understand, he might sound very fluffy and idealistic but he was candidly able to put that on the ground and make it work and that's what we should all be trying to do.

Meng Jinghu is a very famous young maverick guy in Beijing right now, but I think what's significant for us is his adaption of Western works, ranging from The Balcony to Bedbugs to two films adapted to the stage that could not be more different, Love is Colder Than Death and Billy Wilder's The Apartment, so he's what we'd call interesting. But he's also innovated actual films within China. So his 《空中花园谋杀案》(The Murder Case Of The Hanging Gardens Apartment) Is a new kind of musical in China and also 《三个橘子的爱情》(The Love Of Three Oranges), which include three love story of Utopia , but he didn't borrow too much from Love Utopia except the title and he had kind of a rock band on stage and he used the instruments as they played their roles. He tried to innovate with both Western and Chinese forms. Si Fan or longing for worldly pleasures is a mixture of Giovanni's text with an old Ming Dynasty 昆曲 (Kunqu Opera). So he is experimenting with both cultures, but I wanted to say more about bringing Western forms to China and making them their own.

And finally, Yu Rongjun, a playwright in Shanghai. He has an interesting dual role, because he's a very productive playwright, almost too productive. He writes plays really quickly and they get produced very quickly. And I'm actually bringing him to Duke in the spring for a residency for six weeks so that we can slow him down in a workshop to write one of his plays in English. And in China there's no dramaturgy so the idea is to work with the playwright and actor and the director involved in making these plays because there are other models that they've adopted from other places. So he's also, though, the marketing director and program director for a major production company in Shanghai, the Drama

& Arts Center. And so he has an administrative role and an artistic role. And one of his jobs that he's so affective at is fostering international cultural exchange and also, inter-Asia cultural exchange. He started the Asian Theater Festival that happens every Fall. He jumpstarted the college theater festival that happens in Shanghai and Meng Jinghui was a big factor in starting that in Beijing a few years ago. But Yu Rongjun is constantly traveling abroad to festivals and bringing productions back to Shanghai and trying to bring productions from Shanghai to the US. So, beginning to close, our exchanges need to go both ways. We're very good at bringing foreigners to China, to direct a play, to be a foreign expert, to show the Chinese how to do something and that's somewhat problematic. It's a wonderful thing, but we need to bring more Chinese work to the United States, we need Chinese directors and not require them to speak English in order for them to work here because they don't require foreigners to speak Chinese to work in China.

And we really need to take care to pay attention to the role of translation and language. The first spoken drama to the West from China ever come to the United States was not until 2005 after many decades of foreigners going to China and doing work. That was Tea House that tour in USA. I did try to bring the Meng Jinghui play to Santa Barbara in 2002, 2003, and it was all set to go and then SARS happened and the American side cancelled and wouldn't bring the Chinese in because of SARS, it was very unfortunate. But it's a really new thing for us to bring Chinese plays. And I think one of the reasons is that we feel that the audience was reluctant to see a play in another language or the problem that we're always looking at Chinese traditional art, Beijing Opera, and other forms that we think are Chinese. While modern theater is very Chinese, too. There's a very exciting, urban work happening in China and other types of theater and we should be interested in how they adapt Western classics and how they write their own stories about their own experiences and we should want to see them. So I want to see more of that happening as well as people striving for mutual respect, you know, common ground and deeper understanding of each other's cultures as they enter into partnership and cultural exchanges.

To close with one sentence, when Billie Tsien said yesterday that great works of art just are, I think this is somewhat illusory. I think great works of art appear to just be, if they're done well, but they don't just happen. They happen through sensitivity, deep knowledge, and mutual collaborative spirit and real consideration of diverse audiences and effective communication among these artists and to these audiences. So I hope that we will all strive for that in our future work.

中美舞蹈交流的回首、现状与未来建议

欧建平

中国艺术研究院舞蹈研究所副所长，研究员

内容提要： 中美两国虽然远隔重洋，但人民间百余年来的交往和友谊却在不断地超越着意识形态上的差异甚至分歧，并明显地推动了世界文化的发展，极大地影响了世界和平的进程。仅就笔者20多年来直接参与、组织和推动中美两国舞蹈交流的经历，以及从事这方面研究的结果而言，中美两国的亲密程度远远超出了所有人的想象。本论文将以大量真实可信且趣味横生的史实为例证，轻松愉快地告诉诸位这个事实！

"理解构筑和平"。举世公认，在世界的版图上，中美两国虽然远隔重洋，但人民间百余年来的交往和友谊却在不断地超越着意识

舞在全球化的进程中

形态上的差异甚至分歧，并明显地推动了世界文化的发展，极大地影响了世界和平的进程。仅就笔者20多年来直接参与、组织和推动中美两国舞蹈交流的经历，以及从事这方面研究的结果而言，中美两国的亲密程度远远超出了所有人的想象。

"身体从不扯谎"。古往今来，作为"非文字"的艺术，舞蹈身心并举、一目了然的特征使它在人与人之间坦诚相见、彼此沟通、互爱互信、世界和平等方面，发挥了不可替代的神功，而中美舞蹈交流的丰硕成果则在两国人民间的交往和友谊中，扮演了重要的大使角色。仅就笔者近30年来专门从事中外舞蹈交流的经历和研究成果而言，任何宏观上的"国际"交流，实质上，都是微观上的"人际"交流；而就在这些频繁的人际交流中，不用文字，只用动作加以表达的舞蹈，在沟通彼此的过程中，其实效超过了其他的艺术和语言。

我将在下文中，从自己进行了20多年的课题《中外舞蹈交流史》中，摘取几段中美舞蹈交流的历史，并配上珍贵的图片或视频，来形象地说明以上的基本观点，并愿同与会者分享我最初发现这些史料时的震撼与快乐。

百年回首

裕容龄表演邓肯风格的《蝴蝶舞》。

1902年，清末驻法国大使裕庚的爱女裕容龄（1882—1973），曾就学于伊莎多拉·邓肯的门下，地点是她在巴黎维利亚大街的舞蹈工作室。她学舞的时间虽不长，却深受邓肯返朴归真的生活态度与崇尚自然的艺术风格之影响，甚至敢于违背父母之命，身披白纱长裙，裸露半个臂膀，像邓肯那样，在公众面前赤脚表演《希腊舞》和《玫瑰与蝴蝶》这两个典型的邓肯风格的舞蹈，表现出中国人对邓肯舞蹈思想的深层理解和出色诠释，因而受到巴黎观众的好评。后来，她又先后进入法国国立歌剧院和巴黎音乐舞蹈学院深造，拜萨那夫尼等名师学习过芭蕾。4年后，她随父亲回国，并按宫廷规定，做了慈禧太后的御前女官。在此期间，她一面潜心学

埃德温·邓比的肖像

习中国的民间舞蹈和戏曲舞蹈，一面创作并表演自己的舞蹈，其中包括中国风格的《扇子舞》、《荷花仙子舞》、《菩萨舞》、《如意舞》，以及邓肯风格的《希腊舞》、《蝴蝶舞》和《西班牙舞》等，因而成为在近代中国舞蹈史上，最早直接学习了西方舞蹈，并将其带回祖国之人，受到舞蹈史学家们的高度重视。

1903年，美国最著名的舞蹈评论家和理论家之一埃德温·邓比（1903—1983）出生在中国的天津。或许是中国文化那充满诗意的特征从小便对他发生了耳濡目染的熏陶作用，或许是中国艺术那大写意的诗性风格为他日后的写作打下了烙印，反正，他最令西方舞蹈界、文艺界和普通观众赞叹不已的优势，就是用符合舞蹈特征的诗意，去观察并撰写舞蹈评论和理论文章。

早在20世纪初，当中国近代改良派领袖康有为提出"强身救国"的教育思想之时，以体操和舞蹈为内容的欧美近代体育就以"强健身体"、"顽固精神"的实际功用，满足了我们的身心需求，其中贡献最大者当为美国威斯康星大学的女教师梅爱培——1915年8月，上海基督教女青年会创办上海女青年体育师范学校时，她出任了校长的要职，该校的舞蹈课程在技术课中占有相当大的比重，而教授舞蹈的美国和中国教师则有五六位之多，其中包括担任副校长的陈英梅，她曾留学美国，是中国人中第一位接受过高等教育的专职体育女教师。梅爱培不仅在天津、南京、上海教授过欧洲土风舞，而且还从上海女青年体育师范学校，选派了优秀毕业生高梓、张汇兰赴美留学；她们两人学成后均回国任教，为发展中国舞蹈事业做出了贡献，并为欧美舞蹈在中国建立了良好的口碑。

1925至1926年，美国现代舞创始人露丝·圣—丹妮丝和泰德·肖恩夫妇曾两度率舞团来中国大连、天津、北京、上海（两次）演出。在北京，丹妮丝在天坛翩跹起舞时，构想出了自己的独舞《白玉观音》；而肖恩则根据中国传统哲学中的"阴阳"观念，创作并演出了《哦，太阳哥哥，月亮妹妹》这个舞蹈，使美国现代舞在宇宙观和世界观等哲学层面上，与中国的传统文化精神完美地融为一体。此外，全团舞者还与中国戏曲舞蹈大师梅兰芳做了深入的专业交流：梅先生为美国舞蹈家们做了专场演出，而丹妮丝和肖恩夫妇不仅做了大量笔记，而且还安排了舞者安·道格拉斯随梅先生学习虞姬的双剑舞，进而为他们随后以梅先生的代表作《霸王别姬》为灵感，创作和表演的同名舞蹈做好了充分的准备，不仅首开美中专业舞蹈交流之先河，而且也为梅先生1929年的访美成功，奠定了重要的基础。

丹妮丝自编自演的舞蹈《白玉观音》　　丹妮丝－肖恩夫妇与梅兰芳在北京的合影

　　1926年末，美国舞蹈家、"现代舞之母"伊莎多拉·邓肯在俄罗斯的弟子们曾专程来到哈尔滨、天津、北京、上海、汉口等城市，演出了大批带有炽热革命激情的节目，其中包括专门创作的歌舞《中国妇女解放万岁》，尤其是他们在"辛亥革命"的发源地——武汉公演的节目对如火如荼的中国革命，起到了推波助澜的积极作用。

　　此外，《邓肯自传》1928年在美国问世，6年后的1934年在中国出现了第一个汉语译本，接下来则在1935、1938和1939年，接连出版了三个汉语译本！中华人民共和国成立后，由于中美关系进入冷战时期，邓肯这本被各国艺术家和女大学生们争先拜读的"思想解放的《圣经》"一度无人问津，直到1976年文化大革命结束、1978年改革开放开始后的1981年，出现了两个不同的译本，而1990年代以来，由于中国人阅读量的俱增，陆续出版的译本则数不胜数，其中有些则是对以往译本的改写。《邓肯自传》这段在中国传播的历史不寻常处就在于，它始终以作者无拘无束的传奇人生、自尊自爱的独立人格、返璞归真的精神境界和优美畅达的笔触文风，对有着几千年封建思想定势的中国民众，形成了温柔而剧烈的冲击。

1929年，在美国好莱坞歌舞片的影响下，上海拍摄的故事片《压岁钱》明显效仿了美国的踢踏舞童星秀兰·邓波尔，并推出了当年不到10岁的中国踢踏舞童星胡蓉蓉。实际上，胡蓉蓉足以自豪的资本不仅包括出演了4部电影，并在3部中展示了舞蹈才艺，而且还天生了一副好嗓子，并从5岁开始随俄罗斯芭蕾老师索科尔斯基学习，由此打下的童子功为她日后主创国际舞台上最出名的两部中国芭蕾舞剧之一《白毛女》奠了基础。从笔者进行了20多年的"舞蹈交流史"研究来说，这条史料足以证明，中国人对好莱坞歌舞片热潮的学习速度是惊人之快的。

胡蓉蓉儿时拉手风琴演唱的照片

胡蓉蓉编导的中国芭蕾舞剧《白毛女》剧照

朱德与史沫特莱在延安的合影　　　毛泽东与贺子珍在延安的合影

1937年1月，美国女记者史沫特莱（Agnes Smedley）前往中国革命的大本营延安，做了长达7个月的采访，因同情中国人的抗日战争而与毛泽东、周恩来、朱德等中国共产党的领袖人物结下了深厚友谊，并在向全世界宣传抗日真相的同时，耐心地教他们跳美国弗吉尼亚的土风舞和西方的交际舞，结果形成了每个周末都要在延安的剧场举办交际舞会的惯例，不仅改变了他们以往将跳交际舞看做是资产阶级生活方式的看法，而且还被当做是向封建思想的挑战；这种健康的自娱自乐方式一直在他们中间持续到1966年文化大革命的爆发。

有趣的是，史沫特莱在她的回忆录《中国的战歌》中细致地描写说："朱德同我破除迷信，揭开了交际舞的场面。周恩来接着也跳了起来，不过，他跳舞就像一个人在算数学题似的。彭德怀喜欢在一旁看，就是不肯下来跳。贺龙在青砖铺就的地面上随着音乐的旋律跳，并经常光临现场，他是唯一身上有节奏感的中共高级领导人物。"史沫特莱说，毛泽东开始也比较矜持，甚至有些放不下架子，不愿跟我跳舞，但最终还是爱上了跳交际舞，并且一发而不可收，甚至因此与其夫人贺子珍发生了尖锐的矛盾……

美籍犹太作曲家和编导家阿龙·阿甫夏洛穆夫（1894—1965）出生于原为中国领土的乌苏里江畔的尼克拉耶夫斯克，从小深受中国文化的浸染，会唱一些中国歌曲，更迷恋于唱念做打并举、表情丰富异常的京剧。1918年苏黎世大学音乐系毕业后来到中国发展，先后在天津的洋行、上海的屠宰场和工部局（Municipal Council for British, French & American Concessions）图书馆谋生，同时搜集中国民间音乐，创作、指挥并演出了多部中国现代器乐、歌剧、舞剧和音乐剧。1941年，由美籍犹太人谢尔出资，久居上海研究中国文学艺术的美国女作家华尼亚克编剧，阿甫夏洛穆夫作曲，并特邀了几十位京剧演员，先后在上海当时灯光设备最全和音响效果最好的兰心大戏院（Lyceum Theatre），以及规模最大的大光明大戏院（Grand Theatre），成功上演了一部三幕的大型舞剧《古刹惊梦》。

默斯·堪宁汉运用《易经》思想和"机遇编舞法"创作的舞蹈《空间点》

舞剧的灵感取自中国民间神话，讲述了青年男女慧莲和邻家少年如何在观音菩萨的指点下，冲破封建恶势力，最终收获圆满爱情的故事。由于编排了《千手观音舞》、《长袖舞》、《玉盘舞》、《扇子舞》等中国风格、古色古香的舞段，借用了京剧的武打场面表现善恶之争，首次使用了西式管弦乐队做现场伴奏，并由中国红十字会举办义演，这部舞剧总共演出了四场，可谓盛况空前，由此使得"中国舞剧"（当时直译为"中国芭蕾"）的名称得到公认。

1951年，当中美关系处于低谷时，美国现代舞大师默斯·堪宁汉开始了他研究和运用中国《易经》的伟大历程，而由他据此首创、以"变"为本的美学思想和"机遇编舞法"已成为国际舞蹈界最具影响力的舞蹈创作方法之一。

1978年，中国开始推行改革开放的新国策，中国舞蹈界由此开始了"走出去、请进来"的学习与交流的进程，而美国的舞蹈，尤其是现代舞，则在随后的10年中，开始进入神州大地：

1978年6月，首个中国艺术团赴美访问，先后在纽约、华盛顿、明尼阿波利斯、旧金山、洛杉矶演出30场，并观看了纽约市芭蕾舞团、玛莎·格莱姆现代舞团、默斯·堪宁汉舞蹈团、埃里克·霍金斯舞蹈团、哈莱姆舞蹈剧院各具风采的演出，从技术风格到美学特征等各个方面，都

中国艺术团访美期间,中央芭蕾舞团团长李承祥与美国现代舞大师玛莎·格莱姆聊天。

中国艺术团访美期间,卡特总统、福特总统夫人贝蒂·福特分别热情地接见了团员。

接触到完全不同于前苏联芭蕾的样貌。

本·史蒂文森与米歇尔·沃斯珀:美中舞蹈交流的重要桥梁

1979年,美国艺术界代表团首次访华,成员中有时任休斯顿芭蕾舞团艺术总监的英国舞蹈家本·史蒂文森(Ben Stevenson),并引发了他随后长达30年之久的"中国情结"——他从1980年开始,多次来到中国北京、沈阳、西安等地,教授芭蕾基训和舞蹈编导,并以个人的热情和财力,多次邀请中国优秀的芭蕾表演和舞蹈编导人才赴美深造,而最近由澳大利亚拍摄的芭蕾故事片《毛泽东时代的最后舞者》(Mao's Last Dancer)中的主人公——李存信(Cunxin Li),就是他在中国的首批学生之一。"老本"对中国舞蹈发展的贡献有目共睹,笔者1985年10月曾为他在北京舞蹈学院编导系创办初期的两周教学担任过助教和口译,亲眼见证了他孜孜不倦的无私帮助,更庆幸北京舞蹈学院特聘他为首位外籍教授!

需要特别给予褒奖的,是为这个美国艺术界代表团担任口译的美国小姐米歇尔·沃斯珀（Mitchelle Vosper）。她毕业于哥伦比亚大学，能说一口流利的普通话和广东话，曾在周文中教授(Prof. Zhou Wen Zhong)在哥大主持的"美中艺术交流中心"(American-China Arts Exchange Center at Columbia University) 工作。她不仅出色地协助完成了这次美国艺术代表团来华交流的任务，而且还确保了以霍华德·加德纳教授（Prof. Howard Gardner）为首的哈佛大学《零点项目》（Project Zero of Harvard University）首次访华的圆满成功，更深化了她与中国文化结下了不解之缘——她此前已定居香港，随后不仅嫁给香港中文大学教育学院的一位中国教授，而且还出任了总部设在纽约的"亚洲文化协会"驻香港分会(Hong Kong Office of the New York City-based Asian Cultural Council)的主任。30多年来，她以始终如一的热情和不知疲倦的努力，促成了包括本人在内的大批中国内地及港澳台的艺术家前往美国深造，为中美两国的文化艺术交流默默无闻地做出了巨大的贡献！

笔者在本届《中美文化论坛》上与米歇尔·沃斯珀（右）、美国总统艺术与人文委员会副主任堪达斯·卡兹的合影

1980年底，由"美国舞蹈节"主席查尔斯·莱因哈特率领的首个美国舞蹈家代表团来华访问并讲学24天，其中的现代舞蹈家斯图亚特·霍兹、贝拉·刘易斯和劳拉·迪恩则首次为我们带来美国现代舞的第一手信息。

美国舞蹈家代表团在北京恭王府的合影

　　1981年夏，北京舞蹈学院代表团首次访问美国，黄伯虹和曲皓两位教授回国后系统介绍"美国舞蹈节"和"美国国际芭蕾舞比赛"的文章，为我们这些后来者提供了最早的参考资料。

　　1983年的7月14日至8月7日，在美籍华人舞蹈家王晓蓝教授的精心安排下，美国舞蹈资料馆的创始馆长珍妮维也芙·奥斯瓦尔德来京讲学，她在北京舞蹈学院播放了美国现代舞大师玛莎·格莱姆训练体系与经典剧目《天使的欢乐》《悲歌》《拓荒》《心之窟》《阿帕拉契亚的春天》的影像，以及格莱姆的资深舞者罗斯·帕克斯同时在京教授的"格莱姆技术"，首次让中国舞蹈家亲身感受到了美国现代舞的巨大震撼，而刘敏、华超、杨华、蒋齐等学员都是当时中国舞蹈界最优秀的青年舞者。

　　1985年10月底至11月上旬，艾尔文·艾利美国舞蹈剧院来华公演，其将欧洲芭蕾的

艾尔文·艾利美国舞蹈剧院来华公演的《启示录》

欧哈德·纳哈林根据王方宇先生书法创作的《墨舞》

线条、美国现代舞的张力、美国爵士舞的顿挫与非洲原始舞的能量完美合一的特殊魅力，首创了现代舞门票进入中国黑市的惊人记录。

同年11月17日至18日，崔士·布朗舞蹈团来京做内部交流与演出各一场，首次让中国舞蹈家领略了"纯舞蹈"的魅力与困惑。

同年12月中下旬，美国现代舞蹈家玛丽安·萨拉克来京教授玛莎·格莱姆技术，并表演邓肯的自由舞，首次让中国舞蹈家亲睹了这位"现代舞之母"师法自然的自由舞风。

1986年6月24日至7月7日，美国现代舞大师默斯·堪宁汉的舞者艾伦·古德和帕特里西亚·兰特来到北京的中国歌剧舞剧院，在两周的时间里，不仅教授了"堪宁汉技术"，而且还为舞者们量身打造了作品《北京1号》，首次让中国舞蹈家感受了这种风格融芭蕾的腿脚和现代舞的躯干于一身，再用"机遇法"随时变换方向的显著优势。

同年的8月23日，美国现代舞蹈家欧哈德·纳哈林率舞团来京交流，并内部演出了根据王方宇先生新书法创作的《墨舞》，让中国观众看到了中西合璧的种种可能性。

1987年5月21日，美国现代舞蹈家伊丽莎·蒙蒂和戴维·布朗来京教学并内部表演了自编的现代舞《劈波斩浪》和《梦幻时光》，让中国舞蹈家瞠目结舌于格莱姆舞者腹肌的强大表现力。

1989年10月27日和29日，美籍韩国现代舞蹈家洪信子率领她在纽约的"笑石舞蹈团"来北京和天津演出2场舞剧《小岛》，其全部从生活提取的舞蹈动作语汇，以及高度诗意的结构、超级简约的音乐和舞美，令中国观众耳目一新。此后，她还曾为汉城市立舞蹈团的来京公演编舞《走向2001》，并应邀来上海戏剧学院做独舞表演，并先后3次来北京舞蹈学院、广东现代舞团教学，为中国现代舞的发展注入东西合璧的魅力。

洪信子笑石舞团演出的《小岛》

而在这一切中美舞蹈交流开始之初，商如碧、江青、董亚麟、王晓蓝、王仁璐等美籍华裔舞蹈家就纷纷回到中国教学，并将纽约"亚洲文化委员会"的资金和"美国舞蹈节"的师资带进了中国，更引发了中国首个专业现代舞团——广东实验现代舞团的诞生。

从1984年开始，先后拿亚洲文化协会的奖学金，去美国舞蹈节学习现代舞，由此改变了他们个人的人生，并促进了中国舞蹈繁荣的内地舞蹈家有：蒋华轩、门文元、赵明、杨美琦、张鹰、欧建平、金星、陈维亚、高成明、桑吉加、邢亮、李捍忠、马波、文慧、侯莹、段妮等30人。

现状一瞥

回首中美舞蹈交流百年来的历史，值得记录的流水账的确可以罗列出不少，比如继上述于1980年代发生的舞蹈交流活动之后，我们在中国内地又陆续看到了丹·瓦格纳、道格拉斯·尼尔森等美国现代舞蹈家的出色教学，保罗·泰勒（3次）、艾尔文·艾利（又来了2次）、玛莎·格莱姆、霍塞·林蒙、拉·鲁波维奇、珍妮弗·穆勒等美国现代舞团，哈莱姆舞蹈剧院、休斯顿芭蕾舞团、旧金山芭蕾舞团、美国芭蕾舞剧院等美国芭蕾舞团，以及《猫》、《美女与野兽》、《42街》、《发胶》、《妈妈咪呀》等美国百老汇音乐剧的精彩演出，而美国观众也在1991、1997、2001年的"美国舞蹈节"和纽约市，三次看到了广东现代舞团的精彩演出；2005年更在首都华盛顿肯尼迪艺术中心举办的"中国文化周"，看到了北京现代舞团、中央芭蕾舞团的几台中国舞蹈演出。

但由于没有得到两国政府大力且稳定的支持，整体上必然缺乏短、中、长期的规划，这些舞蹈演出大多以散兵游勇的方式，断断续续、民间为主的方式进行，即使是中国国家大剧院于2008年的开张，多少缓解了这种无序，也没有形成同中美这两个大国相匹配的规模。

对比法、英两国政府在舞蹈交流和整个文化输出上的高度重视与巨额投入，中美两国政府或许应该惊醒！而回顾上个世纪的50年代，前苏联芭蕾教学与编导的先进思想与方法通过政府的文化交流协定系统地进入中国，为新生的共和国迅速建立起完整舞蹈体系的成功案例，我们更会对政府间的舞蹈交流寄予厚望！

未来建议

我的建议将分为微观的与宏观的两个部分：

针对美国现代舞自1980年以来对中国舞蹈产生的积极影响与尚不够系统与深入的实际问题，以及美国舞蹈家和其他艺术家自1960年代后现代主义以来争相学习中国《易经》却大多浅尝而止的美中不足，并根据美国现代舞"善于创新"和中国《易经》"长于变通"的公认优势，我建议，中美两国政府可将"系统学习、科学总结、长期化、制度化地交流与传播美国现代舞的创新机制和中国易学的应用研究"等内容，纳入未来的文化交流协定之中；

与此同时，我更建议中外两国政府共同策划并出资，建立"中美交流基金会"，以便使两国各个领域的交流进入一个更长远、更全面、更大规模的新时期。

早在1988年，笔者接受美国"亚洲文化协会"资助，首次访美期间，接受纽约《报刊新闻》的整版专访时曾指出："中国向西方先锋派舞蹈形式开放，无伤社会主义的大雅。在我看来，中国的强大足以不被任何外来影响所吞没。跨文化交流的重要性就在于，如果人们相互理解，便不会再有战争。"

22年过去了，笔者对此依然坚信不疑。

欧建平1988年接受纽约《报刊新闻》的整版专访

【参考书目】

一、汉语：

王克芬、刘恩伯、徐尔冲、冯双白主编：《中国舞蹈大词典》[M]. 北京：文化艺术出版社，2010.

中华人民共和国文化部对外联络局编. 中国对外文化交流概览 [M]. 北京：光明日报出版社，1993.

王克芬、董锡玖、刘凤珍.《中国古代舞蹈家的故事》[M]. 北京：人民音乐出版社，1983.

史沫特莱. 中国的战歌 [M]. 江枫，译. 北京：作家出版社，1986.

李承祥. 对美国舞蹈的初步印象 [J]. 北京：舞蹈，1979年第一期.

沈致隆. 加德纳·艺术·多元智能 [M]. 北京：北京师范大学出版社，2004.

杨美琦. 我与美国舞蹈节 [M]. 广州，2010.

姜椿芳. 创立中国舞剧的最早尝试 —— 忆阿甫夏洛穆夫的音乐创作活动 [J]. 北京：舞蹈论丛，1981年第四辑.

陈钟. 三十年代的中国新舞剧活动 —— 忆阿龙·阿甫夏洛穆夫 [J]. 北京：舞蹈论丛，1983年第四辑.

焦雄屏. 歌舞电影纵横谈 [M]. 台北：远流出版公司，1993.

史蒂文森, B. 美国休斯顿芭蕾舞团艺术指导本·史蒂文森在北京舞蹈学院编导系讲学记录 [J]. 欧建平，译. 北京：北京舞蹈学院，1985.

欧建平. 现代舞的理论与实践 [M]. 北京：光明日报出版社，1994.

欧建平. 世界艺术史·舞蹈卷 [M]. 北京：东方出版社，2003.

欧建平. 外国舞蹈史及作品鉴赏 [M]. 北京：高等教育出版社，2008.

索雷尔, W. 西方舞蹈文化史 [M]. 欧建平，译. 北京：中国人民大学出版社，1996.

二、英语：

邓比, E. 观舞 —— 舞蹈评论集锦 [M]. 纽约：舞蹈地平线出版社，1949.

舍曼, J. 一位丹妮丝-肖恩舞蹈团舞者1925—1926年在远东的日记和家书 [M]. 美国康州米德尔城：威西里安大学出版社，1975.

邓肯, I. 邓肯舞者：自传 [M]. 美国康州米德尔城：威西里安大学出版社，1965.

欧建平. 从"洪水猛兽"到"百花一支"：中国现代舞的起源、发展与先天不足. 露丝·索罗门、约翰·索罗门. 东西方相遇在舞蹈中：跨文化对话中的声音种种 [J]. 瑞士舒尔：哈伍德学术出版集团，1995.

科恩, S.J. 国际舞蹈百科全书 [M]. 牛津、纽约：牛津大学出版社，1999.

布莱姆瑟, M. 国际芭蕾舞辞典 [M]. 底特律、伦敦、华盛顿特区：圣詹姆斯出版社，1993.

本博-普法尔兹格拉夫, B. 国际现代舞辞典 [M]. 底特律、纽约、伦敦：圣詹姆斯出版社，1998.

科格勒, H. 简明牛津芭蕾词典 [M]. 牛津、纽约：牛津大学出版社，1987.

克雷恩, D., 麦克雷尔, J. 牛津舞蹈辞典 [M]. 牛津、纽约：牛津大学出版社，2000.

Dance Exchanges Between China and U.S.A.: 100 Years' Retrospective, Present Situation & Suggestions For the Future

Ou Jianping

Research Fellow
and Deputy Director
of Dance Research
Institute,
Chinese National
Academy of Arts

Abstract: : China is separated far, far from the United States of America by oceans. However, it's also universally acknowledged that the mutual contacts and friendship between these two great peoples have constantly surpassed the ideological differences and even disputes all this 100 years, thus obviously pushing forward the development of the world culture and greatly affecting the process of the world peace. Merely from this speaker's personal experiences while directly participating, organizing and promoting the dance exchanges between our two countries for the past over twenty years, and from the results of my historical and theoretical studies into this extremely interesting and important subject, I'd like to make bold to say that the degree of intimacy between our two peoples could easily go beyond everyone's imagination. Believe it or not, follow me into these reliable and interesting historical facts, and I bet, you'll give me an even more enlightening conclusion of your own!

"Understanding constructs peace." As everyone could tell from reading any version of the world map, China is separated far, far from the United States of America by oceans. However, it's also universally acknowledged that the mutual contacts and friendship between these two great peoples have constantly surpassed the ideological differences and even disputes all this 100 years, thus obviously pushing forward the development of the world culture and greatly affecting the process of the world peace. Merely from this speaker's personal experiences while directly participating, organizing and promoting the dance exchanges between our two countries for the past over twenty years, and from the results of my historical and theoretical studies into this extremely interesting and important subject, I'd like to make bold to say that the degree of intimacy between our two countries could go beyond everyone's imagination.

"Body never lies." Since time immemorial, dance, as a "non-verbal" language and with its simultaneous body-and-soul function and first-glance understanding, has always played an irreplaceable role in frankly facing and closely connecting each other among different peoples,

Dancing in this globalized world

effectively building up mutual love and trust, and eventually leading to the world peace while the rich fruit of the dance exchanges between China and U.S. has played the decisive role of an ambassador in the mutual contacts and friendship among the artists and common people of our two countries. And as far as my personal experience in conducting the dance exchanges between China and the outside world and my scholarly researches in this field for almost 30 years are concerned, the so-called "inter-national" exchange is conducted always as a kind of "inter-personal" exchange! Therefore, among all this increasingly more and more exchanges, the person to person expression and face to face understanding in the dance exchange to bridge different nations are far more natural and effective than any other art forms.

In the following paragraphs, I'd love to select a few historical events from "Dance Exchange History between China and the Outside World," one of my over twenty year research projects, and illustrate them with rarely seen photos and video clips, for the purposes of proving my concepts mentioned above, and sharing with all of you at this Second China-U.S. Cultural Forum my shocked pleasure when I first discovered all this materials.

100 Years' Retrospective

In 1902, Miss Yu Rong-Ling (1882-1973), the daughter of Mr. Yu Geng, the Chinese Ambassador of the Qing Dynasty to France, went to study dance with Isadora Duncan in her studio in Paris. Although her study didn't last long, she was fascinated with Duncan's simply life attitude and natural dance style, and even made bold to dance Greek Dance and Rose and Butterfly, two of typical Duncan dances, in the public, which was obviously against her parent's will but won a praise from the local audience. Later on, she went to study dance respectively at National Opera of Paris and Paris Conservatoire of Music & Dance. Four years later, she followed her father back to Beijing, became Empress Ci Xi's Lady-in-Waiting and in this capacity, she carefully studied Chinese folk dances and traditional opera dance on the one hand while choreographing and dancing her own dances for the Empress, such as the Chinese styled Fan Dance, Fairy Lotus Dance, Bodhisattva Dance, Good Luck Dance, etc. and Greek Dance, Spanish Dance, etc. in the Duncan genre, thus being highly regarded by the Chinese dance historians as the first Chinese who studied the Western dances abroad and brought them back to China.

In 1903, Edwin Denby (1903-1983), one of the most famous U.S. dance critics and theorists, was born in Tianjin (formerly as Tientsin), the most important international harbor city in northern China at the time, and I believe that the poeticism of the Chinese ancient culture has possibly played a subtle role in paving the way for him to write such poetic dance reviews and articles when he grew up to become a dance writer.

As early as the beginning of the 20th Century, when Kang You-Wei, the political leader of innovative movement in China's early modern period, put forward the educational ideas like "strengthening the body to save China," the practical functions such as "strengthening the body" and "consolidating the spirit" of the European and American physical education nicely represented by its gymnastics and dance, exactly satisfied the physical and spiritual needs of the Chinese people of that particular time. Among these pioneering contributors, the most influential one should be the American teacher Miss Abby Shaw Mayhew of University of Wisconsin: in August of 1915, she was appointed Principal of the Shanghai-based YWCA Teachers School for Physical Education where the dance classes took a quite large percentage in the practical curriculum while the Chinese and American dance teachers were as many as five to six, one of whom was Chen Ying-Mei,

Yu Rong-Ling's dancing her Isadora Duncan styled Butterfly Dance

Portrait of Edwin Denby

who was the first Chinese sent to study physical education at higher educational level in the States and became an assistant to Miss Mayhew in the position of Vice Principal. In addition to teaching in Shanghai, Miss Mayhew also taught European folk dances in other Chinese cities such as Tianjin, Nanjing (formerly as Nanking) etc. and sent Miss Gao Zi and Miss Zhang Hui-Lan, two best of her girl students to study in the States; and what is more, both of them came back to China after their graduation in the States, made great contribution to the development of Chinese dance as the teachers of Jinling University in Nanjing for many years, and won a public praise for the European & American dances among the Chinese people.

From 1925 to 1926, Ruth St. Denis and Ted Shawn, the founders of American Modern Dance, took their "Denishawn" company to dance twice in the Chinese cities such as Dalian (formerly as Dairen), Tianjin, Beijing (formerly as Peking), Shanghai, etc. on their Far East tour, and it was in Beijing where St. Denis got her inspiration for choreographing a female solo for herself White Jade while posing for photography in front of the Temple of Heavens, and the title role is the Goddess of Mercy who has been extremely popular among the Chinese people for being able to help young couples to have children. Also in China, Ted Shawn made good use of the Chinese "Yin and Yang" concept and choreographed O Brother Sun and Sister Moon for himself, thus combining the American modern dance and the Chinese culture on a philosophical level. Also in Beijing, they conducted professional exchanges with Mei Lan-Fang, the world famous Chinese Peking Opera master, in which, Mei and his group performed particularly for them and St. Denis and Shawn took a lot of notes, and then asked their dancer Ann Douglas to learn the Double Sword Dance from Mei, which became the basis for choreographing their own version of General Wu's Farewell to His Wife later

Ruth St. Denis dancing her White Jade

Ruth St. Denis and Ted Shawn with Mei Lan-Fang in Beijing in 1925

on, thus not only starting the professional exchanges between U.S. and China, but also laying down some kind of foundation for the Mei's successful tour of the U.S. in 1929.

By the end of 1926, the Russia-based disciples of American modern dancer pioneer Isadora Duncan (1877-1927), the "Mother of Modern Dance," came to dance in the Chinese cities of Harbin, Tianjin, Beijing, Shanghai and Hankow, the latter of which being the birthplace of the "Revolution of 1911," which was the Chinese bourgeois democratic revolution led by Dr. Sun Yat-Sen and ended the over 2000 year history of feudalist society in China. The Duncan dancers performed many pieces of revolutionary passion, including a song-and-dance named as "Long Live the Liberation of Chinese Women," created and performed particularly for this China tour in order to support the fiery Chinese revolution then.

In addition, Isadora Duncan's autobiography My Life has become the most popular book in the Chinese dance field, and a best seller for general readers, with six different translations six years after its English publication in 1928, that is, four ones respectively in 1934, 1935, 1938 and 1939 before the People's Republic of China was founded in 1949 and two more since 1981, and many more since 1990s when the Chinese readership has greatly increased. The significances of this book's popularity in China could be well summarized into two at least: firstly, generally speaking, China was never that far from U.S., and the Chinese people have always got beautiful feeling for the American people, together with their strong curiosity in their culture, and the best example of this could always be cited that we translated the name of the "United States of America" into the "Beautiful Country" in Chinese characters (while, as an interesting and provocative contrast, the Japanese used the "Rice Country" in Chinese characters to represent the States); secondly, the Duncan's autobiography, with her unrestrained and legendary life, her open and independent character, her simple and natural spirit, and her beautiful and fluent writing, has always been a soft and strong cultural attack to our Chinese way of thinking that could not be easily separated from our over 2,000 years history of feudalism.

In 1929 when the Hollywood musicals swept across the whole world, a Chinese young girl named Hu Rong-Rong became famous because of her skilful tapping on both the floor and the staircase in the Shanghai-made film Gift Money at the Lunar New Year, which obviously followed the example of Shirley Temple, the U.S. child prodigy in tap dancing. However, what Hu could be very proud of herself for is that she was not only born with a sweet voice, but also started her ballet training with Nicola Sokorsky, a good Russian teacher in Shanghai since she was five, which paved the way for her future career as the chief choreographer for The White Haired Girl, one of the two famous Chinese ballets on the international stage. And what means more to me in studying the history of dance exchanges is that it took us almost no time to catch up with the latest trend of the Hollywood musicals.

Since January, 1937, the American journalist Agnes Smedley has visited Yan'an, the major basis for the Chinese revolution and stayed there for seven months during which she not only built up deep friendship with the Chinese Communist Party leaders like Mao Ze-Dong, Zhou En-Lai, Zhu De among

Hu Rong-Rong's choreography The White Haired Girl

Hu Rong-Rong's singing while playing her accordion

others, owing to her great sympathy for the War of Resistance Against Japanese Invasion which they were leading, and told the truth to the outside world, but also taught the western social dances such as the Virginia Dance from the U.S., and the European social dances to all this revolutionaries and even started ballroom dance as a ritual every weekend in there, thus greatly changing their attitude towards these western dances as a kind of bourgeoisie life style, and at the same time regarding them as a good way to challenge the feudalist ideology. In addition, this ballroom dance tradition had lasted until the Cultural Revolution broke out in 1966.

Interestingly enough, Smedley recalled many details in her memoirs such as, "General Zhu De took the lead in joining me to break the mystery and opening the social dance scene, which was followed by Zhou En-Lai who, however, danced like doing math exercises. ... Mao Ze-Dong was somewhat reserved at first and didn't like to dance with me, but eventually, he fell in love with social dancing, and simply couldn't stop it, which aroused severe conflicts with his wife He Zi-Zhen …"

In 1940s, Aron Avshalomov, the Jewish-American composer and choreographer made bold to stage a three-act and Chinese fairy tale-based dance drama named The Shocking Dream in An Ancient Temple at Lyceum Theatre and Grand Theatre, the best venues in Shanghai at the time, with himself as the

Ages Smedley with Zhu De in Yan'an

Mao Ze-Dong with his wife He Zi-Zhen in Yan'an

composer, in addition to other short dances of Chinese themes and movements, thus paving the way for the later comers in well combining the Western music and Chinese stories.

In 1951 when the relationship between China and U.S. was dropped into the lowest tide, the American modern dance master Merce Cunningham began to study and use I Ching, namely the Book of Changes, the best of Chinese philosophical wisdom, and the Chance Method he has invented, based on his understanding of the book and his "change"-based aesthetics, has become one of the most effective and creative tools of choreography all over the world.

In 1978 when China has begun to adopt its new policy of "Open-Door &

Points in Space, a modern dance choreographd by Merce Cunningham with the concept of The Book of Changes and the Chance Method.

uring their stay, Mr. Li Cheng-Xiang, former Artistic Director of the National Ballet of China, was chatting with Martha Graham, the American Modern Dance Master

While visiting the States for the first time, the Chinese Performing Arts Company was warmly received by President Jimmy Carter and the First Lady Betty Ford

Reform," the Chinese dance circle has begun its study and exchange process precisely by "Going out and inviting in," and it was mostly during the coming ten years that the American dance, and particularly the modern dance, came into China.

In June of 1978, the first Chinese Performing Arts Company visited U.S., giving 30 performances respectively in New York, Washington D.C., Minneapolis and Los Angeles, watching the various styles of performances respectively by Martha Graham Dance Company, Merce Cunningham Dance Company, Erick Hawkins Dance Company, Harlem Dance Theater, and getting to know the completely different techniques and styles from those of the Soviet ballet.

In 1979, the first U.S. Arts Delegation visited China and among its members was Ben Stevenson, the former Artistic Director of Houston Ballet, who has started his profoundly loving complex with China ever for the next 30 years. He not only kept teaching ballet technique and choreography respectively in Beijing, Shenyang, Xi'an, and kindly invited many young and talented Chinese dancers to further their training with him in the U.S. with great enthusiasm, and the recently projected film Mao's Last Dancer was in fact the story he started from the very beginning and the blue print of the main character Cun-xin Li was one of his most favored Chinese students. Fortunately, this author helped him teach at Beijing Dance Academy in 1985 for two weeks when the Choreography Department was newly founded, thus getting to know lots of interesting details behind the story and why he was appointed the first Guest Professor by Beijing Dance Academy.

This author with Mitchelle Vosper (right) and Candace Katz, Deputy Director of The President's Committee on The Arts and The Humanities at this Second China-U.S. Cultural Forum

History has kept recording the great contributions of the delegation's interpreter Mitchelle Vosper, who had graduated from Columbia University, was fluent in both Mandarin and Cantonese, had worked at American-China Arts Exchange Center at Columbia University founded by Prof. Zhou Wen-Zhong and therefore guaranteed the success of the delegation. Ever since then, she has tirelessly bridged the cultural relations between the U.S. and China as Representative first and Director then of the Hong Kong Office of the New York City-based Asian Cultural Council, such as successfully arranging for Prof. Howard Gardner to give lectures on his Multi-Intelligent Theory in Hong Kong, and carefully selecting the best artists, critics, historians, art managers from Hong Kong and Mainland China, and sending them to do their advanced studies in the States.

By the end of 1980, the first U.S. Dance Delegation visited China for twenty four days and nights, with Charles Reinhart, Director of American Dance Festival, as its leader, and the members included modern dance choreographers and teachers Stuart Hodes, Bella Lewitzky and Laura Dean, ballet directors Arthur Mitchell and Michael Smuin, and dance historian Susan Shelton, and their lectures on the U.S. modern dance provided us with the vivid, precise and direct information for the very first time.

In the summer of 1981, the Delegation of Beijing Dance Academy visited U.S. for the first time, and the articles Prof. Huang Bo-hong and Prof. Qu Hao respectively published in Beijing became the earliest written information on the American Dance Festival in Durham, North Carolina, and the International Ballet Competition in Jackson, Mississippi, for us later comers to read for reference.

The first U.S. Dance Delegation visited Dance Research Institute at The Prince Gong's Mension in Beijing in 1980

From July 14 to August 7, 1983, and carefully arranged by Prof. Lan-Lan Wang, the Chinese-American dance educator, Madam Genevieve Oswald, founding curator of Dance Collection at Performing Arts Research Library attached to New York Public Library, came to visit Beijing and Shanghai for three weeks, giving lectures on the U.S. modern dance and showing the films of Martha Graham's master pieces such as Diversion of Angels, Lamentation, Frontier, Cave of the Heart and Appalachian Spring while Rose Parks, one of Graham's veteran dancers, gave master class of Graham Technique for three weeks, and the students like Liu Min, Hua Chao, Yang Hua, Jiang Qi were the best Chinese dancers selected from all over China. These two events physically and psychologically shocked the Chinese dance artists with the dynamics of the U.S. modern dance for the first time.

From the end of October to the beginning of November of the same year, Ailvin Ailey American Dance Theater came to dance in China and created a shocking record when its tickets went into black market with its great combination of beautiful lines of European ballet, strong dynamics of American modern

Alvin Ailey American Dance Theater in Ailey's signature piece Revelations

dance, percussive pizzazz of American jazz dance and unexhausted energy of African dance.

On November 17 and 18 of the same year, the US post modern dance master Trisha Brown took her company to Beijing where they respectively gave a lecture-demonstration and a performance to the dance professionals in Beijing, simultaneously pleasing the younger ones with their dynamic momentum while puzzling the older ones with their "pure dance" concept for the first time.

In the middle and last ten days of December, 1985, the U.S. modern dancer Marian Sarach came to Beijing and Shanghai where she respectively gave master classes of Graham Technique and performed Isadora Duncan's free dances which were perceived by the Chinese dancer professionals for the first time.

From June 24 to July 7, 1986, Alan Good and Patricia Lent, two dancers of Merce Cunningham Dance Company, came to Beijing where they not only gave technique classes everyday, but also choreographed a piece named Beijing No. 1 on the dancers of China National Opera & Dance Drama Theatre, the biggest professional dance company in Beijing and in China. And for the first time, the Chinese dancers got a chance to learn the advantages of Cunningham Technique which well combines the balletic legs-and-feet and the Graham torso, plus his constant changes of directions.

On August 23, 1986, the former Graham dancer Ohad Naharin took his NYC-based dance company to perform to the dance professionals in Beijing and half of his concert was Dancing Ink, which he had choreographed based on

Ohad Naharin's choreography Dancing Ink, inspired by Prof. Wang Fang-Yu's calligraphy

his inspiration from Prof. Wang Fang-Yu's contemporary Chinese calligraphy, and showed us more possibilities on how to combine the Western and Chinese cultures into one entity.

On May 21, 1987, the former Graham dancers Elisa Monte and David Brown came to dance their own works Treading and Dream Time for the dance professionals in Beijing, and what astonished us most was the powerful expression of their belly muscles, which we witnessed with your own eyes and kinesthesia.

On October 27 and 29, 1989, the Korean-American modern dancer Sin Cha Hong took her NYC-based Laughing Stone Dance Theater Company to perform her master piece Isle in Beijing and Tianjin, and the Chinese audiences were thrilled by her dance language which was composed totally of daily movements nicely selected from improvisation, as well as her highly poetic structure, minimalist music and stage sets. Later on, she choreographed a piece named as 2001 on Seoul City Dance Company for its public performance in Beijing, which reminded us of the new millennium for the first time, did a solo show at Shanghai Theatre Academy, and gave modern dance workshops three times respectively at Beijing Dance Academy and Guangdong Modern Dance Company,

Sin Cha Hong's Laughing Stone Dance Company in Hong's master piece The Isle

the first professional modern dance company in China, etc. thus in-putting lots of vitality into the Chinese modern dance.

And before all this China-U.S. dance exchanges got started, these Chinese-American modern dance artists such as Ruby Shang, Chiang Ching, Dong Ya-Lin, Lan-Lan Wang, Ren-Lu Wong, took the lead in bringing the U.S. modern dance into China, together with the funding of the Asian Cultural Council (ACC), and the teachers of the American Dance Festival (ADF), which led to the establishment of Guangdong Modern Dance Company.

Since 1984, the ACC grantees in mainland China, mostly studying modern dance at the ADF, have not only changed their own lives by doing lots of creative things they had never dreamed of, but also promoted the prosperity of Chinese dance, and they are respectively Jiang Hua-Xuan, Men Wen-Yuan, Zhao Ming, Yang Mei-Qi, Zhang Ying, Ou Jian-Ping, Jin Xing, Chen Wei-Ya, Gao Cheng-Ming, Sangjijia, Xing Liang, Li Han-Zhong, Ma Bo, Wen Hui, Duan Ni, Huang Xin among others.

Present Situation

Looking back at the history of dance exchanges between China and U.S. for the past 100 years, I've realized that there are still more events to be mentioned, particularly those that have happened since the late 1980s, such as the modern dance workshops given by the U.S. teachers like Dan Wagner, Douglas Nielson in Beijing, three tours of Paul Taylor Dance Company in 1996, 2000 and 2007, two more tours of Ailvin Ailey American Dance Theater in 2004 and 2007, Martha Graham Dance Company in 2008, Jose Limon Dance Company and Jennifer Muller Dance Company both in 2009, Lar Lubovitch Dance Company in 2010; Houston Ballet in 1995 and 2003, Harlem Dance Theater in 2006, San Francesco Ballet and American Ballet Theater both in 2009; as well as the Broadway musicals like Cats, Beauty and Beast, the 42nd Street, Spray, Mama Mia, High School Musical, etc. in China while the U.S. audience saw the performances of Guangdong Modern Dance Company respectively at the ADF and in New York City in 1991, 1997 and 2001, and Beijing Modern Dance Company, Central Ballet of China in The Chinese Culture Week at Kennedy Center for Performing Arts in Washington D.C. in 2009.

However, as we have failed to get any regular and strong support from either Chinese or U.S. government, nor have we made any short term, middle term, long term plans, the dance exchanges between our two big countries have happened only in a sporadic, casual, disjointed and non-governmental way, even the establishment of our Beijing-based National Center for Performing Arts in 2008 has decreased or relaxed this disordered situation, the scale of dance exchanges has failed to match the size, scope, dimensions and importance of our two big countries!

Compared with the great attention and big budget for the dance exchanges and the cultural export as a whole the French and British Governments have given and provided, our Chinese and U.S. Governments should be wakened up! Looking back at 1950s when the advanced concepts and methods of the Soviet ballet training and choreography systematically came into China through two governments' exchange agreements, and helped us successfully set up a complete dance system of our own for the newly born People's Republic of China, we're naturally expecting this kind of long-termed governmental exchanges would take place between our two countries!

Suggestions for the Future

My suggestions would be given on two levels, that is, a microscopic one and a macroscopic one as follows:

Considering the influence of U.S. modern dance to develop the creativity in the Chinese dance is quite positive but far from systematic, and the U.S. dancers and other artists have always been anxious to study I Ching (The Book of Changes) and to use its principle to make unexpected and artistic changes since the post modernism in 1960s but easy to get confused about its philosophy and methodology, I suggest that we should put the "In-depth study of both the U.S. Modern Dance and the Chinese I Ching" into the next cultural exchange agreement between our two governments;

At the same time, I would love to suggest that my Chinese Government and the U.S. Government should join effort to establish a "China-U.S. Exchange Foundation," for the purpose of enabling the exchanges in all fields on both sides to develop with a long termed and more comprehensive plan, and on a larger scale.

Back to 1988 when I visited the U.S. for the first time with a fellowship from the NYC-based Asian Cultural Council, I talked to the reporter of The Journal News in New York like this, "Opening up China to avant-garde dance forms doesn't hurt socialism. To me, China is strong enough not to be swallowed up by any outside influences. The importance of cross cultural exchanges is that if people understand each other, there will be no more wars."

Although twenty two years have passed by now, I still believe so.

The full page interview with Ou Jian-Ping, this author, in The Journal-News, New York, 1988

Bibliography:

I. In Chinese:

Wang, Ke-Fen, Liu, En-Bo, Xu, Er-Chong, Feng, Shuang-Bai.A Grand Dictionary of Chinese Dance[M]. Beijing: Art & Culture Press, 2010.

Bureau for Cultural Relations with Foreign Countries of The People's Republic of China.A Complete Guide to Cultural Exchanges between China and the Outside World[M].Beijing: Guangming Daily Press, 1993.

Wang, Ke-Fen, Dong, Xi-Jiu, Liu, Feng-Zhen.Stroies of The Dancers in Ancient China[M].Beijing: People's Music Press, 1983.

Smedley,Agnes.The Chinese Battle Songs[M].Jiang, Feng. trans. Beijing: Writers Press, 1986.

Li, Cheng-Xiang.My First Impression of The American Dance.[J].Beijing: Dance, No.1, 1979.

Shen, Zhi-Long.Gardner, Arts and Multi-Intelligence[M].Beijing: Beijing Normal University Press, 2004.

Yang, Mei-Qi. Me and The American Dance Festival[M].Guangzhou: Self-printing, 2010.

Jiang, Chun-Fang. The First Experiments in Creating Chinese Dance Dramas: Avshalomov's Music Creations[J].Beijing: Dance Forum, No. 4, 1981.

Chen, Zhong. The New Dance Drama Creations in 1930s' China: A Memoir of Aron Avshalomov[J]. Beijing: Dance Forum, No. 4, 1983.

Jiao, Xiong-Ping. Lectures on The Musical Films[M]. Taipei: Yuanliu Publishing Company, 1993.

Stevenson, Ben. Lectures on Choreography at Choreography Department[J].Ou, Jian-Ping, trans. Beijing: Beijing Dance Academy, 1985.

Ou, Jian-Ping.The Modern Dance: Theory & Practice[M].Beijing: Guangming Daily Press,1994.

Ou, Jian-Ping.World Arts History: Dance Volume [M].Beijing: Oriental Press, 2003.

Ou, Jian-Ping.The History and Appreciation of Foreign Dances[M].Beijing: Higher Education Press, 2008.

Sorell, Walter.Dance In Its Time: A Cultural History of Western Dance[M]. Ou, Jian-Ping, translated. Beijing: Remin University Press, 1996.

II. In English:

Denby, Edwin.Looking at Dance. New York:Horizon Press, 1949.

Sherman, Jane. Soaring: The Diary and Letters of A Denishawn Dancer in the Far East, 1925 – 1926. Middletown, Connecticut: Wesleyan University Press, 1976.

Duncan, Irma. Duncan Dancer: An Autobiography. Middletown, Connecticut: Wesleyan University Press, 1965.

Ou, Jian-Ping.From "Beasts" to "Flowers" : Modern Dance in China. Solomon, Ruth, Solomon, John ed. East Meets West in Dance: Voices in the Cross-Cultural Dialogue. Chur, Switzerland: Harwood Academic Publishers, 1995.

Cohen, Selma Jeanne. International Encyclopedia of Dance[M].Oxford: Oxford University Press, 1999.

Bremser, Martha. International Dictionary of Ballet[M].Detroit, London & Washington D.C.: St. James Press, 1993.

Benbow-Pfalzgrav, Taryn. International Dictionary of Modern Dance[M]. Detroit, London & Washington D.C.: St. James Press, 1998.

Koegler, Horst. The Concise Oxford Dictionary of Ballet[M].Oxford & New York: Oxford University Press, 1987.

Craine, Debra, MacKrell, Judith. The Oxford Dictionary of Dance[M]. Oxford & New York: Oxford University Press, 2000.

有意义交流的关键——参与

达米安·沃策尔

美国维尔国际
舞蹈艺术节主任

内容提要： 此次论坛是促进此类交流的重要对话时机，而有在座各位参与，便变得更具意义。参与目的有所不同，并非都只关注问题，而是参与其中，积极引导，寻求保持在当下的方法，并积极参与使文化交流实际生动的有意义交流。我信赖参与，我认为这才是实现有意义交流的关键所在。

    本人跳舞已经很多年，而作为芭蕾舞者业已25年左右。我记得，上次来伯克利的时候，我还在跳舞。2008年，我退休不再跳舞。我曾多次在加州跳舞，在我事业开始起步时是跳独舞，之后则作为领舞者，因此可以这么说，在此之前，我已从另一不同角度对伯克利有所体验。钱以佳对艺术做出评论，克莱尔又简短提到这个问题，我非常感兴趣。我认为这以不同方式引起我们的共鸣。对我来说，确切理解艺术以及艺术内涵是非常困难的。我是一名舞者，我的艺术就在当下时刻之中。艺术即是表演，而进行表演就是最重要的，即是一切，就其本身而言，即代表整个世界。不要说没有准备等等，但那就是关键，那就是一切。现在我不再跳舞，这不仅仅涉及艺术可成为什么，可能成为什么，将成为什么，重要的是当前我们能够怎样以及将怎样使艺术变得有趣而重要。很多人都谈到历史，确实如此，但很少人谈到现在。

    但克莱尔却重点强调了这一点，那些观点在某种程度上可能会让人感到紧张，但那确实不该让人感到不舒服，但中国与美国之间在历史艺术遗产的广度和厚度之间的差异确实是现实。对我来说，现在重要的或许是活着的虚无，但这确实是目前的状态。那么现在到底是什么？如今的艺术代表什么？这包括本人论述中的我来自何方、以及我马上会做什么。对我而言，艺术是一系列事情，涉及娱乐，涉及启迪，这就是我们能够从艺术当中学到的东西。另外，艺术也涉及交流。而这些可能是最为重要的。因为对我而言，这是生存和繁荣兴旺的唯一方式，回到当下，艺术就是体验。在我的世界里，体验有两种方式。一种是我们刚刚进行的，每个人都坐下观看，在我们坐下观看的同时，脸上体现的表情各不相同。总的来说，观看时有幽默、开心和愉悦。另一种为真正体验并以另外方式真正参与其中。我所做的事情之一是与马友友合作开展一个教育计划，去年春天即着手进行此项计划。纽约市共有450个六年级班级，在班加罗尔合为一个班。我们所进行的即是，让所有这些孩子在一年当中通过音乐、舞蹈和讲故事等形式接受多种文化介入实践。并且，他们在艺术的帮助下学习课程，就像通过音乐来学习地理。从这点上看，类似丝绸之路项目，我们正在谈论一种印度舞，而这些孩子都曾学过这个舞蹈，现在他们将进行表演。最近，我一直都在班加罗尔与这些孩子待在一起。对我而言，这即是在体验，与仅仅观看一场印度舞极为不同。这就是我所认为的体验的含义。当然，这只是在孩子的角度上，而这很棒。

而对于艺术，我认为尤其涉及交流，比如国家之间和社团之间的交流。有人提到使艺术成为人们生活的组成部分，不仅属于精英人群，这点在先前有所提及。当然，这点极为必要。这不仅从一个美国视点来看我的表演以及我的创作工作，而更重要的是，我们怎样才能扩大观众群？如何让这触及所有人？而非只是社会的一小部分，并走向世界。

这是一个班级。每所学校都被要求做点什么，以说明其如何相互联系。而这所学校，即布鲁克林的青年妇女领袖学院，决定通过舞蹈讲述移民这一主题。孩子们在马友友伴奏下起舞，这场舞蹈是孩子们与老师合作完成的。这引领他们走上迁移路径。现在，您们应该了解，他们通过进行DNA测试发现这一迁移路径。这也是其中一部分。因此他们了解到了自己的历史，并且将通过艺术、舞蹈和音乐获得一次难以忘怀的学习经历。

他们与音乐家合作共同完成此次舞蹈。同龄学生齐聚一堂，而5所学校中各所学校都采取不同方式。其中一些学校通过戏剧，一些通过舞蹈，另一些则通过音乐进行。实施方法各有不同。他们迁移至中东，最终他们将抵达中国,然后他们将解释具体通过何种方式在纽约集结以及他们的故事。现在,我确实认为,他们已通过舞蹈学到其迁移模式。而我认为这是我们能够真正连接交流的方式之一。

在此次会议开始时,利奇主席引述孔子关于音乐和礼仪的一句话,大致意思是说,如果对音乐和礼仪加深理解,就不会发动战争。非常神奇的是,这句话流传甚久。是否确实如此?让我们稍作考虑。近代的约翰·肯尼迪总统在哈佛大学一次毕业典礼致辞中谈到:"如果更多政治家欣赏诗歌,我们的世界将会更加美好。"但他也说过另一句话:"如果更多诗人了解政治,我们的世界则会更加美好"。我确实认为这与我们在座的实践者密切相关,我们知道,我们并非生活在某种短暂且似象牙塔般的艺术世界里。当然,它非常重要!我的意思是,我们刚刚看到的一些东西在文化意义上非常有趣,但有时在艺术上并非必要,仅仅因其时效性而在文化意义上有必要。在有些方面,艺术变得更具相关性。

今天我想讲的最后一点是,我认为此次论坛是促进此类交流的重要对话时机,而有在座各位参与,便变得更具意义。参与目的有所不同,并非都只关注问题,而是参与其中,积极引导,寻求保持在当下的方法,并积极参与使文化交流实际生动的有意义交流,在某种意义上说,我们因自己的参与而有所成长。我信赖参与,我认为这才是实现有意义交流的关键所在。

Damian Woetzel

Director of the Vail
International Dance
Festival, USA

The Key to Meaningful Exchange —— Participation

Abstract: This forum is an incredible valuable occasion to enable the exchanges, but they become far more valuable at the level at which you participate. There's a ratio of participation in it. Not nearly studying the problem, but participating in it and looking for ways to remain current and to be available for the kind of meaningful exchange that makes cultural exchange actually living. I believe in participation, I believe that's the key to meaningful exchange.

I was a dancer for many years. I was a ballet dancer for about 25 years. I realized that the last time I arrived here at Berkeley, I was still dancing. I retired in 2008. I danced over here at a number of times, and personally at the beginning of my career and later on as a principal dancer, so I've kind of seen it from a different angle than I'm seeing it today, shall we say. When Billy made the comments about what art is, which Claire brought up briefly, it is interesting to me. I think it struck a chord with a bunch of us in different ways. For me, it was hard to understand exactly what it was and that was exactly what it was. I was a dancer, I was in that moment. It was a performance. And doing the performance was the paramount, that was everything and in its own way, the world. Not to say that there wasn't preparation and all, but that really was the point, that was everything. Now that I don't dance, it's much more about what art can be, what art might be, what art will be, how can we, what will make it interesting and important in our day. There's been so much talk about history, and rightly so, maybe not quite as much talk about currency.

But Claire really brought that to the fore, the ideas that I think there's an uncomfortable tension in a way, which really shouldn't be uncomfortable, but it is the reality between the breadth and weight of the Chinese historical artistic legacy in comparison to the American.

And for me, what's important now, and perhaps it's the vanity of being alive, but it's what is now. What is it about now? What are the arts today? And that encompasses where I come from in my comments and what I'm going to do in a minute. To me, the arts are a bunch of things. They're about entertainment. They're about enlightenment, what you can learn from the arts. They're about exchange as well. And they're probably most importantly, because to me this is the only way they live and flourish, getting back to that currency, they are experience. How did they get this experience? There are two ways to experience in my world. There's the way in which we just did, where everybody's sitting down and watching and there's great variety of expression on your faces as we sit here and watch it. By and large, there's humor, joy, and pleasure in watching. There's another to experience and that's to actually experience and to actually participate in another way. So what I want to do is show a tiny clip. One of the things I do is I work with Yo Yo Ma on an education program and this is a thing we did last spring. There are 450 sixth grades in New York City and they're being joined by a class from Bangalore. And what we did is these kids, over the course of the year, were given various cultural interventions through music, through dance, through storytelling. And they learned their curriculum with the aid of the arts. So it's like learning geography through music. In this sense, it's the Silk Road project and we're talking about an Indian type of dance and these kids have all learned it and now they're going to do it. I'm currently with these kids in Bangalore. To me, that is experiencing and is very different than just seeing an Indian dance. It may or may not have an effect. So that's what I mean when I say experience. So this is on a children's level. And that's great.

So that's a point about education where the arts now and I think that's particularly relevant to exchange, certainly, between countries, between societies. It was mentioned about making the arts a part of the people's lives and not just the elite that was mentioned earlier today. And, of course, that's direly necessary. Not only from an American point of view, in terms of my performative works, my producing works. It's all about, how can we expand the audience? How can we make this relevant to everybody? Not just a little certain section of society. Well, that goes for the world as well.

So this is a class. Every school was asked to do something that illustrated how they connected, so to speak. And this school, the Young Women's Leadership Academy in Brooklyn, decided to depict migration through dance. And the kids are being accompanied by Yo Yo Ma and this is a dance that they made together with their teachers. And it's taken them on their path of migration. Now, you should know that they discovered this path of migration by doing DNA testing. That was a part of this as well. So they learned their history, if you will, and they're getting a memorable learning experience through the arts, through dance, through music.

And they collaborated with the musicians to make this dance. And then they came together for their peers. And each school of the five schools did a different thing. Some of them explored it through theater, actually, and some through dance, some through music. There are all different kinds of ways to do it. So I'm just going to let this play as I continue talking. This is them migrating to the Middle East and eventually they're actually going to go to China and then they're going to depict how they all came together in New York, which is their story, if you will. Now I would definitely argue that they learned their migratory patterns by doing dance. And this is one of the ways that I believe we can connect exchange in a meaningful way.

We started this conference with the wonderful Confucius quote that Chairman Leach mentioned about music and courtesy and Confucius said, to the effect, he said if there's an increased understanding of music and courtesy we would not have to deal with war. It is an amazing thing to have come down through the centuries. Is it true? Well, let's think about that for a second. Latter day John Kennedy, in a Harvard commencement, said, "If more politicians knew poetry, we would have a better world." But you know the other interesting thing he said was, "If more poets know politics, we'd actually have a better world." And I actually think that's very relevant to the practitioners in the room that we have awareness, we're not living in some ephemeral other ivory tower artistic world. Of course it matters! I mean, some of the things we just saw are very interesting culturally, and not necessarily just artistically at times, but culturally because of their timeliness. There are places where the arts become a more relevant point.

I feel like I should wrap quickly. My ultimate message here to you today is that I think this is an incredible valuable occasion to enable these exchanges, but they become far more valuable at the level at which you participate. There's a ratio of participation in it. Not nearly studying the problem, but participating in it and looking for ways to remain current and to be available for the kind of meaningful exchange that makes cultural exchange actually living, We grow out of our ability to participate, in a sense. I believe in participation, I believe that's the key to meaningful exchange.

跨文化交流中的理解误差

贾磊磊

中国艺术研究院院长助理、文化发展战略研究中心主任,研究员

内容提要: 实现不同文化背景下人与人之间的相互理解与相互认同,克服跨文化交流中的理解误差,进而改变相互之间的文化偏见,是保护和发展文化多样性的重要保证。过去由于种种原因,中国在国际舞台上所处的被动地位造成了我们在文化交流方面的失语状态,进而失去了我们与西方主流社会进行文化对话的机会。现在随着我国综合国力的提升,使我们赢得了重新展现中国形象的历史机遇,为此我们应当塑造的是一个与经济中国相互统一的文化中国的形象,使中国在摆脱了贫穷、落后的经济形象的同时,彻底改变封闭、僵化的文化形象。在这个历史过程中如何消除跨文化交流中的理解误差,校正历史造成的文化偏见,拆除强势文化的壁垒,是实现文化多元化发展的重要问题。

在多元化的文化语境中,不同文化之间的相互接纳、相互融合有赖于各自对文化的正确理解,特别是对于那些相对陌生、相对隔膜乃至于相互对抗的文化,更需要加强相互之间的交流、对话,本着一种客观、平等、公正的态度坦诚相待。坦率地说,不论是国家之间还是民族之间都不可能没有利益上的冲突,也不可能没有文化上的矛盾,这些都是不可避免的客观现实 —— 即便就是在国家的核心利益方面没有根本的对立与冲突,在文化领域也难免产生各种程度不同的异议与摩擦。面对这种境遇,立足于国家长治久安的未来发展,我们在文化领域需要特别关注的是,不能把国家、民族之间的冲突建立在一种相互猜忌、相互误读的基础上,更不能够把文化矛盾建立在一种理解的误差上,不同国家即便就是在经济领域、政治领域存在着这样或那样的竞争与分歧,也不应当单向度地以己度人,误读对方的话语意义。正是本着这样的精神,在文化交流中应该尽量消除理解的误差,避免文化在传播过程中产生意义的偏移,进而消除不必要的对抗与冲突。

一

人类不同文化之间的冲突有时并不是因为相互之间不能接受,不能认可,而是因为相互之间的不能理解,不能认同。这种不理解、不认同有时源于不同的价值观念,有时又源于交流过程中的理解误差。这种理解的误差尽管并不一定会导致尖锐的利益冲突,但在特定的语境下则可能诱发深度的文化对立。

不同文化之间的交流和对话是相互理解与相互认同的前提。但是,在相互交流的过程中,由于交流媒介、交流方式、交流模式的不同,有时可能会产生与交流的初衷未必一致的交流效果。英国的文化学者伯克在分析文化演进的历史变迁时曾经说:"当不同的文化相遇时,每种文化对其他文化形成的形象有可能成为一种固定程式(stereotype)。固定程式本身可能并没有错误,但它往往会夸大事实中某些特征,同时又抹杀其他一些特征。固定程式多多少少会有些粗糙和歪曲。可以肯定地说,它缺乏细微的差别,因为它是将同一模式运用于相互之间差异很大的文化状况。例如,欧洲人所画的美洲印第安人往往是一种合成的形象,把不同地区的印第安人的特征结合在一起,创造出一种简单的总体形象。"这种合成往往是根据不同国家既定的文化习俗来进行的。在国际文化交流的语言平台上,很多发展中国家的民族形象都曾经面临着这样一种被"固定程式"化的历史经历。除了恶意的曲解和丑化之外,文化本身的表述形态与接受方式也可能产生歧义,要改变这种现状,发展中国家只有通过不断地加强文化产品的输出,不断地增进对于自己国家文化形象的建构才能够逐渐实现,而不能够指望其他国家自动放弃他们固有的文化立场,或是改变他们的阐释理念。

也许,在不同文化的互译中,被"改写"与被"固定程式"化的情形似乎是必然的 —— 只有像葡萄酒、香烟这种没有生命的物质消费品才有可能原汁原味地被接纳,凡是文化符号的转译与传播,都不可能百分之百地与原有的文化形态相互对位。在这种情况下如何消除文化符号在转译与交流中被歪曲、被误解、误读的现象，即成为消除不同文化对立与冲突的重要问题。

其实，在文化交往中任何国家往往都是把自己置于中心地位来权衡与其他国家的关系。从中世纪开始许多国家的地图，就把本国置于世界的中心位置。像著名的赫里福德地图，把耶路撒冷置于世界的中心，提供了宗教有关中世纪如何看待世界版图的有力证据。包括16世纪威尼斯的木刻，从表面上看都是写实的，但作为一种文化符号实际上标明了绘制者自我中心的文化观念，是"伦理地理学"的典型范例。现在大家都可以共同确认地球的物质形态，可是在不同国家印制的地图中都会把本国的位置定在世界的中心，这已是不争的事实。

二

我们亟待有一批映现真实中国形象的作品对过去影片所造成的负面影响进行历史的校正，对国际影坛上中国的旧形象进行全面的覆盖，才能够逐渐改变中国在国际文化交流中所造成的文化误读。

在我们跨文化交流的历史经验中，中国的形象被西方传播媒体"改写"与"置换"的例证举不胜举。中国人的形象在西方艺术作品中过去总是被扭曲、被丑化、甚至被妖魔化的。在西方早期的美术作品中就反映出这种倾向。作者在描绘荷兰东印度公司的一名使节到来中国的情形时，就把西藏的喇嘛画成了天主教的教士，把喇嘛手中的念珠画成天主教的念珠。与版画相配的说明文字进一步反映了这种同化中国的倾向。把喇嘛的宽袖比作修士的袖子，把他的"念珠"比作修士的念珠。显然，这是因为该书的读者大多是天主教徒。事实上，就连西方人也很清楚铜版画中所画的帽子与传统的尖角喇嘛帽根本不是一回事，可是他们偏偏要按照自己的意志把中国的形象"西方化"。

进入改革开放的历史时代以后，中国打破了封闭、僵化的文化局面，在思想解放运动的推动下，我们在大量汲取发达国家先进的科学技术的同时，开始引进西方的文化产品。同时，利用各种渠道向海外展示当代中国的历史性变化。但是西方社会对中国选择性的文化态度，使中国的文化形象依然没有摆脱旧时的那种落后、封闭的面貌。加之我国在国际上获奖的主要作品是第五代电影人的民族寓言式的影片。这些影片在文化反思与文化寻根的时代潮流中对于中国内地的思想解放运动起到了推波助澜的积极作用，特别是在大众文化领域所展开的拨乱反正的思想变革产生了不可磨灭的历史作用。但是，这些影片在叙事空间的封闭状态与时间上的停滞状态很容易使观影者把影片表述的故事内容与中国封建社会的文化形象联系在一起。由于西方没有一个文化反思的社会历史背景来阅读第五代电影，他们会把我们作为批判对象来揭示的内容作为我们的现实内容来看待，这种阅读背景的文化落差，造成了我们与他们在影片意义建构方面的偏移。第五代导演以悲怆的人文情怀探索传统文化的痛楚和民族心理的深层结构的主观意图，不管是有意还是无意大都被国际电影节忽略了，他们更愿意看到的是在这些影片中所表现的那种带有落后、封闭色彩的文化符号，来满足他们对于中国的历史想象。我们至今也不认为第五代的那些艺术电影是专门拍给西方人看的，他们影片中所具有的强烈的文化反思意图，对于西方人来讲可能根本就没有阅读的兴趣。也许处于后工业时代的西方社会并不知道中国电影在改革开放的历史进程中所肩负的文化使命，也不知道中国电影要摆脱"文革电影"影响的严峻现实，在这样一种文化语境的落差中，中国电影在国际电影节上获奖的诸多作品不可避免地被误读，使这些影片在客观上成为满足西方对于东方文化想象的一种现实文本。我们固然不能否认这些电影在影像艺术的表述层面对于世界电影界的冲击，但就其对中国文化形象的深远影响而言，这些影片提供的并不是一个令人欣慰的佐证。

尽管这些获奖影片使我们的电影在国际电影界有了一席之地，可是对于国际舞台上的中国形象而言其影响却令人担忧。目前，在不能改变双方历史背景的情况下，在无法填平不同时代形成的文化落差的境遇下，怎样弥合文化交流的这种理解错位是一个极为紧迫而又重要的问题。目前，我们在国内得奖的影片在国际上同时得奖的只有11.4%，可见国内和国际的评价标准并不一样，这种现象对任何一个国家的电影可能都在所难免。可是差异如此之大，使我们必须认真寻找其中的根本原因。

三

我们对于中国文化在海外的译介、推广显然需要加大力度，特别是需要通过大众传播媒介以商业化的方式，避开西方社会有形无形的各种屏蔽，深入到普通受众的视野，让他们在休闲娱乐的氛围中直接感受到中国文化的真正魅力。

除了历史境遇的差异所造成的不可避免的文化误读之外，强势国家常常容易将弱势国家的文化神秘化、低俗化。如果再加上意识形态的壁垒、文化立场的差异，发展中国家，特别是东方国家的形象过去时常被曲解和改写，在信息单向流动态势下，中国的文化形象被丑化和妖魔化的事件时有发生，以致西方的民众很难通过主流传播通道认识中国文化的真正面貌。现在就像我们不能放弃对于疆域的政治主权一样，我们也不能够丧失对于语言符号的文化主权。现在好莱坞电影进入中国电影市场，就连配音演员的资质都要经过他们的审定才能够通过，以此来保证影片能够完整意义的有效传播，而我们的经典文化文本却近乎随意地被译为与西方文化趋同的概念在国际文化交流中普遍使用。

中国的京剧被西方人翻译为"北京歌剧"（Beijing Opera），其实歌剧原本是一种以歌唱为主的舞台演出形式，而中国京剧则是一种集"唱、念、做、打"为一体的表演艺术，单纯的歌剧理念显然无法覆盖京剧的丰富内涵。现在，京剧中的"唱、念、做、打"已经被直译为英语中的汉语拼音，而北京歌剧的概念依然被沿用。也许，在跨文化的交流中根本就不存在一个能够与中国京剧相互衔接的英语词汇。就像当年周恩来用"中国的罗密欧与朱丽叶"来形容梁山伯与祝英台令西方人欣然认可一样，把中国京剧翻译为北京歌剧也未尝不可。可是，这种根据类似原则将中国独有的文化形态嫁接到西方文化模式中的交流方式，不仅曲解了中国文化艺术的原生意义，而且导致了语言交流过程中的理解偏差，特别值得注意的是这种模式造成了在文化价值观上中国文化被"西方化"的倾向，它使我们民族的文化在跨文化交流中失去了它最为宝贵的独特意义。西方对中国文化最具代表性的误读是对"功夫"的译介。当年李小龙主演的功夫片风行海外，中国功夫随之扬威世界，致使许多外国词典里都出现了一个新词："功夫"（Chinese Kung Fu）。现在在许多外国人心目中，功夫就是中国武术的代名词，而实际上中国武术在北方通常被称为武术，而在南方则被称之为功夫。后来西方人又把中国以武术技击为主导动作、以侠义精神为核心内容的武侠电影称之为功夫电影，并且拍摄了《功夫之王》、《功夫熊猫》这类以功夫命名的影片。在这些影片中，中国武术博大精深的文化内涵基本被眼花缭乱的外部的技击动作所覆盖，特别是中国武术禅武合一、内外兼修的文化精神被西方人忽略了。在影片《功夫熊猫》中，憨态可掬的熊猫练就武艺的过程，是一个不断地满足它贪吃欲望的过程，它在物质欲望的诱惑下不断提升武术技艺的表述与中国武侠电影中英雄的成长历程在文化取向上已经完全背道而驰。可见西方人看中的是中国功夫在技艺层面所表现出来的那种奇异的击打技艺与抗击打能力，而中国武侠电影的真正要义并不在于外部的技击动作如何精彩，而关键要看的是其内在的精神品质怎样升华。中国武侠文化中那种其言必信、其诺必诚、其行必果的侠义精神，那种舍生取义、捐躯忘亲的阔大胸襟都不是靠外部的技击动作能够完全体现的。

比对功夫的翻译更为严重的是对于"龙"的转译。龙在中国文化里是吉祥、尊贵的象征；有时甚至与帝王与皇权的威严联系在一起。在英语中龙被翻译成 Dragon（怪兽、恶魔），用之于人，常常描述的是凶猛、暴戾、凶恶的形象。最为突出的是西方文化里常爱把龙与撒旦、魔鬼相提并论，有时甚至就是一个词。西方人甚至曾经把纳粹法西斯也称之为 Dragon。在第二次世界大战中，美国国内的反日宣传海报根据日本领土的形状，把日本画成一头张牙舞爪的 dragon。其目的是想借此告诉美国民众："日本是一头恶魔（dragon）。1941年6月2日的《下午》报（纽约的一家日报，现已停刊）也刊登了一幅漫画，上面画着有着希特勒面部特征的 Dragon，它正横跨大西洋向美国本土游来，它身上画着明显的纳粹标志。 特别值得注意的是，由于 Dragon 在基督教文化中代表着恶魔——撒旦，所以敌对的双方经常把对方妖魔化，而这种妖魔化的方式就是把对方比喻为 Dragon。德国法西斯当时也曾经在海报和宣传标语中以 Dragon 来比喻他们的主要敌人，并且把它描绘成吐着火舌的多头怪兽。不知道究竟是什么原因使得在中国至尊无比的龙，在西方变成了一种传说中的怪兽。直到现在的好莱坞电影《木乃伊3》中，由死而复生的中国帝王"丘王"变成的依然是一只凶神恶煞的多头怪兽，在嘶叫与怒吼中带着杀人的军队涂炭生灵。包括在《哈利·波特》系列片中，龙的变异形象也总是邪恶、凶残的代表。这种情况说明，我们与西方主流文化之间在许多重要领域还存在着明显的理解误差，对于那些容易产生歧义的文化符号，不论是作为民族的象征还是作为企业的形象广告都应该慎用，以免引起负面影响。

四

随着文化交往的不断深入，相互之间并不一定都会认同与接受。如果在文化交往中不注重交往的有效方式，不选择恰当的文化产品，不尊重对方的文化个性，那么，交往的频率越高，诱发的冲突与对立可能就会越大。

目前，在全球化的历史语境中，如何通过有效的文化交流方式，来缩小和弥合人类社会在文化领域的对立与冲突，是个十分紧迫而又重要的问题。经济贸易的合作对于贸易的双方并不只是带来互惠，而且还会带来利益的对立与纷争，由于深度的经贸讨论很可能会超越单纯的经济领域而进入到文化领域，在文化交流并不充分的情况下，必然会产生贸易双方的疑虑与分歧。所以，我们不能期待仅仅通过经济的方式来加强国家之间的联系，国家之间的文化问题必须通过有效的跨文化交流方式来解决。经济贸易的交往只能够加强双方的利益合作，可是并不能"购买到"对方的文化价值观，文化的理解必须通过文化的交流才能够实现，尤其是经济贸易本身可能还会带来双方在经济利益方面的讨价还价、甚至在议价过程中由于双方各持己见还可能产生摩擦。所以，国家与国家之间的经贸交往更多只能够促进经济的互惠，而不能取代文化的交往与对话。

现在，不同国家在国际交往中往往把经济贸易放在首位，国家间都希望通过经济的互惠来加强相互的共同利益，以实现国家间长久、稳定的政治关系。如前所述，经济的交往并不能够取代文化的沟通和价值观的相互认同。卢森堡皮埃尔·维尔纳学会顾问委员会主席让－雅克·叙布纳在"第一届中欧文化对话"中指出，文化的最高成就是避免战争。现在欧洲一体化进程中通过政体、语言、金融的全面合作使欧洲成员国之间发生战争的可能性几乎降到零，这不能不说是一个伟大的历史性创举。在这个过程中文化其实起到了决定性的作用。2009年4月29日在四川省成都市举行"中国——西班牙论坛"第五次会议上，西班牙文化部政治与文化产业司司长吉耶尔莫·科拉尔提到了目前欧洲正在实施的"欧洲文化宪章机制"，欧盟通过这个机制对欧盟国家的历史名胜、古代遗迹、旅游圣地进行重新确认。这表明欧洲正在从经济、金融的一体化走向文化价值观的一体化进程。其目的就是要强化欧盟国家的共同文化价值观，他们把这个机制的实施看做是欧盟和平稳定发展的基础。尽管文化有利于经济的可持续发展，但是人们不希望文化仅仅成为财富增长的工具，强调整体的文化价值观，会加强基于文化多样性基础上的相互联合，使欧盟的一体化建设进程得到文化的有力支撑。

　　随着文化交往的不断深入，相互之间的不断了解并不一定都会带来认同与接受。就像一对日益加深了解的恋人一样，往往是接触的越密切、了解的越深入，产生摩擦的概率可能会越高，引发的矛盾会越尖锐，分手的可能性越大。固然，国家与国家之间的关系不像个人之间的关系那么容易被情绪所左右，但是可以肯定的是，如果在文化交往中不注重交往的有效方式，不选择恰当的文化产品，不尊重对方的文化个性，那么交往的频率越高，诱发的冲突与对立可能就会越大。中国古代的美学家刘勰在一千多年前就曾经感叹道："知音其难哉！音实难知，知实难逢，逢其知音，千载其一乎！"这位以《文心雕龙》而永垂千古的伟大艺术家，其历史的慨叹至今仍然不绝于耳，可见我们在探寻人类相互理解与相互认同的途径上是如此任重道远，值得欣慰的是中国改革开放所创立的历史伟业，使世界上的许多国家、特别是发达国家不得不躬下身来倾听中国的声音，思忖中国的力量。如果说，过去由于种种原因我们在国际舞台上所处的被动地位造成了我们在文化交流方面的失语状态，进而失去了我们与西方主流社会进行文化对话的机会，那么，现在随着我国综合国力的提升，使我们赢得了重新展现国家形象的历史机遇。为此，我们应当塑造的是一个与经济中国相互统一的文化中国的形象，使中国在摆脱了贫穷、落后的经济形象的同时，也彻底改变封闭、僵化的文化形象，努力消除跨文化交流中的理解误差，用事实改变海外对我们的文化偏见，实现中国文化繁荣发展的伟大理想。

Misinterpretation in Cross-cultural Exchange

Jia Leilei

Research Fellow and
President Assistant
of Chinese National
Academy of Arts
Director of Cultural
Development
Strategy Research
Center, CNAA

Abstract: It is crucial to realize the mutual understanding and recognition between peoples in different cultures, clear up misinterpretation in cross-cultural exchange, and eliminate the existing cultural bias, so as to ensure the protection and development of cultural diversity. In the past centuries, China has been in a status of cultural aphasia in cultural exchange and further lost the opportunity of cultural dialogues with the Western mainstream societies due to its passive position in the international arena. Presently, it is high time for China to show the world a new image with its growing comprehensive national power. Therefore, we shall shape a cultural image corresponding to China's economic power, so that the country will completely change its previous cultural image of being self-enclosed and ossified and get rid of the poverty-stricken and economically-backward image. It is critically needed to clear up misinterpretation in cross-cultural exchange, rectify the historically-formed cultural bias, and remove the barriers imposed by cultural powers, in order to realize the development of multiculturalism.

In a multicultural context, mutual acceptance and integration of various cultures are based upon the true understanding of different cultures, especially the strange and less-understood ones, and even in opposition to one's own. More importantly, it is necessary to strengthen exchange and communication between cultures, and treat each other objectively, equally and fairly. Frankly speaking, it is unavoidable to have either conflict of interest or cultural contradictions between countries or ethnics, and differences and frictions will exist more or less in cultures, even though countries have no fundamental confrontations or conflicts in their core interest. Against such a background, we shall start from the future development of the country for long-term peace and stability, and avoid putting the conflicts between countries and ethnics into a context full of suspicion or misunderstanding, or treating the cultural contradictions based upon misinterpretation. Even though there are economic competitions and political differences between countries, one country should not judge the others by itself or misread the others' discourse meanings. In line with this principle, more efforts shall be put in cultural exchange to clear up misinterpretation, prevent cultural meanings from bias during communication, and eliminate unnecessary confrontations and conflicts.

I

Cultural conflicts may be resulted from mutual misunderstanding and non-recognition, instead of mutual non-acceptance or non-approval. The mutual misunderstanding and non-recognition is sometimes from differed values, and sometimes from misinterpretation in communication. The misinterpretation may not necessarily lead to sharp conflicts of interest, but is likely to induce deepened cultural confrontations in specific contexts.

It is on the premise of cross-cultural exchange and dialogues that peoples in different cultures can understand and recognize each other. Nevertheless, due to the differences in media, methods and modes of communication, the results may turn against the original intentions. In his analysis of cultural evolution, the British scholar Burke once said, "When different cultures meet, each may form a stereotype for the image of another. A stereotype may not be wrong itself, but it usually overstates some aspects of fact, while obliterating others. A stereotype is more or less rough and misrepresenting. Definitely, it lacks subtle differences, as it applies a same mode to various cultural situations that greatly differ from one another. For example, the American Indians painted by Europeans were actually a compounded image, in which features of Indians in different regions were integrated into a simplified general image." Such compound is often made in accordance with the existing culture and customs in a country. On the international discourse platform for cross-cultural exchange, many developing countries used to be faced with such a "stereotyped" image of nation. In addition to malicious distortion and defamation, the form of expression of a culture and the way it is accepted by others may also produce ambiguities. To change the current situation, a developing country has to continuously strengthen the output of its cultural products and improve the construction of its cultural image, instead of looking to the other countries to give up their established cultural standpoint voluntarily, or change their ideas of interpretation.

Maybe it is unavoidable for a culture to be "rewritten" or "stereotyped" in cross-cultural exchange, and only lifeless material goods such as wine and cigarettes can be accepted as they are. No cultural icons are able to be translated or communicated fully corresponding to the original cultural forms. In these circumstances, it is important to clear up all the twisted, misunderstood and misinterpreted translations of a cultural icon during cross-cultural exchange, so as to eliminate confrontations and conflicts between different cultures.

In cross-cultural exchange, a country, in fact, usually judges and weighs the relations with the others with itself as the center. Since the Middle Ages, many countries have placed themselves in the center of the world on their versions of maps. For instance, Jerusalem is placed in the world's center on the well-known Hereford Map, showing a religious attitude toward the world in the Middle Ages.

And the Venetian wood carving of the 16th century, though seeming to be made from life, as a cultural icon, actually indicates the makers' self-centered cultural concepts and is typical of "ethical geography". Even though the international communities have got to a common view about the world's material form, it cannot be denied that a country will still try to place itself in a central place when drawing a map of the world.

II

It is in urgent needs to make some new films truly reflecting China's image and rectifying the negative impacts the previous films have made, so that the old image of China in the international movie circle can be covered, and the cultural misinterpretation of China gradually cleared up in international cultural exchange.

In the past cross-cultural exchange, the image of China has been repeatedly "rewritten" or "replaced" by the Western media, and that of the Chinese people has always been twisted, smeared, and even demonized. The tendency was clearly reflected through the early Western paintings. In a painting depicting the arrival of a commissioner of the Dutch East India Company in China, the Tibetan lamas are painted as priests and the prayer beads into rosaries. The tendency of assimilation of China was further reflected in the descriptions to the woodcut print. That the wide sleeves of a lama's clothes were described as those of a priest's clothes and a string of "prayer beads" in a lama's hand as a priest's rosaries was obviously because that most readers of the book were Catholics. In fact, even Westerners themselves well knew that the hat drawn in the copperplate was completely different from a traditional lama's pointed cap. Nevertheless, they still "Westernized" the image of China according to their own wishes.

Since the epoch-making reform and opening-up, the previous cultural enclosure and stagnation have been broken in China. With ideological emancipation, the Western cultural products have been introduced into the country, which also learns huge amount of advanced science and technology from developed countries. Meanwhile, China has shown via various channels the other countries its historical changes. However, the Western societies have selective acceptance of the Chinese culture, and remain impressed with the old cultural image of China of being backward and self-enclosed. Additionally, the Chinese films winning international awards and known to the outside world were mainly the fifth-generation national-fable-like ones, which played an active role in the ideological emancipation in the mainland China in times of cultural reflections and root-seeking, and had an unforgettable historical significance in the popular culture to bring order out of chaos in people's thinking. Nonetheless, the closed state of narrative space and the stagnation state of time in these films left a wrong impression on audience that the stories told in the films reflected the cultural image of feudalism in China. Unfortunately, as there has been no such a social and historical background of cultural reflections in the West as in China, what was critically revealed in the fifth-generation films was seen by the West as the reality in China. This cultural difference in interpretation has resulted in deviations between the Chinese fifth-generation directors' original intentions and the Western understanding of their films. The fifth-generation directors' intentions to explore, in a pathetic and humanist manner, the pains in traditional Chinese culture and the national psychological structure in depth were intentionally or unintentionally ignored in various international film festivals. The Western audience preferred the cultural icons indicating China's backwardness and self-enclosure in these films, to satisfy the age-old imagination of China. We have never thought that the fifth-generation literary films had specially targeted the Westerners, for the strong intentions of cultural reflections in these films may have never interested the western audience at all. Perhaps the western societies in the post-industrial era have no idea at all about the cultural mission undertaken by the Chinese films in the historical process of reform and opening-up, or the harsh reality confronting the Chinese films that they have to get rid of the impacts of the "films made in the Cultural Revolution". In these disparities between the Chinese and western cultural realities, the international-award-winning Chinese films have inevitably been misinterpreted and objectively become an in-reality channel through which the western audience could satisfy their imagination of the Oriental cultures. No doubt we cannot deny the impacts the fifth-generation Chinese films have brought on the expression of video art in the world's movie circle, but they have not played a positive role in changing China's cultural image in the world.

Though some space these award-winning films have won for the Chinese film industry in the world, their impacts on the world's attitudes toward China's image are troublesome. At present, with the historical backgrounds unchanged and the historically-formed cultural gaps unfilled, it is urgent and crucial to find out how to clear up the existing misinterpretation. Currently, only 11.4% of the Chinese films which won domestic awards also won the awards in international film festivals, indicating differed criteria adopted domestically and globally, which can hardly be avoided for the film industry in any country. However, the above-quoted low percentage in China urges us to find the fundamental reasons.

III

We shall put more efforts in translating, introducing and promoting the Chinese culture in the overseas, especially to the ordinary audience, in a commercial way via mass media and trying to avoid those tangible and intangible barriers in the Western societies, so that the ordinary audience can have personal experience of the true charms of the Chinese culture.

In addition to the inevitable misinterpretations caused by historically-formed differences between various cultures, the cultures of disadvantaged countries are often mystified and vulgarized by the powerful countries. Moreover, with ideological barriers and differences in cultural standpoints, the images of developing countries, particularly the oriental ones, have been repeatedly distorted and rewritten in the past. In the unidirectional flow of information, the cultural image of China was so often defamed and demonized, that the western people were unable to know about the true Chinese culture via mainstream communication channels in the Western societies. Nowadays, we shall defend our cultural sovereignty over language and icons, in the same way we defend our political sovereignty over territory. Sharply contrasting with the fact that the qualifications of the Chinese dubbing actors for the Hollywood films in the Chinese market must be approved by the Hollywood film-makers, to ensure the meanings of a Hollywood film are able to be fully interpreted, classical concepts in the Chinese culture have been casually translated into the ones adapted to the Western cultures and widely used in international cultural exchange.

The traditional Chinese drama Jing Ju(京剧) is translated into "Beijing opera" by the West, but opera is a form of stage production with singing as the major method of expression, while Jing Ju(京剧) is a type of performing arts composed of four basic performing techniques of "singing, reciting, acting and martial arts performing". Therefore, the concept of opera is too simple to cover the essence of Jing Ju(京剧). So far, the four basic techniques in Jing Ju(京剧) have been known to the English-speaking population as "Chang(唱), Nian(念), Zuo(做) and Da(打)", directly taken from the scheme for the Chinese phonetic alphabet, while the term Beijing opera is still in use. Perhaps Jing Ju(京剧) has no satisfactory equivalent in English at all. It may be not that bad to have Jing Ju(京剧) translated into Beijing opera, just like that Zhou Enlai once described Liang Shanbo and Zhu Yingtai to the western audience as "the Chinese Romeo and Juliet". Nevertheless, such mode of cross-cultural exchange to graft a cultural form unique to China in the western cultural mode according to a principle of analogy has not only distorted the native characteristics of the Chinese culture, but also led to the misinterpretation in language exchange. It is particularly noteworthy that this mode of communication has resulted in a tendency in which the Chinese culture is "Westernized" on the level of cultural values, so that the uniqueness most precious to the Chinese national culture has lost in cross-cultural exchange. The translation and understanding of "kung fu" by the West has been a most typical example of the misinterpretations of the Chinese culture. Kung fu was first known to the whole world through Bruce Lee's films, and "kung fu" has emerged as a new term in English and the synonym for the Chinese martial arts to many foreigners. However, the Chinese martial arts are actually known as Wu Shu (武术) in North China, and kung fu (功夫) is a term commonly used in the south. Later, the swordsmen films, showing the art of attack and defense in the Chinese martial arts and the spirits of chivalrous swordsmen, were named by the West kung fu films, such as The Forbidden Kingdom and Kung Fu Panda. The extensive and profound cultural connotations of the Chinese martial arts have been clouded by the dazzling display of various techniques of attack and defense. Particularly the West has overlooked the essence of the Chinese martial arts that pays equal attention to internal mind and external techniques. The lovely panda in Kung Fu Panda practices martial arts to satisfy his greedy appetite for food. To practice martial arts encouraged by material desires expressed in this film totally went against the essence of the traditional Chinese swordsmen films. It can be seen that what the West likes about the Chinese martial arts is the amazing techniques of attack and capabilities of strike-resistance, while the essence of the Chinese swordsmen films is the internal mind of a true hero. The external techniques of attack and defense alone cannot truly embody the essence of the Chinese martial arts: honesty in words, faith in promise, resolution in deed and preference to death over disgrace.

The translation of "Long (龙)" in Chinese to the English word "dragon", however, was a much worse case than that of kung fu where Long (龙), a symbol of auspiciousness and respectfulness, and the imperial authority in the Chinese culture, is translated into "dragon" in English, meaning a monster or devil, and if a person is described as "a dragon", it means the person is violent, brutal and cruel. In particular, dragon is usually connected with, sometimes even the synonym of Satan and devils in the Western cultures. Westerners even used to call Nazi dragon. In the Second World War, Japan was drawn, to the shape of its territory, as a threatening dragon in the American anti-Japanese posters, to show the American people that Japan was a dragon. The cartoon published in PM (a New York daily newspaper that has stopped publication now) on June 2, 1941, depicted a Hitler-headed dragon emblazoned with swastikas straddling the Atlantic. It is particularly noteworthy that in the West, opposing sides usually demonize each other as dragon, as dragon symbolizes Satan in the Christian cultures. The German fascists used to describe their enemies as multi-headed dragon with a blazing tongue in the posters and slogans. It has been unknown why the respectful dragon in China has become a monster in the Western legends. Even the reviving Chinese Emperor in the Hollywood film The Mummy: Tomb of the Dragon Emperor is transformed into a malicious-looking multi-headed monster, howling and roaring, and leads his armies to kill people. Variants of dragon were also taken to represent devil and cruelty in the series of Harry Potter. It is indicated that there is significant misunderstanding in many fields between the Chinese culture and the Western mainstream cultures. Therefore, the cultural icons, as national symbols or brand image for an enterprise, shall be used with care, in case there would be any unnecessary negative impacts.

IV

As in-depth cultural exchange is conducted, mutual recognition and acceptance may not be fully realized. The more cultural exchange is conducted, the fiercer conflicts and confrontations will be induced, with no effective communication adopted, no proper cultural products selected, or no mutual respects paid in cultural exchange.

Against the background of globalization at present, it is urgent and crucial to cushion conflicts and confrontations between different cultures by means of effective cross-cultural exchange. Together with the mutual benefits in economic and trade cooperation, there will be conflicts and disputes of interest. In-depth economic and trade negotiations are very likely to go beyond the simply economic issues into the cultural field. Under these circumstances lacking full cultural communication, there must be doubts and disputes between the two parties involved. Therefore, we cannot simply rely on economic means to strengthen the contacts and ties between countries; instead, an effective way of cross-cultural exchange is a more important channel to solve conflicts between different cultures. Contacts through economic activities and trades can only strengthen the mutual cooperation for benefits, but may not necessarily "purchase" each other's cultural values. Cultural understanding cannot be realized without cultural communication. Moreover, the parties have to negotiate for their own economic profits in economic activities and trades, and may have conflicts if both parties stick to their own views in negotiations. Thus, economic and trade cooperation can only promote mutual benefits in the economic field, but is unable to replace cultural exchange and dialogues between countries.

Nowadays, economic and trade cooperation is usually given first priority in international communication. All the countries try to establish and keep long and stable political relationships with the others by strengthening their common interest through economic reciprocity. However, as above stated, economic contacts cannot take the place of cultural communication and mutual recognition of values. As Jean-Jacques Subrenat, Chairman of Scientific Council of the Pierre Werner Institute, said on the First Chinese-European Cultural Dialogue, the highest cultural achievement was to avoid war. The possibility of war between member countries of the European Union has been almost reduced to zero, thanks to the political, lingual and financial cooperation in the integration in Europe, the historical significance of which cannot be denied. During the process, culture has played a decisive role. At the Fifth Meeting of China-Spain Forum held on April 29, 2009, in Chengdu, Sichuan Province, Guillermo Corral, Director of Division of Politics and Cultural Industries of Ministry of Culture of Spain, talked about the ongoing "Mechanism of the European Cultural Charter", through which the European Union could reconfirm the historical sites, ancient monuments and tourist attractions in the EU countries, indicating that the integration of the EU countries was expanding from economy and finance into cultural values. The integration of cultural values is aimed to strengthen the common cultural values of the EU countries. The mechanism is seen as the foundation for a peaceful and stable development of EU. Culture is indeed beneficial for a sustainable economic development; nevertheless, people do not want to see culture simply as a tool for increase in wealth. To place emphasis on the integral cultural values can consolidate the alliance based upon cultural diversity and give strong support to the integration progress in EU.

As in-depth cultural exchange is conducted, mutual recognition and acceptance may not be fully realized. Just like a couple, there may be more and sharper conflicts, as the two get closer and know more about each other, and they are more likely to split. It is true that the relationship between countries is less subject to emotions than that between a couple, but it is obviously that the more cultural exchange is conducted, the fiercer conflicts and confrontations will be induced, with no effective communication adopted, no proper cultural products selected, or no mutual respects paid in cultural exchange. An aesthetician in the ancient China and author of the Literary Mind and the Carving of Dragons, Liu Xie sighed with feeling more than a thousand years ago, "How difficult to find a bosom friend! It's hard to find someone who really understands me. Were there such a person, may we not meet each other the whole life. It may be a chance once in a thousand years to meet a person who really understands me!" The words of this famed author are still echoing in our ears now. There is a long way to go and much to do to reach true understanding and recognition of one another. Fortunately, since the reform and opening-up in China, many other countries, particularly the developed ones, have had to bend to listen to China's voices and think about China's strength. In the past centuries, China has been in a status of cultural aphasia in cultural exchange and further lost the opportunity of cultural dialogues with the Western mainstream societies, due to its passive position in the international arena. Presently, it is high time for China to show the world a new image, with its growing comprehensive national power. Therefore, we shall shape a cultural image corresponding to China's economic power, so that the country will completely change its previous cultural image of being self-enclosed and ossified and get rid of the poverty-stricken and economically-backward image. It is critically needed to clear up misinterpretation in cross-cultural exchange, rectify the historically-formed cultural bias, and remove the barriers imposed by strong cultures, in order to realize the development of multiculturalism.

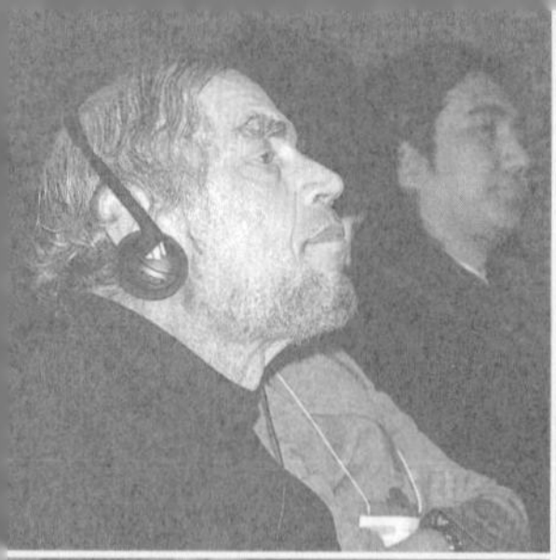
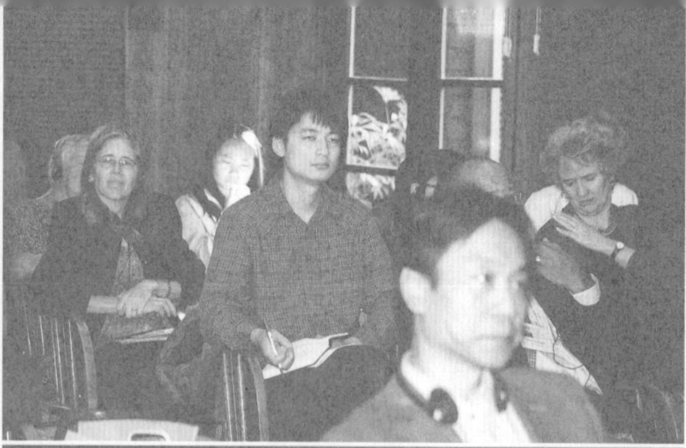
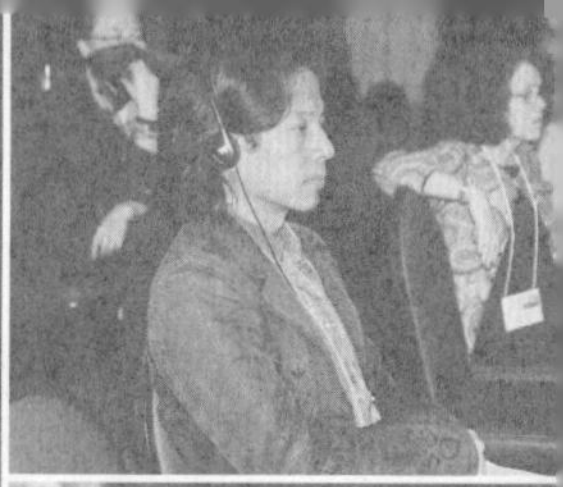
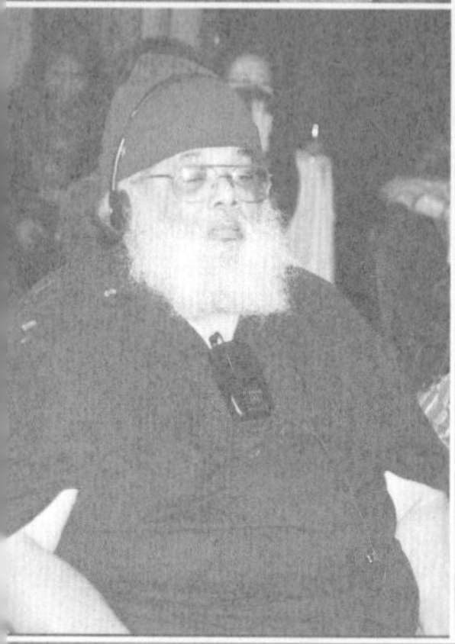
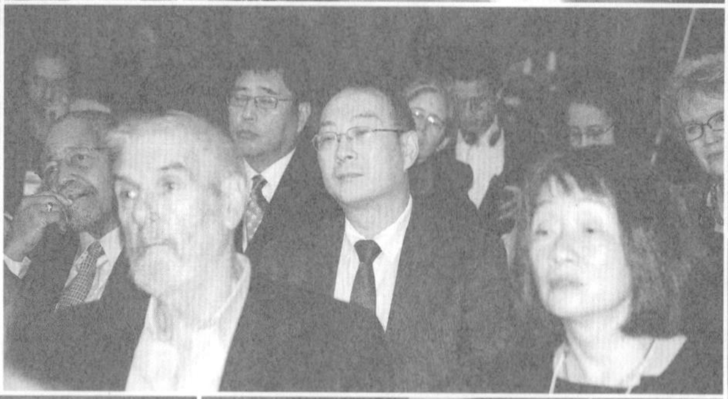
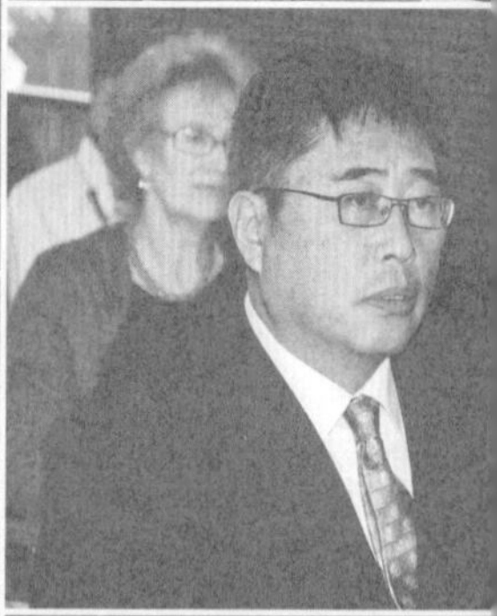
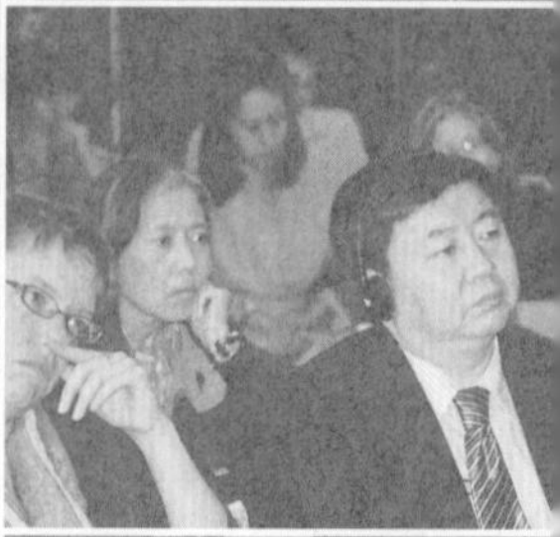
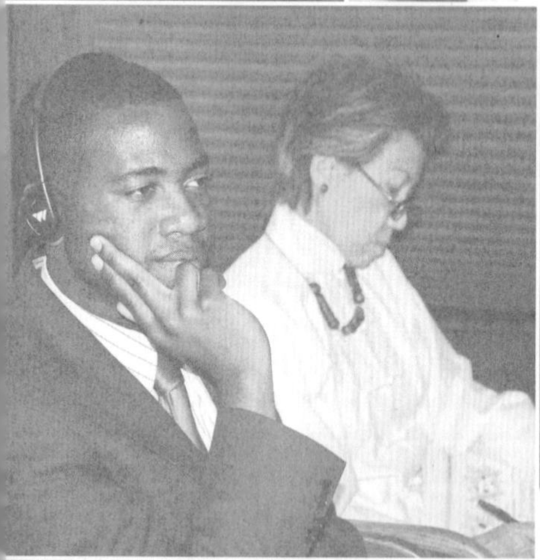
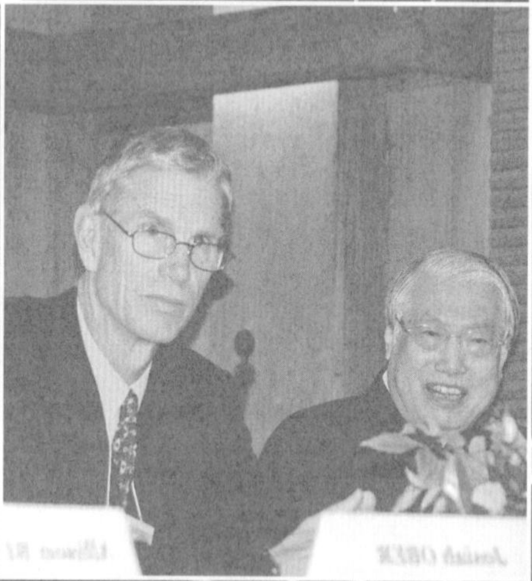
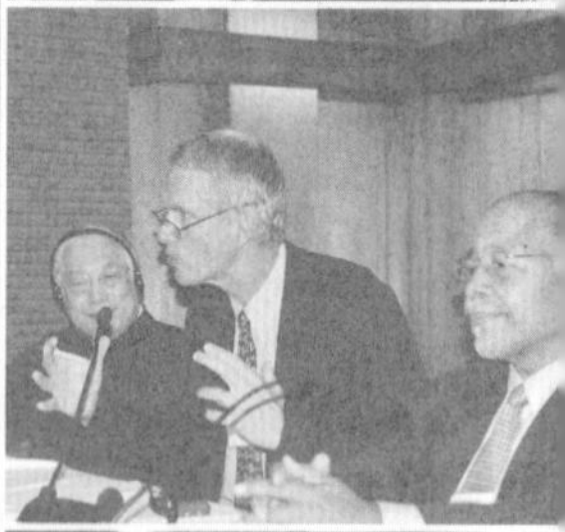
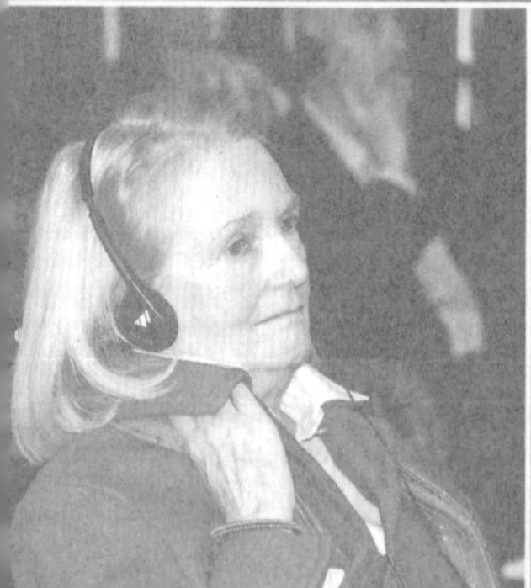
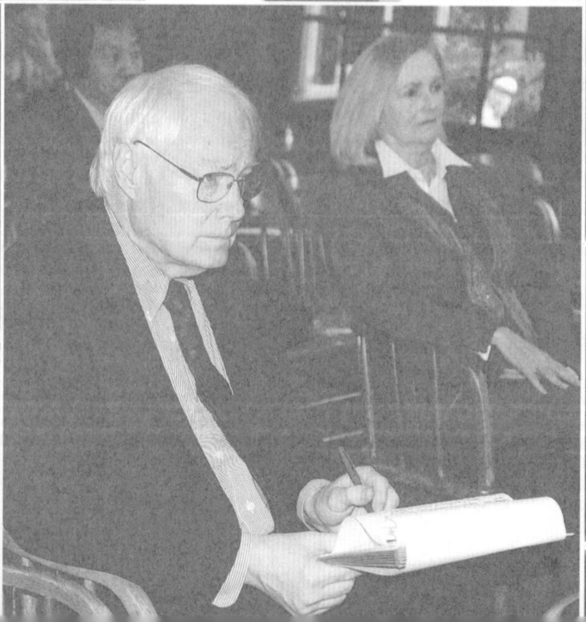
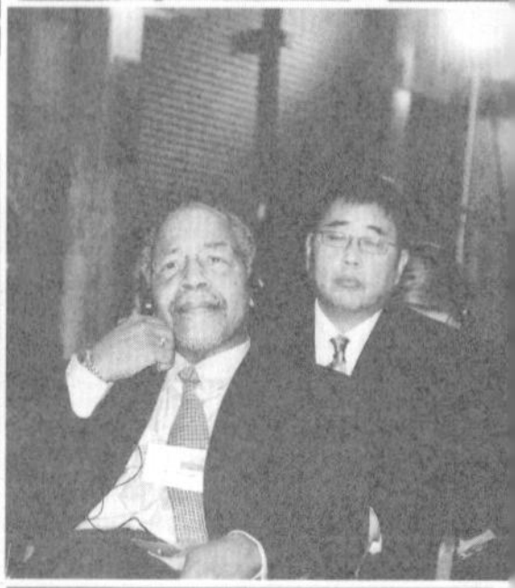
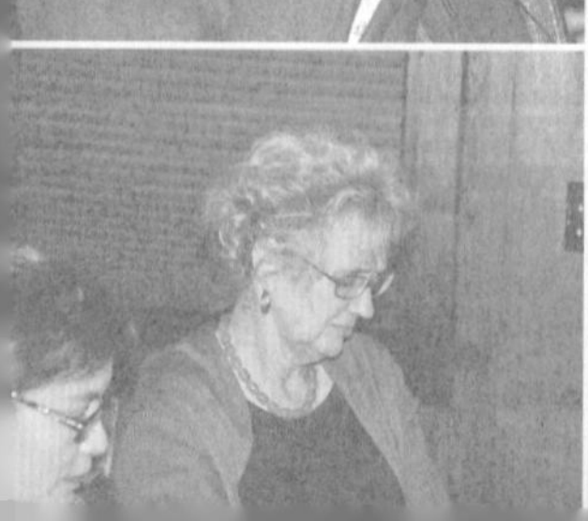
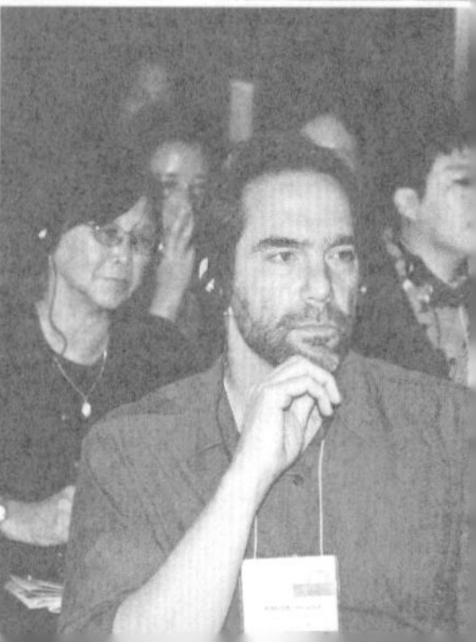

UNIT V:
THE FUTURE OF CHINA - U.S. CULTURAL RELATIONS

第五单元 中美文化关系的未来展望

美国国家人文基金会主席吉姆·利奇
主持人导语
Jim Leach, Chairman of US National Endowment for the Humanities
"Moderator's Introduction"

中国艺术研究院中国文化研究所所长刘梦溪研究员做主题发言
《对话是人类的生活准则》
Liu Mengxi, Research Fellow and Director of Institute of Chinese Culture,
Chinese National Academy of Arts
"Dialogue is a Principle for Human Life"

美国波士顿大学欧洲比较历史学教授埃里森·布莱克利做主题发言
《文化比政治更具影响力》

Allison Blakely, Professor of European and Comparative History, Boston University
"Culture is More Powerful than Politics"

中国人民大学国际关系学院副院长金灿荣教授做主题发言
《未来十年的世界与中国：从国际政治的视角》

Jin Canrong, Professor and Associate Dean of School of International Studies,
Renmin University of China
"The World and China in the Next Decade: A Perspective from International Politics"

美国斯坦福大学古典学、政治科学教授何塞·欧博做主题发言
《文化关系——大国合作的途径》
Josiah Ober, Professor of Classics and Professor of Political Science, Stanford University
"Cultural Relations—The Way of Cooperation Between The Powers"

主持人导语

吉姆·利奇
美国国家人文
基金会主席

在本轮最终的总结座谈会上，我们讨论的可能是最重要的中美事务，即中美未来的文化关系。文化关系如此重要的原因在于所有的问题都是两国人民和两国政府如何看待对方导致的结果。如果两国及其各自的人民不能互相尊重，那么无论两国政府当下的政策如何，都不能保持持续的关系。

在这种情况下，我感觉有三个现象是不言而喻的。第一，本世纪中，甚至可以说是这一千年中，最重要的双边关系将是中美关系。如果其发挥建设性作用，我们便可期许到和平与繁荣的时代。不然，则会出现相反的局面。第二，全球以加速变更为其标志，这涉及了有文字记载以来反复出现的变革，包括倒退回到过去曾经存在的状况。现在，未知的和未经历的情况都成了正常的事。第三，这一变更最独特的特点是，它与科技发展联系在一起，而且最严重的是，会对军事装备造成影响。这意味着在很多方面，最深刻的政治学观察结果来自于爱因斯坦，他曾评论到原子分裂改变了一切，但没有改变我们的思维方式。关于这一点，让我们冷静的是历史仍然可以稍微为我们指点迷津，冲突是不变的，这或许是因为冲突是人类的本性。所以我们如何看待事物已不再重要，要解决的问题是如何约束冲突本能。仅有的乐观回应似乎是人类性格必须改变，或我们要以一种更为深刻的方式了解人类本性，以便开发出能够更好指导我们自身的技术。所以作为这个任务的指导，历史是其一，尽管历史是最不确定的指导。文学是其二，可能相比其他艺术形式而言，文学更适于让人们将自己置身于过去的想象之中，设身处地地从他人角度进行思考。其三，我们有哲学。就中美关系而言，我想说的是，两国之间确实需要关注的最乐观的相似性之一，就是在犹太基督教的世界，强调权利概念。但是存在一个与黄金法则有关的道德支撑，这个法则当然就是"想要别人怎样对你，就要怎样对待别人"。而在儒家传统中，也有类似这条黄金法则的但更委婉的说法，就是"恕"道，这实际上是说"己所不欲，勿施于人"。

我提到这些通用原则的原因在于，文化差异可能仍然涉及到自我利益的差异，这几乎是无可争议的。中国人可能想要我们更加遵奉孔子学说，而我们则想要中国人更了解杰佛逊的思想，毋庸置疑，这就需要我们扩大相互之间的尊重。因此，在这个背景下，问题就是如何促进尊重，这是这次最终座谈的目的。

James Leach

Chairman of US
National Endowment
for the Humanities

Moderator's Introduction

In this final summation panel we're dealing with what maybe the most important issue of US and Chinese affairs, which is the future United States and Chinese cultural relations. And the reason cultural relations are so significant is that all other issues are ramifications of how our two peoples and our two governments look at each other. If countries and their respective peoples cannot respect each other there can be no sustaining relations whatever the policies of two governments may be in the moment in time.

In this context, it strikes me that there are three phenomena that are self evident. One is that the most important bilateral relationship in this century and quite possibly in this millennium will be the United States and Chinese relationship. If it's constructive we're looking at the potential era of potential peace and prosperity. If not, the reverse could well be the case. Secondly, the world is hallmarked by change in its acceleration and involved much of recorded history which has been repetitive with revolution involving change back to circumstances that existed before. Now the unknown and the inexperienced is the norm. And so the thirdly, the most unprecedented aspect of all of this change that we see around this relates to advances in science and technology and the most sobering relates to the ramifications for military hardware. And that means that in many ways the most profound political science observation comes from Einstein who once commented that splitting the atom had changed everything except our way of thinking. And what's sobering about this is that to the degree that history remains a partial guide conflict can be noted as a constant and presumably because human nature is a conflict. And so how we think about things has never mattered more. And so the question that has to be addressed is how the instinct for conflict can be contained. And it would appear that the only optimistic response would be that human nature has to change or we'd have to understand human nature in a much deeper way in order to develop techniques to better direct human beings themselves. So what are the guides to this task, history is one although the more unprecedented circumstance of the last less sure guide history is. Literature is another and probably literature is better suited to having people place themselves in the imagining of the past and to put themselves into people's shoes than almost any other art form. And thirdly we have philosophy. And I just want to say in the context of US and Chinese relations one of the most optimistic similarities truly demands attention and that is the Judeo-Christian world there is a great deal of emphasis on the concept of rights but there is a moral underpinning which relates to the golden rule which is of course that we should do unto others and as we want others to do unto us. In the Confucian tradition, there is a similar but less obtrusive framing of this golden rule which is the doctrine of 'Shu' (Forgiveness) which in effect says that one should not do unto others what one would not want others to do unto themselves.

And I mention these universal principles because while differences in cultures are likely to remain involve differences in self interest are almost certainly to be the case. And while the Chinese might like us to be more Confucian and we might like the Chinese to be more Jeffersonian, there is no reason what-so-ever that there cannot be an expansion of mutual respect. And so it is in the context of the question of how you advance respect that this final panel has been convened.

对话是人类的生活准则

刘梦溪

中国艺术研究院中国文化研究所所长,研究员

内容提要: 真正说来,我看不到中美之间有那么多严重得不得了的分歧。差异,文化的、经济的、政治的,当然存在。但差异不等于不能相处,更不必因差异而形成冲突。那么中美之间的问题来自何方?问题出在哪里?我以为来自不够了解。不是说中国对美国已经全部了解,但问题主要不是由于中国对美国的不了解,而是美国对中国的历史文化,对中国人的文化性格,对近三十年中国的新发展和新思维,没有真实的了解和真正的了解。

今天圆桌会议讨论的主题,我的角色应该是"客串",或者如佛教所说的"随喜",总之属于边缘人物。因为我研究的领域,主要是中国文学和中国历史,而且主要是思想史和学术史。我并不研究国际关系,也不研究中美关系。按照学者的专业态度,我不应该作出位之思,在这里就中美关系的展望发表什么意见。但我对自己国家的前途,对人类的命运,包括中美关系,是有深深的关切的。因为我是学者,也是一名知识分子。我想所有的知识人和文化人,也都会关注我们今天讨论的这个话题。

中国不是美国的威胁

我觉得从中国和世界的关系来讲,我们对中美关系有很高的期待,希望这是一个健康的、有趣的、美好的关系。记得有一个数据统计,说近30年来,中国的家庭里面,一共有多少家庭,有多少人,都来过美国。他们来美国,有的读书,有的工作,有的经商,有的观光旅游。总之这个数字，这个频率，是非常之高非常之大的。

而且事实上，中美自1972年尼克松访华以来，两国有过非常美好的时期。但是不知为什么，也不知道出于什么理由，中美关系后来不那么美好了。然后再好一段，然后再不好。就像是一对不太和谐的夫妻，说吵架就吵架，而且没有想象中的那么深层的原因。以为发生了什么大事，其实仔细一想，并没有什么了不起的大事发生。可是这样两个国家，就是喜欢不断地吵架怄气，甚至有时要摔东西，甚至剑拔弩张到要离婚。

真正说来，我看不到中美之间有那么多严重得不得了的分歧。差异，文化的、经济的、政治的，当然存在。但差异不等于不能相处，更不必因差异而形成冲突。那么中美之间的问题来何方？问题出在哪里？我以为来自不够了解。不是说中国对美国已经全部了解，但问题主要不是由于中国对美国的不了解，而是美国对中国的历史文化，对中国人的文化性格，对近30年中国的新发展和新思维，没有真实的了解和真正的了解。

我不明白，美国人，当然主要是政界，包括那些智库，我想不包括在座的各位教授，为什么会觉得中国是一个威胁呢？这不符合现实，也不符合历史，更不符合中国文化。中国文化的特点是富于包容性，而不具有侵略性。中国在历史上从来没有威胁过别人，即使非常强大的时期，比如汉代，比如唐代，那时是非常强大的国家。可是，当时非常强大的汉代，在处理跟北方的民族的关系的时候，把中国皇宫里面一个最漂亮的小姐送了出去，送给了北方的可汗王，作他的王妃。这就是中国历史上有名的"昭君出塞"，那个小姐叫王昭君。那么唐代呢？同样是非常了不起的时期，非常的繁荣，文化上多元开放，艺术、文学、诗歌，灿烂辉煌，国力也非常强大。可是唐代的时候，你们了解，又把一位美丽的公主送到了西藏，就是文成公主入藏，这不是文学的虚构，是真实的历史。

昨天一位教授讲到，当中国弱的时候如何如何。其实在中国最强大的时期，把中国的非常美丽而有身份的的女子送给偏远的部族，希望跟具有不同文化背景的国家民族建立良好的和平的关系，而不是互相冲突的关系。这是大家都知道的历史事实。以我的历史知识，我不知道中国在历史上任何一个时期，大家可以举例，曾经威胁过美国、威胁过英国、威胁过法国、威胁过意大利、威胁过西班牙、威胁过荷兰？我想没有这样的事实。

因此现在很流行的一个假设，说中国居然可以成为美国的敌人，我认为这是一个没有根据的假设,没有理由的假设。错了,朋友! 中国和美国不是敌人,他们完全可以成为朋友。你看今天上午几位学者的发言,一位是杜克大学研究中国戏剧史的教授,她讲到了英若诚。我虽然不研究戏剧,但戏剧我喜欢。你说的英若诚先生,我倒是认识他,他英文非常好,他能表演,也会导演,还懂文化,他是一位很有名的学者。他喜欢中国文化,也喜欢美国文化。还有欧建平教授讲的,中美在舞蹈方面的那些有趣的链接,我听了以后很感动,这是非常美好的影响互动。

我几次来美国,我接触的美国学者,他们都非常之好,我们可以很快成为朋友。如果说中美之间出现了分歧,我认为大部分是由于误解,由于美国对中国的历史文化不够了解。如果有更深一点的了解,怎么会得出"中国是美国的威胁"这样一个违背历史也违背常识的不真实的结论呢?

文化的"异""同"问题

但在众说纷扰的背后,的确还有我所关注的更为根本的学理问题,这跟我昨天的演讲有关,也可以说是人类的哲学认知的问题。具体说,是关于人类文化的"同"和"异"的问题。几乎所有的人,在中国也是如是,包括许多学业有成的学者,他们在涉及这个问题的时候,观察的重点和重心,主要是"异",而不是"同"。可是他们忘了,学术研究对于"异"即"不同"的解释分疏,最终的结果是为了寻找到"同"。

我个人很尊敬的一位前辈学者,他是很了不起的学问大家,他已经故去了,就是钱钟书先生。他一生写了很多著作,他的太太杨绛先生,也是了不起的作家学者。钱先生有一个基本的观点,你可以看他晚年的四卷本的著作《管锥篇》,或者早年的《谈艺录》,所有这些著作里面的一个核心的理念,叫做"貌异心同"。长相不一样,心理是相同或相通的。他的《谈艺录》的开篇序言里,有一句很有趣也很经典的话,叫做:"东海西海,心理攸同;南学北学,道术未裂。"就是东方和西方,各个国家民族的不同的人群,大家的心理结构和心理指向,常常是相同的。我们都不喜欢灾难,不喜欢挫折,不喜欢疾病,不喜欢丑恶。我们都喜欢美好和美丽,都喜欢大海和草地,都喜欢雨露和阳光,都喜欢健康,都喜欢美的艺术。

刚才讲舞蹈艺术的那位教授，我们大家立刻就学会了他的表演，不约而同地跟他翩翩起舞。世界上最美好的东西，我们的喜欢是相同的。我看不出人类有那样根本的南辕北辙的天上地下的彼此完全不能相容的不同。当然我说的是文化和族群的整体，不是指哪一个具体的个别的人。我觉得在哲学上要破除对"异"的偏执病。只有承认人类的共同性和共通性，文化的跨文化沟通才有可能。所以不同国家、不同民族的男女，即使语言不通，也可以发生爱情。爱情的依据是爱情本身和人类的爱情心理。这是共通的人性问题和哲学的共同性问题。

对话是人类的生活准则

我们作为人类的一分子，都需要面对我们共同的世界。人与人之间，族群与族群之间，国家与国家之间，最适合人类本性的文化态度，我以为是沟通与对话。我有幸结识哈佛大学的一位研究中国历史文化的学者，我称他为西方的大儒，就是很多人都不陌生的史华兹教授，Benjamin I. Schwartz。他已经故去了。他是犹太人，精通多种语言，早期研究日本，"二战"期间有过功劳，日本袭击珍珠港的那个信号密码就是他破译的，但未引起军方的重视。史华兹教授一生坚持不懈的的一个文化理念，就是跨文化沟通。他说文化是一个松散的整体，里面充满了张力。为了论证跨文化沟通的可以成立，他甚至提出，语言对思维并不像人们想象的具有那么大的作用。他说人与人之间是可以沟通的，不同的文化之间也是可以沟通的。而在我看来，人与人之间的沟通与对话，不同文化之间的沟通与对话，不仅是可能的，而且应该成为人类生活的一个准则，甚至对话与沟通就是人类生活本身，就是人类的一种生活方式，再没有其他方式比对话与沟通更有益心智，更有益于人类的健康。

我们做学问的人，经常离不开两个方面的沟通与对话，一是作为现代人，我们需要跟古人对话；二是作为中国的学人，需要跟不同文化背景的学人对话。古代的那些文化典范，是我们建构新的文化的灵感的源泉，我们离不开他们。不仅中国古代的典范具有此种作用，西方的古代典范同样有此作用。我们可以不了解古希腊罗马的文化吗？我在给我的学生开必读书目的时候，总是把苏格拉底、柏拉图、亚里士多德放在很前面，下面还有康德、黑格尔，尤其康德的三大批判著作，那是必读而又必读的书籍。康德的了不起,在于他的著作永远不会过时。他的那句名言,他说道德理性具有绝对价值,这是真正经典的大判断,常读常新,永远不会成为过去。

今天的学人,如果只局限于本民族的文化背景,而不了解"他者"的文化,不与不同背景的文化交流对话,就不能成为一个通博的学人。国际间的关系,文化是最好的溶解剂。采取对话的方式解决分歧,处理争端,增加了解和理解,是再自然不过的事情。中美之间,为了两国人们的利益,为了人类的福祉,为了世界的安康幸福,难道还有比对话更好的交往方式吗?

人类面临空前的危机

我近来对我们这个世界的前途颇感忧虑,我觉得人类其实是太不聪明了。不是我们大家不聪明,主要是那些跟政治权力的杠杆连接在一起的人,他们太不聪明了。噢,也不是他们天生不聪明,是世俗的利益蒙住了他们的眼睛。他们是利令智昏! 那些丝丝缕缕的私利,那些纠缠不清的利害得失,让他们的头脑变得傻瓜起来。他们竟然完全不了解这个世界已经或者将要发生什么事情。

世界气候的变化是惊人的。冰山在加速溶化,企鹅很快就要失去家乡。地震频发,好几个大洲都接连有地震发生,七级以上的地震就有多起。地震引起海啸造成的灾难,大家都看到了。今年夏天中国的南部,南亚的好几个国家,出现了空前的洪水泛滥。而正当亚洲的南部陷入泽国的时候,亚洲北部的俄罗斯,莫名其妙地燃烧起了熊熊大火,持续近一个月的时间,人们由于眼睛盯着洪水,忘记了还有大火在北方肆虐。很多国家的天气预报都显示,2011年的冬季,欧洲、俄罗斯、中国北方,还有北美,将迎来寒冷的冬天。寒冷和冰雪给人类带来的影响,今年晚些时候我们能够看到。

大自然看来是不耐烦了,正在对人类的无限索取做出激烈的回应。可是人类自己呢? 看不出有丝毫的醒悟。他们自己还在那里互相挤压,鸡争鹅斗,制造恐怖,兵戎相见。为什么不能够和平相处呢? 为什么不作深层的反思呢? 对十年前的那个事件,我不想使用那个事件的直接名称,当然那是人类都不愿意看到的巨大灾难,是大家共同反对的,而且严厉谴责它。但是怎么来解开事件的心理扭结呢？怎样做才能避免人类的仇恨重叠增加呢？我认为这是美国政治家需要认真考虑的问题。可是他们似乎并不想认真考虑。

他们以为武器的打击力可以解决人类的一切问题。是这样吗？武力能解决人们的感情问题吗？能解决人类的爱憎取向吗？具体说，武力能够改变人类的宗教信仰吗？没有任何一种强力可以消灭人类的宗教信仰。宗教情感是人类最神圣的情感，宗教信仰是个体生命的终极归宿。洲际导弹、航空母舰，能改变人类的信仰吗？为什么聪明的美国政治家不考虑这个问题呢？

我觉得中国的民众、中国的知识分子，在中美关系问题上受到了情感的挫折。中国人对美国够好的了。他们喜欢这个国家的开放现代，喜欢美国人的文化性格，直爽热情，而且诚实不撒谎，不像中国人有的时候还要做一点小伪。为什么美国的政治家不能把美国人的文化性格在他们的身上反映出来呢？奥巴马总统的上台，一度给美国人也给世界带来了希望，他提出了化解仇恨的一些理念。他的支持率那么高啊！当然他的有一些想法，我要是美国人我也不会赞成，比如想在某一个特殊的地方建立某一个建筑，其实我不认为在那个地方建立那样的建筑是一个好主意。我想我不明确说大家也会知道，我讲的是哪个地方和要建什么建筑。奥巴马开始的一些理念，他没有继续，甚至现在全部都退回去了。有人说他退回去是为了中期选举，为了他的支持率能够得到提升。

但我们真是很遗憾，我愿意中美有很好的关系，有一切条件成为好朋友。假如彼此的感情有点不和的话，可以吵架，但不要摔东西，可以摔东西，但不要动手，实在不行，即使离婚，也应该好离好散，做不成夫妻，也不要做敌人。

Liu Mengxi

Research Fellow and Director of Institute of Chinese Culture, Chinese National Academy of Arts

Dialogue is a Principle for Human Life

Abstract: To be honest, I see no serious differences between China and the US, in culture, in economy, in politics, or in many other aspects, even though we are always talking about differences. Difference does not necessarily kill co-existence or trigger confrontation. What is the problem between China and the US? Why is that? I don't think it stems from China's lack of understanding of America, but from Americans' lack of genuine understanding of Chinese history and culture, Chinese cultural character, and the new development and mentality of China presented in recent three decades.

As far as today's topic is concerned, I am supposed to be a "guest" at the round table, or a visitor. Anyway, I should not be in the spotlight for I am engaged in Chinese literature and Chinese history mainly about ideology and academy. I do not involve in international relations or Sino-US relation. A meticulous scholar does not allow himself to comment out of his professional limit. However, I would like to prospect Sino-US relation out of concern over the future of my country, destination of mankind and Sino-US relation. I am convinced that all scholars and intellectuals, like me, are concerning about today's issue.

China is not a Threat to USA

Talking about China's relations with the outside world, I always think that the world has very high expectations on Sino-US relationship. People hope that it is a healthy, amazing and good relationship. Statistics shows that, in the recent thirty years, numerous Chinese have been to the US to study, to work, or for business or sightseeing. The number of that population is really big.

And as a matter of fact, the Sino-US relationship, since President Nixon visited China in 1972, had been through its good times. But it got cold for unknown reasons, and warmer, and cold again. They somehow, like a couple, sometimes, fight for no reason; we have no idea what has happened—in fact, nothing has happened. They just bicker and sulk, and throw things around and even declare to divorce each other.

To be honest, I see no serious differences between China and the US, in culture, in economy, in politics, or in many other aspects, even though we are always talking about differences. Difference does not necessarily kill co-existence or trigger confrontation. What is the problem between China and the US? Why is that? I don't think it stems from China's lack of understanding of America, but from Americans' lack of genuine understanding of Chinese history & culture, Chinese cultural character, and the new development and mentality of China presented in recent three decades.

I don't know why Americans—mainly politicians and the Think Tank of course, nothing to do with us professors—feel that China is a threat? The facts, the history and Chinese culture have proved them wrong. Chinese culture is inclusive, not aggressive. Throughout its long history, China has never threatened anyone even when it was really powerful—during the Han and Tang Dynasties, for example, when China was a great power. But in the Han Dynasty a beautiful girl was married to the head of the northern minority for the sake of border relations. This story is generally known as 'Wang Zhaojun went beyond the Great Wall as a bride'. The Tang Dynasty was also a remarkable period. China was extremely prosperous. And that prosperity, in art, in culture, in literature, especially poetry, was enjoyed by different ethnic groups. Like the Han Dynasty, the Tang Dynasty was the time when China was the most powerful in the world. But it was during this dynasty that a Chinese princess named Wencheng was married to a Tibetan ruler. This is a historical fact, not simply a legend.

Yesterday one of our professors talked about what China did when she was weak. In fact, even when she was strong, she married beautiful Chinese princesses away for the sake of peace. She hoped that countries and nationalities of different cultural backgrounds could establish good, peaceful relations instead of confrontation. This is what China has been like in her history. I study history. Could any one of you cite one single example to prove that, in any period in history, China threatened America, or Britain, or France, or Italy, or Spain, or the Netherlands? No, you could not.

Today there is a popular hypothesis that China could be an enemy of the US. No, this is a groundless, false hypothesis. My friends, we are not enemies, but friends. This morning I was here when the scholars delivered their speeches. Among them was an expert on history of Chinese drama from Duke University. I do not study drama, but I like drama. She talked of Mr. Ying Ruocheng, whom I happen to know. He spoke English well; he was a great actor and director, having a profound understanding of culture. And of course, he was a scholar. He loved both American and Chinese cultures. Prof. Ou Jianping spoke of the ties between the two countries in dance. When I heard this, I felt excited. That was very good interaction.

I have visited US frequently. The American professors I know are all very nice; and we become friends instantly. The gaps between the two countries mainly come from misunderstanding. The US does not well understand Chinese history and culture, and mistook China as a threat, a ridiculous conclusion that violates historical facts and common sense.

Cultural Similarities and Dissimilarities

Behind varying opinions there is a theoretic topic I have followed with interest. It is somewhat related to my speech yesterday. It is a topic in the sphere of philosophy, concerning similarities and dissimilarities of cultures. Back in China, when scholars approach this issue, nearly all of them, even established ones, will focus on 'dissimilarities'. However, they have forgotten that the ultimate goal of their studies of differences is to attain a common ground.

I extremely respect a distinguished late Chinese scholar. He is Qian Zhongshu. He was exceptionally learned and wrote a series of dissertations and papers. His wife, Ms. Yang Jiang, was also a great writer. In his works of late years, such as Guan Zhui Pian, or in his works of early years such as the Collection of Talks on Art, there is a consistent philosophy—'The mind is the same despite different appearances'. In his preface to the latter book, he makes an interesting remark, saying, 'People from the East and West have the same mind; sciences from the North and South have the same rule'. In other words, whether you are from the East or West, we have things in common intellectually: we dislike disasters, frustration, illness, or ugliness; we like beauty, the sea, the lawn; we like to be healthy and we love art.

The dancing art talked about by that professor—we perceived its beauty instantly. Everyone danced after him. We all love beautiful things in the world. On this point, we are not dissimilar; on this point, I see no incompatible difference between different peoples. Of course I am talking about cultures and nationalities as a whole, not individuals. In the sphere of philosophy, I feel that we should shake off the stereotyped obsession with difference. Inter-cultural communication could be possible only when we recognize 'commonness' and 'similarities' among human peoples; I see that people from different countries or different ethnic groups speak different languages and fall in love with each other. Love is built on the basis of love itself and love psychology. This is a matter of commonness of humanity and similarity of philosophy.

Dialogue Is a Principle for Human Life

As part of Human beings, we have to face our common world. In my point of view, communication and dialogue between people, between nationalities and between countries are attitudes in culture that best suits human nature. It is an honor that I knew a professor engaged in Chinese history and culture from Harvard University. A Confucian in the West, late Benjamin Schwartz runs his fame around the world. He was a Jew, commanding several languages. He studied Japan in his early age and had rendered service of merit during the World War II by deciphering the code system used by the Japanese when they attacked the Pearl Harbour, which unfortunately failed to alert the US military. Throughout his life, he had insisted on cross-cultural communication. He stated that culture was a loosely defined concept full of tension. In order to support his idea, he even asserted that the effect of language on one's mind was not as great as people have imagined. People can communicate with each other; communication is possible between different cultures. As I see it, dialogue and communication between people and cultures are not only possible, but a principle we should uphold in human life, and are life itself--it is a lifestyle. You could never find anything that better help our mind and health.

For us intellectuals, there are two kinds of communications: first, living in the modern era, we should communicate with our ancestors; second, as a Chinese, I need to communicate with scholars with different cultural background. We can not live without ancient classics, both Chinese and Western, which give us cultural inspirations. Shouldn't I learn something about ancient Greek and Roman culture? On the list of must-read books I hand out to my students, I always place Socrates, Plato and Aristotle on the top; names below them also include Hegel and Kant. Kant's three criticism works should never be missed. His theories will never be out of date. One of his most famous quotes says, 'morality is of absolute value'. Such classical things will never go obsolete.

Today's intellectuals could never be knowledgeable if they stayed within their own cultural background, refused to get to know other cultures and communicate with other cultures. Culture is the best solution to international relations. It is natural to settle disputes and enhance understanding via dialogue. Sino-US dialogue is the best means of communication for the sake of mutual interests, and welfare of human and the world.

We Face Unprecedented Crisis

Recently I always worry about the world's future: I feel that we are not clever. I do not mean us; I mean those politicians—they are not clever. Or they are not born to be so. They have been blinded by greed, or lust of gains. The gains have made their mind numb. They are entirely oblivious to what has and what is happening to the world.

The recent years have seen alarming climate changes. Icebergs are melting, penguins are getting homeless. There are always earthquakes around the world. We have recorded several earthquakes of magnitude above 7.0. We have witnessed drastic tsunamis caused by earthquake. In this summer, South China and South Asian countries suffered from severe flood, and Russia, which lies in the north of Asia, was somehow forgotten by the world for a month, during which fires were raging there. Many countries' weather forecasts have reported that this winter is going to be unusually cold in Europe, Russia, North China and North America. We will see the influence of the freezing winter later this year.

It seems that Nature has lost her patience and is giving drastic answers to our greed. And human? We learn nothing. We keep quarrelling and even come to war. Why shouldn't we stay in peace? Why shouldn't we reflect upon our past doings? I do not wish to mention that incident ten years ago, which mankind has been unwilling to see, and which everyone opposes and condemns. But how can we disarm enmities? How can we curb the incrementing accumulation of hatred? These are, I think, the questions American politicians should consider but are ignored by them.

They believe that arms can settle all problems of mankind. Is that realistic? But can arms settle emotional issues? Can they guarantee love or hatred? Can they resolve the differences between religions? No, no force can do that. Religion is the most sacred affection and the ultimate home of the individual's soul. Can intercontinental missile or aircraft carrier change my faith? Why don't clever American politicians think about these questions?

I often think that Chinese people and Chinese intellectuals are frustrated by Sino-US relation. Chinese people think highly enough of the United States. We like the open and modern country, as well as Americans' character: they are straightforward and hospitable; they are honest, unlike Chinese who are a little hypocritical sometimes. Why can't American politicians project this part of American character? When Barack Obama took the office, he filled many Americans and the rest of the world with expectation. He put forwards many constructive concepts to dissolve hatred. He enjoyed high support rates. Of course, I would not agree to some of his ideas if I were an American. For example, he wishes to build some buildings at some place. I don't think it is a good idea. I won't specifically point out which buildings and which place, but I am sure you know what I am talking about. He has failed to hold his stance and he withdrew. Some have attributed this to the results of the mid-term election, in order to pick up his support rate.

But we are genuinely sorry for that. I wish that China and the United States could keep up their good terms, and be good friends. Even if they had friction, quarrels are acceptable, do not throw things around, and do not fight. Or even they divorced, they should not be enemies.

文化比政治更具影响力

埃里森·布莱克利

美国波士顿大学
欧洲比较历史学教授

内容提要：关于文化多样性，美国和中国是否可以互相吸取经验。我希望我们能够劝说各自的领导人，告诉他们这是一个建立相互尊重文化多样性，甚至更有建设性地致力于强大的国际合作的良好基础，以此代替对文化问题的争论。

  我的所见都让我相信，文化比政治更有影响力。我希望本次会议中的任何报告都强调这种联系。21世纪是第一个在全球所有主要社会中都面临新水平文化多样性挑战的世纪。比如，我自己目前的主要研究项目就是关于欧洲社会如何努力处理种族和身份问题，这些问题曾经被认为仅存在于美国，毕竟美国是唯一一个在国内曾真正实施奴隶制的国家。现在，在国外曾深陷于奴隶贸易、殖民和法律歧视的欧洲民主政治面临着他们为保持经济活力所需要的大量移民。他们第一次被迫处理这种传统优势群体在态度与实践之间的真实差距问题，并让新的非欧洲成员融入其社会，保持与其民主理想一致。换句话说，美国已在这一困境中奋斗了两百年，有趣的是，欧洲的某些个人和群体有时想要以美国为榜样，误以为我们已经解决了所有这些问题。

  作为一个历史学家，我教授比较文化课程已有30多年，我仍然敬畏中华文明的悠久历史及其形成的哲学和体制，惊讶于在欧洲之前中国实际上已经拥有技术和能力去探索全世界，但出于种种原因，他们却选择没有。这一情况的突出实例就是郑和的壮举，他在15世纪早期就带领成百上千条船和上万人7次远征国外，最远达到东非，即如今的中东和南非。这比广为人知的克里斯托弗·麦哲伦航行要早一百年。之后欧洲人的航行令欧洲人确认了其未来的文化多样性，即便这不是他们所想。在我了解的关于中国历史的基础知识中，还让我惊讶的一点是中国也有着长期的管理文化多样性的历史，比如郑和，他是穆斯林，比如19世纪中叶的太平天国运动，同一时间我们发生了全面的美国内战，太平天国运动的特点是宗教冲突，导致大约有两千万人丧生。此外，众所周知，美国的历史短得多，只有3个世纪，但同样发生了与文化差异有关的大量遗留问题，包括最近对移民政策的特别关注，和继续解决长期的种族和有色人种歧视这种思想的相关挑战。

基于这种历史观，我给大家提出的问题是，关于文化多样性，美国和中国是否可以互相吸取经验。在过去的一天半中，我们目睹了大量关于文化影响力在我们这两个国家中得以体现的证据。我希望我们能够劝说各自的领导人，告诉他们这是一个建立相互尊重文化多样性、甚至更有建设性地致力于强大的国际合作的良好基础，以此代替对文化问题的争论。

Culture is More Powerful than Politics

Allison Blakely

Professor of
European and
Comparative History,
Boston University

Abstract: There are lessons that the United States and China can learn from each other concerning cultural diversity. I hope we can persuade our respective leaders that this is a good foundation upon which to build mutual respect for cultural diversity and even more constructive engagement for strong international collaboration in place of contention over cultural issues.

Everything that I've seen has convinced me further and further that culture is more powerful than politics and I hope any report that comes as a result of these proceedings will emphasize that connection. The 21th century is the first in which the entire world was challenged with new levels of cultural diversity within all the major societies. For example, my own current major research project concerns the struggle of European societies to now deal with problems of race and identity that once pretended were solely applicable to the United States, which was after all the only western society that actually practiced slavery at home. Now the European democracies that were the most deeply involved in the slave trade and colonization and legal discrimination abroad are confronted with a high level of immigration they need in order to keep their economies vibrant. And for the first time they are forced to cope with the same type of very real gap between the attitudes and practices of the traditional dominant group and full integration of the new non-European members of their societies consist with their democratic ideals. In other words, the same dilemma the United States has been dealing with for over two centuries and, interestingly, some individuals and groups in Europe are looking to the United States for models for guidance at times under the false assumption that we've solved all those problems.

As a historian, who for more than three decades taught courses on comparative civilizations, I've remained in awe of the long duration of the Chinese civilization, the philosophies and institutions it has shaped. And over the discovery that China actually had the technology and capacity to explore the whole world prior to the Europeans and for various reasons elected not to. The most spectacular example of this were the exploits of the Admiral Zheng He who lead seven expeditions abroad in the early 15th century reaching as far as East Africa present day Middle East and South Asia with fleets numbering hundreds of ships and combined crews of ten's of thousands. All this is a century before the more widely known voyages of Christopher Columbus. One result of the later European voyages is that Europeans ensured a greater cultural diversity for their future even if not intended. Among other surprises for me as I acquired a rudimentary knowledge of Chinese history is that China too nevertheless has a long history of managing cultural diversity, for example Admiral Zheng He happened to be a Muslim. The Taiping Rebellion in the middle of the 19th century around the same time as our devastating American Civil War and the Taiping Rebellion there was featured religious conflict and it resulted in a loss of some 20 million lives. Meanwhile we all know that the United States in a much briefer history spanning three centuries has also produced a rich legacy of issues regarding cultural diversity including the current special attention to immigration policy, and continuing resolution of long standing challenges surrounding this concept of race and color prejudice.

Based on this type of history perspective the question that I have for us is are there not lessons that the United States and China can learn from each other concerning cultural diversity. We've witnessed over the past day and a half a tremendous amount of evidence regarding the powers of cultural influences that have manifested in both directions between our two countries. I hope we can persuade our respective leaders that this is a good foundation upon which to build mutual respect for cultural diversity and even more constructive engagement for strong international collaboration in place of contention over cultural issues.

未来十年的世界与中国：
从国际政治的视角

金灿荣

中国人民大学国际关系学院副院长，教授

内容提要： 未来十年的世界与中国都将发生复杂深刻的变化。世界将进入体系转型和秩序重塑的关键期，国际权力结构呈现出西方与非西方相对均衡、新老大国合作与竞争并存的新局面，这将导致全球议题、决策体制和发展理念出现新的变化。中国在未来十年将经历一个实力增长的黄金期和问题多发的脆弱期，如何使用不断增长的实力以及能否控制住国内矛盾决定着中国崛起的基本前景。未来十年，中国与世界的关系处于重新调适和相互建构的过程之中，彼此之间的战略疑虑和认知差距将大为加剧，中国崛起的外部环境更加复杂。中国外交需要在国家利益与国际责任、自我发展与他者共赢之间显示更多的平衡和灵活性，进而推动中国与世界的关系继续朝着和平、合作的方向发展。

21世纪的头一个十年在世界总体稳定、格局深刻变动的大势下落下帷幕。回顾过去十年，全球化、信息化和民主化的世界潮流在困惑和质疑中继续前进；国际权力和财富自近代以来首次出现了西方向东方转移的历史性趋势；多种力量、不同议题和竞争性的理念纷纷参与到国际博弈中来，世界政治的复杂和不确定性前所未有。过年十年也是中国迅猛发展、加速崛起的重要十年。通过国内改革的持续推进和进一步融入国际体系，中国不仅积累起强大的国家实力和战略影响，而且实现了国家身份的重大转变，成为现行国际秩序的积极参与者、合作性建设者。站在新的历史起点上，思考未来十年的世界与中国对于把握世界的变动趋势以及中国崛起的基本前景具有前瞻性意义，对中国当前的政策制订和战略调整也深具启发。

一、未来世界的基本走向

在国际金融危机、新兴经济体崛起以及全球性问题空前凸显等因素的作用下,世界正加速步入后金融危机时代。对于后金融危机时代世界的基本走向,学者们多有思考,见仁见智。笔者试图以国际结构为基本变量,分析变动中的国际结构对全球议题、决策体制和发展理念的深刻影响,以期为分析未来世界的基本走向提供管窥之见。

西方与非西方在国际关系中的基本分野为我们理解当前和未来的国际结构提供了独特视角。冷战结束以来,世界一度进入了由美国霸权定义的单极时刻。以美国为首的西方阵营成为全球规则的制订者和国际公共产品的主要提供者,在东西和南北关系中占据全面的优势。然而,冷战结束短短二十年的时间,西方的中心地位就出现了明显动摇,其国际权威和全球影响受到相当程度的削弱,尤其是西方霸权的核心支柱——美国因对外政策失误和内部经济困难而出现了严重的实力透支。与西方阵营相对应的则是一个相对分裂和弱势的非西方世界,它们在世界权力结构中处于边缘位置,不仅没有制度决定权和利益分配权,还不时受到西方世界的肆意干涉和战略挤压。冷战结束之后,非西方世界在全球化普遍拓展、技术革命广泛扩散的时代背景下,成功开启或加速推进了基于现代化取向的改革进程。然而,由于历史遗产、资源禀赋、政治能力等方面的巨大不同,这些国家(群体)现代化努力的结果差别甚大,进而导致了它们在国际关系中不同的地位处境、利益诉求和战略选择。

未来十年,西方与非西方的力量对比态势将继续发生变化,国际结构将加速从西方主导到东西方相对平衡的方向转变。从西方阵营来看,美国在力量和权势上仍处于优势地位,科技能力和军事实力令其他国家难以望其项背。奥巴马的变革措施一定程度上改善了美国的经济状况和国际形象。美国最新出台的《国家安全战略》报告与小布什时期的"单边主义"和"先发制人"战略划清了界线,在强调军事实力重要性的同时,明确了外交、发展和国际机制在解决争端、防止冲突和维持和平中的优先性。这证明美国具有强大的自我纠错和战略反思能力。然而,美国所面临的内外困境短期内仍难以得到根本性缓解。在内部,虽然迅速出台的救市计划和经济刺激方案避免了美国经济自由落体式的深度衰退,但相对于新兴经济体的高速增长,美国经济在相当时期内将处于增长乏力的状态,这无疑会极大制约奥巴马再造制造业辉煌的雄心；美国政治上的"极化"现象加剧了两党、府会之间的政策分歧，不利于塑造政治行动所必需的统一意志和战略共识。在外部，反恐战争的久拖不决还将耗费美国相当的实力资源，美国与外部世界的矛盾短期内也没有彻底解决的可能，华盛顿通过"笑脸外交"和多伙伴合作而进行责任外包的战略意图收效甚微。这些都决定了美国未来的国际地位很难再回到新世纪初期的状态，华盛顿不费力气和低成本行使国际领导权的日子成为历史。作为西方阵营重要成员的日本和欧盟都将面临着内部的政治博弈和社会治理难题，难以为西方中心地位的维系提供有力支持。因此，尽管西方在一段时期内仍将处于国际结构的中心，但其内部阵营的三大支柱各自都存在众多问题，其未来发展非常不确定，其主导世界的能力总体呈现下降的趋势。

在非西方世界，新兴市场经济国家由于国内改革的相对成功，国家实力和战略影响显著增强，呈现出群体性崛起的态势。未来十年，尽管新兴市场经济国家都面临各自内部的结构调整和治理难题，但它们仍能够保持高于发达经济体的经济增长速度，成为后金融危机时代世界经济增长的新动力。其结果是新兴市场经济国家在世界经济和政治版图中地位将得到实质性提升，它们与现行国际俱乐部的关系决定着未来世界的稳定与否。俄罗斯在经历了后冷战时期衰败和混乱的十年后，通过强人领导和资源优势重新确立起世界大国的地位，并通过对外政策中的强硬姿态维护其战略利益。近一年多来，俄罗斯受国际金融危机的影响在国际政治中的鲜明立场有所后退，希望通过在伊朗核问题、国际核裁军等现实议题上对美让步来换取美俄关系的修复。然而，两国相邻的地理边界状况、"弥赛亚"式的文化心理结构和不同的历史认知决定了美俄关系改善的限度。未来十年，俄罗斯在内部面临着政策稳定可持续性和市场再改革的难题，在对外战略上则将继续游离于西方与非西方之间，不断地在"希望—失望"的情绪圈中徘徊。因此，俄罗斯在国际结构中的地位具有极大的不确定性，其政策动向将成为影响国际格局变动的重要变量。就伊斯兰世界的未来而言，具有决定性意义的事项在于能否对现有的社会体制结构进行调整，进而在伊斯兰传统和世俗价值、本土文化和西方影响之间达成总体平衡。也就是说，伊斯兰世界能否开启内生力量驱动的现代化转型，决定着其未来的前途命运。失败国家的未来前途既取决于自身能否建立起普遍化的政治权威，也受制于国际社会的援助共识和力度。未来十年，反美主义国家的对抗姿态将随着美国对外政策的调整而有所缓解，但也因美国霸权的相对维持而长期存在，并构成国际政治图景中的一支独特力量。

西方与非西方的发展态势和互动关系意味着后冷战时期西方中心主义的国际结构将出现重大变动，西方的相对衰落与非西方的群体崛起将同时出现，并伴之以各自内部力量对比的显著变化，即美国在西方阵营中的优势地位得到进一步巩固，而新兴市场经济国家在非西方世界中的分量将更加凸显。未来的世界将进入一个西方与非西方相对均衡、新老大国竞争与合作并存的阶段，新兴大国与西方，尤其是与美国的关系决定了国际政治的未来基调和发展取向。具体而言，变动中的国际结构将对未来世界的全球议题、决策体制和发展理念产生深远影响。

第一，具有现代性的全球议题将重新回归到国际政治的中心。冷战结束至今，世界上出现了三种不同类型的国家，即前现代国家、现代国家和后现代国家。包括美国在内的绝大多数国家都位于现代国家的行列，相当多的欧洲国家在社会形态和政治理念上进入到了后现代，而非洲、中亚、拉美的一部分国家则在现代化的博弈中出局，回到前现代的状态，成为典型的"失败国家"。它们因处于现代化的不同历史阶段而具有不同的议题重心和利益诉求。前现代国家面临的首要问题是基本生存，现代国家关注的是物质利益，后现代国家则追求着各种抽象性的权利。冷战结束初期的西方中心主义时代，以抽象权利为核心的全球议题在国际政治中的地位显现，出现了现代国家与后现代国家争夺话语权的局面，而失败国家的生存要求在相当时期内受到漠视。随着新兴国家的崛起、美国的重新制造业化、欧洲出现治理危机，以及失败国家进行现代化重建的努力，强调物质利益的现代性话语将重新占据全球议程的中心。也就是说，尽管后现代权利由于其道德高调和政治正确不仅不会消失，反而将成为未来国际互动的主要形式，但国家间博弈的实质仍将是物质资源、战略利益之争。

第二，全球决策体制将在合法性和有效性之间寻求新平衡。冷战结束以来，以美国为首的西方阵营主导着世界范围内的规则确立和议程设定。然而，西方整体能力的下降和全球性问题的增多导致了西方决策体制在合法性和有效性上的双重危机，国际金融危机的爆发和蔓延进一步加速了既有决策体制的式微。相反，新兴市场经济国家在推动全球经济增长、化解国际金融危机方面发挥着越来越重要的作用。如何释放制度空间来满足新兴国家的利益诉求，进而建立起基于新老大国平等地位和广泛协商的治理模式，成为未来全球决策体制变革的基本方向。20国集团的异军突起不仅提高了新兴国家的发言权和影响力，而且为新老大国进行政策协调提供了有利平台，全球经济决策体制在合法性和有效性之间达成了新的平衡。然而，在涉及范围更广泛的国际和地区问题上，全球决策体制的改革仍然进展迟缓、行动乏力，难以适应急速变动的形势需要。未来全球决策体制一个重要的发展趋向是各国为了占据后金融危机时期的制高点，都在积极组建类别繁多的临时性和非排他性的集团。由于不同集团的利益整合和规范塑造能力不同，那些共识稳固、功能强大的集团将在激烈的竞争中得以存活，并成为未来全球性体制确立的起点。

第三，国际发展理念的多样化和自主性将是大势所趋。在西方中心主义时代，西方不仅建立起物质实力上的绝对优势，更垄断着对发展模式和现代性的话语解释。西方话语的核心在于对现代化模式唯一性（即西方模式）的先验认定，以及对民主包治百病的浪漫式理解，进而导致根据道德标准而非事实判断形成对民主与专制的简单划分。它们将基于特殊情景下积累起来的经验当做普世性的价值选择，并在救世主意识的驱使下在全球范围内不顾一切地大力推广，导致众多后发国家政治失范、乱象丛生。在扎卡里亚看来，第三波民主浪潮所及的多数国家所进行的民主尝试最终都蜕变成了"非自由的民主"，世界对西方模式的可移植性产生了强烈质疑。美国对外政策的战略失误、国际金融危机的爆发，以及欧洲主权债务危机的蔓延等一系列西方本身问题的放大，更使得其作为现代化领航者和民主价值捍卫者的权威形象面临破灭。相反，非西方世界的崛起，尤其是新兴国家在经济发展和危机应对中的相对成功使得其自信心开始增加，更加强调根据自身特性，从本土实际和现实国情出发构建基于内在需要的治理模式。

二、未来中国的发展态势

经过改革开放三十年来的经济增长和实力积累，中国的国家能力得到全面提升。北京奥运会显示了中国强大的组织动员能力和现代化成就，

60周年国庆大阅兵意味着中国军事和国防能力的稳步提升,上海世博会展示的是中国巨大的科技和创新能力,而从抗击汶川地震到应对金融危机则反映出中国超强的抵御灾难和抗打击能力。如果说长期以来中国的国家能力只能由GDP的增长速度和总量来定义,那么现在的力量结构则更加全面和实在。2009年,面临外部危机蔓延和实体经济下滑的严峻挑战,中国通过强有力的政策刺激和内外协调率先走出了国际金融危机,成功实现了"保八"的政策目标。2010年,中国的国内生产总值将确定超过日本,成为世界第二大经济体,其结果是中国被推到了国际舞台的中心,成为世界竞相关注的焦点。

未来十年,中国的总体实力仍将保持快速增长的势头。在经济层面,中国正处于工业化中期阶段这一历史进程中,继续推进现代化建设仍是中国压倒性的战略任务。由于中国的劳动力供给在相当时期内仍然充足,中国不仅有可能而且必须保持经济的高速增长。经过几十年的现代化努力,中国建立起完整的工业体系和发达的基础设施,这为实现增长方式转变和产业结构升级提供了坚实基础。同时,中国具有广阔的市场空间和消费潜力,政府拥有雄厚财政基础和多元政策杠杆。一旦体制性障碍得以消除,国内需求将为经济增长提供强力支撑。随着创新型国家战略的实施,战略性产业将得到大力扶持,中国的科技实力和自主创新能力将会有实质性提升。这不仅有利于大幅提高中国经济的内涵和质量,而且将从根本上改变中国长期处于国际产业链条低端,只能提供简单加工和贴牌生产的格局,进而建立起中国在世界资源配置和分工体系中的优势地位。

在军事层面,复杂、多元的安全威胁决定着未来十年仍是中国国防现代化的快速增长期。首先,尽管近年来两岸关系有所缓和,双方博弈由主权之争回归到治权之争,但台湾问题在相当时期内仍然存在,并随着岛内政治生态的演变和外部势力的持续干预而存在激化、异变的可能;"藏独"、"东突"等分裂主义势力正处于猖獗活跃期,构成对国家安全和领土完整的重大威胁。其次,随着中国进一步融入世界以及"走出去"战略的实施,国家利益的边界不断向外拓展。然而,中国的战略保障能力和军事自卫手段严重不足,如何保护和实现日益增长的海外利益成为新时期国家安全战略谋划的重要内容。最后,中国面临的外部安全环境趋于复杂,在传统大国对华军事防范力度持续增加的同时,非传统安全的威胁也显著上升。这些都意味着中国的国家安全任务将进一步加重,中国将在积极防御的总体战略指导下加强武器装备、科技水平和军队素质,国防能力建设会迈上一个新的台阶。

中国未来能力的增长同时也体现在软实力层面。中国所开启的人类史无前例的工业化进程,不仅实现了经济持续的高速增长和社会生活的根本性改观,而且为整个世界带来了机遇和福祉,而这一切是在超短时期且没有向国外输出战争和转移矛盾的前提下实现的。从日常用品到工业制造,从联合国维和到国际系列峰会,"中国元素"在国际社会日益凸显,"中国模式"成为世界范围内热议的话题。中国发展所遵循的基本经验、政策思路对后发国家如何确定国内优先议程并处理外部经验和本土关怀的关系提供了重要启示,在回应诸如战争与和平、文明冲突、环境保护等当今世界面临的根本性挑战方面也具有独特的影响力。从这个意义上讲,中国崛起同时也是政治软实力的崛起。当然,中国仍面临着软硬实力发展失衡、力量和影响相互分离和国际话语权缺失等难题,进而制约着中国整体能力的持续增长。正是基于此,软实力建构已经成为国家整体发展战略和外交战略布局的重要内容。未来十年,中国将继续"内强素质、外塑形象",在建立良好国内治理、重塑核心价值观和提高外交动员能力方面加大作为,进而为国家整体能力的增长提供支撑。

当然,未来十年也是中国内部矛盾最为突出、发展环境日益复杂的时期。首先,国家财富的迅速增长并没有自动带来整个社会系统的全面进步。相反,长期以来的经济优先主义导致了贫富差距、社会失衡、资源短缺、环境恶化等一系列问题。如何防止这些问题进一步恶化,进而导致社会矛盾的"共振"和集中爆发考验着决策者的政治智慧。其次,随着中国从魅力型领导到技术专家治国的过渡,领导者的个人威望和意识形态整合能力都出现下降趋势,能否以新的共识加强党内团结是一个不可回避的重大问题。如果再考虑到西方对华"分化促变"的压力、权贵利益集团的不断固化,以及民众持续的政治参与要求,中国在政治整合和社会稳定上将面临更加严峻的考验。再次,三十年来国家与社会关系的变化导致了社会力量的显著成长,这在激发社会活力和彰显个性独立的同时也带来了国家决策环境的复杂化。政府越来越需要在慎重理性决策与回应民族主义情绪之间保持平衡,以避免出现重大的战略性失误。因此,可以说,中国内部治理所面临的问题之复杂、挑战之严峻不亚于世界上任何国家。

综合来看，中国在未来十年还将经历一个实力增长的黄金期，并可能在21世纪第二个十年结束时成为一个综合实力仅次于美国的世界第二大国。但如果不能够通过制度调整和社会改革控制矛盾或降低问题带来的冲击效应，中国实力增长的乐观前景也存在反复甚至中断的可能。实力和问题的并存意味着在相当时期内中国是一个具有双重特性的国家，既将自己定位为发展中国家，又在具体事务中与发达国家拥有广泛的共同利益；既经历着经济的高速增长和物质财富的迅速积累，又面临着前所未有的内部挑战和国际风险；既需要回应民众对公正和平等的基本诉求，建立更加和谐的国内社会，又需要消除外部社会对中国的战略疑虑，维持和平稳定的国际环境。这就决定了中国外交也具有复杂的两面性。在战略层面，外交仍将"韬光养晦"，保持内向型的防御姿态，为国内问题的优先解决创造条件；在战术层面则需保持积极的"有所作为"，以维护不断拓展的国家利益。在总体视野上，中国将继续坚持开放合作、互利共赢的国际大局观，但在不同的问题领域则进退有别，尤其更加坚决地维护关涉中国核心利益和战略空间的问题。

三、重构中国与世界的关系

改革开放以来，中国与世界的关系发生了历史性变化。世界体系转型与中国的崛起同步进行、相互影响。世界体系的和平转型为中国崛起提供了重要战略机遇，中国正是在开放性的全球体系和总体稳定的外部环境下实现了国家综合实力的持续增强。同时，中国也以自身力量推动世界体系的不断变迁，成为现存体系的重要参与者和合作性力量。未来十年，中国的发展态势依然迅猛，但"大而不强"、"将起未起"的战略处境难有根本改观；世界权势将加速转移，但制度化的全球体系却远未确立。国家、制度和非国家行为体作用重叠、错综复杂，政治身份千差万别，不确定性和困惑感有增无减。这意味着中国与世界的关系将处于一个重新调适和相互建构的过程之中，彼此之间的战略疑虑和认知差距大为加剧，中国崛起的整体外部环境将更加复杂。

从中国的视角看，中国迅速崛起并进入国际舞台的中心使得国人的心态异常复杂。一方面，中国的这一次崛起是自近代一百多年来经历无数次曲折探索和失败后取得的重大阶段性成功。它表明拥有悠久农业传统的中国在崭新的工业文明形态下同样具有强大的适应能力，国人对实现中华民族的伟大复兴从来没有像现在这样信心满满；但另一方面，高歌猛进的工业化进程带来了前所未来的问题和挑战，中国在转型过程中凸显出来的利益失衡、社会矛盾和信仰混乱使得国人对未来前途充满担忧，而这种担忧又往往在与西方发达社会的对比中进一步放大。国人心态的复杂性还体现在对外部世界的认知上。由于长期处于国际体系的底端，中国渴望通过自我努力得到外部世界的承认，但又深怕陷入他者别有用心的捧杀和过度承担责任的陷阱，因而难免出现面对外部指责过度敏感，出现赞扬之声却又处处设防的情况；在面临事关世界和平和人类福祉的问题时，中国善于进行泛道德化的理想主义宣示，但在具体的行动中却又极度实用主义，力求避其锋芒，徐图自保。这种自信心与自卑感、大国情结与弱者心态的复杂交织使得中国的国际行为摇摆不定、前后不一，增添了外部世界认识中国的难度。

外部世界面对中国崛起时的心态同样复杂。基于超巨型的物理面积、人口规模和持续三十年的经济高速增长，中国崛起正在重塑着外部世界认知中国的集体心理：承认中国崛起的事实但难以认同和真正接受作为独特异质的中国方式，期待中国承担更多的国际责任又对中国的影响拓展和力量使用充满疑虑，相信中国是理解未来世界的关键却始终不愿放弃自我中心的固有观念。反映在不同国家的具体政策行为上，这种复杂认知又具有多样化的表征。在权力加速转移的背景下，美国为首的西方对其中心地位和优越感的丧失倍加担忧，对中国的迅猛崛起存有疑虑、恐慌、排斥的复杂心态和"过激反应"。"中国强硬论"、"中国傲慢论"的国际舆论不时出现，在战略应对上更加强调对华的防范制衡，在制衡战略中又特别强调软、硬手段同时并用；由于在非西方国家群体中的突出地位，新兴国家对中国的嫉妒感不断上升，进而成为双边关系新的麻烦来源；周边国家对华心态面临着从俯视到平视，再到仰视的痛苦调整过程，对中国不断增强的实力影响"欲迎还拒"；发展中国家的心态也很复杂，积极欢迎中国的投资、技术和商品，但又恐惧中国的强大竞争优势，"新殖民主义"的论调时有出现。

由此可见，中国崛起的"地壳运动"效应正在开始显现，不仅改变着世界的客观权力结构，而且也影响着中国和外部世界各自的心理结构。

中外双方都需要经历观念形态和具体政策上的调适过程，建构起更具理性和现实的战略框架。在观念层面，外部世界，尤其是西方社会需要从长期形成的自我中心主义和道德优越感中解放出来，反思基于西方经验建立起的现代性范式在认识中国问题上的局限性，进而放弃改造中国成为典型西方阵营一员的雄心和幻想，真正正视中国因多重身份和多种进程共存而显出的异常复杂性。中国则需要扫除百年的历史悲情和虚骄的民族主义，培育出健康、理性的国民心态，既确信中国取得成就的伟大意义，又对中国所面临的艰巨挑战时刻保持清醒，将一个客观、多元的中国展现给世界。

在具体政策层面，外部世界，尤其是西方需要改变非此即彼的二元对立逻辑，放弃防范、遏制的对抗性思维，真正接纳中国作为多元全球体系中的重要一员，理性看待双方的合作空间和利益冲突，既不能因相互合作而对对方产生不切实际的心理期待，又要避免将功能性领域的争端上升到政治原则、是非善恶的高度。对中国而言，力量增长意味着责任承担，中国很难再坚持独善其身或"搭便车"式的政策选择，承担起与其国力相适应的国际责任不仅是回应外部社会指责、非议的应景之举，更是中国争取国际话语权、提高政治动员能力的长远之道。中国需要在国内优先的总体战略下在国家利益与国际责任、自我发展与他者共赢之间显示更多的平衡和灵活性，以推动中国与世界的关系继续朝着和平、合作的方向发展。这不仅是维护中国国家利益的工具性考量，更涉及到中国能否为全球问题解决提供新选择的价值性思考。

The World and China in the Next Decade: A Perspective from International Politics

Jin Canrong

Professor and Associate Dean of School of International Studies, Renmin University of China

Abstract: In the next decade, both the world and China will undergo complex and profound changes. The world will enter a critical period featuring the transformation of current world system and the remodeling of current world order. The international power structure is taking on a new look that demonstrates a relative balance between Western and non-Western powers, and the coexistence of cooperation and competition between traditional and emerging powers. The change will soon spread to areas like global issues, policy-making mechanisms, and the ideas of development. For China, the next decade will witness a huge increase in its comprehensive strength, and a heavy burden of multiple vulnerabilities. The prospect of China's rise is determined by how it utilizes the ever-growing power and whether it can control the internal conflicts. The rise of China faces a much more complex environment in the next ten years due to the readjustment and mutual construction of the relations between China and the world, and an increase in strategic concerns, and gaps in understanding. As a result, the diplomacy of China should find a flexible balance between its national interests and international responsibilities, and between self-development and a win-win development strategy with other countries, and in turn push the relations between China and the world towards peace, cooperation and development.

In the first decade of the 21st century, a growing trend of changes in current International configuration is taking hold in a world that is generally stable. Over the past decade, global trends such as globalization, information technology, and democratization moved on amid confusions and doubts. For the first time in modern times, a historical shift from the West to the East appeared in international power and wealth. World politics now faces unprecedented complexity and uncertainty as various forces, diversified topics, and competitive ideas permeated the international game. The last ten years witnesses the rapid development of China. By carrying on domestic reforms and further integrating into the international system, China has not only built up powerful national strength and strategic influence, but also improved its international identity by actively participating and building the current international order with other countries. It's of equal necessity to look forward to the future of the world and China in the next decade, which will offer China the foresight to grasp world trends and develop successfully in the future, and will greatly inspire China's policy formulation and strategic adjustments at present.

I. Future trends of the world

Under the joint influence of the international financial crisis, the rise of emerging economies, and the upsurge of global problems, the world is accelerating into the post-financial crisis era. Concerning the future trends of the world in this ear, various scholars have proposed diversified ideas. This paper attempts to study the future trends of the world by using the international structure as a basic variable, to analyze the deep impact the changing international structure has on global issues, decision-making systems, and the ideas of development.

We can draw a distinct perspective into the current and future international structures from the split of Western and non-Western powers in international relations. After the end of the Cold War, the world temporarily entered a unipolar moment defined by American supremacy. Becoming the formulator of global rules and the leading provider of international public goods, the US-led Western camp took full advantage in East-West relations and North-South relations. Nevertheless, the post-Cold War Western-centric position was quickly shaken in only two decades. By now, the international authority and global influence of the Western camp has shrunk considerably. Being the leading force of Western primacy, the power of US is severely weakened for its foreign policy blunders and internal economic difficulties. In contrast, the non-Western world is relatively divided and weak. Marginalized in the world power structure, non-Western countries are deprived of the rights to make decisions and distribute benefits, and constantly suffer from interference and extrusion by the West. Against the great post-Cold War background of the expansion of globalization and the spread of technological revolution, the non-Western world has successfully initiated or accelerated the process of reform and modernization. Nonetheless, because of sharp differences in historical heritage, natural resources, and political abilities, non-Western countries or country blocs have achieved different end results in the pursuit of modernization. This in turn makes them differ in their status, interest appeals and strategic choices in international relations.

In the next decade, the balance of power between the West and the rest will continue to change, and the Western dominance in international structure will soon give way to a more balanced power system in which both the Western and non-Western powers have their say. As the most powerful and dominant country in the Western camp, US still enjoys unparalleled technology and military strength. To some degree, Obama's reform measures have improved the US economy and its international image. For instance, the latest report on national security strategy not only stressed the importance of military might, but clarified the priority of diplomacy, development, and international mechanism in resolving disputes, preventing conflicts and maintaining peace. By distancing itself from the strategy of unilateralism and pre-emptive strike advocated by the Bush administration, the report demonstrates that US is good at correcting mistakes and reflecting on its strategies. However, the internal and external difficulties in front of US are unlikely to be fundamentally relieved within a short period of time. Domestically, despite that the quickly launched bail-out plan and economic stimulus package help to avoid an economic free-fall, US economy will grow, but sluggishly in comparison to the rapid expansion of emerging economies. The slow recovery will certainly curb President Obama's ambition to revitalize US manufacturing sector. Besides, the polarization of American politics leads to stronger disagreements between Democrats and Republicans, and between the White House and Capitol, making it hard to seek unity of will and form strategic consensus, which are key to the formation of political actions. Externally, US has to spend considerable resources on the prolonged battle against terrorism, and its conflicts with other countries is impossible to be solved immediately. To outsource its responsibility, Washington carried out the smile diplomacy and cooperated with many partners, but the strategy failed to meet the expected outcome. Therefore, in the future, US is unlikely to enjoy the same prominent international status it had owned at the beginning of this century, and it will have to expend enormous efforts and costs to exercise its international leadership., As two other important members from the West camp, Japan and EU are unable to maintain the status of Western-Centrism, for they are dragged by internal political games and social governance challenges. Thereby, although the West will remain at the center of the international structure, but in general, as the three pillars of the camp are facing lots of problems and uncertainties, its ability to lead the world will decline.

The non-Western world is rising as a whole. The comprehensive strength and strategic influence of emerging market economies have rose significantly due to their successful internal reforms. In the next decade, although these countries have to deal with internal restructuring and governance problems, they will continue to grow at a faster speed than developed economies and grow into new drive engines of world economy after the financial crisis. As a result, the status of emerging market economies in world economy and politics will see a substantial rise. Their relations with existing major powers will determine the stability of the future world. After the Cold War, Russia fell into a decade of decline and chaos. But after it re-established its status as a world power via strong leadership and resource advantages, it began to adopt a tough stance in its foreign policy to protect its strategic interests. Suffering from the international financial crisis over the last year, Russia softened its stance and made concessions on issues like Iran's nuclear program and international nuclear disarmament so as to re-set US-Russian relations. Nonetheless, the effort is largely limited in consideration of their different geographic situations, different understandings of the history, and the messianic cultures and mindsets of the two countries. In the coming decade, amid internal calls for stable and sustainable government policies and a second reform of the market, Russia will carry on its foreign policy of drifting between Western and non-Western powers, and will remain in the circle of hope and disillusionment. Thus, Russia's status in international structure is quite uncertain, but the orientation of its policies can significantly influence the international situation. When it comes to the future of Islamic world, the most decisive point is to readjust existing social system so as to balance Islamic traditions with secular values, local cultures and western influences. That is to say, the future destiny of Islamic countries is determined by whether they can embark on the transition to modernism driven by the endogenous forces. As for the failed states, their future needs a commonly recognized political authority, as well as assistance based on international consensus and efforts. The anti-Americanism will be eased in the next ten years as US adjusts its foreign policies, but it is unlikely to diminish because the long-term US supremacy will continue.

The development trends of Western and non-Western powers, together with their interactive relations, foretell significant changes of the post-Cold War international structure dominated by the West. The West will decline relatively, while non-Western powers will rise as a whole. In the meantime, the power distribution within the two worlds will also change. That is, the US dominance in the Western camp will be further strengthened, while emerging market economies will play bigger roles in non-Western world. The world will enter an era featuring a relative balance between the West and the rest, and the coexistence of competitions and cooperation between traditional and emerging powers. The relations between emerging powers and the West, with US in particular, will set the tone and the trend of international politics in the future. Specifically, the changing international structure will deeply affect the global issues, decision-making systems, and ideas of development in future world.

Firstly, modern, global issues will return to the center of international politics. Since the end of the Cold War, three different types of countries have coexisted in the world, which are pre-modern state, post-modern state and modern state. Most countries, including US, belong to the class of modern state. A considerable number of European countries have become post-modern states in social formation and political philosophy. Some countries in Central Asia and Latin America, failing to get modernized in time, are downgraded to pre-modern states, or the so-called failed states. The three types of countries, on different historical stages of modernization, focus on different issues and appeal for different interests. Pre-modern states strive to meet basic survival needs, modern states emphasize on material interests, and post-modern countries are pursuing a variety of abstract rights. The early years after the Cold War were dominated by Western-Centrism. At that time, global issues in international politics were centered on abstract rights, leading to a fight for discourse right between modern states and post-modern states. In contrast, the survival-based needs of the failed states were unfortunately ignored for quite a long time. Nevertheless, with the rise of emerging countries, the return to manufacturing in US, the governance crisis in Europe, and the efforts of failed states to modernization, the modern discourse of material interests will reoccupy the centre of global agenda. In other words, the nature of power game is still the competition for material resources and strategic interests, although post-modern rights, thanks to its strong morality and political correctness, will not diminish, but become the main form of international interaction in the long run.

Secondly, the global decision-making system will seek a new balance between legitimacy and effectiveness. Since the end of the Cold War, the US-led Western camp dominated the process of making rules and setting agendas in the world. Nonetheless, with the decline of the overall ability of the West and the rise of global problems, the Western decision-making system is now facing a twin crisis in both legitimacy and effectiveness. The spread of international financial crisis further accelerated the decline of the existing system. On the contrary, emerging market economies are playing increasingly important roles in promoting global economic growth, and resolving international financial crisis. Consequently, the basic trend of future policy-making system is to find the space to meet the demands of emerging countries, and in turn establish a governance model based on extensive coordination and equal status between traditional and emerging powers. The rise of G20 not only strengthens the discourse power and influence of emerging countries, but provides traditional and emerging powers with the platform to coordination their policies. In this way, the global economic decision-making system achieves a new balance between legitimacy and effectiveness. But the system still needs swifter and deepened reforms to satisfy demands by the ever-changing situation, and counter global and regional problems on a broader scale. To take the high ground in the post-financial crisis era, different countries will establish various temporary and exclusive blocs, which will be an important trend in the development of future global decision making system. As these blocs differ in the ability to integrate different interests and to set up standards, only those with strong consensuses and powerful functions will survive the fierce competition, and becoming the starting point for establishing a global system.

Thirdly, ideas of international development will inevitably become diversified and independent. Back in the era of Western-Centrism, besides building an absolute advantage in physical strength, the West monopolized the right to interpret mode of development and modernity. The heart of the Western intercourse lies in the presumption of a unique way to modernization, or rather, the Western mode, and in the belief in the almightiness of democracy. That is why the world was simply divided into democratic states and autocratic states. Drawn from moral standards rather than fact-based judgment, the division considered the experience accumulated under specific scenarios as the universal choice. Driven by a messianic mindset, the West vigorously promoted their experience across the globe, resulting in political turmoil and social instability in many late-coming countries. Zakaria holds that many of the democratization attempts by countries involved in the third wave of democratization eventually evolved into illiberal democracy, stirring up worldwide suspicion of the portability of the Western mode. The Western image as the pioneer in modernization and defender of democracy is now shattered by the exposure of a series of internal problems in the West, such as strategic blunders in US foreign policy, the out-break of financial crisis, and the spread of European sovereign debt crisis. Contrastingly, the non-Western world is now on the rise. Emerging countries are relatively successful in economic development and crisis prevention. Increasingly confident, these countries put more emphasis on their own characteristics, and form their own governance mode according to internal needs, local realities, and current national conditions.

II. Future trends of China's development

After the implementation of the reform and opening up policy in 1979, three decades of economic growth and accumulation witnesses China's national strength increasing in every aspect. The Beijing Olympic Games displays China's modernization achievements and the strong capacity of organization and mobilization. The military parade on 2009's National Day evidences the steady improvement of China's military and national defence. The 2010 World Expo in Shanghai demonstrates China's advanced technology and innovation capacity. Other events, from the earthquake relief work in Wenchuan to countermeasures against the financial crisis, shows that China excels at disaster relief and damage resistance. For a long time, China's national strength can only be defined by the growth rate and total amount of GDP. But now, the present power structure of China is comprehensive and concrete. In 2009, despite of the spread of financial crisis and the downturn in real economy, China stepped out of the international financial crisis first and realized the goal of 8% growth in GDP thanks to its powerful stimulus policies and fine coordination between internal and external markets. In 2010, China surpassed Japan to become world's second largest economy, and thereby became the highlight of the world.

In the next decade, China's overall strength will continue to grow at a fast rate. Economically, China is in the middle stage of industrialization. In this historical process, it is overwhelmingly important to carry on the strategic mission of modernization. Sufficient supply of labor forces in the long term makes it a possibility and a must for China to keep its rapid growth. After decades of efforts to build a modernized country, China has established a complete industrial system and developed infrastructures, preparing the way to transform the pattern of economic growth and to upgrade the structure of industry. Meanwhile, China boasts a vast market with numerous potential consumers, and the government has a strong financial base and various regulatory policies. Once the institutional obstacles are removed, China's economic growth will be greatly motivated by its domestic demands. With the implementation of national strategies for innovation, China will give full support to strategic industries, leading to a substantial growth in its scientific and technological strength and innovation capacity. It will not only greatly increase the content and quality of China's economy, but also help China move up from the bottom of international industrial chain to the upstream. Then, China will take the upper hand in worldwide resource allocation and division of labour.

Militarily, China will accelerate the modernization of its national defence in response to complex and diversified security threats. Firstly, although the cross-strait relations is easing in recent years, and the two sides has put aside at the moment the dispute over sovereignty, yet the Taiwan issue is unlikely to be solved very soon. Besides, there is the potential for the issue to get intensified and altered by interference from outside forces or changes in the internal political environment. What's more, the rampant activities of Tibetan separatists and East Turkistan secessionists pose a huge threat to China's national security and territorial integrity. Secondly, as China goes global and further integrates into the world, the boundary of its national interests is also expanding outward.

But China severely lacks the ability of strategic support and the military means to defend its interests. In the new era, it will become an important part of China's strategic planning to protect and fulfil the growing overseas interests. Finally, China is facing an increasingly complex external security environment with soaring non-traditional security threats, and an ever-increasing opposition military presence by traditional powers. These means China has to shoulder a much heavier duty of national security. Under the grand strategy of active defense, China will step up the construction of national defense by improving the weaponry and equipment, as well as the technological level and quality of the army.

In the future, the soft power of China will also grow rapidly. The scale of China's industrialization is unprecedented. It has not only achieved sustained rapid economic growth and fundamental changes in social life, but also brought opportunity and welfare to the whole world. The most remarkable point is that the whole process is done in a very short period of time, and has not brought wars or conflicts to other countries. From daily supplies to industrial fabrications, from UN peacekeeping operations to a string of international summits, China is now an outstanding element in international community, while the Chinese Mode has become a hot topic around the world. The basic experience and thinking of China gives new-coming countries a revelation on how to set the priority of domestic agenda, and on how to treat the relationship between external experience and local care. The Chinese Mode also has a distinct influence over how to counter such fundamental challenges in the world today as war and peace, clash of civilizations, environment protection, and so on. In this sense, the rise of China equals the rise of its political soft power. Of course, the comprehensive growth of China's national strength is constrained by some harsh problems in that the development of soft and hard powers is imbalanced, that its limited influence does not match its power, and that it lacks international discourse power. Thus, the construction of soft power has become the country's overall development strategy and an important part of China's foreign policy. In the coming ten years, China will keep improving quality of life at home and image outside, attach greater emphasis on national governance, the core values, and diplomatic relations, and thereby provide support to the development of its comprehensive national strength.

Of course, China in the next ten years will be full of internal conflicts and external complexities. Firstly, the rapid growth of national wealth does not mean the overall progress of the entire social system. On the contrary, the long-time focus on economic growth has led to a series of problems like economic disparity, social imbalance, resource shortages, and environmental degradation. Policy makers need to muster all their political wisdom to prevent the escalation of these problems, which are often the prelude to the eruption of social conflicts. Secondly, the transition from charismatic leadership to technology-based leadership will inevitably reduce the personal prestige of leaders and ideological cohesiveness. The transition poses a severe challenge on finding new consensus to keep the unity of the ruling party. Secondly, the test on China's political integration and social stability will be even more severe if we consider the pressures from the West, the formation of vested interests group, and the continuous public demand of political engagement. Thirdly, three decades of changes in the relations between the state and the society has caused a remarkable growth of social forces. Although the social forces do vitalize the society and highlight independent personality, yet they make national decision-making much more complex. To avoid major strategic mistakes, the government has to strike a balance between making rational decisions and responding to nationalist sentiments. Therefore, suffice it to say China, like any other country in the world, is facing complex problems and severe challenges in its internal governance.

On the whole, China will experience in the next decade a huge increase in its comprehensive strength, and may become world's second largest country, only behind US, in comprehensive strength by the end of 2020. Nevertheless, the optimistic prospect may be darkened or even dimmed if the country fails to control conflicts and solve problems through system adjustments and social reforms. The coexistence of power and weaknesses discloses the twofold nature of China in a considerable period of time. Although positioned as the largest developing country, China nonetheless shares wide common interests with developed countries in practical affairs. Experiencing a rapid economic growth and accumulation of material wealth, China faces unprecedented internal challenges and international risks. Shouldering the responsibility to build a harmonious society where the public demand of justice and equality are fulfilled, China has to ease foreign doubts towards its strategy and take the responsibility to maintain a peaceful and stable international environment. These facts determine the twofold nature of China's diplomacy. Strategically, to concentrate on internal issues, China needs to keep a low profile and maintain an inward-looking defensive posture. Tactically, China should actively defend its broadening national interests. In the overall perspective, China should expand its horizon to the international level, stick to openness, cooperation, mutual benefit, and a win-win strategy, treat different issues with different approaches, and be determined to safeguard its core interests and strategic space.

III. Restructuring of the relations between China and the world

Since the reform and opening-up in 1979, the relations between China and the world have undergone historic changes. The transformation of the world system runs parallel to the rise of China and the two processes are continuously influencing each other. The peaceful transformation of world system offers an important and strategic opportunity for the rise of China. The increase in China's comprehensive strength is inseparable from a generally stable global system. Meanwhile, China has been pushing the world system towards change and has become an important participant and collaborator in the existing system. Despite of the fast development of China in the next ten years, the country, big but not so strong, is unlikely to bring fundamental changes to its strategic situation and remain in the starting phase of its rise. Likewise, although the transfer of world power will be accelerated in the coming decade, the sense of uncertainty and confusion will not cease, because of the over-lapping impacts from actors with diversified political identities, such as states, institutions, and non-state actors. As a result, China will face a much more complex environment in the next ten years due to the readjustment and mutual construction of the relations between China and the world, and an increase in strategic concerns and gaps in understanding.

From China's perspective, the rapid rise of China and its entry into international arena complicates the mindsets of the Chinese people. For one thing, the rise of China today is a major success after over a century of twists and turns. It proves that the traditionally agrarian country is able to adapt to the brand new industrial civilization. Thus, it is unsurprisingly that the Chinese people are more confident than ever to realize the revival of the nation. For another thing, the rapid development of industrialization brings about unprecedented problems and challenges, such as imbalanced interests, social contradictions, and confused beliefs. Therefore, during the transition period the people are anxious about the future. The anxiety is often amplified in contrast with the Western developed countries. The understandings of outside world also reflect the complex mindset of the Chinese people. Staying at the bottom of international system for decades, China wishes to be recognized through self-efforts. But at the same time, China is afraid of getting conceited by those with ulterior motives or be forced to take excessive responsibilities. That is why China is sometimes oversensitive to external blames, or is wary of praises. When an issue is related to world peace and human well-being, China always considers it morally and takes an idealistic stand. But when it comes to concrete actions, the country would resort to pragmatism, take evasive actions, and put self-preservation first. The combination of confidence and inferiority, of power complex and weak mindset make China's international actions inconsistent and swaying, and thus adding the difficulty for the outside world to know China.

Similarly, the outside world has a mixed feeling toward the rise of China, which, in combination with China's gigantic land mass, huge population, and three decades of rapid economic growth, is restructuring the group mindset of the outside world towards China. People from other countries respect the fact of China's rise, but find it difficult to accept the unique approach taken by China. They wish China could take more international responsibilities, but doubt the expansion of its influence and the use of its power. They regard China as a key member of the future world, but are reluctant to cast aside the self-centered prejudice. Under this complicated mindset, different countries have formulated diversified policies on China. For the US-led Western countries, they are extremely worried about the loss of their central position and sense of superiority against the background of rapid power transition. Thus, a mixed feeling of doubt, fear, rejection arouses among these countries. They often overreact to the rise of China, saying that China has got more arrogant and tough. Strategically, the West tries to use the stick and the carrot to check and guard against China. In non-Western countries, the emerging powers are increasingly jealous of China's outstanding status in the non-Western world. The mindset creates a new barrier in bilateral relations. The neighbouring countries are painfully adjusting their attitudes towards China, who once was inferior to them, gradually caught up with them, and eventually surpassed them. No wonder they are very hesitant to embrace China's increasing power and influence. It is the same with other developing countries, which on one hand welcomes China's investment, technology, and commodities, and on the other hand fear China's strong competitive strength. Thus, they sometimes call China's influence the neo-colonialism.

From the above analysis, we can see that the rise of China is exerting tremendous influence over the power structure in the world as well as the mindset of China and the outside world, both of whom needs time to adjust their ideologies and concrete policies so as to construct a more rational and realistic strategic framework. Conceptually, the outside world, especially the West, should break away from traditional self-centrism and moral superiority, reflect on the practices of learning China via the modern paradigm based on Western experience, abandon the ambition and imagination of transforming China into a typical member of the Western camp, and face squarely the unique complexity displayed by China due to its multiple identities and the coexistences of several processes in the country. China, however, needs to nurture a healthy and rational national mindset by wiping out arrogant nationalism and the century-long tragic sentiment concerning the nation's latter-day history. The Chinese people should be convinced of the significance of China's achievement, recognize the daunting challenges in the way, and introduce to the world an objective and diversified China.

In consideration of concrete policies, the outside world, especially the West should change the logic of binary opposition, abandon the antagonist mind of curbing and guarding against China, and accept China as an important player in a diversified global system. They ought to take a rational view of the room for collaboration (space) and conflicts of interest between the two sides by avoiding unrealistic expectations of China in cooperation, and separating disputes in functional areas from political principles and the dichotomy of good and evil. As for China, the growth in strength means more responsibilities. Rather than standing aloof to world affairs, China needs to actively shoulder international responsibilities in accordance to its national strength rather than regarding it as a passive way to respond to external criticism, for the action is actually a sustainable way to gain international discourse power and to improve China's ability of political mobilization. With internal affairs high on the agenda, it is of great necessity for China to strike a flexible balance between its national interests and international responsibilities, and between self-development and a win-win development strategy with other countries, and in turn push the relations between China and the world towards peace, cooperation and development. This is not only to safeguard the national interests of China, but also determines whether China can provide new options to solve global problems.

文化关系——大国合作的途径

何塞·欧博

美国斯坦福大学
古典学、政治科学教授

内容提要： 中国和美国都是大国。大国确实会有竞争，但也必须寻找合作途径。当西方文化的有魅力的部分已在中国得到认可的同时，中国文化的美丽瑰宝在西方正得到更多认可。这种创造性竞争的可能性，和最终建立不但有更多的了解，并更多地综合世界上最好的最持久的传统这样一个世界的可能性，是我对中美文化关系未来的最终期望。

我的学术领域是政治学和人文学科，所以我将努力把这两个问题放在一起讲。作为一个政治学家，我们必须面对的事实是，中国和美国都是大国。大国确实会有竞争，但如同诸位所说，大国也必须寻找合作途径。权力是关系的一部分，是中美双方关系中的一部分。问题是，哪种权力是值得提倡的，我们如何使用权力。我想的是，金灿荣已经告诉我们需要为这种权力寻找途径，这就是文化力量——约瑟夫和我所说的软实力——而不是军事和经济制裁这种硬实力。

那么我们想象一下，让我们一起做个欧洲旅行，比如在意大利，转到法国、越过英国、达到德国、罗马尼亚，到希腊、阿里巴尼亚，横渡非洲，去埃及、利比亚、阿尔及利亚和摩洛哥。在这次旅行中，你将见到巨大的差异，会遇到许多不同的文化。表面上，这些不同的文化极端地、非常地不同；但表面之下，这些差异事实上有着类似的基础。如果你从考古学水平上看，如果你到过庞贝、里昂、巴斯、大莱波蒂斯等伟大的考古遗迹，你会看到基本相同的罗马地层、罗马建筑，这些差异巨大之地的城市曾经看起来非常相同，所以罗马是一个文明社会。西方一种观点认为，实际上有一个世界级的文明，在拥有真正的广泛性的世界文明这一点而言，西方唯一一次真正与中国相当。罗马帝国因其硬实力而出名，因其军团而出名，因其军队而出名。但罗马帝国显然又是由软实力所延续的，是由文化、帝国机制、语言 —— 罗马帝国常见的几种语言 —— 共同的建筑风格、共同的法律体系、文学、艺术 —— 视觉艺术和表演艺术 —— 所延续的。罗马文化反过来又是软实力的产物。罗马文化是借鉴，或者可以说是接收希腊文化而在罗马世界中部分地加以融合的产物。因此，我们认为，罗马文化的许多东西实际上是从希腊借鉴过来的，它是软实力的一种形式，可以说是一种征服。所以文学、表演、语言，甚至字母、神话，对文明形成内涵的了解，对罗马人而言，至少是希腊和罗马之间这种软实力关系的产物。希腊的流行文化从何而来？它也不全是本土文化，它不仅仅开始于希腊，而是现在的伊拉克、美索不达米亚和埃及之间的软实力关系。

希腊文化自身部分来自于与其他伟大文明的互相交流。希腊文化开创了一个灿烂的新纪元，我们尤其可在雅典看到古典时期的例证。在那个时代，如今西方人所了解的历史、戏剧和哲学首次得以发展，那个时期，人这一概念在一个与众不同的政治体系中改变了一切，这个体系有着独特的机构 —— 民主机构，为人类自由和富人、穷人共同参与创造一个共同文明的可能性奠定了基础。希腊雅典和罗马的软实力、文化和体制成功地改变了他们的世界，因为这些文化形式和体制的吸引力很大，人们受到这些体制文化的发展潜力吸引。在游览了雅典和罗马之后，古老世界的人们对他们在这些体制中发现的有价值的一些文化感兴趣，因此这些文化就得以扩展。这就是软实力如何起作用的方式。不是通过军队，不是通过入侵，而是通过吸引力，通过美与丑、善与恶这些东西的对比。这样，来自不同文化的人们一同分享他们认为美好出色的东西，这就是软实力的作用方式。软实力最终会起到作用，只要它起作用，它的作用就会持久稳固。所以希腊和罗马的文化和体制尽管在西方不再占据绝对的主导地位，但在西方社会中仍然有着巨大的影响力。对西方世界而言，它们仍在许多方面发挥着基础作用，涉及范围仍然十分广泛。这是西方的一个独特的文化特性，在伊斯兰世界有着很高的影响力，也无疑传播到了南亚和东亚。中国学者与西方学者一样阅读苏格拉底和柏拉图的作品。所以我认为，软实力提供了一种思考大国之间相互关系的途径。这种关系，在某种意义上说，既有竞争性又有合作性，但它不需要以任何方式牵扯到硬实力，不需要牵涉军队，我想这种力量将不可避免地成为未来中美关系的一部分。

但我认为我们在此可以呼吁的、可以畅想的是软实力关系，应将其推至前景。与硬实力不同，软实力不需要寻求霸权。软实力关系不必是零和博弈。罗马人采纳希腊文化时，并不表示罗马人输了；希腊人采纳美索不达米亚和埃及文化时，不代表希腊人是失败者。同样，中国人学习柏拉图和亚里士多德时，不表示中国人输了；而当我们将中华语言和儒家传统的研究纳入进来，将中国历史融入我们的传统时，不代表西方学者输了。当西方文化有魅力的部分已在中国得到认可的同时，中国文化的美丽瑰宝在西方也得到更多认可。这种创造性竞争的可能性，和最终建立不但有更多的了解，并更多地综合世界上最好的、最持久的传统这样一个世界的可能性，是我对中美文化关系未来的最终期望。

Josiah Ober

Professor of Classics and Professor of Political Science, Stanford University

Cultural Relations —The Way of Cooperation Between The Powers

Abstract: China and the United States are both great powers. Great powers will indeed compete but must also find a way to cooperate. The beautiful things of Chinese culture are more recognized in the west just as the beautiful things of the Western culture have been recognized in China. I think the possibility for the kind of creative competition and ultimately for building a world in which not only there is a greater understanding but there is a greater integration of world's finest and most enduring traditions that is what I think ultimately I would hope for of future of Chinese-American cultural relations.

My academic fields are political science and humanities and so I'll attempt to bring these two together. Speaking as a political scientist we must face the fact that China and the United States are both great powers. Great powers will indeed compete but must also, as my fellow panelists have said, find a way to cooperate. Power will be part of the relationship, any mutual relationship between the US and China. The question is what sort of power will be exemplary, how will we use power. And I think that as Jin Canrong has already suggested we need to find ways for that power to be cultural power, the soft power, as Joseph Nye talked about, rather than the hard power of military and economic sanctions.

So imagine just take a little trip with me across much of Europe, start in Italy, move to France, go across to Britain, to Germany, to Romania, to Greece, to Albania, cross over to Africa, visit Egypt, Libya, Algeria, Morocco, in that trip you will have seen remarkable diversity. You'll see many different cultures; on the surface these different cultures look awfully different. And yet underneath all of that diversity there is in fact a substratum of similarities if you look at the archaeological levels, if you visit the great archaeological sites of Pompeii, or Leon, of Bath, of Leptis Magna, of Suphetula, and so on you'll see the same basic Roman stratum, Roman architecture, the cities of these remarkably diverse places once all look very much the same. So Rome was a civilization, arguably the West's one claim that actually held a world class civilization the one time the West really equaled china in terms holding a really extensive world civilization. The Roman empire was famous for its hard power, for its legionaries, for its army, and yet the Roman empire was clearly sustained by soft power, by the culture and the institutions of the empire, by the language, by the several languages that become common to the Roman Empire, by a common architecture, by a common system of law, by literature, and by art, both visual art and performing art. Roman culture in turn was a product of soft power. Roman culture was borrowed from, or perhaps one would say, a product of the takeover of and the partial integration of Greek culture in the Roman world. So a lot of what we think of as Roman culture was in fact as the Romans knew very well was borrowed from the Greeks. It was a form of soft power, a conquest one might say, so literature, once again performance, language and even the alphabet, mythology, the very understanding of what it was to be civilized was at least in part for the Romans a product of this soft power relationship between Greece and Rome. Where does Greek pop culture come from? Once again it's not all just indigenous it didn't just begin in Greece, it was soft power relations between what is now Iraq, Mesopotamia, and Egypt. Greek culture was in its own part borrowed from part of an interchange with other great civilizations. Greek culture crystallized in a brilliant epoch that we call the classical period exemplified especially in Athens, this was a time in which history drama philosophy as we in the west now understand it were first developed. It's a period in which the very conception of what it is to be human was transformed all in the context of a distinctive political system, a system with distinctive institutions, democratic institutions which celebrated the possibility of human freedom and the participation of both rich people and poor people in creating a common civilization. Well the soft power, institutions and culture, of Athens, Greece and Rome succeeded in transforming their world because it was these cultural forms and institutions were deeply attractive, people were attracted by the possibilities of this culture of these institutions. After visiting Athens and Rome, people in the ancient world wanted some of that culture, they saw value in those institutions and therefore these cultures spread. That's how soft power really works. Not by force, not by intruding upon but by attraction, by making something that is beautiful as opposed to ugly, that is good as opposed to evil, that shares something that people from different cultures can recognize as fine and excellent, that's how soft power works. Soft power ultimately works, if and when it does, in a way that is persistent. So Greek and Roman culture and institutions, although no longer absolutely dominant in the west remain highly influential in the west, remain foundational in many ways for the western world and they also travel very widely. That's not only by the west, that's a unique cultural attribute of the west and was highly influential in the Islamic world and travel easily to south and East Asia as well. Socrates and Plato are read by Chinese scholars as well as by western scholars. So soft power I think, gives us a way to think about an interrelationship between great powers that is indeed in some sense competitive as well as cooperative, but it need not in any way involve the hard power, need not involve force. I think that power will inevitably be part of the US-Chinese relations in the future.

But I think that what we in this room can call for and hope for is ways in which that soft power relationship is the one that is put to the foreground. Unlike hard power there is no need for soft power to seek hegemony. Soft power relations need not be zero-sum. The Romans were not the losers when the adopted Greek culture, the Greeks were not the losers when the adopted the culture of Mesopotamia and Egypt, and likewise Chinese people are not the losers when they learn something from Plato and Aristotle, western scholars are not losers when we incorporate the study of Chinese language and Confucian tradition, the history of China into our traditions. When the soft power, the attractive, the beautiful things of Chinese culture are more recognized in the west just as the beautiful things of the Western culture have been recognized in China. I think the possibility for a kind of creative competition and ultimately for building a world in which not only there is greater understanding but there is a greater integration of world's finest and most enduring traditions that is what I think ultimately I would hope for of future of Chinese-American cultural relations.

The Second U.S.-China Cultural Forum

A Binational Conversation on Bridging Cultures

The National Endowment for the Humanities in cooperation with the Chinese Ministry of Culture is hosting a day-and-a-half program on the role of art and culture in Sino-American relations. A series of roundtable conversations will take place among prominent scholars, artists, writers, and other representatives from the two nations.

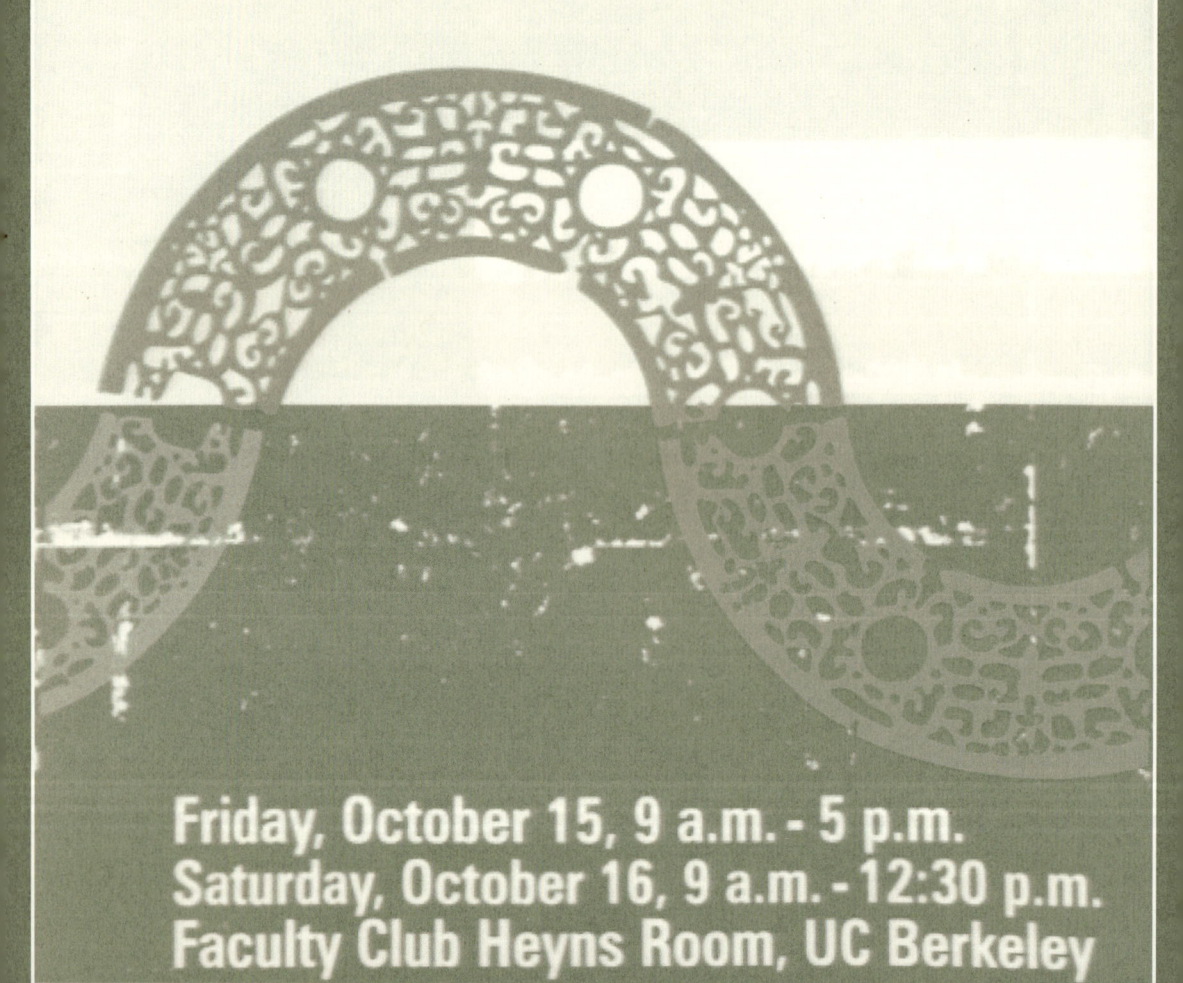

Friday, October 15, 9 a.m. - 5 p.m.
Saturday, October 16, 9 a.m. - 12:30 p.m.
Faculty Club Heyns Room, UC Berkeley

NEWS ROUNDUP

新闻综述

构筑新世纪的巴比伦通天塔
——"跨文化双边对话：第二届中美文化论坛"述评

贾磊磊
中国艺术研究院
院长助理、文化发展
战略研究中心主任

内容提要： 2010年10月15日至16日，在美国旧金山的加利福尼亚大学伯克利分校，由中华人民共和国文化部和美国国家人文基金会共同主办的"跨文化双边对话：第二届中美文化论坛"隆重举行。此次论坛的成功举行证明中美文化交流所拥有的坚实基础和通畅渠道，双方提出了中美文化交流的伦理起点与历史起点，以及中美文化沟通与互动的基本原则。论坛为进一步深化中美两国的文化交流，开辟中美文化合作的新领域，迈出了重要的历史步伐。

据《圣经》里记载，初始人类想要建一座通向天堂的"巴比伦通天塔"，上帝为了防止人类到达天庭，让人们说各种不同的语言，使他们之间无法相互沟通，最终导致了通天塔的坍塌，人类建造通天塔的宏大理想就此化为泡影。可是，人类并没有就此放弃构筑通天塔的梦想，更没有放弃相互交流与沟通的希望……

时至今日，在建筑人类建立了无数耸入云天的摩天大楼，它们就像现代社会的巴比伦通天塔一样，尽管解决了人们人们居住的空间需求，但是却没法消除人们之间的隔阂，进住到钢筋水泥"森林"里的人们相互之间变得更加冷漠；在科技界人类创造了人造地球卫星，人类仿佛拥有了"上帝之眼"，通过它可以鸟瞰地球的任何一个角落。然而，人造卫星覆盖一切的天眼，却无限放大了人类窥视的欲望，使战争的危险从地面、天空延展到了天宇；在信息传播领域，人类具备了有史以来最神奇的沟通工具——互联网，它比周幽王

本文转载自《民族艺术研究》2010年第6期。

指挥的烟火、拿破仑手中的报纸、希特勒控制的电影、布什关注的电视都更快捷，也更有效。可是，就在我们几乎拥有了一切沟通的技术手段之后，世界上的人们就能真正地相互沟通、相互理解了吗？今天，人类越来越发现巴比伦通天塔距我们如此遥远，以至于我们难以接近到它的根基……

什么能让我们在困境中确信希望的光芒？什么能让我们免遭相互的隔阂与猜忌而产生的灾难？站在新世纪的历史地平线上，我们必须重新构筑它的历史根基，在文化交流领域寻找它的现实可能——跨文化的双边对话：第二届中美文化论坛的如期举行，建构的就是这样一座跨越时空的文化交流的世纪根基，它正为中美两国在文化方面的相互沟通建起一条通衢大道。

一、并行不悖——中美文化交流的现实通道

2010年10月15日至16日在美国旧金山的加利福尼亚大学伯克利分校绿树掩映的教授俱乐部里，来自中美两国的政府官员和专家学者聚集一堂，饶有兴趣地在讨论关于新世纪"巴比伦通天塔"的有关问题——"跨文化双边对话：中美文化交流的过去现在与未来"，这是由中华人民共和国文化部和美国国家人文基金会共同主办的此次中美文化论坛的中心命题。

作为此次论坛的主办方中方主席、中华人民共和国文化部副部长、中国艺术研究院院长王文章在论坛的开幕致辞中指出，"中美两国虽然远隔千山万水，但两国人民之间并没有因为空间的距离而相互阻隔。今天的中国处在改革开放的新的发展时期，开始以开阔的胸襟和高远的目光吸收世界优秀文化，包括美国电影等在内的多种文化产品进入中国民众的视野，美国当代艺术也越来越为中国人民所熟悉及借鉴。中美文化交流正在迈向一个不断升华的历史时代。它不但沟通两国人民的心灵与情感，增进相互之间理解和信任，还对维持中美两国关系健康、稳定的发展起到重要作用。中国有句老话"万物并育而不相害，道并行而不相悖"（中庸·礼记），讲的就是世间的万事万物都可以相互依存，相互促进共同发展。不同文化之间的交流，会使我们更了解对方而尊重对方，会使我们学习对方而更具创造性"。

论坛的美方主席美国国家人文基金会主席吉姆·利奇，是奥巴马总统2009年7月任命的国家人文基金会的第9届主席，他也是美国亚太事务委员会主席以及中国事务的执行主席。他曾在普林斯顿大学的伍德罗·威尔逊学院、哈佛大学肯尼迪政治学院就职。他在论坛的致辞中说："19世纪的美国诗人沃尔特·惠特曼曾经说过，他有一个梦想，他希望有一天全世界的诗人还有诗歌有机会聚集在一起，集合所有的个人及其作品，一起为世界带来和平。"此前，他曾经问过中国代表莫言，对于世界更好的理解是来自政治家的言论，还是来自小说家的作品？ 莫言说："来自对文化有深刻理解的人，来自世界各地的优秀文学作品。"利奇主席对此番话欣然认同。作为论坛的主持人之一，美国学术团体联合会主席余宝琳女士也表示："我们必须坚持文化和人文知识作为中美文化和经济联系的基础。美国是全世界有关中国文化及其古代和现代表达最重要的知识库之一。我们终究是在各种文化之间建立桥梁，目的不是消除不同的价值观，而是欣赏、理解和解释这些价值观。她指出，事实上，1872年出任加利福尼亚大学第一任校长的丹尼尔·科伊特·吉尔曼就主张伯克利应成为一个真正的跨文化研究中心。让美国人和东方人、欧洲人各自学到对方的语言、文学、历史和科学知识。所以，当年在校内即建立了第一个中国研究中心，教授东方语言和文学。吉尔曼校长的这一作为实际上是密切美国和东亚人民联系的开拓之举。美方此次将第二届中美文化论坛的举办地选在加利福尼亚大学伯克利分校，除了该校悠久的教育历史和显赫的学术地位之外，显然是在对100多年前建立的跨文化研究中心的先见之举表示敬意。

二、知行合一 —— 中美文化交流的伦理起点与历史起点

世界上不同民族、不同国家之间究竟能不能相互理解，如果可以，那么它的途径又在哪里呢？北京师范大学影视艺术与传播学院副院长于丹教授，首先表达了她对中美文化之间可能相互沟通的独到见解，她说：在今天的世界里，文化作为动词存在，作为行为存在，作为过程存在。可以说儒家、道家、佛家，对现实都不提供现成的结论，不提供统一的行为准则，但是它们提供思考方式。中国的文化思想在今天，跟美国文化的对话中，能够呈现出来的普世价值主要包括三个方面：其一，中国儒家孔

子所提倡的作为君子的方式，实际上提供了一种个人融入社会取得自律的可能；其二，中国提倡和而不同，就是说和谐的前提是尊重不同的个性。每一个人不同的取向，融合在社会中才是一种正确的文化选择。文明不以完成统一的强制标准去泯灭每个人的个性，每一个人的个性要在大社会体系中达到均衡，这是一种现代法律和制度下理想的公民社会的状态；其三，就是中国儒家提供了一个知行合一的伦理起点，可以实现个人生命经验平衡和提升的一种现实方式。孔子说的仁爱，就是己欲立而立人，己欲达而达人。一个人用立自己的心帮别人树立价值观，用发达自己的心去帮别人一起发达，这就是仁爱。所以，他既是一个理念，又是一种行为。

在中美文化交流的历史上，有许多身体力行的先行者，他们为中美两国人民的沟通与理解做出了切实的贡献。美国学者克莱尔·康塞逊女士，就是将自己的职业生涯放在中美文化交流史的见证人和阐释者的位置上。她说，我初识中国的时候正是20世纪80年代中国和中国戏剧实力不断增强的时候，当时中国正在改革开放，戏剧艺术家在国内试演，并开始到国外巡演。我亲自见证了中国观众的活力、艺术家的创新能力。我想起了劳伦斯·林德的深刻见解，即大多数外国人将中国文化等同于传统文化，将西方文化等同于现代文化。可实际上，并非如此。对西方来说，2005年话剧第一次从中国传到美国，那是在外国人到中国几十年之后的事。对于美国来说，将中国话剧带到美国真是一件新奇的事。我认为其中的一个原因是我们的观众不愿意观赏另一种语言的话剧，或者说更大的问题是我们一直都在看中国的传统艺术，包括京剧以及其他我们认为是中国作品的其他戏剧形式。而我们应该对他们改编西方经典作品及如何写关于自己经历的故事感兴趣，我们也应该看看这些故事。所以我希望能看到更多这样的事以及人们为了获得共同尊重所做的努力奋斗。要知道，在建立合作关系和文化交流时，强调双方的共同点、深入了解对方的文化是非常重要的。

亲身参与与中国的文化交流活动的美国爱荷华大学国际写作项目主任克里斯多弗·梅里尔教授回顾了自己在中国云南组织的一次学术交流活动，在这项活动中大家每天阅读相同的作品，并就中国作家讨厌而美国作家喜欢的角色进行讨论。美国作家与中国作家发生激烈争论，相互还为对方布置写作练习。经过几个星期的共同旅行、观光、阅读相同的书籍、辩论和探讨，大家对彼此都有了深刻的了解。通过这项活动，让我们开始思考作为作家我们应该做些什么，以及了解来自大洋彼岸的同仁们在做些什么。看看我们能不能邀请对方写一些在他们看来被忽视的事情，以及他们看起来没有兴趣的事情。那么对于我们美国人来说，我们注意到了我们的中国同仁非常注重和谐。我们邀请中国朋友以一些含有矛盾的事物为主题进行写作，并尝试解决这些矛盾。最后我们发现大家阅读的作品都是他们有史以来读到的最有趣的作品。

三、风云际会 —— 西方对中国形象的历史认知

在跨文化交流中，对于一个国家形象与文化认知是极其重要的内容。为此，它也成为第二届中美文化论坛的重要主题。美国耶鲁大学历史系斯特林荣誉教授乔纳森·斯宾塞认为对一个国家形象的认同及其跨文化关系的建立，实际上会受到初遇这个国家时历史状况的影响。1784年，美国开始和中国联系时，当时正是中国处于弱势地位的时期。这就与在此之前欧洲人所看到的中国情形有所不同，他们看到的是清代早期强盛的中国，而美国与中国建立联系时，中国则处于一片混乱之中。包括更多的美国人对中国的印象是美国唐人街的建立时期得来的。他们眼中的中国是一个衰弱、贫穷和四分五裂的国家，包括更早19世纪末的种族歧视和非法移民的景象。所以，那时美国人经常以消极的观点来看待中国。如今，美国对中国的认可和尊重，承认中国现已成为一个强大的贸易合作伙伴，这样的景象可能其他国家的人以前曾见到过，而美国人之前却不太有这样的经历。所以，不同的国家选择了不同的方式看待中国，是由于它们不同的历史起点所决定的。

作为本届论坛视觉艺术的传统和创新学术讨论单元的主持人亨利·亚当斯指出，事实上，美国人首先是根据日本人的观点了解中国的。众所周知，日本在很长的一段时间内把中国作为模板，所有的日本人尝试的只是模仿中国的艺术，但是日本人并没有完全理解中国艺术和中国文化，而两国之间的紧张局势成为20世纪早期非常显著的问题。中国拥有世界上最古老、最伟大并延续至今的文明，中国绘画直到最近才被真正理解。这些画突出个人化的风格并且与书法和诗歌紧密相联。中国绘画的发展方式与西方非常不同。在西方，人物画是主要的表现形式，而

中国在唐朝之后，人物画并不是主流中国艺术家所青睐的题材，而风景画成为主要的表现方式。中国的艺术家通过风景能够重新建立与世界的和谐关系。中国艺术家最精彩的方面之一就是他们愿意放弃表现现实世界而去实现表达自己内心和谐景象这个目的。

跨文化交流其实并不仅仅是一个外向性的命题，而且同时也是一个内向性的使命。中国艺术研究院中国雕塑院院长、美术研究所所长吴为山强调：在跨文化交流中雕塑对于提升国家形象，对于增强公共自豪感、归属感以及凝聚力具有非常重要的作用。雕塑作为国家形象的一个重要组成部分，已经日益受到公众的重视。国家和城市中分布的形形色色、形态各异的雕塑，诉说着这个地区的文化特征，并以无声的方式改变着环境以及人们的生活品位。吴为山还指出中美双方作为全球化的共同受益者，在应对全球性挑战上具有大量的共同利益。同时，中美在发展阶段上存在落差，经济结构、要素优势和自然资源都具有极强的互补性。这就决定了中美文化交流有着广泛的合作前景。中美文化交流应互相尊重并充分体谅对方在保障各自文化安全方面所作的努力。一是在处理文化开放与文化保护关系时，互相尊重对方的利益关切和现实选择；二是在处理文化引进与文化输出关系时，互相理解对方的文化价值体系，彼此尊重双方抉择的权力。

关于中国的国家形象，美国加利福尼亚大学英语与美国研究教授唐纳德·麦奎德多年观察到的现实是：创造力已成为了中国的一项国家使命。其最深刻的表现是北京奥林匹克运动会的开幕式，当时所展现出来的令人惊叹而优美的富有创造力的表演使多年以来外国人对中国的陈旧观念在2008年8月8日晚奥运火炬点燃的一瞬烟消云散。中国充满创造力的基础设施建设速度也非常惊人。中国创新随处可见，不仅存在于设计、时尚、媒体等商业艺术，也在咖啡馆、艺术工作室和画廊、以及剧院、人行道和街角等地方有丰富的体现。到2020年，中国的高速公路系统规模将超过美国，居于世界前列。

四、山水相映 —— 中西艺术表现的相似进程

中西文化艺术的相似与相异一直是跨文化研究领域的主要议题，此前中外学者发表过诸多的论述。在这次中美文化论坛上，哥伦比亚大学

东亚艺术系的多恩·荷·德尔班科教授强调,西方艺术是以人物画像为主,而与此相反我们看到中国的艺术则以自然为中心。从事物的表面上看,传统中西方文化中好像有着不可逾越的鸿沟。诚如凯普林·怀特所宣称,东方就是东方,西方就是西方,二者不可混为一谈。而事实上,在两个艺术传统中,我们发现了很多惊人的相似性和重叠。他通过范宽为代表的北宋山水画与法国13世纪的绘画作品《哥特式大教堂》进行对比,人们可以看到在两幅图画上有相同的层次,看到相似的表达。对于画作《哥特式大教堂》而言,人类可以获得神圣感;而在北宋绘画中,人能够离开他那个崇山峻岭的世界,处于一种与上天相互认同的关系之中。我曾经问学生:"艺术家如何展现自身无形的东西,精神的东西?你如何通过可视的媒介展现自我?"人们只能通过一种外化的方式来展现自我,审视自我。因此,从这个角度来说,14世纪中国画家倪瓒的《竹树野石图》,与17世纪的荷兰画家伦勃郎的作品其实都是一种自画像,他们有着异曲同工之妙。我们可能会说,这是有关自然的绘画,是有关人物的绘画,但是归根结底,它们的落脚点都是艺术家的自画像。所以,人们可以看到在东西方传统中有着相似的进化过程。

不仅在绘画领域中美画家有相同的艺术志趣,在文学方面作家也在相互影响。中国艺术研究院文学院院长、著名作家莫言先生就自己亲身创作经历讲述了中西艺术表现的相互影响问题,他认为:一个作家受别的作家影响的情况是非常复杂的,一个国家的文学受另一个国家的文学的影响情况更加复杂。在当今这个信息共享、交流频繁的时代,几乎可以肯定地说,没有一个作家是没受过别的作家影响的,更没有一个国家的文学是在封闭的状态下自然生成的。中国文学要走向世界,让世界了解我们首先要解决好民族的或者本土的特殊性与人性的普遍性的辩证关系。作家是人民需要的代言人,是社会良知的唤醒者。正如西方是通过我的作品来了解当代中国社会一样,我们也把其他国家的作品翻译过来了解世界,这样可以防止一个国家文学不至于变得民族主义色彩太浓,地域的特点太强,中国文学与世界其他地区的文学之间的边界必将是开放的,交流也必将是双向的。

在谈到中西文化的交融时,亨利·亚当斯指出,英语与中文是两个非常不同的语言,事实上来源于不同的语系。我们要明白我们的语言代表两种不同的社会现实。为了相互了解,我们需要超越互不熟悉的思考和语言的界限。我希望能够通过讨论考虑到这些事实。这次会议不应该是孤立的而应该是更长时间对话的开始。希望这次会议能够达到两个目的，首先是中国学者怎样把灵感推广到西方或者西方学术界，中国人也从自己的文化传统去表现现代社会，并且从西方借鉴，扩大自己的视野以满足人们的基本文化需求，确保这些文化不是西方的而是中国自己的。其次，西方人应当学习中国文化，中国的主流艺术帮助我们重新激活西方艺术、激活西方历史，来表现现在的世界。中国人能帮助我们去更深地了解中国人民以及他们的作品，以在中国快速发展到领导阶层的同时实现互利。这可能是这次会议最大的挑战，我们代表纽约的不同职业者，画家、书法家、雕塑家、建筑家、音乐家，以及其他专家表达看法。中国发展迅速，已经成为现代艺术的主要推动力。

  有时，中西文化的相互融合会奇妙地体现在一个人身上。建筑师钱以佳女士以自己美籍华人的亲身经历发表了对建筑艺术与双重文化身份的见解。她说："我并不是一个真正典型的美国人，我总是说文化上我是百分之百的美国人，心理上我是个百分之百的中国人。这意味着我不会轻易表达我的情绪。当我非常生气的时候，我就保持沉默，我越是生气我就越沉默。作为一个建筑师，我认为建筑的力量在内心，这是真正能打动人们，抚慰心灵和值得记忆的。事实是当我们提到一个好的建筑，平衡和满足它从商品到生活的要求，是着重看它基于什么而不是看它怎么表现。如今，在西方和东方，建筑是从外在被评判的，它是一个商品，一个强烈的图像，一种广告的方式。但是一个伟大的建筑师会带给我们一个平和的缓慢的旅程，在这个建筑的内部，就像在我们的内心深处一样，这个地方是一个很个人的地方，它是一种感觉，一种心灵的经历。我设计的东方古代图书馆，当你行走在其中的时候，每个人都惊奇地发现虽然身在其中，但是就像在外面一样，这个内部非常开放，你能感觉到光线穿过户外；当你从林间空地看这个建筑时，光线进入时就变得非常神秘，因为我们想要与自然生活相联系，光线自然地从所有方向落入到底层，它就像一个盒子，打开时充满阳光。我意识到我喜欢自己是两种文化的综合体。有多种方式让你站在两个不同的地方，让你不是具有很强的文化传统，你是个局外人，你是可以移动的，是自由的。我问我的儿子，他是真正的东西方文化对话的作品，我问他认为自己是中国人还是美国人，他回答说'我不是其中任何一方，我就是我'。这是个循环的问题又回到了我们开始的地方。最后,文化就是文化,伟大的作品就是那样。"

五、和而不同 —— 中美文化的沟通与互动原则

如何实现不同文化之间的相互交流也是跨文化研究的核心命题。中国艺术研究院中国文化研究所所长、研究员刘梦溪是在国学研究领域成果卓著的资深学者,他主张,一个国家的现代化进程,不可能在与世隔绝的情况下单独完成,需要有不同文化背景、不同文化系统、不同文化理念的点燃与嫁接。就像一个人不能离群索居一样,一个国家也不可能逸世独存于当代世界。而文明的融合,首先需要文化沟通。文化沟通不仅是文明人的礼仪,而且是文明人的智慧和生存方式。人与人之间是可以沟通的,不同的文化是可以沟通的,而在我看来,不同的文化之间的沟通不仅仅是人类生活的一个准则,而且是生活本身,它本身就是生活方式,这个方式就需要沟通。

跨文化研究的成果表明:"来自不同文化的人们互动时,最明显的差异,乃在于无法共享符号系统(shared symbol system),甚至还会赋予相同的符号相异的意义。这种异质性是跨文化沟通的最大障碍[1]。"所以,如何实现不同文化背景下人与人之间的相互理解与相互认同,克服跨文化交流中的理解误差,是保护和发展文化多样性的重要保证。中国艺术研究院院长助理、文化发展战略研究中心主任贾磊磊认为:在多元化的文化语境中,不同文化之间的相互接纳、相互融合有赖于各自对文化的正确理解,特别是对于那些相对陌生、相对隔膜的文化,更需要加强相互之间的交流、对话,现在不能把国家、民族之间的关系建立在一种相互猜忌、相互误读的基础上,更不能够把文化矛盾建立在一种理解的误差上,正是本着这样的精神,在文化交流中应该尽量消除理解的误差,避免文化在传播过程中产生意义的偏移,进而消除不必要的对抗与冲突。在全球化的历史语境中,如何通过有效的文化交流,来缩小和弥合人类社会

---

[1] (英)阿雷恩·鲍尔德温(ElaineBaldwin)等著,陶东风等译. 文化研究导论[M]. 高等教育出版社,2004。

在文化领域的对立与冲突至关重要。经济贸易的合作对于贸易的双方并不只是带来互惠，而且还会带来利益的对立与纷争，由于深度的经贸讨论很可能会超越单纯的经济领域而进入到文化领域，在文化交流并不充分的情况下，必然会产生贸易双方的疑虑与分歧。所以，我们不能期待仅仅通过经济的方式来加强国家之间的联系，国家之间的文化问题必须通过有效的跨文化交流方式来解决。经济贸易的交往只能够加强双方的利益合作，可是并不能"购买到"对方的文化价值观，文化的理解必须通过文化的交流才能够实现。

中美文化的相互影响应当是一个历史的事实。中国艺术研究院艺术创作中心画家、中国今日美术馆艺术总监徐累，以一位艺术家眼中的"中美文化太极图"为题目讲述了他对中美文化关系的见解。他说：从艺术研究和收藏的角度来看，美国是中国传统艺术最丰富的拥有者，无论大都会博物馆、波士顿博物馆，还是其他公益机构和私人。这一方面反映了美国的多元文化是建立在人类文明的基石上，同时也说明中国文化在美国所收获的认同具有历史的普遍性。以中国文化为代表的东方艺术启发了美国文学艺术在创造方面的部分灵感，如意象派诗歌和抽象表现主义绘画，同时，美国文化对现代中国的影响也是一个重要的事实。其实，中国文化的恒定宇宙观和美国文化的进取精神代表着不同的价值体系，在艺术上预示着不同的文明气质，同样是前行之车，一个是以后望镜作为前进的动力，另一个则是以勇往直前的自由为引领；一个是在历史的记忆中获得文化的新生，另一个则是在利用流行文化的自由精神。在全球化的今天，保持文化的独立性和特点变得越来越重要，这是人类文明生态的现实需要，同时也是伟大的历史传统与今日创新意义的一种平衡。

长期以来从事中外舞蹈艺术交流活动的中国艺术研究院舞蹈研究所副所长欧建平，参与了众多中外舞蹈艺术的互访，他说：自古以来，舞蹈艺术在各族各国文化交流中都起着不可低估的作用，这种作用直到今天的国际交往中还在继续着。中国舞蹈艺术所具有的独特性，在世界舞坛中是独树一帜的。因此，舞蹈作为一种文化现象和一种文化遗存，全体受教育者都应有权来学习它、继承它、参与它。在世界的版图上，中美两国虽然远隔重洋，但人民间的交往和友谊却在不断超越着意识形态上的差异甚至分歧，并明显地推动了世界文化的发展，极大地影响了世界和平的进程。

在中西文化交流的历史中，与陶瓷、青铜、绘画这些直观的视觉艺术相比，汉字的书写艺术，即书法艺术，在西方是最后被认识的。中国艺术研究院中国书法院常务副院长、国家一级美术师李洪胜基于自己对书法艺术的理解，提出在用线形排列的拼音文字读写的西方人眼中，结构复杂多变的方块汉字，就像一幅幅奇妙的图画，它本身的美令人赞叹，而其含义却深不可测。因此，他从艺术史论家的视角阐释中西方艺术观的差异，以及中国绘画和书法所共有的"状物形，表吾意"的功效，提出从"书画同体"的理念介入，引领西方读者踏入中国书法这一陌生的艺术之门，并步步深入，洞悉其深邃的文化内涵。价值观念是任何社会或文化中的民族性格的基石。不同的价值取向必然导致不同的思想方式、言语行为和道德规范。因此在对外文化交往中，如果不了解双方在文化价值取向方面的客观差异，而是用自己的价值观念去评价、判断对方的思想与行为，或把自己的观念直接带入交往过程之中，必然会造成对方误解而导致事与愿违。中美不尽相同的文化价值取向，决定了彼此在思维、行为等方面必然存在明显的差异，中美文化也同时存在着极为重要的相容性，这是中美两国加强沟通和文化交流的坚实基础。

六、殊途同归 —— 艺术对人类心灵的叩问

由于此次汇聚的专家学者中有一批造诣精深的艺术家与艺术理论家，所以对艺术本体的深入探讨是此次中美文化论坛的焦点之一。美国哥伦比亚大学美国研究中心主任、美国文学研究专家安德鲁·德尔班科教授说：文学是我们现在所处的现时观念之外的领域，文学的作用是在我们需要对现时生活进行观察之时为我们提供一个平台，我们可以借之移动方位。换句话说，文学与我们称之为现时的文化的结构从根本上是对立的，并对其持怀疑甚至是批判的态度。文学教育的意义则在于帮助个体批判机制获得精神的创造力和独立性。

在中国画方面颇有建树的著名画家、中国艺术研究院副院长、研究生院院长田黎明以自己亲身的创作体验讲到：中国画的意象特征作为中国文化重要载体，它以中国文化倡导的温柔敦厚为学养，体验"立天之道曰阴与阳，立地之道曰刚与柔，立人之道曰仁与义"的人文理念，逐步建构出独一无二的属于中国画的审美体系。中国画意象特征首先表现为立格，它以追寻人生境界，强调人格纯真为主体。中国画讲"外师造化，中得心源"，从生活中找到文化感知的内核，让心体贯穿着"一月印一切水，一切水映一月"的理念，月是一种最纯净的文化品格。中国文化倡导真、善、美也是对人关于自我修养完善后向一种人文精神境界统一的过程。中国画的笔墨文化正是以此来关照的。中国画的文化性，以中国传统文化的自律性贯穿于每个时代人们生活和生命的审美意识和人格情趣中；中国画的当代性，继承和发展着传统意象文化的精神，使得中国画在今天展现了它独有的人文高尚品质，这是中国人的精神财富，也是属于人类的共同精神财富。

传统与现代的相互关系一直是学术界反复争论的议题，美国伯克利艺术博物馆和太平洋电影档案馆馆长劳伦斯·林德说，传统的艺术史告诉人们在20世纪末，欧洲、美洲艺术以及亚洲、拉丁美洲艺术都经历了一种由现代主义演变出来的变更，来到一种叫做后现代主义的时代。这种转变，从实质上理解，是一种从创新回归传统的转变。后现代艺术从某种意义上来理解，是对传统，对具象艺术的一种回归，由于创新成为艺术创作的主体风格，从而对过去的历史彻底清除，使得历史在对现实的新解读面前，被完全冲刷掉。后现代主义并不是对过去以及对历史的惊天大逆转。也就是说，后现代主义并不仅仅是对早期艺术形式的一种模仿，而是人们通常认为的，它可以通过技艺驾驭一种临界尺寸，它可以凭借自己的能力在新的起点顺利自然地最终取代现代主义梦想。

对艺术本质的追问是艺术史上的经典性的命题。美国维尔国际舞蹈节总监以及爱丁堡国际艺术节的文化执行总策划达米安·怀特曼结合自己25年的芭蕾舞创作体验，指出现在的艺术到底是什么？如今的艺术代表什么？他说艺术是一系列事情：涉及娱乐，涉及启迪，这就是我们能够从艺术当中学到的东西。另外，艺术也涉及交流。这些可能是最为重要的，因为对我而言，这是生存的唯一方式。也许确切理解艺术定义以及艺术内涵是非常困难的，而我是一名舞者，我就在当时，艺术即是表演，表演就是最重要的，即是一切，就其本身而言，即代表整个世界。那就是一切的关键所在。约翰·肯尼迪总统在哈佛大学的一次毕业典礼致辞中谈到："如果更多政治家欣赏诗歌，则我们的世界会更加美好。"我确实认为这关系到在座的实践者，我们知道，在有些方面，艺术变得更具相关性。我想说的是，此次论坛会议是促进此类交流的重要对话时机，而有在坐各位参与，便变得更具意义。

七、继往开来——中美双边文化关系的展望

对中美双边关系的未来展望是每个与会者内心的一种期盼。有30多年比较文化课程教学经验的埃里森·布莱克利教授在谈到中美文化未来的关系时说："我所见的都让我相信文化比政治更有影响力，我希望本次会议中的任何报告都强调这种联系。21世纪是第一个全球在所有的主要社会中都面临着文化多样性挑战的世纪。作为一个历史学家，我仍然敬畏着中华文明的悠久历史和其形成的哲学和体制，惊讶于中国实际上在欧洲之前就拥有技术和能力来探索全世界这一发现，但他们由于各种原因却没有选择。这一情况的突出实例就是郑和的壮举——他在15世纪早期就带领成百上千条船和上万人7次远征国外，最远达到东非、南非。这比广为人知的克里斯托弗·麦哲伦航行要早一百年。之后欧洲人的航行令欧洲人确认了其未来的文化多样性，即便这不是他们所想。在我了解的关于中国历史的知识中，还让我惊讶的一个是中国也有着长期的管理文化多样性的历史，比如对穆斯林，比如19世纪中叶的太平天国运动，同一时间我们发生了全面的美国内战。此外，众所周知，美国同样发生了与文化差异有关的大量遗留问题，包括最近对移民政策的特别关注，和继续解决长期的种族和有色人种歧视这种思想的相关挑战。基于这种历史观，我提出的问题是，美国和中国是否可以互相学习有关文化多样性的东西，我希望各自的领导人，这是一个建立对文化多样性相互尊重，甚至更有建设性地接触强大的国际合作的良好基础，以此代替对文化问题的争论。"

中国人民大学国际关系学院副院长金灿荣教授是研究国际政治方面的权威学者，他指出：未来的世界将进入一个西方与非西方相对均衡、新老大国竞争与合作并存的阶段，新兴大国与西方，尤其是与美国的关系决定了国际政治的未来基调和发展取向。西方需要改变非此即彼的二元对立逻辑，放弃防范、遏制的对抗性思维，真正接纳中国作为多元全球体系中的重要一员，理性看待双方的合作空间和利益冲突，既不能因相互合作而对对方产生不切实际的心理期待，又要避免将功能性领域的争端上升到政治原则、是非善恶的高度。对中国而言，力量增长意味着责

任承担,承担起与其国力相适应的国际责任不仅是回应外部社会指责、非议的应景之举,更是中国争取国际话语权、提高政治动员能力的长远之道。中国需要在国内优先的总体战略下在国家利益与国际责任、自我发展与他者共赢之间显示更多的平衡和灵活性,以推动中国与世界的关系继续朝着和平、合作的方向发展。这不仅是维护中国国家利益的工具性考量,更涉及到中国能否为全球问题解决提供新选择的价值性思考。

如果不同文化的冲突是源于不同的利益冲突,那么它可能是不可避免的。美国政治学家何塞·欧博教授指出:"我们必须面对的事实是,中国和美国两个大国之间确实存在着不可避免的竞争,同时又在寻找相互合作途径。在权力结构中哪种权力是值得提倡的,我们如何使用这些权力。我想是我们需要努力寻找的途径,这就是文化力量——也就是软实力——而不是军事和经济制裁这种硬实力。对于拥有真正的广泛性的世界文明而言,西方唯一次真正与中国相当。我认为,软实力提供了一种思考大国之间相互关系的途径,这种关系,在某种意义上说,既有竞争性又有合作性,但它不需要以任何方式牵扯到硬实力,不需要牵涉军队,我想这种力量将不可避免地成为未来中美关系的一部分。我们在此可以呼吁的、可以畅想的是软实力关系——即本会上所提出的文化的方式,与硬实力不同,软实力关系是不需要零和博弈的。罗马人采纳希腊文化时,并不表示罗马人输了,希腊人采纳美索不达米亚和埃及文化时,不代表希腊人是失败者,同样,中国人学习柏拉图和亚里士多德,不表示中国人输了,而当我们将中国历史文化融入我们的传统时,不代表西方学者输了。当西方文化的有魅力的部分已在中国得到认可的同时,中国文化的美丽瑰宝在西方正得到更多认可。这表明实现世界上最好的、最持久的文化传统的可能性,是我对中美文化关系未来的最终期望。"

在论坛最终的综合论坛上,吉姆·利奇主席发表了致辞。他说:"今天发展中美关系需要特别关注三个方面的问题。第一,在本世纪中最重要的双边关系将是中美关系。如果其发挥建设性作用,我们可以期许的是和平和繁荣时代;如果没有,那么就会出现相反的局面。第二,全球的加速变更——现在未知晓的和未经历的情况都成了正常的事,这种变更最独特的情形是,我们的生活与科技越来越密切地联系在一起,尤其严重的是它对军备的影响。这意味着最深刻的政治学观察结果来自于爱因斯坦,他曾评论到原子分裂改变了一切,但没改变我们的思维方式。让我们冷静面对的现实是冲突是不可改变的，这可能是因为人类天性本身存在冲突的原因。所以我们要思考、要解决的问题是如何约束人类的冲突本能？乐观回应似乎是人类的性格必须改变，或我们要以一种更深刻的方式来了解人类本性，以便开发出更能纠正人类本身的技术。所以，作为这个任务的指导，历史首当其冲，尽管历史是空前的最不确定的指导；文学紧随其后，可能相比其它艺术形式而言，文学更适合让人们将自己置身于过去的想象中，并让自己想象他人的境地。第三，就中美关系而言，我想说确实需要得到关注的最乐观的相似性之一就是在哲学方面。犹太教与基督教所共有的世界大量强调权力的概念，但是存在一个与黄金法则有关的道德支承，这个法则就是'想要别人怎样对你，就要怎样对待别人'。而在儒家传统中，也有类似这条黄金法则，就是'恕'道，实际上是说'己所不欲，勿施于人'。我提到这些通用原则的原因在于文化差异可能仍然涉及到自我利益的差异，这几乎是无可争议的情况。中国人可能想要我们更加遵奉孔子学说，而我们则想要中国人更了解杰佛逊的思想，我们需要扩大对双方的尊重，这是毋庸置疑的。因此，在这个背景下，问题就是如何扩大尊重，这是召开这次论坛的最终目的。"

八、结 语

其实，自上帝用语言把人类分开之后，人类在迈向相互交流与理解的道路上从来就没有停歇过。人类甚至还发明了一种理想化的沟通工具——世界语，遗憾的是现在几乎没有人用这种理想的语言来说话。1954年成立了联合国这个世界大家庭，想使不同种族、不同国家的人可以坐在一起相互磋商各自关心的问题，维护各自的利益，但是，这个大家庭并没有彻底消除人类的种族歧视与利益争端，甚至以它的名义还不止一次地发动过侵略战争。时至今日巴比伦通天塔好像是一个建了又拆，拆了又建的工程，它的工期周而复始，它的成本不断在追加。也许，人类根本就没有回天之力来撼动上帝的巨手，但尽管如此，在构筑巴比伦通天塔的伟大进程中，我们看到中美两国在新世纪迈出了历史性的步伐。"中美文化论坛"是根据2008年中华人民共和国文化部同美国国家人文基金会签署的《关于鼓励人文学科学术性研究和文化遗产保护合作事宜的谅解备忘录》而举办的，其宗旨是为中美两国在文化领域建立一个公共性、学术性、互动性的定期对话机制,通过此机制探讨文化艺术的发展方式和文化遗产保护等问题,加深中美两国在文化艺术和人文科学领域的相互了解,促进双方在文化艺术和人文科学领域的友好合作,推进两国的文化交流得到全面、持续、深入的发展。2009年11月,中国国家主席胡锦涛与美国总统奥巴马在北京举行会谈,发表了《中美联合声明》,其中强调人文交流对促进中美关系具有重要意义,并进一步明确了建立新的双边机制,召开"第二届中美文化论坛",以期全方位推动中美两国文化领域的高端合作。2010年5月,中国国务委员刘延东和美国国务卿希拉里·克林顿在北京联合主持了"中美人文交流高层磋商机制成立仪式暨第一次会议",再次强调办好"第二届中美文化论坛",凸显了两国领导人对此论坛和两国文化领域深层交流的重视。

毕竟,此次中美文化论坛是中美双方艺术界、学术界的一次真正的高端对话。大家倾心尽力要建立的是一种真正的文化对话机制。现在,伯克利校园内的绿树也许已经变成了缤纷的落英,教师俱乐部内也许又在讨论另一个学术问题。然而,在这里举办的中美文化论坛的讨论还将继续 —— 是在2012年的中国一个充满生机的地方。

Building the New Century's Tower of Babel
Review on the Second China-U.S. Cultural Form: A Binational Conversation Bridging Cultures

Jia Leilei

Research Fellow and President Assistant of Chinese National Academy of Arts Director of Cultural Development Strategy Research Center, CNAA

Abstract: Between October 15 and 16, 2010, the Second China-U.S. Cultural Forum: A Binational Conversation Bridging Cultures was held in the University of California, Berkeley, San Francisco, USA, co-sponsored by the Ministry of Culture of the People's Republic of China and the National Endowment for the Humanities of the United States. The success of the Forum shows that China-U.S. cultural exchange enjoys a solid foundation and goes on smoothly. The Chinese and U.S. sides exchanged ideas on the ethical and historical start points of such cultural exchange and proposed the basic principles in the communication and interaction between Chinese and American cultures. The Forum represents a major step forward in promoting China-U.S. cultural exchange and identifying new areas of cultural cooperation between China and the United States.

According to the biblical account, in the beginning, humans resolved to build a Tower of Babel with its top in the heavens but God came down and confounded their language so that they could not understand one another's speech and eventually the tower collapsed. However, humans have given up neither the dream of building a Tower of Babel nor the hope of communicating with each other...

Today human achievements are seen everywhere. In the filed of architecture, towering skyscrapers have been erected just like modern Towers of Babel. They may have met people's needs for residential spaces but have failed to remove interpersonal estrangement because people become more indifferent to each other after moving into the "forest" of concrete and cement. In the field of science and technology, man-made earth satellites have been launched. It's like that humans have the "Eyes of God" through which they can capture the view of every corner on the earth. However, such inventions have amplified humans' desire to peep considerably and thus spread the danger of wars from land to sky and then

---

This article was first published in the journal *Ethnic Art Studies*.

the universe. In the field of information dissemination, humans have created the most amazing communication tool in history, i.e., the Internet, which is more convenient and effective than the beacons used by King You of Zhou, the newspapers in Napoleon's hands, the films controlled by Hitler, and the television that George W. Bush follows closely. But can people in the world truly communicate with and understand one another with all these communication technologies? Actually we are more and more aware of the fact that today we are so far away from the Tower of Babel and it's even hard for us to approach its base...

What can give us hope against the predicament? What can save us from the disaster brought by estrangement and suspicion? In the context of a new century, we need to rebuild the historical foundation for communication and find the answer in the field of cultural exchange. The Second China-U.S. Cultural Forum: A Binational Conversation Bridging Cultures, held as scheduled, serves just as such a foundation for cultural exchange, a bridge between Chinese and American cultures.

I. Different but Compatible---The Practical Channel of China-U.S. Cultural Exchange

From October 15 to 16, 2010, government officials, experts and scholars of China and the United States were brought together in the Faculty Club of the University of California, Berkeley, San Francisco, United States to talk about an issue related to the new century's Tower of Babel, i.e., A Binational Conversation Bridging Cultures: The Past, Present and Future of China-U.S. Cultural Exchange, which is also the core topic of the Second China-U.S. Cultural Forum co-sponsored by the Ministry of Culture of the People's Republic of China and the National Endowment for the Humanities.

As Chairman of the Forum on the Chinese side, Wang Wenzhang, Vice Minister of Culture of the People's Republic of China, and President of Chinese National Academy of Arts, said in his address at the opening ceremony of the Forum, "Geographically, China and the United States are oceans apart, but the peoples of our two countries have never been alienated from each other due to the long space distance. Today's China is at the new stage of reform and opening-up and starts to absorb the best of all cultures from countries around the world with a great breadth of mind and a long-term view. A wide array of American cultural products, including American films are coming into Chinese people's sight and modern American arts are increasingly known and drawn upon by Chinese people. China-U.S. cultural exchange continues to grow and is approaching a historical time. Cultural exchange allows peoples of both countries to better communicate, improves rapport, fosters understanding and builds trust, as well as plays an important role in sustaining a sound and stable bilateral relationship. There is an old Chinese saying: 'All living creatures grow together without harming one another; ways run parallel without interfering with one another', which means that all creatures in the world depend on each other for mutual development. Cultural exchange makes it possible for us to better understand and respect each other. As we learn from each other, we become more innovative."

Chairman of the Forum on the U.S. side Jim Leach is the ninth Chairman of the National Endowment for the Humanities nominated by U.S. President Barack Obama in the July of 2009 as well as Chairman of the House Subcommittee on Asian and Pacific Affairs and Congressional-Executive Commission on China. He used to work in the Woodrow Wilson School at Princeton University and the John F. Kennedy School of Government at Harvard University. In his address at the Forum, Mr. Leach said, "In the 19th century, we had a very great American poet named Walt Whitman. He once suggested that he had a great dream, and the dream was that all of the poets of the world and all of the poems of the world would come together, and that would serve as a greater group of individuals and a body of work to bring peace to the world." Prior to the Forum, he asked MO Yan if he thought greater understanding of the world would come from politicians and assertions of political doctrine or from novelists and writings about culture. MO's answer was that "It would come from those who understand culture, from the great literary works of the world", which Mr. Leach agreed to very much. As one of the moderators at the Forum, Ms. Pauline Yu, President of the American Council of Learned Societies, said, "We must insist on the importance of culture, of humanistic knowledge as a foundation for any China-U.S. cultural and economic relationship. The American Academy is in fact one of the world's great reservoirs of scholarship concerning Chinese civilization and its antiquely and contemporary expressions." She pointed out that, in fact, Daniel Coit Gilman, the first president of the University of California assuming office in 1872, had envisioned Berkeley as a true intercultural study center for Americans, people of the East, and Europeans to learn each other's languages, literature, history and sciences. Therefore, that very year, the first study center was created on campus the legacy of professorship of oriental languages and literatures, a development President Gilman praised as an early recognition of this intimate relationship that must be developed between California and the cultures and people of East Asia. The Second China-U.S. Cultural Forum was held in the University of California, Berkeley not just because of its long history of education and eminent academic profile but also to show due respect to the intercultural study center established over a century ago.

II. Thinking and Action Aligned ---Ethical and Historical Start Points of China-U.S. Cultural Exchange

Is it really possible that different nations and countries in the world understand each other? If yes, how can it be achieved? Professor Yu Dan, Associate Dean of the School of Arts and Communication, Beijing Normal University, offered her unique insights on the possibility of communication between Chinese and American cultures. According to her, in the present day world where civilizations engage in exchanges, culture exists as a dynamic notion; culture is action as well as a process. Confucianism, Taoism, and Buddhism do not provide conclusions; instead, they provide suggestions; these schools of thinking do not provide a uniform standard for conducts; instead, they provide different perspectives. So in the present day, as we engage in dialogue with the United States, three universal values can be brought forward from Chinese culture. First, the way of a gentleman (man of noble character), proposed by Confucius, provides one possible means for an individual to find his place in society and to abide by a set of disciplines. Second, Confucianism proposes the notion of "harmony despite differences". This means that the prerequisite condition for achieving harmony is respecting individual personalities and preferences. Only by firmly adhering to this principle could we have a justified civilization. Civilization is not about achieving a single set of standard and forcing it onto everyone at the expense of individualities; yet at the same time, it is necessary to strike a balance among the various individualities. This is the ideal state of a civil society under the general framework of rule by law and a modern system. Third, Confucianism proposes the notion of "benevolence" which lies at the core of one's moral principles, bringing an individual's moral belief in line with his actions. In such a way, one finds a sense of balance and transcendence. What Confucius calls "benevolence" is to help the other person establish his values the way you would help yourself and help the other person obtain prosperity the way you would help yourself. This is what benevolence is about. Benevolence is not just a concept. It should also be put into action.

In the history of China-U.S. cultural exchange, many forerunners have practiced what they advocate, making real contribution to the communication and understanding between Chinese and American peoples. American scholar Ms. Claire Conceison is one of them. She has spent her careers afar as a witness to, and interpreter of, cultural exchange between the United States and China. She said, "I encountered China and Chinese theater at a point when it was gaining strength, in the mid 1980s, when China was opening, reforming, and theater artists were experimenting domestically and begin to travel abroad. Personally, I see China's audience as having great vitality, urgency, and innovative power. Lawrence Rinder's insightful comments yesterday also brought to mind, for me, the fact that most foreigners equate Chinese culture with quote traditional, and the West with modern. But actually it's not true. The first spoken drama to the West from China ever come to the United States was not until 2005 after many decades of foreigners going to China and doing work. But it's a really new thing for us to bring Chinese plays. And I think one of the reasons is that we feel that the audience was reluctant to see a play in another language or the problem that we're always looking at Chinese traditional art, Beijing Opera, and other forms that we think are Chinese. We should be interested in how they adapt Western classics and how they write their own stories about their own experiences and we should want to see them. So I want to see more of that happening as well as people striving for mutual respect, you know, common ground and deeper understanding of each other's cultures as they enter into partnership and cultural exchanges."

Professor Christopher Merrill, Director of the International Writing Program at the University of Iowa, has participated in many China-U.S. cultural exchanges and reviewed the academic exchange held in by Yunnan Province, China. In the exchange, participants had exercises each day, read works in common, the role which the Chinese hated while the Americans loved. American and Chinese writers had fierce debates and set writing exercises for each other. As he recalled, "on the last night, having gotten to know one another very closely over the course of weeks, traveling together, seeing sights, reading books in common, arguing, trying to figure out what it means to be a writer, we thought let's try just for a final exercise. Let's think about what it is that we do as writers, and what we see at our colleagues from across the ocean, what they seem to do. Let's see if we can invite each side to write about those sorts of things that they seem to neglect, that they seem not to have any interest in. For the Americans, what we noticed in our Chinese colleagues was that there was a great emphasis on harmony. We invited our Chinese friends to try to write about something that would contain a conflict that in some fashion, try to address a conflict. What happened eventually was that every single one of the writers read the most interesting piece they had ever read."

III. Advancing with the Times---Historical Perspectives of the West on the Image of China

In cross-cultural communication, it is essential to recognize the image and culture of a country, which is also an important theme of the Second China-U. S. Cultural Forum. Mr. Jonathan Spence, Sterling Professor of History Emeritus at Yale University, believes that the recognition of a country's image and the establishment of its cross-cultural relations are actually influenced by the status quo of the country when it is first looked at. The relationship between China and the United States started in a period of Chinese weakness in 1784. That was very different from the situation when the Europeans, the first westerners who came to China, when they saw an extremely strong country in the early Qing period. American relations start with China in a period of great disarray. The image of China in many Americans was from the Chinatown. China in their eyes was a country featuring weakness, poverty and disunity. They may even saw the racial discrimination and illegal immigrants at the end of 19th century. Obviously, Americans then often looked at China from negative perspectives. Today, the United States respects China and recognizes it as a major trade partner, which may not be something new to people other countries but is to the Americans. Therefore, different countries have chosen different ways to look at China, which depends on the historical start points they choose.

As the moderator of the Forum's session on Tradition and Innovation in the Visual Arts, Henry Adams said, "The American first came to know Chinese are from Japanese perspective. As we know, the Japanese turn to China is a model in a narrow period and all Japanese are from that time were some degree of model than that of China, but the Japanese did not always fully understand Chinese art and Chinese culture and the political tensions between the two countries had often been a problem noticeably in the early 20th century. China has the oldest, grandest, most continuous civilized culture in the world, but Chinese painting has not been understood until recently. It's more personal and closely associated with calligraphy and poetry. Chinese painting developed in a way very different from the west. While in the west, figure painting became the dominant form of expression, figure painting ceased to be the charmer practice by major Chinese artists after the Tang Dynasty. And landscape became the central form of the expression. By connecting with the landscape, the Chinese scholars could re-establish the connection with the larger harmony of the universe. One of the most fascinating aspects of Chinese artists that they would rather early abandoned the representation of reality as its central goal."

Cross-cultural communication is actually not only an extroversive topic but also an introversive mission. Wu Weishan, Director of the Institute of Fine Arts and the Institute of Sculpture, Chinese National Academy of Arts, stresses that in cross-cultural communication, sculptures have an essential role to play in promoting national image and increasing the sense of pride and ownership and synergy among the public. As an important part of national image, sculptures have drawn growing attention from the pubic. The various sculptures scattered in a city or country tell about the cultural features of the region and improve people's living environment and quality of life in a way that is barely felt. Mr. Wu also pointed out that, both the beneficiaries of globalization, China and the United States have substantial common interests in addressing the challenges presented by globalization. In addition, there is a development gap between the two countries and they are highly complementary to each other in terms of economic structure, strengths in factors, and natural resources. Thus there are bright prospects of cooperation in the field of China-U.S. cultural exchange. In such exchange, the two sides should respect and fully understand each other's efforts to protect its cultural security. On the one hand, China and the United States should respect each other's concerns, interests and choices in dealing with the relationship between cultural openness and cultural protection; on the other hand, both should understand each other's cultural value system and respect each other's right to make the choice in handling the relationship between the import and export of culture.

Regarding China's national image, Donald Mcquade, Professor of English at the University of California, Berkeley, has observed that innovation and innovation have become a national mission for China. A spectacular expression of that is the Opening Ceremony of Beijing Olympic Games, the purposefully and breathtakingly elegant calligraphy of creativity displayed on that occasion sent generations of stereotyped and clichéd ideas about China and images of it up in smoke when the Olympic torch was lit the night of August 8, 2008. China builds an infrastructure of innovation and creativity in an astonishing way. Creativity is surfacing more visibly, not only in the commercial arts in design, fashion, media and the alike, but also with abundant evidence in nearby cafés, art studios and galleries, as well as in the theatres, and sidewalks and street corners. By the year 2020, China's highway system will be larger than that of the United States.

IV. Mirroring Each Other---The Similar Process of the Representation of Chinese and Western Arts

The similarities and differences between the Chinese and western cultures and arts have been a hot topic in the cross-cultural studies and numerous articles on this topic have been published by Chinese and foreign scholars. In this China-US Cultural Forum, Mr. Dawn Ho Delbanco, Professor of East Asian Art, Columbia University, emphasized that the western art focused on figure paintings. On the contrary the Chinese arts, as we perceive, centers on nature.

On the face of things, it might seem that there are unbridgeable differences between traditional Chinese and western arts. Capling Write once declared that "oh, East is East, West is West, they never between should meet." But in fact, we have found that there are surprising parallels and overlapping between the two artistic traditions. By comparing the landscape painting by Fan Kuan, a representative painter of the Northern Song Dynasty and the 13-century French painting Gothic Cathedral, we can find that the two paintings share the same layers and similar way of representation. The painting Gothic Cathedral inspires in the audience a sense of divinity while from Fan's painting, the audience can identify themselves with the heaven regardless of the world of mountains and landscape. I always asked my students, how is an artist to convey extraction, the invisible, the spiritual? How do you convey extraction through a medium that is by definition visible? You can only do it through extraction. So in that sense, the painting of rock and bamboo by Ni Zan, a Chinese painter in the 14th century, and the works of Rembrandt, a Dutch painter in the 17th century, are all amazingly a sort of self portrait of the artist himself. We might say, this painting is about nature, and that is about men. But in the end, all of the paintings are a sort of self-portrait of the artist, which shows us the evolution process shared by the eastern and western artistic traditions.

Chinese and American painters have common artistic pursuit, and likewise Chinese and American writers have influenced each other. Mr. Mo Yan, Dean of the School of Literature of Chinese National Academy of Arts and a famous writer, told us his personal stories to illustrate the mutual influence of Chinese and western art expression. He believes that other authors' influence over one author is very complicated, while other countries' literary influence over one country is even more so. In an era characterized by information sharing and constant exchanges, we are almost safe to say that, every author was or is now under the influence of other author(s), and no country develops its literature in a closed environment and on its own. If we want the world to understand Chinese literature and understand us, then first we have to balance the relationship between the uniqueness of national or local literature and the universality of human nature. Authors are the spokespersons of the common people and have the mission to awaken the social conscience. The people in the western world get to know the contemporary Chinese society by reading my books, and likewise, we get to know the world by reading the Chinese translation of foreign works, which will make the literature of a country less nationalistic or local. Chinese literature and the literature in other parts of the world will be open to each other and the communication between them will be mutually beneficial.

Speaking of the integration of Chinese and western cultures, Henry Adams pointed out that English and Chinese were two different languages and actually came from two different language systems. We have to understand that our languages represent two kinds of social realities. To understand each other, we need to transcend the boundaries of thinking and language between us. I hope that these facts will be included in our discussions. This meeting should not be a single event but a beginning of a long-term dialogue. I also hope that two purposes will be fulfilled through this meeting: first, Chinese scholars should learn to promote their inspirations to the West, specifically the western academia, and the Chinese people should represent the modern society based on their own cultural tradition, learn from the West to expand their horizon, satisfy the basic cultural needs of people and make sure that these cultures are not borrowed from the West but created by the Chinese. Secondly, the western people should study the Chinese culture. The mainstream Chinese art will help us re-invigorate the western art and the western history to represent the current world. The Chinese people will help us better understand them and their artistic works so that we will realize a win-win situation as China is rapidly climbing to the position of power. This might be the largest challenge facing the meeting. We, on behalf of different kinds of artists in New York, including painters, calligraphers, sculptors, architects, musicians and other experts, would like to state that China, which is growing rapidly, has become a major driving force for the modern art.

Sometimes, it is amazing to spot the integration of Chinese and western arts in a single human being. Ms. Billie Tsien, an architect and also an American born Chinese, shared with us her personal stories and her views on the architectural art and the double cultural identities. She said: I am not a typical American. Culturally I am 100% American, and psychologically I am 100% Chinese. This means that I keep much of my feelings inside. When I get angry, I am quiet; the angrier I am, the quieter I am. As an architect, I think that the power of architecture lies in the heart of people, which is really touching, soothing and worthy of remembering. But the fact is when we judge whether a building is good or bad, balance and meet its needs for commercial and life purposes, we value its foundation, not its way of expression. Too often today both in the west and now in the east, architecture is judged from the outside; it is a commodity, a powerful image and a way of branding. But a great architecture will take us on a quiet and slower journey. The interior of a building is like the heart of every one of us, which is very private and personal. It is all about feeling and a spiritual experience. When you walk in the C.V. Starr East Asian Library I designed, you will be surprised by the illusion that you are touring outside of it though actually you are inside of it. Standing in the open interior space, you can feel the light inside reaching to the outdoor world; if you watch it from the woods outside, you will find the sunray sneaking into the building in a mysterious way. Since we all want to be connected with the natural life, that light naturally move all the way down to lower level so that as we said we describe it as a solid boxes, as it is a kind of open with lights. I realized that I like to be a mix of two cultures. In many ways having your feet in two places is a creative place to stand. You are not bounded by the tradition of strong cultural identity, you are an outsider, you can be a ship shifter and you are free. I asked my son, who is truly the product of East-West dialogue, whether he considers himself Chinese or American, and he answered "I am not one or the other, I am just who I am". So in many ways, this is cycle back to where we began, where we started. In the end, culture just is, great work just is.

V. Harmony in Diversity---The Principle for China-US Cultural Communication and Interaction

How to realize the communication between different cultures is also a core subject in the cross-cultural studies. Liu Mengxi, Director and Research Fellow of the Institute of Chinese Culture of Chinese National Academy of Arts, is a senior and accomplished scholar in the field of sinology. He holds that for any nation, the process of modernization cannot be completed in vacuum, cut off from the rest of the world. Modernization is a process that requires different cultural backgrounds, cultural systems and cultural notions to come into contact, and to learn and borrow from each other. A man cannot live in complete seclusion; likewise, a nation cannot exist isolated from the modern world. Cultural communication is the precondition of integration of civilization; it is not only etiquette of civilized people, but also their wisdom and way to live. People can communicate with each other, so do cultures. As far as I am concerned, the communication between different cultures is not only a principle for human life, but is the life itself. It is the way life is, for which communication is essential.

The cross-cultural studies show that, "When people of different cultures interact with each other, the most obvious difference between them lies in that they cannot share the symbol system, and even interpret the same symbol quite differently. Such kind of difference is the largest obstacle for cross-cultural communication."[1] Therefore, realizing mutual understanding and acknowledgement of people from different cultural backgrounds and overcoming the misunderstanding in cross-cultural communication serve as an important guarantee for the protection and development of cultural diversity. According to Jia Leilei, President Assistant of the Chinese National Academy of Arts and Director of the Cultural Development Strategy Research Center, in a multicultural context, mutual acceptance and integration of various cultures are based upon the true understanding of different cultures, especially the strange and less-understood ones, and even in opposition to one's own. Now the relationship between two countries or ethnic groups cannot be based on mutual suspicion or misunderstanding, which will lead to cultural conflicts. In line with this principle, more efforts shall be put in cultural exchange to clear up misinterpretation, prevent cultural bias during communication, and eliminate unnecessary confrontations and conflicts. Against the background of globalization at present, it is urgent and crucial to cushion conflicts and confrontations between different cultures by means of effective cross-cultural hexchange. Together with the mutual benefits in economic and trade cooperation, there will be conflicts and disputes of interest. In-depth economic and trade negotiations are very likely to go beyond the simply economic issues into the cultural field. If there lacks full cultural communication, there must be doubts and disputes between the two parties involved. Therefore, we cannot simply rely on economic means to strengthen the contacts and ties between countries; instead, an effective way of cross-cultural exchange is a more important channel to solve conflicts between different cultures. Contacts through economic activities and trades can only strengthen the mutual cooperation for benefits, but may not necessarily "purchase" each other's cultural values. Cultural

---

[1] Baldwin, Elaine. *Introduction to Cultural Studies* [M]. Trans. Tao Dongfeng. Higher Education Press. 2004.

understanding cannot be realized without cultural communication.

It is a historical fact that Chinese and American cultures have influenced each other. Xu Lei, Research Fellow of Research Center for Creation of the Chinese National Academy of Arts and Art Director of Today Art Museum, told us his opinions on the relationship between Chinese and American cultures from an artist's perspective with the speech entitled "The Taiji Diagram of Chinese and American Cultures." According to him, in terms of art research and collection, the United States --- specifically the Metropolitan Museum of Art, the Boston Museum and other non-profit organizations and private collectors --- owns the richest resources of traditional Chinese arts. On the one hand, it shows that the diverse culture of the United States is based on human civilization, and on the other, it indicates that the Chinese culture has long been accepted and recognized by the American society. The oriental art represented by Chinese culture was one of the sources for the artistic and literary creation of the United States, such as imagist poetry and paintings of abstract expressionism. At the same time, the American culture's influence on modern Chinese culture is a historical fact that cannot be ignored. In fact, the Chinese culture's perception of the universe as stable and permanent and the entrepreneurship of the American culture represent two kinds of value systems and will be represented by different artistic qualities. If we compare the two cultures to a speeding car, then the car of Chinese culture is driven by the rear-view mirror while the car of American culture by fearless freedom; the Chinese culture is drawing new energy from the tradition while the American culture absorbs new energy from the freedom of pop culture. In the context of globalization, maintaining the cultural independence and characteristics has become more and more important, which is the need of the human civilization and also a balance between the historical tradition and today's innovation.

Ou Jianping, Deputy Director of Dance Research Institute, Chinese National Academy of Arts, has long been engaged in the dance exchanges with foreign countries and participated in numerous visits of dance troupes. According to him, since the ancient times, dance has played and is still playing a role that cannot be underestimated in the cultural exchanges between countries and peoples. The Chinese art of dancing is unique among all the dance cultures in the world. Therefore, as a cultural phenomenon and heritage, dance should be learnt, passed down and participated in by all the educated people. As everyone could tell from a world map, China is separated from the United States of America by oceans. However, it's also universally acknowledged that the mutual contacts and friendship between these two great peoples have constantly surpassed the ideological differences and even disputes all these 100 years, thus obviously pushing forward the development of the world culture and greatly affecting the process of the world peace.

In the history of cultural exchanges between China and the western world, calligraphy, the art of writing with brushes, was the last to be introduced into the western world. It was preceded by direct visual arts such as ceramics, bronze and paintings. Li Shenghong, Deputy Dean of School of Chinese Calligraphy of the Chinese National Academy of Arts, based on his understanding of calligraphy, pointed out that in the eyes of western people who are used to alphabetic writing, the pictographs of changing and complicated structures seem like an amazing picture. The beauty of its appearance is astonishing and its connotations are profound. Based on that, Mr. Li, from the perspective of an art historian, illustrated the differences between the Chinese and western views on art, the function of Chinese painting and calligraphy to express the author's opinions and feelings by representing the appearance of objects, and suggested that we should, based on the similarities between calligraphy and painting, lead western audience into the door of less-understood calligraphy, and teach them step by step to appreciate the profound cultural implications of calligraphy. Values are the foundation of the national character of any society or culture. Different values will, with no doubt, lead to different ways of thinking, words and behaviors, and ethnic codes. Therefore, in foreign cultural exchanges, if we don't understand the objective differences between the cultural values of each other, but use our own values to judge the other's thought and behaviors, or impose our values upon the exchange process, misunderstanding will inevitably arise and it is the last thing we want. China and the United States have different cultural values, and consequently there are obvious differences between the thinking and behaviors of the two peoples. But the Chinese culture and the American culture are also both inclusive, which lays a solid foundation for the two countries to strengthen communication and cultural exchanges.

VI. Achieving the Same Goal through Different Means---Artistic Inquiries into the Human Mind

This forum has attracted a group of highly accomplished artists and art theorists, and their in-depth discussion about art itself has become one of the highlights of the forum. Andrew Delbanco, Director of American Studies of the Columbia University, said: literature is a point outside of our hodiernal circle, and the use of literature is to afford us a platform once we make command a view of our present life, approaches by which we may move it. In other words, literature in this view is fundamentally in opposition, skeptical, and even hostile to the constructions that we call culture of the present moment. The function of literary education then is to assist in the development of an individual critical faculty independence of mind and creativity to use the charge of our present session.

Tian Liming, Vice President of Chinese National Academy of Arts, Dean of the Graduate School of Chinese National Academy of Arts and a master artist in traditional Chinese paintings, shared with us his experience in artistic creation: The symbolism in Chinese painting is a major vessel for the essence of Chinese culture. With the gentleness and kindness advocated by Chinese culture as the fundamental academic and moral attitude, Chinese painting gradually formulated its unique aesthetic system by practicing the humanistic idea that "Yin and Yang are the two basic elements that breed the heaven and the earth; the way to establish the earth consists of hardness and softness, while the way to establish human consists of humanity and justice." The most important characteristic of the images in Chinese paintings is establishing the personality, which mainly refers to pursuing the true meaning of life and emphasizing the pureness of personality. It is the traditional Chinese way of painting that "outer factors create the universe, while the inner factors create the heart". The former originates from daily life, while the latter derives from cultural experience. According to my understanding, the core of deriving cultural experience from life is to follow through on the idea that "the moon casts shadow on all the waters, and all the waters reflect the moon". The moon is the purest cultural representation. Truth, goodness, and beauty promoted by Chinese culture are also about self-perfection and these pursuits are united in the process towards the humanistic ideal. These are the basis of introspection in Chinese painting culture. The essence of culture is embodied in Chinese paintings. This self-discipline of traditional culture is followed through when Chinese people live and conduct aesthetic activities. The modernity of Chinese paintings inherits and develops the spirit of symbolism in traditional Chinese culture, on the basis of which modern Chinese paintings develop their own noble humanistic quality that is the spiritual wealth of Chinese people and all humanity as well.

The relationship between the traditional and the modern has been a controversial topic for the academia. According to Lawrence Rinder, Director of the Berkeley Art Museum and Pacific Film Archive, the traditional art history reveals that at the end of the 20th century, European, American, Asian and Latin American arts all went through a transformation from modernism to post-modernism. The characteristics of post-modernism are demonstrated in the art works created by American artist David Sallid in 2002. Such transformation is essentially a shift from innovation to tradition. Post-modernist art, in a sense, is a return to the traditional and representational art. But since innovation dominates the artistic creation, the past (both texts and images) is completely erased, so is the history in front of the new reality. But what is called the post-modernism did not involve a wholesale reversion to the past, nor to tradition in their original state; that is to say, it did not generally involve the expression that merely simulated the earlier artistic forms. Instead, as it is commonly held, post-modernist artists are so skilled that they are able to manage the critical dimension and at its own capacity to finally and coherently displace the modernism dream at the new beginning.

The quest for the essence of art has been a classical subject in the art history. Damiann Woetzel, Director of the Vail International Dance Festival, USA, and Executive Cultural Planner of the Edinburgh International Festival, shared with us his 25-year experience in ballet choreography and pointed out what art is now and what it represents. He said that: art is about a series of things, about entertainment and enlightenment, and that is why we could learn from art. Art is also about communication, which is probably the most important. For me, it is the only way of life. It is hard to understand exactly what it was and that is exactly what it is. I am a dancer, and I am in that moment. It is a performance. And doing the performance is the paramount, that is everything and in its own way, the world. As far as performance is concerned, it represents the whole world, and is the key to everything. Now that I don't dance, it's much more about what art can be, what art might be, what art will be, how can we, what will make it interesting and important in our day. John Kennedy, in a Harvard commencement, said, "If more politicians knew poetry, we would have a better world." I do think that it is related to all the artistic practitioners present. We all know that art had become more relevant in some aspects. What I want to say is that I think this is an incredible valuable occasion to enable these exchanges, but they become far more valuable at the level at which you participate.

VII. Carrying Forward the Tradition and Looking into the Future: Outlook for China-US Cultural Relations

All participants want to look into the future of China-US cultural relations. Allison Blakely, a professor with more than 30 years of experience in teaching comparative cultures, made the following points regarding the future of China-US cultural relations: Everything that I've seen has convinced me further and further that culture is more powerful than politics and I hope any report that comes as a result of these proceedings will emphasize that connection. The 21st century is the first in which the entire world was challenged with new levels of cultural diversity within all the major societies. As a historian, I've remained in awe of the long duration of the Chinese civilization, the philosophies and institutions it has shaped, and also over the discovery that China actually had the technology and capacity to explore the whole world prior to the Europeans and for various reasons chose not to. The most spectacular example of this were the exploits of the Admiral Zheng He who lead seven expeditions abroad in the early 15th century reaching as far as today's East Africa and South Asia with fleets numbering hundreds of ships and combined crews of tens of thousands. All this is a century before the more widely known voyages of Christopher Columbus One result of the later European voyages is that Europeans ensured a greater cultural diversity for their future though not intended. Among other surprises for me as I acquired a rudimentary knowledge of Chinese history is that China too nevertheless has a long history of managing cultural diversity, such as their Muslim policies and the Taiping Heavenly Kingdom Movement in the mid 19th century. Around the same period, the Civil War broke out in the United States. Besides, as we all know, the American government still has to deal with a lot of issues related to cultural diversity, including the special attention to immigration policies recently, and relevant challenges to eradicate the discrimination against colored people. Based on this type of history perspective, the question that I have for us is: are there not lessons that the United States and China can learn from each other concerning cultural diversity. I hope we can persuade our respective leaders that this is a good foundation upon which to build mutual respect for cultural diversity and even more constructive engagement for strong international collaboration in place of contention over cultural issues.

Jin Canrong, Associate Dean of the School of International Studies of Renmin University of China and an authority in the research of international politics, pointed out that: in the future the world will enter into a stage which demonstrates a relative balance between Western and non-Western powers, and the coexistence of cooperation and competition between traditional and emerging powers. The relationship between emerging powers and the West, in particular the United States, will determine the future keynote and development orientation of international politics. The West should change the logic of binary opposition, and accept China as an important player in a diversified global system. They ought to take a rational view of the room for collaboration and conflicts of interest between the two sides by avoiding unrealistic expectations of China in cooperation, and separating disputes in functional areas from political principles and the dichotomy of good and evil. As for China, the growth in strength means more responsibilities. Rather than standing aloof to world affairs, China needs to actively shoulder international responsibilities in accordance to its national strength rather than regarding it as a passive way to respond to external criticism, for the action is actually a sustainable way to gain international discourse power and to improve China's ability of political mobilization. With internal affairs high on the agenda, it is of great necessity for China to strike a flexible balance between its national interests and international responsibilities, and between self-development and a win-win development strategy with other countries, and in turn push the relations between China and the outside world towards peace, cooperation and development. This is not only to safeguard the national interests of China, but also determines whether China can provide new solutions to global problems.

If the conflicts between different cultures are about interests, then they might be inevitable. Josiah Ober, Professor of Political Science in the United States pointed out that: A fact we must face is that China and the United States inevitably compete with each other, but seek for cooperation opportunities at the same time. In the power structure, which power deserves to be advocated and how should we use such power? I think we should try to answer these questions. The answer is the power of culture, also known as the soft power, not the hard power of military and economic sanction. For the world civilization which is truly universal, the West, for once, is considered truly equal to China. So soft power I think, gives us a way to think about the relationship between great powers that is indeed in some sense competitive as well as cooperative, but it need not in any way involve the hard power, need not involve force. I think that power will inevitably be part of the US-Chinese relations in the future. But I think that what we in this room can call for and hope for is soft power relationship. Unlike hard power, the soft power relations need not be zero-sum. The Romans were not the losers when they adopted Greek culture, the Greeks were not the losers when they adopted the culture of Mesopotamia and Egypt, and likewise Chinese people are not the losers when they learn something from Plato and Aristotle, western scholars are not losers when we incorporate Chinese history and culture into our traditions. The attractive, the beautiful things of Chinese culture are more recognized in the West just as the beautiful things of the Western culture have been recognized in China. It shows the possibility for the best and most enduring cultural tradition in the world, which is my ultimate hope for the future of Chinese-American cultural relations.

In the last session, Jim Leach, Chairman of US National Endowment for the Humanities, delivered a speech. He said: in developing the China-US relations, we need to pay special attention to the following three aspects. First, the most important bilateral relationship in this century will be the United States and Chinese relationship. If it's constructive, we're looking at the potential era of potential peace and prosperity. If not, the reverse could well be the case. Secondly, the accelerating global changes --- now the unknown and the inexperienced is the norm. The most special thing about such changes is that our life has been more and more closely connected with science and technology, in particular, the influence of science and technology upon armament. And that means that in many ways the most profound political science observation comes from Einstein who once commented that splitting the atom had changed everything except our way of thinking. And what's sobering about this is that conflict can be noted as a constant and presumably because human nature is a conflict. And so the question that has to be addressed is how the instinct for conflict can be contained. And it would appear that the only optimistic response would be that human nature has to change or we'd have to understand human nature in a much deeper way in order to develop techniques to better direct human beings themselves. So what are the guides to this task? History is one although it is the unprecedented less sure guide. Literature is another guide and probably literature is better suited to having people place themselves in the imagining of the past and to put themselves into people's shoes than almost any other art form. And thirdly, I just want to say in the context of US and Chinese relations, one of the most optimistic similarities truly demands attention, and that is philosophy. In the Judeo-Christian world there is a great deal of emphasis on the concept of rights but there is a moral underpinning which relates to the golden rule that we should do unto others and as we want others to do unto us. In the Confucian tradition, there is a similar but less obtrusive framing of this golden rule, that is the doctrine of 'Shu' (Forgiveness) which in effect says that one should not do unto others what one would not want others to do unto themselves. And I mention these universal principles because while differences in cultures are still likely to remain, involving differences in self interest is almost certainly to be the case. And while the Chinese might like us to be more Confucian and we might like the Chinese to be more Jeffersonian, there is no reason what-so-ever that there cannot be an expansion of mutual respect. And so it is in the context of the question of how you advance respect that this forum has been convened.

VIII. Conclusions

In fact, since God uses the language as the tool to divide human beings into different groups, they have never ceased to seek for communication and mutual understanding. They even created an idealized communication tool --- Esperanto, which unfortunately is barely used for communication nowadays. In 1954, the United Nations was founded, with the purpose of bringing people of different races and from different countries together, to discuss their own concerns and protect their interests. But the big family of nations hasn't completely erased the racial discrimination and disputes over interests in the human society. And even more than one war have been waged in its name. The construction of the Tower of Babel seems to be an endless process with an ever-increasing cost. Perhaps the human beings have no power at all to change their destiny. But in the great process of constructing the Tower of Babel, we can see that China and the US have made historical progress in the new century.

The China-US Cultural Forum was initiated according to the Memorandum of Understanding signed by the Ministry of Culture of People's Republic of China and the US National Endowment for the Humanities in 2008 to promote academic exchange and cooperation in the humanities and the protection of cultural heritage. Its mission is to establish a public, academic and interactive mechanism for regular dialogues for China and the United States in the cultural field. And through this mechanism, the two countries will discuss issues such as the development mode of culture and art and the protection of cultural heritages, deepen mutual understanding in the cultural field, art, humanities and science, and promote their cooperation in the abovementioned fields and the comprehensive, sustainable and in-depth development of cultural exchanges of the two countries. In November 2009, Chinese President Hu Jintao and the US President Obama held talks in Beijing and announced the China-US Joint Statement, which emphasized the significant role of humanistic exchanges in the China-US relations. They also made it clear for the need of a new bilateral mechanism and the opening of the 2nd China-US Cultural Forum, so as to promote the high-level cooperation of the two countries in the field of culture in an all-around way. In May 2010, Liu Yandong, State Councilor of the People's Republic of China, and the US Secretary of State Hillary Clinton jointly presided over a ceremony marking the Establishment of the China-United States High Level Humanities and Arts Consultative Institution and its First Conference, and stressed again the importance to hold the 2nd China-US Cultural Forum. It shows that the leaders of the two countries attach great importance to this forum and the in-depth cultural communication between the two countries.

After all, this forum provides an opportunity for the artists and the academia from China and the US to hold truly high-end dialogues. What we are trying to do is to establish a true mechanism for cultural dialogue. Now the leaves on the Berkeley campus might have turned yellow and the faculty might be discussing another topic. But today's China-US Cultural Forum will be continued, in a lively place in China in 2012.

建构中美文化交流的世纪桥梁
——"跨文化双边对话：第二届中美文化论坛"述评

潘源
中国艺术研究院文化
发展战略研究中心
副研究员

2010年10月15日至16日，由中华人民共和国文化部和"美国国家人文基金会"共同主办、"美国国家人文基金会"和中国艺术研究院共同承办的"跨文化双边对话：第二届中美文化论坛"在"美国总统艺术人文委员会"和加利福尼亚大学伯克利分校"中国研究中心"的大力支持下，于美国加利福尼亚大学伯克利分校隆重举行。

"中美文化论坛"缘起于2008年8月中华人民共和国文化部与美国国家人文基金会共同签署的《谅解备忘录》，该备忘录鼓励两国在人文与文化遗产保护方面进行学术合作。据此，同年12月，中华人民共和国文化部和美国国家人文基金会共同主办、中国艺术研究院承办的"第一届中美文化论坛：数字化时代文化遗产的保护和展现"在中国北京召开，并取得了巨大成功。2009年11月，中国国家主席胡锦涛与美国总统奥巴马在北京举行会谈，发表了《中美联合声明》，其中强调人文交流对促进更加紧密的中美关系具有重要意义，并提出建立新的双边机制，召开"第二届中美文化论坛"，以期全方位推动中美两国文化领域的高端合作与交流。在此背景下，"第二届中美文化论坛"如期在大洋彼岸的美国加利福尼亚大学伯克利分校隆重召开，该校从19世纪以来一直是中美文化交流的中心，且是最早设立"中国研究中心"的美国高校，可谓中美文化交流的策源地之一。

中华人民共和国文化部副部长、中国艺术研究院院长王文章和

本文转载自《艺术评论》2010年第12期。

美国国家人文基金会主席吉姆·利奇莅临论坛并致辞。

王文章副部长在致辞中回顾了中美文化交流的历史,积极肯定了中美文化交流在两国关系健康、稳定的发展中起到的重要作用。他指出"召开第二届中美文化论坛具有独特的时代意义,标志着中美两国文化交流和合作正在不断深化,此次论坛以'跨文化双边对话'为主题,旨在从文化艺术的各个领域,全面回顾中美交流的历史,探讨两国文化交流的现实路径,展望中美文化关系发展的未来,通过多途径文化交流,增进中美两国在社会文化和科学技术领域中的交流与合作,从而推动文化的多样化协调发展,开辟中美文化交流与合作的新境界。"

吉姆·利奇主席在致辞中指出,"在本世纪,甚至可以说是这一千年中,最重要的双边关系将是中美关系。如果其发挥建设性作用,我们可以期许到和平和繁荣的时代。如果没有,就会出现相反的局面。"他强调中美文化联系是最重要的中美事务,文化比政治更为重要,政府只是文化的一部分,而要解决文化差异,就要扩大双方之间的尊重。如果两国及其各自的人民不能互相尊重,那么无论两国政府当下的政策如何,都不能保持持续的关系。因此,在这个背景下,问题就是如何扩大尊重,而这便是此次论坛的最终目的。

此次论坛采取圆桌会议形式,在"跨文化双边对话"主题下分为"中美文化关系的历史回顾"、"文学遗产与创造性"、"视觉艺术的传统与创新"、"表演艺术比较观"以及"中美文化关系的未来展望"五个专题展开,来自两国文学艺术各个领域近30位杰出艺术家和学者从自己的专业领域和视角出发作了主旨发言,近二百位来自不同国家和文化背景的文化艺术界人士参加了论坛,并积极参与讨论。

与第一届中美文化论坛重点探讨代表现代科技水平的数字技术在文化遗产保护和当代艺术创新中的作用不同,此次论坛突出了文学、艺术等人文元素在跨文化交流中的重要作用。文化的面貌通过艺术的发展呈现,而艺术是文化精神的凝聚,文化、艺术相依共生的关系在此次论坛中得到了充分体现。

消除文化隔阂与理解误差:沟通文化价值观

中美两国之所以积极推动文化对话,是因为双方分属东、西两大文明范畴，有着不同的文化脉络和根基。而异质文化面临着沟通危机。正如美国波士顿大学埃里森·布莱克利教授指出的那样，"21世纪是第一个全球所有主要社会中都面临新水平的文化多样性挑战的世纪。"

而消除跨文化交流中的理解误差、弥合不同文明之间的鸿沟，则需要寻找有效的交流途径。对此，中国艺术研究院中国文化研究所所长、著名学者刘梦溪研究员指出，"世界是多元的、文化是多元的、现代文明模式的建构是多元的。各个国家的经济模式和文明类型却不必也不可能完全整齐划一，但文化精神的理性之光是永恒的。文化交流的实质，应该是理念的交流和普适价值的交流。"中国艺术研究院院长助理、文化发展战略研究中心主任、影视评论家贾磊磊研究员强调通过有效的文化交流方式缩小和弥合人类社会在文化领域的对立与冲突的紧迫性和重要性。他指出，"不同文化之间的交流和对话是相互理解与相互认同的前提。但是，在相互交流的过程中，由于交流媒介、交流方式、交流背景的不同，有时可能产生与交流的初衷未必一致的效果。在多元化的文化语境中，不同文化之间的相互接纳、相互融合有赖于各自对文化的正确理解，特别是对于那些相对陌生、相对隔膜的文化，更需要加强相互之间的交流、对话，本着一种客观、平等、公正的态度坦诚相待。"北京师范大学艺术与传媒学院副院长、知名学者于丹教授亦谈到："所有文化的语言是国际的，但文化的语法是民族的，我们只不过以本民族的语法去诠释世界文明的语言。中国的儒家、道家、佛家提供的是一种思考方式，与世界交流的则是这些文化思想中呈现出来的普适价值。"美国学术团体联合会主席余宝琳教授也表述了类似看法。她说，"我们需要中国学者们多样化的视角和见解，以进行真正意义上的成功合作。我们终究是在各种文化之间建立桥梁，目的不是消除不同的价值观，而是欣赏、理解和解释这些价值观。"

可见，消除文化隔阂的有效途径是以具有普适性的价值观和人类共通的情感来弥合差异，而文学艺术作品正是承载这些价值观和情感的重要介质。

美国南卡罗来纳大学哥伦比亚分校的萨拉·辛纳克劳斯教授在抒发自己对绘画的观感时指出，"绘画是表达我们周围世界以及我们内心世界的一种方法，是内部、外部以及其他事物之间的联合体，是文化的枢纽。"中国艺术研究院雕塑院院长、著名雕塑家吴为山研究员亦以自己的雕塑作品《睡童》、《老子》、《孔子》和《侵华日军南京大屠杀遇难同胞纪念馆主题雕塑》为例，说明文化交流"最重要的是要了解彼此的情感和彼此的文化价值观"，即从"同化自然"的稚童、到"上善若水"的先哲、再到苦难中的芸芸众生，都拥有普遍共通的情感，而这便是文化交流的基础。

中美创作理念的异同：在碰撞中求同一

文学、艺术不但是承载价值观与情感的介质，其本身呈现的技法和理念亦是中美文学、艺术家沟通与交流的热点。两国文学、艺术家藉此良好的交流机会，一方面探寻对方文化中同领域的创作手法和心法，一方面诚恳介绍本国的艺术精髓；同时，他们也有意识地将两国的同类艺术加以比照，分析不同文化背景下，各尽其妙的艺术创造中是否存在呼应之处，从而在艺术创作的实践领域寻找文化的同一性。

基于这一目的，中国艺术研究院副院长、研究生院院长、著名画家田黎明研究员介绍了最能体现中国画独特审美理念的意象文化美学，指出该美学思想以"澄怀观照、寓物取象、心与象合"的人文体验、以及注重"人格立足、以德观物、立象尽意"的表达方式，传颂了中国画的特色和中国文化的本源，并通过文例从"立格"、"品物"、"返照"、"形神"、"心象"五个层面简述中国画所蕴涵的人文品质和精深的中国文化内涵。

中国艺术研究院中国书法院副院长、著名书法家李胜洪研究员也对中国的传统艺术——书法和刻字——做了必要阐述，因为它们已成为中国文化的代表性符号。而两者结合而成的中国"书刻"则以其构成之美、力度之美、色彩之美和肌理之美，成为中国传统艺术语言的崭新表达。中国艺术研究院戏曲研究所所长刘祯研究员认为，"文化时代"是人类社会发展的更高形态。通过梳理中国戏曲的发展，他阐述了传统文化艺术是文化时代的基础和本质的观念。

美国伯克利艺术博物馆和太平洋电影档案馆馆长劳伦斯·林德介绍了西方的艺术流变，说明了现代艺术向后现代艺术的转换，并阐释了后现代艺术与传统艺术的关系，即创新与回归之间的辩证联系。

对于中国的文学与艺术，美国克利夫兰市凯斯西储大学亨利·亚当斯教授也谈及自己的理解。他认为，"由于中国绘画与书法和诗歌、以及与学者的紧密联系，其发展方式与西方绘画非常不同。在西方，人物画是主要的表现形式，而中国在唐朝之后人物画便不再是主流艺术家青睐的实践，风景画成为主要的表现方式。通过联系风景，中国学者能够重新建立与世界的和谐关系。中国艺术家最精彩的方面之一，就是愿意放弃表现现实世界而去达到这个目的。"

美国哥伦比亚大学副教授恩·荷·德尔班科通过实例，将中、西绘画中的具体作品加以比较，认为虽然表面上看，中西方文化好像有着不可逾越的鸿沟，但两个艺术传统中却有很多惊人的相似与重叠之处。她举出欧洲与中国传统绘画的诸多实例，如在11世纪郭熙的作品中发现了与希腊雕像相类似的"平衡力"原则，而这种"平衡力"又与中国的"阴"、"阳"概念相仿；此外，她还将倪瓒、王崇明和石涛等画家与欧洲其他一些著名画家的画作进行比对，所显示的相似性将东西方文化结合起来，从而很好地诠释了"文化构筑桥梁"这一课题，也证明20世纪西方现代主义艺术家们所持的正是中国艺术家业已践行几个世纪的艺术理念。

美国著名建筑师钱以佳更是从自身的文化背景出发，进一步阐释了这种"桥梁关系"。作为美籍华人，中国式的内敛风格也体现在她的建筑上，"我认为建筑的大部分力量在内部，这是真正能打动人们、抚慰心灵和值得记忆的。"所以，中西结合的文化背景不但塑造了她独特的个人气质，也构成了她重内在的建筑风格。

美国总统艺术人文委员会执行主任瑞秋·格斯林斯是一位著名的纪录片导演和制作人，她亦谈到，"这两天我们讨论过的所有艺术学科中，在绘画、雕塑、诗歌、戏剧方面，中国领先美国至少四个世纪。但电影是在中、美两国近乎同时诞生的唯一艺术门类。因此，我认为对这方面的必要分析非常有趣，可以了解到两国怎样采用相同的媒介、却以不同或相似的方式塑造其文化。"

中美文化的相互影响与借鉴：采彼之长以厚己

中美两国在文化艺术领域的交流与合作由来已久，且深深影响了两国艺术家的创作，并烙印在各自文学艺术作品中。在此次论坛上，两国艺术家分析彼此之间的文化渊源，认为跨文化影响能够衍生新的创作灵感，给双方文学、艺术注入创作活力，从而为自身文化吸纳优秀的异质文化基因创造条件。

中国艺术研究院舞蹈研究所副所长欧建平研究员认为，中美近百年舞蹈交流的丰硕成果在两国人民间的交往和友谊中，扮演了重要的大使角色。

中国艺术研究院创作研究中心艺术家徐累研究员通过其个人的观察和实践，指出美国是世界上收藏中国传统艺术资源最丰富的国家，其对中国传统文化的研究和推广也颇有成就。以中国文化为代表的东方艺术启发了美国文学艺术的部分创作灵感，如意象派诗歌和抽象表现主义绘画；同时，美国文化对现代中国的影响也是一个重要的事实，尤其从20世纪80年代开始，中国艺术上的观念性变革许多得益于美国现代主义的启发。

中国艺术研究院艺术创作研究中心著名作家莫言研究员谈到，包括自己在内的一批作家深受美国文学的影响，并期望"假以时日，中国作家的作品也会对外国的、包括对美国的年轻作家产生影响"。与之相呼应，美国爱荷华大学国际写作项目主任克里斯多弗·梅里尔教授也谈到自己受到中国作家的影响，并指出唐诗几乎影响了所有的当代美国诗歌。他进而介绍了中美两国"发现之旅"文学交流项目，总结了其中的收获，并希望中美两国做出更多的类似交流。

美国耶鲁大学高级讲师金安平以《诗经》对孔子的影响为例，认为这样的"早期文本"倘若呈现给西方读者，他们一定也能得出同样的感悟，并就此谈到中国古典文学的翻译及流通问题，希望能够以一种有趣而吸引人的方式将这些知识结合起来，呈现给西方读者，通过"能够真正触及更多西方读者的文本"，使其获得"更深的文学影响以及更丰富的历史接触"。

中美双边关系的未来展望：以文化促进认同

关于中美文化关系的未来展望，中国人民大学国际关系学院副院长金灿荣教授认为，应将之放在中美关系的框架中考虑。而对中美关系的未来预测，很大程度上要看政治、经济、军事与社会文化四个关系的发展。这四个关系都具有两面性，前两者的竞争面大于合作面，而后两者的合作面更大。所以，"文化是中美关系中的一个稳定因素。我们应有效利用两国文化中的共同性，发掘文化深层的相似性，促进中美关系的发展"。

美国斯坦福大学何塞·欧博教授从"软实力"角度对中美文化关系寄予厚望。他认为，在中美关系中，应提倡基于文化、艺术、文学、语言、国家机制等体现出来的软实力。他强调，"中国人学习柏拉图和亚里士多德时，不表示中国人输了，而当我们将中华语言和儒家研究以及中国历史融入我们的传统时，不代表西方学者输了。当西方文化有魅力的部分在中国得到认可时，便拥有了软实力；而中国文化的美丽瑰宝在西方也正得到更多认可。这种创造性竞争，是我对中美文化关系未来的最终期望。"

诚如瑞秋·格斯林斯所言，中美艺术家正是以相同的介质，却以迥然相异、或是异中有同的方式塑造着各自的文化。当两国文学、艺术家将自己的创造成果展示出来时，他们交流的是内心的感悟和创新的愉悦。当他们在切磋技艺时热情相和、在智慧碰撞中惺惺相惜时，文化的隔膜和界限已经悄然消失。美国著名舞蹈家达米安·沃策尔谈到，对他而言，艺术涉及娱乐和启迪，更涉及交流，因为这是其生存和繁荣兴旺的唯一方式。而"此次论坛是促进此类交流的重要对话时机，有在座各位参与，使它变得更具意义。参与的目的有所不同，且并非都只关注问题，而是参与其中，积极引导，使文化交流实际生动而有意义。"当全体与会者在达米安·沃策尔的带动下起舞时，第二届中美文化论坛的会场已成为一个圣洁的艺术殿堂，跨文化的双边对话已不仅仅是艺术的交流、学术的探讨，而是在同一和谐文化生态中的愉快相聚。

Pan Yuan

Associate
Research Fellow
from the Cultural
Development
Strategic Research
Center of Chinese
National Academy
of Arts

Constructing A Century Bridge of China-U.S. Cultural Exchange

Overview of "A Binational Conversation Bridging Cultures: The Second China-U.S. Cultural Forum"

Abstract: "A Binational Conversion Bridging Cultures: The Second China-U.S. Cultural Forum", co-sponsored by the Ministry of Culture of the People's Republic of China and the U.S. National Endowment for the Humanities and presented by the U.S. National Endowment for the Humanities and Chinese National Academy of Arts, was opened in the University of California, Berkeley USA (UC Berkeley) between October 15 and 16, 2010, under the generous support of President's Committee on the Arts and the Humanities (PCAH) and the Center for Chinese Studies at the UC Berkeley.

It is the Memorandum of Understanding signed by U.S. National Endowment for the Humanities and the Chinese National Academy of Arts on August 2008 that initiated the idea of establishing China-U.S. Cultural Forum. The memorandum encouraged academic cooperation in cultural heritages protection between the two sides. Under such a spirit, "Protection and Presentation of Cultural Heritage in a Digital Era: The First China-U.S. Cultural Forum", co-sponsored by China's Ministry of Culture and the U.S. National Endowment for the Humanities and presented by Chinese National Academy of Arts, was opened in Beijing in December of the same year and made a great success. In November 2009, Chinese President Hu Jintao and U.S. President Barack Obama held talks in Beijing and issued the China-U.S. Joint Statement. The Statement emphasized the importance of cultural exchanges to promoting closer China-U.S. relations, proposed to establish new bilateral mechanisms and said the two countries would jointly hold the second China-U.S. Cultural Forum to promote high-end cultural cooperation and exchange between both sides. Against such a backdrop, the Second China-U.S. Cultural Forum was opened as scheduled in UC Berkeley. This university is among the origin places of cultural exchanges between the two countries, as it has always been a China-U.S.

This article was first published in the 12th issue of *Arts Criticism* in 2010.

cultural exchange center since the 19th century and was the first university in U.S. to set a Center for Chinese Studies.

Wang Wenzhang, Vice Cultural Minister of China and President of Chinese National Academy of Arts, and Jim Leach, Chairman of U.S. National Endowment for the Humanities attended and addressed the forum.

Wang Wenzhang reviewed the history of China-U.S. cultural exchange and affirmed its importance in the healthy and sound development of the bilateral relationship. He said the opening of the Second China-U.S. Cultural Forum "bears unique significance of our time". "It signifies that bilateral cultural exchange and cooperation between China and the United States will continue to be deepened". "The theme of this forum is A Binational Conversation on Bridging Cultures. The purpose of this forum is to, through various aspects of culture and different forms of arts, review thoroughly the history of China-U.S. exchange, seek a practical path for bilateral exchange, and discuss the prospect of China-U.S. cultural exchange. Through various means of cultural exchange, this forum hopes to strengthen bilateral communication and cooperation in the areas of humanities and social sciences, culture and arts. This will in effect promote cultural diversity and create a new chapter in China-U.S. cultural exchange and cooperation".

Jim Leach said in his speech that "the most important bilateral relationship in this century and quite possibly in this millennium will be the United States and Chinese relationship. If it's constructive we're looking at the potential era of potential peace and prosperity. If not, the reverse could well be the case." He emphasized the most importance of China and U.S. affairs in the cultural relationship between the two countries, and said cultural was more important than politics, as the latter was only a part of the former and cultural differences should be solved through better mutual respect. If countries and their respective peoples cannot respect each other there can be no sustaining relations whatever the policies of two governments may be in the moment in time. Therefore, what we should do is to enhance the mutual respect, which is also the ultimate goal of this forum.

This forum held round-table meetings to discuss such topics as "Historical Perspectives on China-U.S. Cultural Relations", "Literary Heritage and Creativity", "Tradition and Innovation in The Visual Arts", "The Performing Arts: Comparative Perspectives" and "The Future of China-U.S Cultural Relations" under the theme of "A Binational Conversation Bridging Cultures". About 30 outstanding artists and scholars in literature and art from both countries made key-note speeches based on their own fields and perspectives, and about 200 people from culture and art communities from different countries and cultures attended the forum and actively participated in the discussions.

The first forum focused on the role of digital technology, which represents the level the modern technology, in the protection of cultural heritages and the innovation of contemporary art. Differently, this forum emphasized the importance of culture, literature and other cultural factors in cross-cultural exchanges. Culture is manifested by art, while art is the cream of art. Such interdependence was fully displayed in this forum.

Remove Culture gap and Misinterpretation: Communicate Cultural Values

China and U.S has made active efforts to promote the bilateral cultural dialogue, because cultures of the two countries, Oriental and Occidental respectively, have different systems and values and such differences cause communication crisis. As Allison Blakely, professor from Boston University pointed out, "The 21th century is the first in which the entire world was challenged with new levels of cultural diversity within all the major societies."

Effective ways of communication should be found to remove misunderstandings in cross-cultural exchange and narrow the gap between different civilizations. To this question, Liu Mengxi, research fellow and Director of the Institute of Chinese Culture at the National Academy of Arts and a famous scholar, said: "I tend towards a diverse world, diverse cultures and diverse modern civilizations." Although economic patterns and civilization types of different counties are unnecessary and impossible to be the same, "the rationality of cultural ethos is long lasting." The essence of cultural exchange is the communication of ideas and universal values. Research fellow Jia Leilei, President Assistant of Chinese National Academy of Arts, Director of Cultural Development Strategy Research Center and a movie critic, emphasized the urgency and importance of narrowing and eliminating cultural conflicts and contradictions through effective cultural exchange. He said: "It is on the premise of cross-cultural exchange and dialogues that peoples in different cultures can understand and recognize each other. Nevertheless, due to the differences in media, methods and modes of communication, the results may turn against the original intentions."" In a multicultural context, mutual acceptance and integration of various cultures are based upon the true understanding of different cultures, especially the strange and less-understood ones, and even in opposition to one's own. More importantly, it is necessary to strengthen exchange and communication between cultures, and treat each other objectively, equally and fairly. " Professor Yu Dan, Associate Dean of School of Arts and Communication, Beijing Normal University and a renowned scholar, also said, "It can be said that all cultures share the same language, but every culture has its own grammar. We use the grammar of our own nationality to engage in an international dialogue, for the purpose of finding a new cultural sphere." Confucianism, Taoism, and Buddhism in China provide us a way of thinking, while exchanges with other cultures in the world reflect the universal values in these cultures. Pauline Yu, President of American Council of Learned Societies, expressed a similar idea. She said, "We will need these multiple facets of perspectives of scholars here and scholars in China for truly successful collaboration. We build bridges between cultures after all, not to eradicate differences in values, but to appreciate, understand and interpret them."

Obviously, the effective way to remove the cultural misinterpretation is to make up differences through universal values and shared emotions by human beings, while literary and artistic works are important carriers of such values and emotions.

Sara Schneckloth, Professor of Drawing from University of South Carolina,

Columbia, said drawing as an idea of taking the world around us and the world within us and translating it into a image that allow the access for others to entering to the world and our experience□to our minds, and is a hub of culture. Wu Weishan, Director of Institute of Sculpture, Chinese National Academy of Arts and a famous sculptor, took his sculptures like Sleeping Child, Laozi, Confucius and Theme sculptures for the Memorial Hall of the Victims in Nanjing Massacre as examples to convey an idea that the most important part of cultural exchanges is to understand the emotions and cultural values of each other. That means emotions and feelings shared by the naïve child, philosopher and all living creatures that suffer are the basis for cultural exchange.

Creation Concepts' Similarities and Differences between China and U.S.: Pursuing Identity in Cultural Collision

Not only carriers of values and emotions, literature and art present skills and ideas that are also hot issues in the communication and exchange between Chinese and American literary scholars and artists. Through this precious opportunity, they, on the one hand, explored and studied creation techniques and expertise in the cultural sphere of each other, and sincerely introduced the best part of their own culture and art on the other hand. Meanwhile, they consciously compared arts of the same kind in both countries, to find out similar among diverse artistic creations under different cultural background, so that they can find identity in practical artistic creation.

Bearing this in mind, research fellow Tian Liming, Vice President of Chinese National Academy of Arts and Dean of the Graduate School, Chinese National Academy of Arts, introduced image aesthetics which can best reflect the unique aesthetic concept of the Chinese painting. He pointed out that together with humanistic experiences of observing with a peaceful mind, creating images according to objects and achieving harmony between mind and images, and with ways of expression emphasizing being personality-oriented, integrating moral with paintings and conveying thoughts with images, the concept demonstrates the characteristics of Chinese paintings and the origin of Chinese culture. His paper briefly describes with examples the humanities qualities and profound culture contained in Chinese paintings from the five perspectives of establishing the pattern, observing the objects, imitating the objects, forms and spirit, and mind and images.

Li Shenghong, research fellow and Deputy Dean of School of Chinese Calligraphy, Chinese National Academy of Arts and a famous calligrapher, also expounded calligraphy and lettering, traditional Chinese arts, as they have become a symbol of the Chinese culture. Chinese calligraphy engraving, the combination of the two arts, is a new expression of traditional Chinese culture with its beauty of constitution, stereoscopic impression, color and texture. Liu Zhen, research fellow and Director of Institute of Traditional Operas, Chinese National Academy of Arts, held that the "cultural era" was the highest form of human society. By reviewing the development of Chinese opera, he conveyed an idea that the traditional culture and art is the basis and essence of the cultural era.

Lawrence Rinder, Director of the Berkeley Art Museum and Pacific Film Archive, introduced the artistic schools in the western world, described the transfer from modern art to post-modern art, and explained the relation between the post-modern art and the traditional art, namely a dialect relation between innovation and returning to the tradition.

Henry Adams, professor from Case Western Reserve University in Cleveland, U.S., talked about his understanding about Chinese literature and art. He said that: "Because of the close connection with calligraphy and poetry, and because of its close connection with the scholar class, Chinese painting developed in a way very different from the west. While in the west, figure painting became the dominant form of expression, figure painting ceased to be the charmer practice by major Chinese artists after the Tang Dynasty. And landscape became the central form of the expression. In contrast to the west, they never play an important role in Chinese art. The reasons for this are hard to pinpoint. By connecting with the landscape, the Chinese scholars could re-establish the connection with the larger harmony of the universe. One of the most fascinating aspects of Chinese artists that they would rather early abandoned the representation of reality as its central goal."

Dawn Ho Delbanco, Associate Professor of East Asian Art, Columbia University, compared specific Chinese and western paintings. According to her study, "on the face of things, it might seem that there are unbridgeable differences between traditional Chinese and western arts. And in fact there are surprising parallels and overlapping between the two artistic traditions." She cited many examples of European paintings and traditional Chinese paintings: The "counter-balance" principle in Green sculpture was found in Chinese artist Guo Xi's painting in the 11th century, which is quite similar to "yin" and "yang", philosophical concepts in Chinese tradition. Besides, she compared paintings by Chinese painters like Ni Zan, Wang Chongming and Shi Tao with that by some famous European painters. The shared part thus found and the similarities between eastern and western cultures give a reasonable interpretation of her subject "Bridging Cultures with Art", and also proved that artistic concepts followed by modern western artists in 20th century are exactly what Chinese artists have practiced for centuries.

Billie Tsien, a famous American architect, further explained such "bridge" on the basis of her own cultural background. As a Chinese-American, she followed the introverted Chinese style in her design. She said the power of architectures mostly lied in its inner part, and that is what really touches, comforts and should be memorized by people. Therefore, her Chinese-American cultural background not only shaped her unique personality but also her priority to the inner power in her architectonic design.

Rachel Goslins, Executive Director of the President's Committee on the Arts and Humanities and a famous documentary director and producer, also said, "In almost all of the artistic disciplines we've discussed over these two days, painting, sculpture, poetry, theater - well, the Chinese have a head start on the Americans by at least four centuries. But film, film is the only discipline that was born in both of our countries at the same time. So this is an area where, I think, it's imperative analysis will be especially interesting, to learn about the different ways our two countries have taken the same tool and used it to shape their culture in different or similar ways."

Mutual Impact and Learning between Chinese and American Cultures: Drawing the Strong Points of Others to Make Oneself Rich

The long-standing cultural exchange and cooperation between the two countries has imposed profound influence on the artistic creation in both of them and left traces in respective literary and artistic works. In this forum, artists from both sides analyzed the cultural origins of each other, and agreed that cross-cultural exchanges can derive new inspirations, bring new vigor to culture and art of each other, and thus lay the foundation for absorbing heterogeneous culture.

Ou Jianping, research fellow and Deputy Director of Dance Research Institute, Chinese National Academy of Arts, held that the fruits in century's exchange in dance between the two countries served as an ambassador in the communication and friendship between two peoples.

Xu Lei, research fellow of Research Center for Creation, Chinese National Academy of Arts, pointed out based on his personal observation and experience that, U.S. owns the richest resources of traditional Chinese arts and has made considerable contribution for the research and promotion of traditional Chinese arts among all countries. The Oriental culture represented by Chinese culture has partially inspired of American literature and art, for example, imagist poems and abstractionist painting. Meanwhile, American culture has also influenced China at the same time. Particularly, reforms in artistic concepts since 1980s own a lot to the modernism in U.S..

Mo Yan, a famous writer and research fellow from Artistic Creation and Research Center of Chinese National Academy of Arts, said many writers including himself were influenced by American literature. He hoped that given more time, the exchange can become more bilateral, where the works of Chinese authors will influence authors from other countries, including young authors in America. In response, Christopher Merrill, Director of the International Writing Program at the University of Iowa, also said Chinese writers' influence on himself, and said Chinese poems in the Tang Dynasty have influenced almost all contemporary poems in the U.S.. He then introduced the Life of Discovery, a literary exchange program, listed achievements thereof, and wished more of such exchange programs.

Annping Chin, Senior Lecturer from Yale University, taking the influence of Book of Poetry on Confucius as example, said that the western reader certainly could have the same feelings as Chinese do if an early text like Book of Song was presented to him in this way. He then talked about the translation and popularization of Chinese classic literature, and hoped to find an interesting way to integrate such knowledge and present to western readers. Such classics should reach more western readers so that they can get deeper literary influence and know more about the history.

Prospect of China-U.S. Relation: Promote Identity through Cultural Exchange

Jin Canrong, professor and Associate Dean of School of International Studies,

Renmin University of China, held that China-U.S. cultural ties should be put into the framework of the bilateral relation, while the future of the bilateral relation significantly depends on the development of relations in politics, economy, military affairs and culture. All the four relations have twofold nature: the former two are more of competition than cooperation, while the latter two are more of cooperation. Therefore, cultural is a factor than can benefit stable bilateral relation. We should make full use of the shared part by the two cultures and find similarities at the deeper level, so as to promote the development of China-U.S. relation.

Josiah Ober, professor from Stanford University, expressed his high hopes to China-U.S. cultural relation from the perspective of the "soft power", and advocated the soft power manifested by culture, art, literature, language and national mechanism. He emphasized that, "Chinese people are not the losers when they learn something from Plato and Aristotle, and western scholars are not losers when we incorporate the study of Chinese language and Confucian tradition, the history of China into our traditions. When the soft power, the attractive, the beautiful things of Chinese culture are more recognized in the west just as the beautiful things of the Western culture have been recognized in China, I think the possibility for a kind of creative competition is what I think ultimately I would hope for of future of Chinese-American cultural relations."

As said by Rachel Goslins, both Chinese and American artists have taken the same tool and used it to shape their cultures in different or similar ways. When they display their creative works, they share with each other their feeling and pleasure of innovation. They feel nothing at all about their cultural differences and boundaries, when they discuss with each other and admire each other's talent and wisdom. Damian Woetzel, a famous dancer in U.S., said arts, for him, are a bunch of things. They're about entertainment. They're about enlightenment, what you can learn from the arts. They're about exchange as well, because to him this is the only way they live and flourish. He said: "This forum is an incredible valuable occasion to enable the exchanges, but they become far more valuable at the level at which you participate. There's a ratio of participation in it. Not nearly studying the problem, but participating in it and looking for ways to remain current and to be available for the kind of meaningful exchange that makes cultural exchange actually living." When all participants danced together with Damian Woetzel, the venue for the Second China-U.S. Cultural Forum has become a sacred heaven of art. Bilateral Cross-cultural dialogue is not only artistic and academic exchange, but a happy gathering in a harmonious cultural sphere.

重构全球化语境下的
文化交流模式
——"跨文化双边对话：第二届中美文化论坛"述评

肖庆
中国艺术研究院
文化发展战略研究中心
助理研究员

　　为了进一步深化中美两国的文化交流，开辟中美文化合作的新境界，由中华人民共和国文化部和美国国家人文基金会共同主办的"跨文化双边对话：第二届中美文化论坛"于10月15日至16日在美国加利福尼亚大学伯克利分校隆重举行。

　　第二届中美文化论坛由中华人民共和国文化部和美国国家人文基金会共同主办，美国国家人文基金会和中国艺术研究院共同承办，并在美国总统艺术人文委员会和加利福尼亚大学伯克利分校"中国研究中心"的大力支持下举行。中华人民共和国文化部副部长、中国艺术研究院院长王文章，中国驻美国大使馆公使衔文化参赞李冬文，文化部艺术司司长董伟，中国艺术研究院副院长、研究生院院长田黎明，中国艺术研究院院长助理、文化发展战略研究中心主任贾磊磊，美国国家人文基金会主席吉姆·利奇，美国总统艺术人文委员会执行主任瑞秋·格斯林斯等出席开幕式。出席论坛的中方学者还有中国艺术研究院中国文化研究所所长刘梦溪，文学院院长、著名作家莫言，戏曲研究所所长刘祯，美术研究所所长吴为山，书法院常务副院长李胜洪，舞蹈研究所副所长欧建平，创作研究中心画家、北京今日美术馆艺术总监徐累，北京师范大学艺术与传媒学院副院长于丹，中国人民大学国际关系学院副院长金灿荣。美方出席论坛的有来自哈佛大学、斯坦福大学、耶鲁大学、哥伦比亚大学、波士顿大学以及美国总统艺术人文委员会、美国学术团体联合会等

本文转载自《中国文化报》（2010年11月9日）

著名高校和艺术机构的专家、学者和艺术家。

"中美文化论坛"是根据2008年中华人民共和国文化部同美国国家人文基金会签署的《关于鼓励人文学科学术性研究和文化遗产保护合作事宜的谅解备忘录》而举办，其宗旨是为中美两国在文化领域建立一个公共性、学术性、互动性的定期对话机制，通过此机制探讨文化艺术的发展方式和文化遗产保护等问题，加深中美两国在文化艺术和人文科学领域的相互了解，促进双方在文化艺术和人文科学领域的友好合作，推进两国的文化交流得到全面、持续、深入的发展。2009年11月，中国国家主席胡锦涛与美国总统奥巴马在北京举行会谈，发表了《中美联合声明》，其中强调人文交流对促进中美关系具有重要意义，并进一步明确了建立新的双边机制，召开第二届中美文化论坛，以期全方位地推动中美两国文化领域的高端合作。2010年5月，中国国务委员刘延东和美国国务卿希拉里·克林顿在北京联合主持了"中美人文交流高层磋商机制成立仪式暨第一次会议"，再次强调办好"第二届中美文化论坛"，凸显了两国领导人对此论坛和两国文化领域深层交流的重视。

在为期两天的论坛中，来自中美两国的50余名专家、学者和艺术家就"中美文化关系的历史回顾""文学遗产与创造性""视觉艺术的传统与创新""表演艺术比较观"以及"中美文化关系的未来展望"等多个论题展开了深入的交流与探讨。

回眸历史是为了更好地关注当下。文化的交流不但沟通中美两国人民的心灵与情感，增进理解和信任，还对推动两国关系健康、稳定的发展起到重要作用。

中华人民共和国文化部副部长王文章在论坛开幕致辞中引述中国古语"万物并育而不相害，道并行而不相悖"，并指出不同文化的交流会使双方文化更具创造性。中美两国虽然远隔千山万水，但两国人民之间开始交往的历史已有190多年。今天的中国处在改革开放的新的发展时期，开始以开阔的胸襟和眼光吸收世界优秀文化，包括美国电影等在内的多种文化产品进入中国民众的视野，美国的现当代文化艺术也为中国的学者和艺术家所熟悉、了解及借鉴。中美文化交流正在迈向一个不断升华的历史时代。

美国国家人文基金会主席吉姆·利奇在致辞中说，19世纪著名的美国诗人沃尔特·惠特曼曾经有一个美好的梦想：有一天全世界的诗人都聚集在一起，将他们充满不同个性的诗歌汇聚在一起，用他们的诗为世界带来和平。中国的先贤孔子认为，如果有更多的人欣赏音乐，世界上就不会有战争。吉姆·利奇认为，文化的作用巨大，人们从对世界了解比较深刻的作家的作品中，能够了解和认知我们的世界。文化的发展离不开彼此的交流。他祝愿本次论坛取得丰硕成果。

美国学术团体联合会会长余宝琳女士认为：中国文明的迅速扩展及其文化的深刻内涵吸引了美国人对中国进行研究。美国学术团体联合会在1919年成立之后不久即成为了中美学术交流研究的推动者之一。中美两国即使政治关系紧张，学术和文化的交流也兴盛不衰。如今，大批中国学生来到我们美国北部的院校学习，最新的统计数字为10万，表明中美两国的学术互通充满了生机与活力。在今天，中国和美国在经济方面有着千丝万缕的联系，这一联系比以往任何时候都更为紧密。每年约有1.5万名美国学生前往中国学习，奥巴马总统希望这一数字上升到10万，我相信这一目标将会实现。

耶鲁大学历史系斯特林荣誉教授乔纳森·斯宾塞回顾了中美文化交流的历史，认为由于选择的历史时期不同，美国学者所得到的关于中国历史的结论差别非常显著。中美建交之初，更多的美国人印象中的中国是从19世纪末的移民和20世纪70年代末期在美国建立的唐人街得来的。他们眼中的中国是一个衰弱、贫穷和四分五裂的国家。而现如今，我感受到了美国对中国的尊重、认可，以及承认中国现已成为一个强劲的经营合作伙伴，一个强劲的贸易合作伙伴。

凯斯西储大学美国艺术教授亨利·亚当斯在演讲中说，中文与英语不仅在词汇上不同，在组织现实和与事物的联系方面也不同。我们要明白我们的语言代表两种不同的社会现实。为了相互了解，我们需要超越互不熟悉的思考和语言的界限。亨利·亚当斯认为中美文化论坛有两个目的：首先是促进中国学者把灵感推广到西方学术界；其次，要推动西方人学习中国文化。中国发展迅速，如今已经成为现代艺术的主要推动者，中国的主流艺术帮助我们重新激活西方艺术的灵感来表现当前的世界。中美文化论坛应当是我们两国之间更长时间对话的开始。

"双边对话"为文化艺术研究提供了全新的视角，促使人们从动态开放的视点考察不同文艺形态的发展，并在此基础上探求共同的文化建构。

美国总统艺术人文委员会执行主任瑞秋·格斯琳斯认为，在绘画、雕塑、诗歌、戏剧方面，中国领先于美国至少四个世纪。当这些艺术在我们美国的艺术创始人眼前闪过时，中国人已经在完善这方面的工艺了。但是对于电影艺术是一个例外，电影是同时在中美两国诞生的唯一一个学科。1896年，美国第一部电影问世。1905年，中国制作了第一部记录京剧的电影。我认为从这个角度对中美文化艺术进行必要的分析是非常有趣的，可以了解到两国艺术家塑造其文化的不同方式。

著名作家莫言在演讲中说："上个世纪80年代初期，很多美国翻译家翻译中国小说时，主要选择的是中国小说的政治性和思想性，他们希望读者能从中国作家的作品里读到中国社会政治的变化或经济的变化。当然，这种选择的视角无可厚非，但我认为真正好的文学翻译应该把艺术性放在第一位。我作为一个作家，希望外国读者能够从中国作家的作品里读到我们在艺术方面的创新和发现，截止到目前，我们更多从外国文学里受到影响。我想假以时日，中国作家的作品也会对外国的包括对美国的年轻作家产生影响。我期盼着这一天。"

著名画家田黎明认为，中国文化遵循"人法地，地法天，天法道，道法自然"的人文思想，以"道生一，一生二，二生三，三生万物"的自然规律来运行。中国画的意象特征作为中国文化的重要载体，以中国文化倡导的温柔敦厚为学养，体验"立天之道曰阴与阳，立地之道曰刚与柔，立人之道曰仁与义"的人文理念，逐步建构出独一无二的属于中国画的审美体系。中国画的文化性贯穿在每个时代人们生活和生命的审美意识和人格情趣之中，中国画的当代性继承和发展着传统意象文化的精神，使得中国画在今天展现了它独有的人文高尚品质，这是中国人的精神财富，也是属于人类的共同精神财富。

哥伦比亚大学东亚艺术系的多恩·荷·德尔班科教授从20世纪表现主义艺术家的一些画作中发现，它们与中国画有着密切的联系。西方现代主义艺术家们在20世纪所遵循的正是中国艺术家已经践行了几个世纪的艺术理念。当下，绘画的普遍性能够使绘画与所有的人群进行交流，从而使人们理解绘画。

著名书法家李胜洪认为，艺术交流在文化交流中起着非常重要的作用，我们了解一个国家，可能首先始自艺术的角度。在中国五千年文明发展史中，书法艺术和我们中华传统中包括有容乃大、与时俱进、和而不同的思想都是息息相通的。随着时代的发展，书法艺术的语言越来越丰富。在现代书刻艺术所做的尝试中，通过借鉴西方色彩学的一些理念，可以创造一种非常独特的视觉效果。

刘祯研究员在主题发言中对目前中国文化的发展历史进行了梳理。他说，随着昆曲艺术2001年被列入联合国教科文组织"人类口头和非物质文化遗产代表作"以来，越来越多的年轻人、大学生喜欢昆曲，喜欢京剧，喜欢地方戏和传统艺术，传统艺术丰厚的底蕴将极大地丰富人民群众的文化、精神需求，增强时代文化的历史感、厚重感，成为文化前行不竭的源泉和动力。

著名画家徐累认为，在中国当代艺术的发展进程中，有几个关键的节点与美国的艺术有很紧密的关系。从艺术研究和收藏的角度来看，美国是拥有中国传统艺术资源最丰富的西方国家，这一方面说明了美国的多元文化是建立在人类文明的基石上，同时也反映了中国文化在美国所受到的认同。

杜克大学戏剧研究教授克莱尔·康塞逊作为一位在戏剧研究和翻译方面颇有建树的学者，很自豪地将自己的职业生涯定位为中美文化交流的见证人和阐释者。她说，在西方很多学者的眼中，常常把中国文化等同于中国的传统文化，而在她所研究的中国话剧领域，克莱尔·康塞逊教授感受到的是中国文化中非常现代和具有创新性的一面。她指出，话剧是在20世纪初，作为新文化运动的一部分从西方引入中国的，在这一过程中，中国知识分子起到了很重要的作用。这种引进的形式不是通过殖民主义，也不是通过西方影响，而是当时中国知识分子改革中国文化的自发行为。

文化交流的目的不是消除不同的价值观，而是理解和认识这些价值观。如何在东西文化碰撞、融合的背景下，构造良性互动的交流范式，是中美两国文化学者共同关注的现实问题。

贾磊磊研究员认为，不同文化之间的交流和对话是相互理解与认同的前提。但在相互交流的过程中，由于交流媒介、交流方式、交流模式的不同，有时可能会产生与交流的初衷未必一致的效果。目前在全球化的历史语境中，如何通过有效的文化交流方式来缩小和弥合人类社会在文化领域的对立与冲突是十分紧迫而重要的问题。经济贸易的交往只能加强双方的利益合作，但并不能"购买到"对方的文化价值观，文化的理解必须通过跨文化交流的方式才能实现。

加利福尼亚大学英语与美国研究教授唐纳德·麦奎德多年来曾多次走访中国，并与中国政府领导人进行交谈。他认为，创新和创造力已成为了中国的一项国家使命。这一使命最近的一次表现是北京奥林匹克运动会的开幕式。当时所展现出来的令人惊叹而优美的富有创造力的表演使多年来外国人对中国的陈旧观念和印象在2008年8月8日晚奥运火炬点燃的一瞬烟消云散。在与中国竞争的同时需要客观地理解和看待中国的强大。

爱荷华大学国际写作项目主任克里斯多弗·梅里尔以他所组织"发现之旅"项目，展现了两种文化之间相互交流的一种模式。在为时两年的活动中，"发现之旅"项目将12名在25岁至40岁之间的美国作家介绍到中国，中国方面也将相同人数的中国作家到美国。交流的重要性不在于相互派遣代表，而是将作家们集中到一起进行交流、建立合作。

著名雕塑家吴为山在演讲中以他所创作的雕塑作品来说明自己的文化价值观。20多年来，吴为山创造了400多件雕塑作品，分布世界20多个国家，有反映世界重大历史事件和重要历史人物的作品，也有反映普通人生活百态的作品，每件作品的背后，都有自己独特的故事，这些故事是艺术家经历、情感的体现，也是文化价值观的体现。欣赏艺术作品的同时，就是了解彼此情感和分享彼此文化价值观的过程，这也是中美两国之间进行文化交流的意义所在。

欧建平研究员在演讲中提到1988年他接受纽约《报刊新闻》专访时曾发表的言论："中国向西方先锋派舞蹈形式开放，无伤社会主义的大雅。在我看来，中国的强大足以不被任何外来影响所吞没。跨文化交流的重要性就在于，如果人们相互理解，便不会再有战争。"22年过去了，欧建平对此依然坚信不疑。

全球化一方面使世界趋近于"同"，使世界越来越相似；另一方面，又使世界趋近于"异"，使文化间的差别变得越来越大。中美文化交流在促进相互理解、包容和融合的同时，也将是一种涵盖不同价值和共同需求的过程。

对于未来世界的发展趋势，美国国家人文基金会主席吉姆·利奇提出了三个鲜明观点："第一，在21世纪这一千年中，最重要的双边关系将是中美关系。第二，当今世界的加速变化，涉及了有文字记载以来最复杂的情况。第三，这一加速变化最重要的特点是，我们的生活与科技发展联系在一起,而且最严重的是会对军事装备产生影响。爱因斯坦曾评论原子分裂改变了一切,但没改变我们的思维方式。我们必须认识到,由于人类本身存在内在冲突,冲突是不变的,可以改变的是我们思维的方式,或许我们要以一种更深刻的方式来了解人类本性,以便开发出更能纠正人类冲突本性的技术。就中美关系而言,存在一个黄金法则:想要别人怎样对你,就要怎样对待别人。在儒家传统中也有类似的说法,即'己所不欲,勿施于人'。中国人可能想要我们更加遵奉孔子学说,而我们则想要中国人更了解杰佛逊的思想。我们需要扩大对对方的尊重,这也是我们开展"双边对话"的目的。"

刘梦溪研究员在发言中说,一个国家的现代化进程,不可能在与世隔绝的情况下单独完成,需要有不同文化背景、不同文化系统、不同文化理念的嫁接。就像一个人不能离群索居一样,一个国家也不可能逸世独存于当代世界。亨廷顿教授的偏颇,是过分强调了文明的冲突,而轻忽了文明的融合。而文明的融合,首先需要文化沟通。文化沟通不仅是文明人的礼仪,而且是文明人的智慧和生存方式。正是在这个意义上,国与国、区域与区域、民族与民族之间,是互为依存的关系。东方离不开西方,西方也离不开东方。同和异,是就达至目标的途径而言。正如《易经》上所说:"天下同归而殊途,一致而百虑。"

哥伦比亚大学美国文学学者、美国研究中心主任安德鲁·德尔班科教授认为,每一代人都应继承先辈所创造的优势。他将这称为人类历史的接力赛:一代人获得了某种知识的内涵,发现了一些事物,他们需要将这些知识内涵和发现的事物传递给下一代,使下一代不必再花费精力发现同样的事物。那么对知识的寻求就可以从一个比之前更高的起点开始。这是安德鲁·德尔班科教授对于科学发展根本方式的理解,他认为文化的传承同样遵循这样的规律。

斯坦福大学古典学教授政治科学教授何塞·欧博在演讲中提出了对于中美文化关系的期望:与硬实力不同,文化软实力不需要寻求霸权。中国人学习柏拉图和亚里士多德时不表示中国人输了,而当我们将中华语言和儒家传统的研究、中国历史融入我们的传统时,不代表西方学者输了。我期望:当西方文化有魅力的部分在中国得到认可的同时,中国文化的美丽瑰宝也在西方得到更多认可。这种创造性竞争的可能性和最终建立,有待中美两国之间进行更深入的对话。

于丹教授认为，中美文化论坛以一种对话的方式来呈现各自对于当今社会和历史文化的一种态度。态度的交流，比我们的结论更重要。于丹教授以中国儒家思想中"君子"的标准、"和而不同"的理念以及"知行合一"的例子，说明中国传统文化中的精华不仅仅是中国的，也是世界的。我们完成这种呈现，是为了最后在全球化的范围中让一种新文化的奇迹，化成天下，带我们去解决共同的迷惑，走向大同世界。

建筑师钱以佳是美籍华人，她在演讲中满怀感情地谈到东西两种文化传统给自己带来的影响："当我年轻时，我对两种文化带来的冲击有些困惑，当我逐渐成熟，我开始喜欢自己是两种文化的综合体。这样可以有多种角度审视世界。我的儿子是真正的东西方文化对话创造的'作品'，我问他是中国人还是美国人，他回答说：'我不是其中任何一方，我就是我。'这是一个文化的轮回，在经过一个漫长的循环周期后，又回到了直指内心的本源，伟大的艺术作品同样是这样。"

金灿荣教授认为："世界192个联合国成员国当中，双边贸易超过4000亿美元的只有两家，一是美国和加拿大，一是美国和中国。贸易的相互依存度证明我们事实上已不可分离了。中美关系有四根支柱，即政治关系、经济关系、军事与安全关系和社会文化关系。在这四个支柱中，既有竞争又有合作。未来中国对美国的重视程度，只会提升而不会下降。我认为，未来中美关系的问题，不取决于中国的态度，很大程度上来自于美国的态度，当然也来自于以后客观存在的第三方因素。"

波士顿大学欧洲比较历史学教授埃里森·布莱克利在主题发言中展望了中美文化的未来关系。他说，文化比政治更有影响力。21世纪是全球所有国家都面临着新水平的文化多样性挑战的世纪。他敬畏中华文明的悠久历史和其形成的哲学体系，惊讶于中国很早就拥有技术和能力来探索世界，如郑和在15世纪早期就带领成百上千条船和上万人7次远征国外，这比麦哲伦航行要早一百年。埃里森·布莱克利提议两国学者督促各自的领导人建立对文化多样性的相互尊重，并更有建设性地进行全方位的国际合作，以此替代对文化问题的争论。

作为本届中美文化论坛的延伸活动，参加论坛的中方学者还参加了由芝加哥大学东亚系举办的学术研讨活动，受邀在哥伦比亚大学教育学院进行了主题演讲，并参加了联合国教科文组织的相关活动，为本次中美文化交流画上了完美的句号。第二届中美文化论坛的会标是由中国传统剪纸图案画意而成的一道彩桥，希望这道彩桥能不断延伸，架起中美两国文化艺术沟通与交流的桥梁，成为东西文化交流、融合、碰撞的盛会。

Xiao Qing

Assistant Research Fellow of Cultural Development Strategy Research Center, Chinese National Academy of Arts

Reconstructing the Pattern of Cultural Exchange under the Context of Globalization
An Academic Review of "A Binational Conversation Bridging Cultures: the Second China-U.S. Cultural Forum"

To promote the China-U.S. cultural exchange and open up the new horizon for binational cultural cooperation, the Second China-U.S. Cultural Forum themed A Binational Conversation on Bridging Cultures, was jointly held by the Ministry of Culture of the People's Republic of China and the U.S. National Endowment for the Humanities from October 15-16th at the University of California, Berkeley.

The Second China-U.S. Cultural Forum was jointly held by the Ministry of Culture of the People's Republic of China and the National Endowment for the Humanities of the U.S and jointly sponsored by the National Endowment for the Humanities and Chinese National Academy of Arts with strong support from the President's Committee on the Arts and Humanities of the U.S. and the Center for Chinese Studies at the University of California, Berkeley. The following guests attended the opening ceremony: Wang Wenzhang, Vice Minister of Culture of P.R.C and President of Chinese National Academy of Arts; Li Dongwen, Cultural Minister Counselor of the Chinese Embassy in the U.S; Dong Wei, Deputy Director-general of the Department of Arts, Ministry of Culture; Tian Liming, Vice President of Chinese National Academy of Arts and President of the Postgraduate School; Jia Leilei, President Assistant of Chinese National Academy of Arts and Director of Cultural Development Strategy Research Center; Jim Leach, Chairman of National Endowment for the Humanities; and Rachel Goslins, Executive Director of President's Committee on the Arts and Humanities. Chinese scholars attending the forum also included Liu Mengxi, Director of the Chinese Culture Research Center of Chinese National Academy of Arts; Mo Yan, Dean of the School of Literature and renowned writer; Liu Zhen, Director of the Institute of Traditional Operas; Wu Weishan, Director of the Institute of Fine Arts; Li Shenghong, Executive Deputy Dean of the School of Chinese Calligraphy, Ou Jianping, Deputy Director of Dance Research Institute, Xu Lei, Painter

This article was first published in *China Culture News* on November 9th, 2010.

of the Research Center for Creation and Art Director of Beijing Today Art Museum; Yu Dan, Deputy Dean of the School of Art and Communication, Beijing Normal University; and Jin Canrong, Deputy Dean of the School of International Studies, Renmin University of China. Experts, scholars and artists from Harvard University, Stanford University, Yale University, Columbia University, Boston University, President's Committee on the Arts and Humanities, American Council of Learned Societies and other prestigious universities and arts institutions also attended the forum.

The China-U.S. Cultural Forum was held in accordance with the 2008 Memorandum of Understanding on Cooperation to Encourage Academic Research and Cultural Heritage Protection signed between the Ministry of Culture of the People's Republic of China and the National Endowment for the Humanities of the U.S. It aims at establishing a public, academic and interactive dialogue mechanism on a regular basis for the cultural exchange between China and the U.S. With this mechanism, we will be able to discuss issues such as the development pattern of arts and culture and the protection of cultural heritage, etc., deepen the mutual understanding of China and the US, and promote the cooperation in culture and arts, so as to facilitate the comprehensive, sustained and profound development of the cultural exchange between the two countries. In November 2009, the Chinese President Hu Jintao and the US president Barack Obama held a meeting in Beijing and delivered the China-U.S. Joint Statement, emphasizing the significance of cultural exchange in the China-U.S. relationship and declaring that a new bilateral mechanism will be established and the second China-U.S. Cultural Forum will be held with a view to fully promoting the high-end cooperation between the two countries in the field of humanities. In May, 2010, Chinese State Councilor Liu Yandong and U.S. Secretary of State Hillary Clinton jointly hosted a ceremony marking the Establishment of the China-United States High Level Humanities and Arts Consultative Institution and its First Conference. Both sides reiterated their common wish for the success of the China-U.S. Cultural Forum, which showed that leaders in both countries attached great importance to the forum and the deepening of cultural exchange between them.

During the two days of the forum, more than 50 experts, scholars and artists from China and the U.S. had deep discussions and exchanges on the topics of Historical Perspectives on China-U.S. Cultural Relations, Literary Heritage and Creativity, Tradition and Innovation in The Visual Arts, The Performing Arts: Comparative Perspectives and The Future of China-U.S. Cultural Relations.

Reflection on the past helps us to get a better view of the present. Cultural exchange will not only have people of the two countries connected spiritually and emotionally, but also improve mutual understanding and trust. In this way, it will contribute to a healthy and stable binational relationship.

Wang Wenzhang, Vice Minister of Culture, PRC, quoted an old saying when addressing the opening ceremony that "all living creatures grow together without harming one another; ways run parallel without interfering with one another" and noted that exchange between different cultures can make us more innovative. Geographically, China and the United States are oceans apart, but the peoples have been in contact for more than 190 years. China today, in the new era of reform and opening up, has begun to learn from the good cultural elements around the world with an open mind. Various cultural products, including movies from the U.S. have come to China and modern and contemporary arts of the U.S. have become familiar to and inspired many Chinese scholars and artists. The cultural exchange is moving towards a new epoch.

Jim Leach, Chairman of US National Endowment for the Humanities said in the address that Walt Whitman, a famous US poet of the 19th century, once suggested that he had a great dream that all of the poets of the world and all of the poems of the world would come together, and that would serve as a greater group of individuals and a body of work to bring peace to the world. He also cited the ancient Chinese philosopher Confucius that if peoples of the earth would spend more time appreciating music and understanding courtesy, there would be no war. He believes that culture plays a big part in the world and works of an author who holds a profound view of the world will help people understand our world. No cultural development may be made without exchange. He wished the forum a fruitful success.

Pauline Yu, President of the American Council of Learned Societies, noted that "it was upon the rapid expansion of Chinese civilization and the impressive substance of its cultural productivity that fuel the American people to study China. And I'm very proud that my own organization, the American Council of Learned Societies has been one of the major promoters of research on the scholarly exchange with China, began shortly after our Council was founded in 1919. Even though the China-U.S relationship suffers tension sometimes, the academic and cultural exchanges have never been dampened. Recently, as many as 100 000 Chinese students have come to study in northern US, showing the vitality of the mutual academic exchange between the two sides. Meanwhile, with the economic connection of the two countries closer than ever, 15 000 American students come to study in China each year and President Obama wish the number could one day reach 100 000. I believe this is quite attainable."

Jonathan Spence, Sterling Professor of History Emeritus of Yale University, reviewed the history of China-U.S. cultural communication and proposed that U.S. scholars have reached quite different conclusions about Chinese history since they have focused on a different period in history. In the early days after China and the United States established formal diplomatic relations, people in the U.S. got most of their impression on the Chinese people from the immigrants of the late 19th century and the Chinatowns established in late 1970s. This resulted in a perspective that China was weak, poor and fragmented. Today, American people have shown respect and recognition to China, acknowledging China as a capable business and trade partner.

Henry Adams, Professor of American Art from Case Western Reserve University said, "The Chinese and English languages are different not only in the words but in the way of organizing reality and making connections between things. Let's remember that our languages present two different pictures of reality. To understand each other, we need to reach beyond the way of thinking and speaking which were not most familiar". He believed that the China-U.S. Cultural Forum held two separate purposes. It first helps Chinese scholars to spread their inspirations among the academic community in the West, and secondly, attracts more western people to learn the Chinese culture. With rapid development, China has now become a main force in pushing forward contemporary arts. Mainstream Chinese arts can inspire western artists to present the current world. The China-U.S. Cultural Forum should serve as a threshold for a long-lasting dialogue between the two countries.

The "Binational Conversation" provides a brand-new perspective for the cultural and artistic research and inspires us to observe the development of various artistic forms in an open manner. Based on this, we may quest for a common cultural construction.

Rachel Goslins, Executive Director of the President's Committee on the Arts and Humanities, said, "The Chinese have a head start on the Americans by at least four centuries in painting, sculpture, poetry and theatre; the Chinese were perfecting the craft in many of these disciplines before they were even a gleam in the American founding fathers' eyes; but film is an exception as the only discipline that was born in both of our countries at the same time. The first moving pictures were shown to an American audience in 1896. And by 1905, the first Chinese film was made, which was a recording of the Beijing Opera. So this is an area where, I think, it's imperative analysis will be especially interesting, to learn about the different ways our two countries have taken the same tool and used it to shape their culture in different or similar ways."

Mo Yan, a famous writer said, "During the early 1980s, many American translators translated what they thought were Chinese novels that above anything else carried certain political messages and ideologies, in an attempt for readers in their own countries to read about changes taking place in China's society, politics and economy. There is of course nothing wrong with this approach. But I think literature translation should place aestheticism above everything else. As an author myself, I hope that readers who do not speak Chinese can enjoy the aesthetic explorations in our works. Up until now, there have been more Chinese readers that have been influenced by foreign literature than foreign readers by Chinese literature. I hope that given more time, the exchange can become more bilateral, where the works of Chinese authors will influence authors from other countries, including young authors in America. That's something I'm looking forward to."

Tian Liming, a famous painter believes what Chinese culture follows is the Chinese humanistic idea, namely, "Man models himself after the Earth; The Earth models itself after Heaven; The Heaven models itself after Tao; Tao models itself after nature". What Chinese culture operates on is the natural law that "Out of Tao, One is born; Out of One, Two; Out of Two, Three; Out of Three, the created universe." The symbolism in Chinese painting is a major vessel for the essence of Chinese culture. With the gentleness and kindness advocated by Chinese culture as the fundamental academic and moral attitude, Chinese painting gradually formulated its unique aesthetic system by practicing the humanistic idea that "Yin and Yang are the two basic elements that breed the heaven and the earth; the way to establish the earth consists of hardness and softness, while the way to establish human consists of humanity and justice." The essence of culture in Chinese paintings is followed through when Chinese people live and conduct aesthetic activities. The modernity of Chinese paintings inherits and develops the spirit of symbolism in traditional Chinese culture, on the basis of which modern Chinese paintings develop its own noble humanistic quality that is the spiritual wealth of Chinese people and all humanity as well.

Dawn Ho Delbanco, Professor of East Asian Art from Columbia University discovered from the paintings of some 20 century expressionist painters that such works are closely related to traditional Chinese paintings. The art concept that the western modernist artists followed in the 20th century is exactly what Chinese artists have been following for centuries. Currently, since painting is universal, it can be shared among and understood by all people.

Li Shenghong, a famous calligrapher, said: Artistic exchange played an essential role in cultural communication. Our understanding of a country's culture may start from its arts. In the development of the Chinese civilization over the 5,000 years, calligraphy has embodied the spirits of being tolerant, keeping pace with the times and valuing harmony despite differences. The art of calligraphy has been greatly enriched over time. The innovative attempts made by modern calligraphy-engravers, including borrowing Western artistic concepts about colors, may produce a unique visual effect.

Research Fellow Liu Zhen summarized in his keynote speech the history of Chinese culture up to now. He said that since Kunqu opera was inscribed in UNESCO's list of the oral and intangible cultural heritage, more and more young people and college students have developed a liking for Kunqu opera, Peking opera, local operas, and other forms of traditional arts. The time-honored traditional art will address people's cultural and spiritual needs and give historicity and depth to the zeitgeist. It will provide inexhaustible strength and momentum to cultural development.

Xu Lei, a famous painter believed that during the process of modernization of Chinese contemporary art, several key points are related to the penetration of American culture, and that in terms of art research and collection, the U.S. owns the richest resources of traditional Chinese arts; this showed on the one hand, that the multicultural America is based on the broad civilizations of mankind and on the other hand, that the Chinese culture had been recognized in the U.S.

As a scholar famous for her achievements in the study and translation of dramas, Claire Conceison, Professor of Theater Studies of Duke University, proudly took herself as a witness to, and interpreter of, cultural exchange between the US and China. She said that many western scholars took Chinese culture as an equivalent to traditional Chinese culture but she found in her study of Chinese plays that Chinese culture was quite modern and innovative in some way. She pointed out that theater forms were imported deliberately from the West at the turn of the 20th century as part of the new culture movement, in which the Chinese intellectuals played an important role and that this did not occur through colonialism or influence of the West, but as a deliberate attempt made by the Chinese intellectuals to reform the culture.

Cultural exchange is not aimed at eliminating different values, but at mutual understanding. A realistic issue of common concern among Chinese and U.S. scholars is how to establish a constructive exchange or interaction pattern in the context of culture clash and integration between the East and the West.

Research Fellow Jia Leilei held that it was on the premise of cross-cultural exchange and dialogues that peoples in different cultures can understand and recognize each other. Nevertheless, due to the differences in media, methods and modes of communication, the results may turn against the original intentions. Against the background of globalization at present, it is urgent and crucial to cushion conflicts and confrontations between different cultures by means of effective cross-cultural exchange. Contacts through economic activities and trades can only strengthen the mutual cooperation for benefits, but may not necessarily "purchase" each other's cultural values. Cultural understanding can only be achieved through cross-cultural communication.

Donald Mcquade, Professor of English from the University of California, Berkeley has been to China many times over the years and talked with Chinese leaders on several occasions. He believes that innovation and creativity have become a national mission for China. A spectacular expression most recently, the opening ceremony of Beijing Olympic Games, the purposefully and breathtakingly elegant calligraphy of creativity displayed on that occasion sent generations of stereotyped and clichéd ideas about China and images of it up in smoke when the Olympic torch was lit the night of August 8, 2008. While competing with China, people should have an objective view and understanding of its strength.

Christopher Merrill, Director of the International Writing Program at the University of Iowa, presented a model of cultural exchange with a programme he organized—Life of Discovery. The programme brought about a dozen young American writers between the ages of 25 and 40 to China and Chinese sent a like number of writers to America. And the notion was not just in exchange of delegations, but to actually put the writers into conversation together and to try to forge collaboration.

Wu Weishan, a famous sculptor, explained his own works and cultural values. He has created over 400 sculptural works in over 20 years. Behind every work, there is a story. The sculptures reflect the artist's experiences, emotions, and the result of his artistic studies and practices. Furthermore, they reflect his cultural values. By appreciating the works, we get to know the emotions and the cultural values of the artist. And this is what China-U.S. cultural exchange may achieve.

Research Fellow Ou Jianping mentioned in his speech, what he once said in an interview with the Journal News in New York in 1988 that "Opening up China to avant-garde dance forms doesn't hurt socialism. To me, China is strong enough not to be swallowed up by any outside influences. The importance of cross-cultural exchanges is that if people understand each other, there will be no more wars". Although twenty two years have passed by now, he still believes so.

Globalization is drawing the world more and more alike, but in the mean time is also highlighting the differences and broadening the cultural gap. The cultural exchange between China and the U.S. will involve different values and common needs while improving mutual understanding, tolerance and integration.

Talking about the future development of the world, Jim Leach, Chairman of the U.S. National Endowment for the Humanities proposed three points: first, the most important bilateral relationship in this century and quite possibly in this millennium will be the United States and Chinese relationship; second, the world is hallmarked by change in its acceleration and involved much of recorded history which has been repetitive with revolution involving change back to circumstances that existed before; and third, the most unprecedented aspect of all of this change that we see around this relates to advances in science and technology and the most sobering relates to the ramifications for military hardware. Einstein once commented that splitting the atom had changed everything except our way of thinking. We must be aware that conflict is a constant presumably because human nature is a conflict. We'd have to understand human nature in a much deeper way in order to develop techniques to better direct human beings themselves. In the context of US and Chinese relations, there is a golden rule that we should do unto others as we want others to do unto us. In the Confucian tradition, there is a similar but less obtrusive framing of it: one should not do unto others what one would not want others to do unto themselves. He further noted, "While the Chinese might like us to be more Confucian and we might like the Chinese to be more Jeffersonian, there is no reason what-so-ever that there cannot be an expansion of mutual respect. And so it is in the context of the question of how you advance respect that this final panel has been convened."

Research Fellow Liu Mengxi said, for any nation, the process of modernization cannot be completed in vacuum, cut off from the rest of the world. Modernization is a process that requires different cultural backgrounds, cultural systems and cultural notions to come into contact, and to learn and borrow from each other. A man cannot live in complete seclusion; likewise, a nation cannot exist isolated from the modern world. Professor Samuel Huntington puts too much stress on "clash", and not enough on the integration of civilizations. Cultural communication is the precondition of integration of civilizations; it is not only etiquette of civilized people, but also their wisdom and way to live. Mr. Liu believes that, regardless of whether we are talking about nations, regions, or ethnic groups, the relationship is one of mutual dependence. The East cannot exist in isolation from the West, or vice versa. Humanity shares a set of common goals, and different approaches are taken to realize these goals, which is how our similarities and differences may be perceived. This idea can be found in the ancient Chinese classic I-Ching (the Book of Changes): through different paths we walk toward the same destination; though we may disagree on ideas and means, all means point to the same end.

Andrew Delbanco, Director of American Studies from Columbia University believes: each successor of generation of view shall start with all the advantages in which their predecessors have one. He called this a relay race of view of human history, that one generation arrives at certain insides, discoveries, and passes their own to the next generation, so that they don't have to be rediscovered, so that the quest for knowledge can begin anew from a more advanced point from where it was before. Professor Andrew believes that this is fundamentally the way science works, and he supposes that culture takes the same way.

Josiah Ober, Professor of Classics and Professor of Political Science, Stanford University, talked about his expectations on the China-U.S. cultural relationship: Unlike hard power there is no need for soft power to seek hegemony. Chinese people are not the losers when they learn something from Plato and Aristotle;

neither are western scholars when they incorporate the study of Chinese language and Confucian tradition, the history of China into their traditions. He hoped that the attractive, the beautiful things of Chinese culture can be more recognized in the west just as the beautiful things of the Western culture have been recognized in China. He noted the possibility for and the ultimate establishment of a kind of creative competition can only be achieved with deeper conversation of the two countries.

Professor Yu Dan said, "Through civilized dialogue, the China-U.S. Cultural Forum aims to discuss our respective views on the cultural aspect of the modern world, and on the values of our traditions. We might not reach a conclusion, but I think the exchange of our viewpoints is more important than reaching a conclusion." She took the criteria of a gentleman (man of noble character), and the notions of "harmony despite differences" and "unity between cognition and action" for example and illustrated the viewpoint that the essence of traditional Chinese culture does not only belong to China, but is a shared wealth of the world. Within the context of globalization, our purpose is to construct a new cultural structure, in hope of providing a solution for our common challenges, so that one day we will live in a world of harmony.

Architect Billie Tsien, a Chinese American, talked about the influence of both Chinese and western cultures on her with deep emotions, "When I was young, I was somewhat confused by the impact of two different cultures. But as I grew older, I realized that I liked to be a mix of two cultures for being such enabled me to observe the world in various perspectives. I asked our son, who is truly the product of east-west dialogue, whether he considers himself Chinese or American, and he answered 'I am not one or the other, I am just who I am'. So in many ways, this is a cycle back to where we began, where we started, and so is any great work of art."

Professor Jin Canrong said: among the 192 member states of the United Nations, only two pairs of partners have a trade volume over US$400 billion, that is, U.S.-Canada and U.S.-China. The interdependence exists not only in trade. The China-U.S. relationship has four dimensions: the political, economic, military & security, and social & cultural relationship. In all four dimensions, there are both competition and cooperation. China will only consider the U.S. a more and more important peer in the future. Therefore, the future of China-U.S. relationship depends more on how the U.S. take it than the attitude of China, though third-party factors do have an influence as well.

Allison Blakely, Professor of European and Comparative History, Boston University, looked out on the future of China-U.S. relationship in his speech. He said: Culture is more powerful than politics. The 21st century is the first in which the entire world was challenged with new levels of cultural diversity within all the major societies. He has always been in awe of the long duration of the Chinese civilization, the philosophies and institutions it has shaped and the discovery that China actually had the technology and capacity to explore the whole world prior to the Europeans and for various reasons elected not to. The most spectacular example of this were the exploits of the Admiral Zheng He who led seven expeditions abroad in the early 15th century, 100 years before Fernando de Magallanes' voyage, with fleets numbering hundreds of ships and combined crews of tens of thousands. He proposed that scholars from both sides should urge their national leaders to establish respect for cultural diversity and be more constructive in international cooperation of all kinds, so as to ease up the dispute over cultural issues.

The Chinese participants of the forum also took part in an academic symposium held by the East Asian Studies Department, University of Chicago, as a follow-up of the forum. They were invited to deliver speeches and participated in some activities organized by UNESCO. With such activities, the forum drew to a perfect end. The logo of the second China-U.S. Cultural Forum is a colorful bridge in the style of traditional Chinese paper cutting, a symbol of the cultural and artistic exchange between China and the U.S. The forum is expected to become an opportunity for the communication, contact and integration of eastern and western cultures.

翻译与文化
美中两国学者与艺术家齐聚圆桌论坛

梅瑞狄斯·辛德雷
美国国家人文基金会
资深作家

中国小说家莫言翻开威廉·福克纳《喧哗与骚动》的译本时看到了约克纳帕塔法郡，这是福克纳在密西西比州虚构的一个郡，郡中居民的原型都是他在现实生活中遇到的人。

莫言说，"读过福克纳作品之后，我发现自己的经历和生活也可以写成故事和文学作品。我所熟识的人、所了解的村庄都可以变成书中角色。"莫言已经成为中国著作最丰的作家之一，他的小说以位于中国山东省的家乡为原型，将场景设置在一个虚构的村庄中。

2010年10月15日至16日，"第二届中美文化论坛：跨文化双边对话"在加利福尼亚大学伯克利分校举行，莫言在论坛上分享了自己"遭遇"福克纳的经历。论坛由美国国家人文基金会和中华人民共和国文化部共同主办，将两国杰出的艺术家、作家、历史学家和政治理论家齐聚一堂。与会者讨论了中美两国人民对文化的理解有何异同，传统与创新在文化中扮演的角色，以及文化对中美两国关系产生了何种影响。

除了讨论其他主题之外，圆桌论坛还再次强调了翻译在文化交流中扮演的核心角色。爱荷华大学国际项目主任克里斯多弗·梅里尔谈到了埃兹拉·庞德翻译的中国诗作对美国诗人产生的影响。耶鲁大学高级讲师金安平谈到翻译在孔子著作推广方面具有重要性。画家徐累说，在文化大革命之后的几年中，他学习的一部分是阅读美国诗歌中译本和唐代诗作。莫言也坚持这一主题，他说翻译对于

本文转载自美国国家人文基金会官方网站（http://www.neh.gov/news/archive/20101027.html）。

文学而言不可或缺。

中国艺术研究院戏曲研究所所长刘祯指出，中国人已经开始认识到文化对社会的重要性。他说，中国即将进入一个"文化时代"，对此，我们已经万事俱备。这是一项艰巨任务。中国艺术研究院中国文化研究所所长刘梦溪表示赞同。他说，文化对话不仅仅是一条生活法则，更是生活本身。

贯穿整届圆桌论坛的另一项主题是中美文化相互影响的方式。第二代美籍华人建筑师钱以佳谈到借鉴两国文化传统如何推动产生新的词汇和新的思维方式。钱以佳说，处身两地从很多方面而言是居于一个具有创意的位置，文化就是如此，伟大的艺术就是如此。中国艺术研究院中国舞蹈研究所副所长欧建平讨论了美国在20世纪对中国舞蹈文化产生的影响——从中国版的秀兰·邓波（20世纪30年代电影中在楼梯上上下下唱歌跳舞的童星），谈到教党政领导人跳华尔兹，再到引进现代舞蹈技术。

杜克大学戏剧系教授克莱尔·康塞逊鼓励中国剧团赴美演出。她说，我们需要进行双向交流。我们需要将更多的中国著作引入美国。我们还要更加关注翻译和语言。

作为会议的一部分，美国国家人文基金会和中国文化部签署了一项《谅解备忘录》，呼吁将论坛继续举办下去，下一届将于2012年在中国举办。美国国家人文基金会主席吉姆·利奇说，"21世纪乃至新千年中最重要的双边关系是中美关系。我们能否开展建设性合作，弥合彼此之间多项政治和经济差异，将有赖于我们能否尊重彼此的历史和文化。文化大于政治。不建立相互间的尊重，可持续的政治关系便无从谈起。"

美国总统艺术人文委员会和加利福尼亚大学伯克利分校"中国研究中心"为本届会议提供了额外支持。

TRANSLATION AND CULTURE
American and Chinese Scholars and Artists Gather for Roundtable Discussions

Meredith Hindley

Senior Writer at the National Endowment for the Humanities

When Chinese novelist Mo Yan opened a translated volume of William Faulkner The Sound and the Fury, he encountered Yoknapatawpha, the fictional county in Mississippi that Faulkner populated with people like those he knew in real life.

After reading Faulkner, I realized that my own experience and my own life could become stories and literature, said Mo. The people that I am familiar with, the villages, they can all become characters. Mo has become one of China's most prolific authors, setting his novels in a fictional village based on his hometown in China's Shandong province.

Mo shared his encounter with Faulkner as part of the Second U.S.-China Cultural Forum: A Binational Conversation on Bridging Cultures, held at the University of California, Berkeley on Oct. 15-16, 2010. The forum was sponsored by the National Endowment for the Humanities and the Ministry of Culture of the People's Republic of China. The forum brought together prominent artists, writers, historians, and political theorists from both countries. The participants discussed the similarities and differences in how Americans and Chinese perceive culture, the role of tradition and innovation in culture, and how culture has influenced relations between China and the United States.

Among other themes, the roundtable discussions reinforced the central role translation plays in cultural exchange. Christopher Merrill, director of international program at the University of Iowa, touched on the influence of Ezra Pound's translations of Chinese poetry on American poets. Annping Chin, senior lecturer at Yale University, spoke about the importance of translation in making the works of Confucius available. For painter Xu Lei, reading American poems in translation, as well as poems from the Tang Dynasty, was part of his education in the years following the Cultural Revolution. Mo was also adamant on the topic. Translation is indispensable to literature, he said.

This article is quoted from the official website of NEH (http://www.neh.gov/news/archive/20101027.html).

Liu Zhen, director of the Chinese Opera Institute at the National Academy of Arts, noted that the Chinese people have started to realize how important culture is to society. China is looking forward to a cultural era, he said. We have all of the conditions to make it happen. It's a daunting task.Liu Mengxi, director of the Institute of Chinese Culture at the National Academy of Arts, echoed a similar sentiment. The dialogue between cultures is not only a principle of life, but it is life itself, he said.

The ways in which American and Chinese culture have influenced each other was another theme that ran through the roundtable discussions. Architect Billie Tsien, a second-generation Chinese-American, spoke about how drawing on two cultural traditions can lead to new vocabularies and ways of thinking. In many ways having your feet in two places is a creative place to stand,said Tsien. Culture just is. Great art just is.Ou Jianping, deputy director of the China's Dance Institute at the National Academy of Arts, discussed American influences on Chinese dance culture in the twentieth century—everything from China's own version of Shirley Temple (the child star who sang and danced her way up and down a staircase in 1930s films) to teaching the party leadership to how to waltz to importing modern dance techniques.

Claire Conceison, professor of theater studies at Duke University, called for more performances of Chinese theater in the United States. Our exchanges need to go both ways,she said. We need to bring more Chinese works to the United States. We need to pay more attention to translation and language.

As part of the conference, the National Endowment for the Humanities and China's Ministry of Culture signed a memorandum of understanding that calls for continuing the forums, with the next one to take place in China in 2012. The most important bilateral relationship in the twenty-first century and possibly this new millennium is between the United States and China, said NEH Chairman Jim Leach. Whether we can work constructively together and bridge our many political and economic differences will depend on whether we can respect each other's history and culture. Culture is bigger than politics. No sustaining political relationship can develop if mutual respect is not established."

Additional support for the conference was provided by the President's Committee on the Arts and Humanities and the Center for Chinese Studies at the University of California, Berkeley.

中美文化论坛历史沿革

"中美文化论坛"缘起于2007年6月,"美国总统艺术人文委员会"组织美联邦政府五个主要文化机构一行36人访华。此次访问意在开辟美国与中国进行沟通的文化渠道,开启中美政府间文化交流的新篇章。

在中华人民共和国文化部副部长、中国艺术研究院院长王文章的直接领导下,"中美文化论坛"筹备工作开始启动。2007年11月,文化部外联局组织的中美合作项目代表团赴美与美国文化机构会谈,双方就论坛的规模和内容达成共识,为论坛的顺利召开奠定了基础。

2008年4月,应美方邀请,文化部派考察小组出席了美国和意大利在意大利佛罗伦萨召开的"国家认知:历史记忆和文化"学术讨论会。与会期间,小组成员分别与美国总统艺术人文委员会主席阿黛尔·玛戈、美国国家人文基金会主席布鲁斯·科尔进行了会谈,商谈了"中美文化论坛"的有关事宜,确定"中美文化论坛"由美国国家人文基金会和中国艺术研究院承办,就会议论题进行了具体磋商。

2008年8月,美国国家人文基金会与中国艺术研究院共同签订了《谅解备忘录》,确定中美两国在人文与文化遗产保护方面进行学术交流与合作。《谅解备忘录》中提到,美国国家人文基金会和中国艺术研究院期望共同举办"中美文化论坛",将中美两国学者聚集一堂,进行高质量的人文学术研究,促进两国之间的文化艺术交流。

此后,中国艺术研究院与文化部外联局进行多次磋商,拟定了"与美国国家人文基金会进行学术交流的意向书",计划2008年12月在北京召开"第一届中美文化论坛"。希望通过论坛与美方建立一种新的学术合作机制,推动中美两国的文化交流与合作。美方亦申明,美国国家人文基金会非常重视加强中美之间的相互理解，希望促进更深刻的交流与合作，并对我方提出的详尽实施计划表示感谢。

"中美文化论坛"的组织机构就论坛的目的、宗旨、原则、规模、议题、时间、地点等问题进行了反复磋商和详尽规划，为论坛的成功举行奠定了坚实的基础，使之成为中、美两国文化交流与合作的良好开端。

第一届中美文化论坛

2008年12月8日至9日，由中华人民共和国文化部和美国国家人文基金会共同举办、中国艺术研究院承办的"中美文化论坛——数字化时代的文化遗产保护和展现"在北京隆重召开。中华人民共和国文化部部长蔡武，文化部副部长、中国艺术研究院院长王文章、文化部副部长赵少华、美国国家人文基金会主席布鲁斯·科尔、美国总统艺术人文委员会执行主任莫兰·亨利等中美文化管理机构高级官员出席论坛。来自中美双方的50多位官员、专家、学者和艺术家进行了深入而积极的讨论。

在为期两天的会议中，中美两国专家学者围绕"数字技术与文化遗产保护"的中心论题，针对数字技术在文化遗产保护和发展方面的作用、数字技术在历史文化教育方面的作用、如何利用数字技术保护传统文化艺术以及如何利用数字技术保护非物质文化遗产等多个论题进行了广泛对话与深入研讨。

文化部副部长、中国艺术研究院院长王文章在论坛开幕式致辞中指出："中国政府历来重视文化遗产的保护工作，特别是在利用数字技术保护文化遗产方面，做出了诸多富有成效的工作。中国故宫博物院和国家图书馆就利用数字技术在文物和古籍保护方面取得了突出的成就，中国非物质文化遗产保护中心在非物质文化遗产的保护方面也进行了许多有益的实践，中国艺术研究院还利用数字技术对大量的传统音乐资源进行修复和保护。我们希望通过这次中美文化论坛，能够与美方广泛地开展科技和文化之间的交流，挖掘中华文明的优秀传统元素和宝贵遗产，为人类的和谐发展与和平进步做出积极的贡献。"

美国国家人文基金会主席布鲁斯·科尔在开幕式致辞中讲到："我们两国将在支持人文学科以及文化遗产的保护及介绍方面寻求进一步的合作。对于未来两国之间富于成效而重要的文化和学术交流，我充满了热切的期待。运用数字技术能够很简单地处理以往不能解决的问题。在这些领域,数字技术所显示出的巨大力量让我们思考新的问题,寻求能够跨越时间和不同物质的新关系和新模式。在美国人文科学基金会,我们深信数字技术在改变人文学科方面也有巨大的潜力,也会以同样的方式改变人文学科的知识、教学以及规划和设计。我们希望能引领这一'新边疆'的开发。"

文化部副部长赵少华在闭幕式致辞中指出,"此次'中美文化论坛',无论从主办方的规模和规格来看,还是从讨论和交流的深度、广度来说,都堪称是中美文化和学术交流史上的一件盛事,它必将为中美文化交流开启更为辉煌的篇章!"

在此次论坛上,与会的专家学者就文化多元化、文化遗产保护、信息数字化的发展等问题进行了深入的对话与交流,提出了许多富有创见的学术观点,中美文化界人士也进行了广泛深入的沟通,并取得了不少共识。

论坛的召开在促进数字技术与文化遗产保护工作的结合方面发挥了积极作用,它不仅标志着中美两国文化交流与合作达到一个新的阶段,而且对推动两国关系的发展也具有十分深远的意义。

第一届中美文化在热烈而成功的氛围中落幕。会后,美国国家人文基金会主席布鲁斯·科尔和美国总统艺术人文委员会执行主任亨利·莫兰对此次论坛给予了高度评价,并对"第二届中美文化论坛"寄予厚望。之后,根据王文章副部长的指示精神,编纂了题为《数字化时代的文化遗产保护和展现——中美文化论坛文集》,以中英双语、图文并茂的形式出版,使"中美文化论坛"的学术成果社会化,进一步扩大和深化了此次论坛的社会影响。

第二届中美文化论坛

2009年11月,中国国家主席胡锦涛和美国总统奥巴马在北京举行会谈,发表了《中美联合声明》。声明涉及中美关系、建立和深化双边战略互信、经济合作和全球复苏、地区及全球性挑战以及气候变化、能源与环境等几个方面,体现了双方的共识,也为今后两国关系的发展宣示了方向。声明着重强调人文交流对促进更加紧密的中美关系具有重要意义,从而促请建立新的双边机制,并将中美两国将合作举办"第二届中美文化论坛"写入《中美联合声明》,显示出中美双方领导人对此次论坛的高度重视。

2010年5月,中共中央政治局委员、国务委员刘延东和美国国务卿希拉里·克林顿在北京联合主持了"中美人文交流高层磋商机制成立仪式暨第一次会议",并见证了中美人文交流高层磋商机制正式成立。此次会议中,中美双方再次强调要办好"第二届中美文化论坛",凸显了两国领导人对论坛和文化领域深层交流的重视。

在文化部王文章副部长的亲自领导下,中国艺术研究院与文化部外联局就"第二届中美文化论坛"相关事宜进行协商,对论坛的架构提出了初步构想,在与美方协商过程中,双方共同确定了"跨文化双边对话"的论坛主题。

2010年10月15日至16日,"第二届中美文化论坛"在美国加利福尼亚大学伯克利分校举行。论坛之后,中方代表进行了相应的延伸性学术活动,与美国哥伦比亚大学、芝加哥大学和纽约佩斯大学等著名高校的师生进行学术交流,加深了双方的了解,增进了互信,使中美文化论坛走向了更为广阔的领域,为中美文化交流提供了新的路径。

Evolution of China-U.S. Cultural Forum

The China-U.S. Cultural Forum was established in June 2007, when the US President's Committee on the Arts and the Humanities organized a China visit by a delegation of 36 members selected from five main federal cultural institutions. The visit, designed to open a cultural channel for communications with China, represented a new chapter in the cultural exchanges between the Chinese and US governments.

Preparations for the founding of the Forum began under the direct leadership of Wang Wenzhang, the Vice Minister of Ministry of Culture of P.R.C, President of Chinese National Academy of Arts. In November 2007, a delegation on China-U.S. cooperation projects organized by the Bureau for External Cultural Relations of Ministry of Culture held talks with US cultural institutions. The two sides reached consensus on the scale and content of the Forum, which laid the foundation for a smooth opening of the Forum.

In April 2008, invited by America, Ministry of Culture dispatched a special inspection group to the academic symposium "National Recognition: Historical Memory and Culture", which was jointly held in Florence by the United States and Italy. During the meeting, the group members held talks respectively with Margo Lion, Chairman of the President's Committee on the Arts and the Humanities, and Bruce Cole, Chairman of the National Endowment for the Humanities. They discussed matters relating to the China-U.S. Cultural Forum and decided that the Forum would be undertaken by the US National Endowment for the Humanities and the Chinese National Academy of Arts and held specific consultations on the topic of the forum.

In August 2008, the US National Endowment for the Humanities and the Chinese National Academy of Arts signed a Memorandum of Understanding to confirm academic exchange and cooperation between China and the United States in the humanities and the protection of cultural heritage. The document said the US National Endowment for the Humanities and the Chinese National Academy of Arts would jointly host the China-U.S. Cultural Forum, which would bring Chinese and American scholars together to engage in high-quality academic researches on the humanities and promote cultural and art exchanges between the two countries.

Later on, the Chinese National Academy of Arts and the Bureau of External Cultural Relations of the Ministry of Culture held several consultations, worked out the Letter of Intent for the Academic Exchanges with the US National

Endowment for the Humanities and planned to hold the first China-U.S. Cultural Forum in Beijing in December 2008. It hoped that this forum would help establish a new mechanism for academic cooperation with the US side and promote the cultural exchanges and cooperation between the two countries. The US side also declared that the National Endowment for the Humanities attached great importance to promoting the mutual understanding between the two countries and hoped to deepen bilateral exchanges and cooperation. It also expressed thanks to the Chinese side for the detailed implementation plan.

The organizing institutions of the China-U.S. Cultural Forum held repeated consultations and worked out a detailed plan to define the objectives, aims, principles, scale, topics, time and place of the Forum. This laid a solid foundation for the successful holding of the Forum and ensured the Forum would represent a good beginning of the cultural exchanges and cooperation between the two countries.

The First China-U.S. Cultural Forum

The China-U.S. Cultural Forum – Preservation and Presentation of Cultural Heritage in Digital Age was held in Beijing on December 8 and 9, 2008. The Forum was co-sponsored by the Ministry of Culture of the People's Republic of China and the US National Endowment for the Humanities and organized by the Chinese National Academy of Arts. The Forum was attended by Cai Wu, Minister of Culture, Wang Wenzhang, Vice Minister of Culture and President of the Chinese National Academy of Arts, Zhao Shaohua, Vice Minister of Culture, Bruce Cole, Chairman of the US National Endowment for the Humanities, Henry Moran, Executive Director of the US President's Committee on the Arts and the Humanities, and other senior officials of Chinese and US cultural administrative institutions. At the Forum, more than 50 officials, experts, scholars and artists from the two countries held in-depth and lively discussions over relevant topics.

During the two-day meeting, Chinese and U.S. experts and scholars focused their discussions on the central topic "Digital Technology and Cultural Heritage Protection". They held wide-ranging and far-reaching discussions on the roles of digital technology in the preservation and development of cultural heritages, the roles of digital technology in history and culture education, how to use digital technology to preserve traditional culture and art and how to use digital technology to preserve intangible cultural heritage.

In his opening address, Wang Wenzhang, Vice Minister of Culture and President of the Chinese National Academy of Arts, said, "The Chinese government has always emphasized the preservation of cultural heritage and in particular has done a great job in using digital technology to preserve cultural heritage. The Palace Museum and the National Library of China have made remarkable achievements in using digital technology to preserve cultural relics and ancient books. The China Intangible Cultural Heritage Protection Center has made many useful attempts in preserving intangible cultural heritage. The Chinese National Academy of Arts has used digital technology to repair and preserve large amounts of traditional music resources. We hope that through the China-U.S. Cultural Forum, we can have extensive scientific and cultural exchanges with the US side so as to explore the outstanding traditional elements and valuable heritages of the Chinese civilization and to make positive contributions to the harmony, development, peace and progress of mankind."

In his opening address, Bruce Cole, Chairman of the National Endowment for the Humanities, said, "Our two countries will seek further cooperation in supporting the humanities and preserving and presenting cultural heritage. I fully look forward to fruitful and important cultural and academic exchanges between our two countries in the future. Digital technology can be used to easily solve issues that cannot be solved in the past. In these fields, the tremendous strength demonstrated by digital technology prompts us to ponder over new issues and seek new relations and new models that can cut across time and different materials. We at the National Endowment for the Humanities are deeply convinced that digital technology also has a huge potential in changing humanity discipline and can, in the same way, change the knowledge, teaching, planning and design of humanity discipline. We hope we can lead in developing this 'new frontier'."

Vice Minister of Culture Zhao Shaohua also noted in his closing address, "The China-U.S. Cultural Forum is a great event in the history of China-U.S. cultural and academic exchanges, either in terms of the scale and level of the host, or in terms of the in-depth and width of discussions and exchanges. It will certainly open a more splendid chapter in China-U.S. cultural exchanges."

At this Forum, the experts and scholars held in-depth dialogues and exchanges over the issues of cultural diversity, cultural heritage preservation and information digitization, and presented many creative academic views. Cultural figures from the two countries also made wide and deep exchanges and achieved consensus on many issues.

This Forum played positive roles in promoting digital technology in cultural heritage preservation. It not only marked a new stage of the cultural exchanges and cooperation between the two countries, but also had far-reaching implications to the development of the relations between the two countries.

The first Forum ended in a warm and successful atmosphere. After the Forum, Bruce Cole, Chairman of the US National Endowment for the Humanities, and Henry Moran, Executive Director of the US President's Committee on the Arts and the Humanities, spoke highly of the Forum. They placed high hopes on the second China-U.S. Cultural Forum. In accordance with the instructions of Vice Minister Wang Wenzhang, "Preservation and Presentation of Cultural Heritage in Digital Age—China-U.S. Cultural Forum Collection of the Theses" was published and this helped socialize the Forum's academic fruits and further widened and deepened its social impact.

The Second China-U.S. Cultural Forum

In November 2009, Chinese President Hu Jintao and US President Barack Obama held talks in Beijing and issued the China-U.S. Joint Statement. The Statement covered the areas of China-U.S. relations, bilateral strategic mutual trust and economic cooperation, global recovery, regional and global challenges, climate change, energy and the environment. It crystallized the consensus of the two sides and charted the direction for the development of bilateral relations in the future. The Statement emphasized the importance of cultural exchanges to promoting closer China-U.S. relations, urged the establishment of new bilateral mechanisms and said the two countries would jointly hold the second China-U.S. Cultural Forum. This is an indication that the leaders of the two sides attach high attention to the Forum.

In May 2010, Liu Yandong, Politburo Member of CPC Central Committee and State Councilor, and Hillary Clinton, US Secretary of State, jointly chaired the founding ceremony and the first session of the China-U.S. High-Level Consultation Mechanism for Cultural Exchanges in Beijing. They also witnessed the formal launching of this mechanism. During this meeting, the two sides reemphasized the importance of the second China-U.S. Cultural Forum. This indicated that leaders of the two countries attached great importance to this Forum and to deeper cultural exchanges.

Under the personal leadership of Vice Minister of Ministry of Culture Wang Wenzhang, the leaders of the Chinese National Academy of Arts and the Bureau of External Cultural Relations of the Ministry of Culture held consultations over matters relating to the second China-U.S. Cultural Forum and formed preliminary ideas about the Forum's structure. In the course of consulting with the US side, the two sides jointly defined "Cross-Culture Bilateral Dialogue" as the theme of the Forum.

On October 15 and 16, 2010, the second China-U.S. Cultural Forum was held at the US University of California, Berkley Campus. After the Forum, the Chinese delegates made extensive academic activities and held academic exchanges with the teachers and students of the University of Columbia, the University of Chicago, the Pace University and other institutions of higher learning. The goal was to deepen the mutual understanding, enhance the mutual trust , make the China-U.S. Cultural Forum head for a broader field and provide a new path for China-U.S. cultural exchange.

图书在版编目（CIP）数据

跨文化双边对话：第二届中美文化论坛文集/贾磊磊主编.
— 北京：文化艺术出版社，2011.11
ISBN 978-7-5039-5225-8

Ⅰ.①跨… Ⅱ.①贾… Ⅲ.①文化交流－中国、美国－文集 Ⅳ.①G125-53

中国版本图书馆CIP数据核字（2011）第215806号

跨文化双边对话
——第二届中美文化论坛文集

主　　编	贾磊磊
责任编辑	仲　江
书籍设计	顾咏梅
出版发行	文化艺术出版社
地　　址	北京市东城区东四八条52号　100700
网　　址	www.whyscbs.com
电子邮箱	whysbooks@263.net
电　　话	（010）84057658　84057666（总编室）
	（010）84057696　84057697（发行部）
经　　销	新华书店
印　　刷	北京图文天地制版印刷有限公司
版　　次	2011年11月第1版
印　　次	2011年11月第1次印刷
印　　张	26.25
开　　本	710×1000　1/16
字　　数	300 千字
书　　号	ISBN 978-7-5039-5225-8
定　　价	48.00 元

版权所有，侵权必究。印装错误，随时调换。